P9-DVO-346

Neurofeedback in the
Treatment of
Developmental Trauma

A Norton Professional Book

Neurofeedback in the Treatment of Developmental Trauma

Calming the Fear-Driven Brain

Sebern F. Fisher

Foreword by Bessel van der Kolk, MD

W. W. Norton & Company

New York • London

This book is not intended to substitute for medical or psychotherapeutic advice, training, or treatment.

Manufacturing by Quad Graphics, Fairfield
Production manager: Leeann Graham

Library of Congress Cataloging-in-Publication Data

Fisher, Sebern F., author.
    Neurofeedback in the treatment of developmental trauma : calming the fear-driven brain / Sebern F. Fisher ; foreword by Bessel A. van der Kolk, MD. — First edition.
        pages   cm
    "A Norton professional book."
    Includes bibliographical references and index.
    ISBN 978-0-393-70786-1 (hardcover)
    1. Biofeedback training.   2. Electroencephalography.   3. Brain damage—
Treatment.   I. Title.
    RC489.B53F57   2014
    616.8'047547—dc23
                            2013047881

ISBN: 978-0-393-70786-1

W. W. Norton & Company, Inc., 500 Fifth Avenue, New York, N.Y. 10110
www.wwnorton.com
W. W. Norton & Company Ltd., Castle House, 75/76 Wells Street, London W1T 3QT

1 2 3 4 5 6 7 8 9 0

To Johnny

Contents

Acknowledgments

To begin at the beginning, I want to thank the two friends who introduced me to neurofeedback, Barry Zimmer and Kathy Zilberman, with particular gratitude to Kathy, who was the first to train my brain. I owe them both an enormous debt.

I have been guided on this long unfolding path by some of the best minds in the field of neurofeedback, too many to acknowledge individually but all deeply appreciated. I am particularly grateful to Ed Hamlin for his many contributions to me and to this text. He is one of the brightest lights in this field, and he gave of his time and expertise to keep me aligned with the rapid evolutions in neuroscience and in our shared passion, neurofeedback.

Lee Cheek, Sam McClellan, and Bob Myers, each in their own way, introduced me to the trauma body.

I want to thank Ruth Cohn and Sam McClellan for their artistic, technical, moral, and material support.

My patients have each contributed this book. They have weathered my learning curve and shown me what they could do with newly organized and quieted nervous systems; they have taught me how to think about mind, self, and arousal. We have been on a profound journey together, and I want to thank them for staying the course with me.

Andrea Costella Dawson, my attentive, patient, and thoughtful editor at Norton, understood that, in the age of the brain, all too little was written about addressing the disordered brain directly. She had the vision to ask me to write this book and has been there for me at every turn.

John, my partner in life, kept the world at bay and from the beginning, encouraged this book into being. I truly could not have done this without him, nor would I have wished to. John, now you get your study back!

And lastly, my unending gratitude to my "devoted other" (and the author of this term), Edward Emery.

Foreword

How often is an experienced clinician-researcher confronted with a new paradigm that profoundly changes his understanding of what he has done all his professional life? How often does a remarkably novel way of understanding the mind, brain, and body come along, one that has been around for at least three decades yet remains at the periphery of clinical practice and neuroscience?

A few years ago I served on a medical panel in which we all were asked to name the greatest advance we were then involved in. One person mentioned mosquito netting to combat malaria, another that she had found a gene for anorexia (huh?, I thought), and I mentioned that we were working on ways to reconfigure electrical communication patterns in the brain in order to help people feel more fully alive in the present. The audience stared in disbelief, but I had no chance to elaborate on my statement. In her book, Sebern Fisher does so eloquently.

One way in which we judge credibility of new treatment techniques is by the way the bearer of the tidings behaves. If a skittish, intense person pushes me hard into taking an interest in their amazing new therapy that will solve most of mankind's ills, I usually squirm away. However, when a calm, curious, confident, and humorous individual engages me into looking at familiar things from an intriguing new angle, my curiosity is piqued.

I had the good fortune of meeting Sebern Fisher at an attachment conference in Providence, Rhode Island in the fall of 2007. She showed me a series of family drawings sketched by a very impaired 10-year-old boy who had been treated with neurofeedback (see Figure 4.1). The first drawing consisted of a stick figure, which a 3-year-old could have produced. Twenty sessions later his family portrait had taken on complexity, nuance, and character. Another twenty sessions later the drawing looked like the work of a full-fledged young artist. I was intrigued. I had never encountered a treatment approach that could shift the perceptual system of a human being so dramatically in such a short period of time.

My intrigue, combined with Sebern's thoughtfulness, gentleness, and sharp analytical skills, prompted me to eagerly accept her invitation to spend a weekend with her in Northampton, Massachusetts to become more familiar with what neurofeedback could do, specifically with regard to patients suffering from developmental trauma. Sebern explained that she could show me all the electroencephalograms and statistical analyses[1] that had been collected on neurofeedback, but none would be as eloquent as the patients she had treated, and she wanted me to meet them.

One snowy afternoon Sebern hooked me up to a small computer in her home office to display an electroencephalogram (EEG) of my brain waves on the screen in front of me, an EEG that was more sophisticated than what one million dollars worth of equipment could produce in the EEG laboratory in which I had worked in medical school. Nice to see how technological advances had democratized access to brain wave activity.

Subsequently, I interviewed three of Sebern's patients, all of whom had suffered from developmental trauma. One was a woman who had been plagued with intractable epileptic seizures and confined to her apartment in a housing project, waiting for her next seizure to occur, hoping that this would not happen at a time when she was to pick up her baby from daycare. She told me that neurofeedback had cured her seizures after numerous medications had failed to do so, and had helped her to become sufficiently focused to attend college and get a degree in journalism.

The next young woman had been chronically isolated and out of touch with her environment. After neurofeedback training, she came across as vivacious and inquisitive.

The third patient was most familiar: A young woman who had grown

---

1. van der Kolk, B. A. (2005). Developmental trauma disorder: Toward a rational diagnosis for children with complex trauma histories. *Psychiatric Annals 35*(5), 401–408.

up shuttled between residential treatment programs, hospitals, and foster care placements and who, a few years prior to our meeting, had matured out of Child Protective Services, suffering from dissociative identity disorder and chronic self injurious behavior, without any identifiable skills. Young people like her tend to be too confused, frightened, and dysregulated to benefit from most therapy programs, and, lacking more effective interventions, are often managed on mood stabilizing medications, which make them less impulsive but also less able to learn and engage deeply in school, work, or relationships.

A bright woman, she described what it was like to have been plagued by chronic noises in her head and an inability to focus on schoolwork, therapy, or consistent relationships because of a disastrous combination of a chronic state of terror and extreme mental confusion. During our two lengthy interviews she gave me the most lucid description anybody has ever given me of what it was like to have been a chronically dissociated, self-destructive, terrified adolescent.

Of the many memorable things she told me, one in particular stands out: "Yes, I slowly became an attached person. When you are not afraid and confused you can know people differently." When I asked her to summarize what neurofeedback had done for her she said,

> It calmed me down. It stopped the dissociation. I can now use my feelings; I'm not running away from them; I'm not held hostage by them. I can't turn them off and on, but I can put them away. I may be sad about the abuse I went through, but I can put it away. I can call a friend and not talk about it if I don't want to talk about it, or I can do homework, or clean my apartment. I'm not anxious all the time, and when I am anxious I can reflect on it. If the anxiety is coming from the past I can find it there, or I can look at how it relates to my life now. And it's not just negative emotions, like anger and anxiety—I can reflect on love and intimacy or sexual attraction. Neurofeedback freed me up to live my life the way I want to because I'm not always in the thrall of how I was hurt and what it did to me. I'm not in fight or flight physically all the time.

She appeared completely cured, and three years after our interview she graduated near the top of her class in nursing school. Sebern's patients are the sorts of patients who utilize enormous public health resources, usually with very little to show for it. They barely function. These are the treatment-resistant people we know so well, and who have inspired us at the Trauma Center in Boston to explore a whole range of unconventional treatments. What Sebern's patients told me was the sort of anecdotal evidence that we need to inspire us to begin a serious exploration of how—and for whom—these treatments work. I felt in my element: I love to study promising new treatments that have not been tested before, like, over the years, Prozac, EMDR, sensory integration, and yoga for PTSD.

Probably the greatest challenge in mental health is how we can help patients with severe affect regulation problems, like those I interviewed at Sebern's office. This usually results from severe childhood abuse and neglect—otherwise known as developmental trauma—in which lack of synchronicity in the primary caregiver relationship leads to abnormal rhythms of brain, mind, and body. These patients are so chronically hyperaroused or shut down, and unable to filter out irrelevant information, that they have trouble engaging in whatever they are doing in a focused manner (except when they are involved in re-enacting their traumas). Our field has struggled to come up with treatments that can help them to be fully alive in the present, without being hijacked by fear, confusion, or distraction, and thus far we have been painfully unsuccessful.

As Sebern says in this book: "Stress never lies with the events that we identify as stressful—it lies in our reaction to them." Neurofeedback raises the brain threshold and generally increases stress resiliency as it increases stability. We are supposed to learn affect regulation during the first few years of life. However, if the system that regulates emotional arousal does not become hardwired in the brain early in life there is little chance that subsequent experience can engage neuroplasticity to such a degree that it can override the critical periods of development. Research on monkeys and infants raised with sensory and emotional deprivation in orphanages has shown that it is virtually impossible for the brain to acquire such capacities outside of these critical periods. My meetings with Sebern's patients held out the promise that neurofeedback might be able to accomplish what we had thus far failed to do.

Upon my return to Boston we at the Trauma Center arranged to get ourselves trained in neurofeedback, and to start a regular clinical and research program. We were interested in brain function and physiology, and, somewhat surprisingly, one of the strongest groups of supportive colleagues came from Boston University's Department of Sports Medicine. One application of neurofeedback's capacity to change focus and attention has been in the area of performance enhancement.[2] Neurofeedback training has been shown to improve cognitive flexibility, creativity, athletic control, and inner awareness.[3] I do not know of any other psychiatric treatment that can do that.

In Italy, Bruno Demichelis, the head psychologist of MilanLab, a research center established by soccer club AC Milan, taught his players to maintain a state of relaxation while watching video recordings of their errors, which led to increased mental and physiological control. In 2006, several of these players were members of the Italian team that won the World Cup. The following year, AC Milan won the European championship.

Chris Kaman of the Los Angeles Clippers, the 7-foot NBA center, is a poster child for neurofeedback training. In his early years in the NBA he had trouble concentrating and often lost track of what he was doing. After a series of neurofeedback sessions under the supervision of psychologist Tim Royer he averaged a career-high 17.9 points, 13.7 rebounds, and three blocks per game, and became a dominant center in the NBA. Kaman attributes his athletic improvements to neurofeedback.[4]

Some of the best work in the area of neurofeedback and performance enhancement has been done by John Gruzellier in London, who studied the effects of 10 sessions of neurofeedback on a group of music students. A panel of judges from the Royal College of Music evaluated their per-

---

2. Vernon, D. J. (2005). Can neurofeedback training enhance performance? An evaluation of the evidence with implications for future research. *Applied Psychophysiology and Biofeedback, 30*(4).

3. Mason, L. A., & Brownback, T. S. (2001). Optimal functioning training with EEG biofeedback for clinical populations: A case study. *Journal of Neurotherapy 5*(1–2), 33–44.

4. Beauregard, M. (2012). *Brain wars: The scientific battle over the existence of the mind and the proof that will change the way we live our lives.* New York: HarperCollins.

formance of a piece of music before and after neurofeedback training. When compared with five alternative treatment groups, only the neurofeedback group improved their real-life musical performance by approximately 10%, a huge difference in such a competitive field.

These studies on performance enhancement fit in well with the effects of neurofeedback on traumatized individuals: It helps to stabilize and focus attentional systems in the brain. Neurofeedback truly is a different paradigm from what we are accustomed to. Communication patterns in the brain are mediated by chemical and electrical signals. Because of the enormous clinical and commercial potential of psychiatric medications thus far, only the chemical paradigm has received significant interest from the scientific community. The electrical patterns in the brain have been almost entirely ignored. Even brilliant neuroscientists like Antonio Damasio and Jaak Panksepp invariably express the hope that the abnormal brain patterns that they find in their research studies will some day be rectified when somebody discovers the right chemical intervention. Neurofeedback offers an alternative to drugs and seems to be able do things that medications up to now have failed to deliver.

When neuroimaging techniques became available they allowed us to observe metabolic patterns in the brain and localize particular mental activities. However, localization does not necessarily lead to effective intervention—it just gives us a better idea of where things take place. In contrast, sophisticated EEGs allow us to measure shifting communication patterns in real time and can assist us to alter specific brain wave configurations by finding the right locations and frequencies for neurofeedback intervention. By providing brains with feedback we can change brain wave patterns and help people's minds to become more alert, attentive, focused, and organized.

As Sebern says about her patients suffering from developmental trauma, and indeed all those who engage in neurofeedback training,

> When we provide feedback to the brain we are, essentially, providing it with a mirror of its own function and inviting it to make more of some frequencies and less of others, that is, to oscillate differently. In neurofeedback, we seem to be nudging the brain to set up new oscillatory patterns that enhance both its natural complexity and its inherent and

necessary bias toward self-regulation. In effect, we may be freeing up innate but stuck oscillatory properties in the brain and allowing new ones to propagate. In neurofeedback, you see an evolving presence and dimensionality of the person who is training. They expand their focus, think new thoughts about old problems, and typically their vocabulary grows and becomes more nuanced. They are able to escape the ruts of their narrative.

It amazes me that this powerful approach has been available as long as it has without yet finding widespread acceptance. Neurofeedback is applied neuroscience—it is a new frontier in helping innumerable people who up until now have been condemned to just make the best of feeling chronically fearful, unfocused and disengaged. Sebern Fisher, a sensitive clinician and immensely experienced neurofeedback practitioner, is the right person to teach us how to integrate it into clinical practice.

—Bessel A. van der Kolk, MD
Medical Director, The Trauma Center at JRI
Professor of Psychiatry, Boston University School of Medicine

Introduction

We admitted Carl[1] to our residential treatment program for severely disturbed adolescents in the early fall of 1984. He had not yet turned 12. He was a little boy, and there was no other treatment facility in Massachusetts willing to take him.

Carl's angelic, blank face was framed by a tangled halo of burnt umber hair. His pale blue eyes revealed nothing: no fear, apprehension, worry, relief, sadness, or regret. Even when he was agitated and angry, which were his usual states of being, there was no light in his eyes. He was stocky from medications and institutional food, and he walked with the heedless effort of a toddler with a full diaper. He came to my office—which seemed suddenly devoid of cuddle toys and little red cars—accompanied by one of our larger and stronger residential staff. Before I had a chance to say hello or introduce myself, Carl said, looking into the air between us, "I was disadopted." The word sounded too big for his mouth, like new vocabulary for a 4-year-old. It wasn't clear that he knew exactly what the word meant, but his tone suggested that he had picked up on the judgment many had formed about his adoptive parents, and that he wanted to recruit that in me. For better or worse, this wasn't hard to do. I was one of those who, despite knowing what had happened in that family, felt that his parents had abandoned a vulnerable child. I believed deeply that there were no children, particularly this young, who could not be treated, given enough time, skill, patience, and love. I asked him why he had been "disadopted," and he told me that his parents

---

1. All names of patients used in this book are pseudonyms.

didn't like him anymore. When I asked him why, he shrugged his shoulders. He didn't know.

Carl's file filled in some of the story. A yellowed clipping showed that he had been advertised for adoption by the state in a column in the local paper. He was an adorable 9-year-old child, smiling his gap-tooth smile, who had spent his life in residential programs and foster care and who was looking for a permanent family to love him. A childless couple in their late 40s saw the ad and began the process to adopt this beautiful, troubled boy. Apparently the Department of Social Services had reassured them that what Carl needed was what every child needed: a secure home and the love of two parents. They assured them too that his attention-deficit/hyperactivity disorder (ADHD) was not uncommon or that difficult to treat.

Carl was "disadopted" 18 months after the papers were signed. He had just turned 11 when the police took the last of many emergency calls from his home. Carl got angry at his mother when she withheld a snack until he completed a page of his homework. In fact, he became enraged. He banged out of the house, grabbed a 2-by-4 piece of lumber, and knocked her unconscious with a blow across the back of her head as she sat at the kitchen table with his homework in front of her, waiting for him. She was taken to the local hospital by ambulance, and he was taken to the locked facility on the other side of the state in handcuffs and chains. His mother recovered from the blow, but she could not recover from this child. Neither parent wanted to press charges; they just wanted to be done with Carl.

Carl was the sixth of six children, born 7 months after his biological father was sent to state prison for aggravated assault and attempted murder. His three oldest siblings were in foster care. He was born in his mother's broken-down car. When his mother finally took him to the hospital, Social Services intervened, and all of the children were placed in separate foster homes. He had lived in a total of 17 homes and residential programs from infancy until his adoption at age 10.

As the clinical director of this treatment center, I'd worked with many severely troubled kids. Very few could make any use of traditional psychotherapy, whether behavioral or psychodynamic. I had abandoned the futility of these therapies pretty quickly, in favor of just about any approach that would help me reach these children. As disturbed, deprived, and in their own ways, as hopeless as all of these kids were, they could, with enough therapeutic elbow grease, become interested in relating to me, the fundamental prerequisite for therapy.

But Carl was of a different order. Unlike most of his peers, he wasn't resistant to therapy; he just didn't get it. More precisely, he didn't seem to get that I actually existed. His own existence seemed a kind of biologically perpetuated whim. Although he had an average IQ and was clearly not autistic, he had no "theory of mind"—no awareness that I had a mind different than his or that he himself had something called a *mind*.

He would repeat the same antisocial behavior over and over again, oblivious to consequences. He did not seem to learn from experience, whether positive or negative. There were daily incidents, many requiring physical restraint. When he would finally tire and surrender to the restraint, the staff would take him through a detailed behavioral analysis to help him see and then articulate the series of events that led to the restraint. I would repeat this when we were in session, all in a vain attempt to give him some framework for cause and effect, and to instill some sense of responsibility and even morality. He would thump or toddle away from the restraint or the session, usually calmer but none the wiser.

At one point he gave a cognitively impaired schoolmate a cup of his urine, saying it was soda. The boy, pleased to be noticed, took a swallow. When I learned of this incident, I watered down a glass of warm apple juice in a plastic cup, before he arrived, and insisted that he drink it. He smiled. He knew this had to do with what he'd done at school and he was sure I was giving him pee to drink. Looking alternately worried and amused, he refused it. I insisted, reminding him that he'd had no trouble offering this drink to his schoolmate. He looked at me with rage flashing through a crooked smile, and finally, unable to withstand the press of two big staff members and a therapist, he took a small sip, ready to spit it out. "It's just apple juice!" he said, defiantly.

"Then drink it all." He shook his head, ready to bolt.

"So, Carl, how is this making you feel?"

"You're abusing me, making me drink piss. I'll report you!"

"So it doesn't feel good, right?" He did not respond. "How do you think it made Landon feel?" He looked trapped for a split second, then confused, and then distracted. I drank the warm juice and he smiled, as if in on the "joke" the whole time. "I knew you wouldn't do that," he said—a good sign, I thought—and I said that he was right, I would never do that to him or to anyone else. "Why did you?" I asked. He shrugged his shoulders. "It was a joke."

The complex lessons of cause and effect, empathy and kindness were lost on him. It seemed that there was no way to teach him even the basics of human relationship. He could not learn, socially or academically. He was at the second-grade level in most of his subjects. He quickly became the most unpopular kid in the treatment program, a fact that did not seem to penetrate his consciousness. If it did, he showed no signs that it bothered him. He would make temporary alliances to some nefarious end and then inevitably turn on his compatriot. Carl existed, to himself and to me, as a jumble of increasingly predictable and unrelenting destructive behaviors. It wasn't just that he lacked insight or motiva-tion—that was characteristic of most of the kids there—it was that Carl lacked *himself*. There was, to borrow from Gertrude Stein, "no there, there" (1937). Therapy with him was a game of shadows.

Carl frustrated, worried, and exhausted me. Time, patience, skill, and even the possibility of love meant nothing. I couldn't reach him. In some important way, I felt I didn't understand him. Of course, I knew that he was profoundly affected by his tragic history—this was true of every one of my patients. It was the particular way in which he was affected, his soulless absence, which felt different to me.

Carl was approaching 14 and in futile treatment for nearly 2 years when I discovered attachment theory and attachment therapy, which shed light on the origins of his troubled behavior. The teacher who led the workshop on attachment was describing Carl, a child without a con-science, a child preoccupied with blood and gore, a child with a fond-ness for knives, a child ruled by rage and aggression, a child with no friends, a child who lacks empathy, who is hyperactive, who is often cruel to weaker children and animals, who has no cause-and-effect thinking, who feels no regret, and who engages in primary process lying (the denial of his culpability even when he is caught red-handed). In the course of this book we will revisit all of these symptoms as manifestations of brain dysfunction that can be addressed at a neuroelectrical level, but at this point, I knew only to focus on what Carl seemed to be feeling or what he thought or how he behaved. These were conversations, however, that he could not have due to developmental damage to his brain. The therapeutic impasse lay not so much with the child, but with his brain.

Carl spent 6 years with us and "aged out" at 18. Within 5 days of his sparsely attended graduation party he was in jail for sexually harassing a mentally disabled woman.

Due in great part to our experience with Carl, my colleagues and I at the treatment center began to assess every new intake for attachment-related difficulties. It did not take us long to detect a correlation between the level of attachment disruption in early childhood and treatment outcome: The more motherless the child was, or perceived him- or herself to be, the worse the prognosis. We had been focusing on early childhood trauma as a primary indicator of damage done, but it was never as predictive of treatment failure as the internalization of the absence of a mother, of no one taking care of the helpless infant. This feeling can lead to a profound attachment disruption long past the stage of infancy.

It wasn't until Allan Schore's seminal work, *Affect Regulation and the Origin of Self* (1994), and the advent of brain imaging that connections were made between maternal behavior and infant brain development. The single greatest cost of the mother's inability to regulate herself, we learned, is to the development of her child's right hemisphere, the part of the brain that governs regulation of emotion. Poor right-hemisphere development means that the child, like her mother, would be unable to regulate the intensity or expression of her feelings. But Schore's thesis is even bolder. He makes the argument, persuasively, that *affect regulation* is a prerequisite for the development of a coherent sense of self and other. Without the felt experience of the self-regulated mother, the baby is so overtaken by fear for her survival (and perhaps for the mother's too), that she has no capacity to organize a felt, coherent sense of self and other. Schore's work further elucidated the dilemma that was Carl. In the absence of his mother or another caregiver who could "mother" him, Carl had not developed the brain structures that serve to inhibit the subcortical emotions of fear and rage. In the absence of his mother, Carl was absent a self.

Of course, it is rare for children who have attentive mothers to be severely traumatized. The good-enough mother naturally protects her child. When traumatic events occur that are beyond her control, she validates them and helps her child recover from them. This can mean the difference between *experiencing a traumatic event* and *becoming traumatized*. The best that we had to offer these skinless, burning children was palliative care: our concern, our time, our patience, and our drugs. However, because they barely knew that we existed, this giving of ourselves made no difference to the attachment-disordered kids. As for drugs, they were routinely ineffective. As one psychiatrist said, there is no medication for a terrible childhood—but he of course felt no choice but to heavily medicate these children just to maintain some level of control. These kids were, at least for us at that time, untreatable.

Then I was introduced to neurofeedback, also called EEG biofeedback—a process that gives us access to the electrical domain of brain function by training brain waves to operate at "quieter," more stable frequencies—and the paradigm of brain function that underpins it. My view of and approach to treating kids like Carl changed. I came to understand why therapy so often fails these children and the adults they become. We understood what the loss of a mother could mean to the child in our care and to the subsequent attachment problems he may develop. What we didn't know were the ongoing effects of motherlessness, interpersonal violence, profound neglect, and repeated abandonment on his vulnerable developing brain. As is still largely true, we were looking at the impact of neglect and abuse on how the child felt, thought, and behaved. We simply did not know about the grievous toll this took on the child's brain itself.

Discovering Neurofeedback

I was still the clinical director of the residential treatment program in 1996. Our charges were, if anything, becoming more disturbed and more disturbing. A new admission burned down the girl's residence; a newly graduated patient burned down her outpatient treatment center;

a boy who was discharged home to his severely depressed mother, contracted HIV and went on a mission to give it to as many girls as he could. Graduates committed theft, battery, homicide, infanticide, and suicide. All too often we could follow their terrible trajectories in the newspapers. We were considered one of the best treatment centers for severely emotionally disturbed (SED) adolescents, and our tally of successful outcomes was dismal. Most of our graduates joined the swelling ranks of dysfunctional adults, and most had children who became equally or more dysfunctional. Only one or two kids a year, in a census of over 100, went on to live lives of quieter desperation. As their therapists, we managed this with a quiet desperation of our own. We did our best. It was very far from enough.

In early March of that year, something happened that changed my entire approach to this work—and which, in turn, became the genesis of this book. When my friend, Kathy Zilberman, an experienced psychologist, told me about neurofeedback, I felt both skeptical and interested. By the end of dinner, I agreed to be her first "subject." As suggested already, I was deeply interested in matters of the mind, but the brain itself was only faintly inferred and in clinical practice, usually drugged. The relationship between brain and mind was a subject for philosophers, not psychotherapists. Since that weekend in March, that very relationship has become my passion. But better to begin at the beginning.

Kathy and I met to begin a weekend of neurofeedback training. I suffered from insomnia, and she chose a calming protocol. After the first day I had a severe migraine (I was a migraineur), and I considered not making the long drive back to her house the next day. When I woke up—there was no change in my sleep—the decision was made to return. I phrase it that way because it did not exactly feel like *my* decision, just one that was made and to which I did not object. We did several more half-hour sessions on Sunday morning, went out for brunch, and I drove back home.

There was a movie playing in town that many of my feminist friends had recommended, and that afternoon was my last chance to see it. So despite my throbbing, medicated head, I took my seat on the aisle to watch *Antonia's Line*. Until the scene I am about to describe, I was unaware of feeling anything much different as a result of the neurofeedback. After it, there was no doubt that I had had a profound experience. The scene involved a rape and a pitchfork. I had watched the requisite number of violent films in the name of art, politics, or coolness, but this scene, on that day, made me sick, literally sick. I had to leave the theater. I noted being surprised that everyone wasn't leaving. All faces, in fact, were turned toward what seemed to me, at that moment, unprecedented and inexcusable violence. As I walked home, I was aware of feeling a level of vulnerability that I had never experienced. Although unfamiliar and disquieting, it seemed right. I was struck by the cobalt blue sky as day turned to night and noticed the house lights winking on along the street. I found myself neither back at the movie—or with all it evoked— nor already home. I was there, fully present, and exquisitely open. There was, notably for me, no threat in the air. I felt newly safe.

By the time Kathy and I talked the next night, I was in the third day of the migraine, hypomanic, and delivering my report through highly pressured speech. Kathy, as one can easily imagine, was worried. She said this training was meant to calm me and that clearly had not happened. (It would take some evolution in software and in understanding to know that training at 12–15 Hz was too high a frequency for my brain and many others.) Given the pressure in my voice, it was hard to reassure her, but I was not worried. I acknowledged the problems and told her, with confidence, that they would be gone by Wednesday morning. (They were.)

I spoke about my experience in terms of Buddhist teaching. "If I didn't have the vocabulary of the *dharma*, Kathy, I would have to make it up. I understand the teaching now in a way I have never gotten it before [we are both Buddhist meditators]. I understand what it is to be one with everything, because I am." This was, in fact, my experience, but given that I was hypomanic, not at all reassuring to anyone outside of me. Beneath the hyperarousal, I felt something, which, in that initial conversation, I could not yet name. I had lost a hyper-startle response that I had lived with for most of my life. And beneath the wild waves of migraine and mania, I felt collected, even serene. I'd been aware that I would send a stalking horse out before me to deal with new social encounters, but this insight had done nothing to diminish its presence or the innate sense of its necessity. This false self, too, vanished. I had always rehearsed

anticipated conversations and often felt myself floundering in unantici-
pated ones. After the brain training, I was surprised, as were others, by
my sudden, easy spontaneity. Over the next few days, as the negative
effects waned and the positive endured, I realized that I was, simply,
much less afraid. My life—in fact, my *self*—had changed profoundly,
and there was a sense of never going back.

It was this experience that gradually gave rise to my understanding of
the preeminence of fear in all psychopathology and to its normative
potential to highjack all other states of mind. But fear not only grabs the
mind, it overtakes the brain. I knew that I dealt with chronic fear, but I
thought about it exclusively as my *mind*'s reaction to my history. That
weekend, I discovered my brain. I could feel a new reality, that my brain
was separable from my mind and that my mind was inseparable from my
brain. My brain seemed to have a mind of its own. It was this that sent
me back to Kathy's even with the migraine and this that predicted when
the hypomania would end. I had found it through asking my brain, via
feedback, to change the frequencies at which it fired, to find its own
inherent but disrupted rhythmicity. And in the process, I had achieved
significant relief from fear. This had to mean that fear was not only a
mind event; it was a brain event that was somehow encoded in how my
brain fired.

The following October I went to Los Angeles for a 5-day workshop
with Barry Sterman and Susan and Siegfried Othmer. I felt like I understood this process from the inside out, but I was still unclear about the
science that supported this experience. After several eureka moments,
after learning some of the basic science, and after hearing that others had
had experiences similar to mine, I borrowed money and bought a neurofeedback system.

And so, I began to learn how to treat developmentally traumatized
patients in a fundamentally new way. Since then I have integrated neurofeedback into my practice of psychotherapy with most of my patients.
Most of them endure the multiple, in most cases, lifelong aftershocks of
developmental trauma. As adolescents and adults they have been given
a wide range of diagnoses: posttraumatic stress disorder (PTSD), attachment disorder, dissociative identity disorder (DID), ADHD, conduct
disorder, obsessive–compulsive disorder (OCD), borderline personality

disorder (BPD), narcissistic personality disorder, dependent personality disorder, antisocial personality disorder, Asperger's syndrome (now referred to as high level autism), eating disorder, bipolar disorder, and substance abuse. Although they have come for therapy with many different diagnoses and were almost all seen as suffering "comorbidities," they had strikingly similar histories, including failed attachment; neglect; sexual, physical, and/or emotional abuse; and, for some, the insecurities of poverty, homelessness, and inadequate food as young children. They all shared the core problem of affect dysregulation. Fear plays an insidious role in all of these comorbidities, as well as in Axis II diagnoses. In most cases, as neurofeedback training quiets fear, the symptoms of these disorders significantly diminish. After years of neurofeedback, I no longer see these disorders as distinct, but as individual manifestations of overwrought, amygdala-driven and dysregulated nervous systems.

Just as emotion regulation is the first task of good parenting, it is also the first task of effective therapy. All too often, however, the severe states of the patient prevail and despite the best efforts of both the therapist and the patient, despite even the most judicious use of pharmacology, the therapy fails. Through training the brain to seek its own stability, we can ease these terrible sequelae to early childhood neglect and abuse, regardless of the diagnosis given. The fact that these things happened never goes away, but the person's reactivity to them can diminish dramatically. In talking about how early traumatic events had stolen her life, one of my patients said, "I don't know exactly where this is coming from but, somehow, it just doesn't seem relevant anymore."

Several important core assumptions are the foundation of this book:

1. Neurofeedback changes the focus of our attention from the mind to the brain.
2. The brain organizes itself rhythmically in the frequency domain, and it is there that brain plasticity resides.
3. We can access these rhythms through a type of computerized biofeedback to the brain called *neurofeedback*.
4. Fear is the core emotion and the primary dysrhythmia in developmental trauma. Without addressing the brain's fear circuitry

directly, developmental trauma remains highly resistant to treatment.

My aim in writing this book is to share with readers what I have learned about the intricacies of attachment problems and developmental trauma and the role that neurofeedback can play in ameliorating them. In the following chapters I explore what happens to the brain, the infrastructure of mind, in developmental trauma and why and how neurofeedback can be used to help these shattered minds by organizing the dysregulated brain. We tend to think of the brain in terms of its other critical physical and chemical domains. But its plasticity, its ability to change and to learn, seems to lay primarily in its electrical, oscillatory properties—in short, in the way it fires. As Thomas Insel, the Director of the National Institute of Mental Health, noted in his article in *Scientific American*, "The latest research shows that the malfunctioning of entire circuits may underlie many mental disorders" (2010, p. 44). I introduce readers to the electrical domain of brain function because this domain is fundamental to understanding how and why neurofeedback works.

In the chapters to come, I explore the formations of mind and brain of those suffering from developmental trauma, and share the brain-based techniques I have found to be effective. For those readers who are just beginning to investigate this field, I introduce the science of neurofeedback, which suggests that brain plasticity resides in the electrical oscillations of the brain that we access through brain wave training. I share my approach to using neurofeedback with this population, particularly protocols that address fear. I describe my experience of integrating neurofeedback and psychotherapy and explore how each impacts the other. I also introduce you to many patients with these challenging histories who have benefited from neurofeedback training, as well as to several who have not. Ultimately, these stories are important illustrations of the power of neurofeedback to foster positive change, particularly its ability to quiet the repetitive firing of fear circuitry. When fear quiets, these patients can begin to live in their own skins. They feel increasing equanimity and increasing empathy. These are manifestations of the emerging sense of self and other. The well-regulated brain gives rise to a self unafraid to love. In this way, neurofeedback is a relational technology and intervention.

I do not write this book as a neuroscientist or a researcher. I am sharing what I have learned as a psychotherapist over many years of working with very troubled adolescents and adults, before and after I began to use neurofeedback, and as someone who has used neurofeedback extensively with her own brain. It is my hope to make neurofeedback understandable, accessible, and compelling to clinicians and their patients who are struggling to deal with the seemingly unending devastation of developmental trauma.

A final note: I use the word *patient* throughout this book because I cannot think of a better term, particularly for people with these histories. *Patient* has its root in the Greek word for "suffering."

Neurofeedback in the
Treatment of
Developmental Trauma

PART I

UNDERLYING THEORIES

Chapter |

The Mind in Developmental Trauma

Void of Self

Presently we lack the diagnostic language to describe the enduring catastrophe of the child whose mother has turned away. However this comes about—through neglect, abuse, abandonment, mental illness, addiction, or other troubles—the baby is left without a felt sense of the mother's presence and without the experience of an organizing other. When children and adults come to our clinical attention with histories of traumatic events, they are most often diagnosed with either posttraumatic stress disorder (PTSD) or reactive attachment disorder (RAD), and sometimes both, in an attempt to represent what has happened to them and how they manifest their histories. There are problems with these diagnoses.

PTSD joined the diagnostic vernacular in the DSM-III in 1980 (American Psychiatric Association, 1980) to describe anew what therapists had always seen as a common consequence of war: the breakdown of the personality under the assault of unrelenting horror and fear. Initially it was a diagnosis intended for soldiers, like the diagnosis of "soldier's heart" dating back to the Civil War and "battle fatigue" and "shell shock" in wars that followed. PTSD was then quickly adopted to diagnose the effects of civilian trauma such as rape, car accident, or natural disaster. It was taken up as well by those working and living with the multiple aftershocks of early childhood abuse and neglect. This is not the PTSD of international combat, but of in-home terror. The nervous system is stunned in both adults and children with PTSD. Both can have sleep disturbances, nightmares, flashbacks, problems thinking clearly, and trouble regulating intense emotions, all of which undermine their capacity for relationships. When a baby is stunned, however, the child suffers not only these symptoms but the ongoing effects of primary dysregulation on their developing brains, bodies, and core sense of self. Anyone, child or adult, who meets criteria for PTSD is in the grip of unrelenting terror, and terror that never remits disfigures the mind. But it is a quantitatively and qualitatively different experience to be exposed to overwhelming, terrifying events as an adult than it is to be exposed to them as a baby or a child—and then, all too often, at the hands of one's caretaker. As we will see, the concept of *developmental trauma* addresses these differences.

With so much of our thinking turned toward the terrible effects of trauma, it can be easy to lose sight of the fact that a child need not be abused to be in trouble; he needs *only* to experience himself as abandoned by the mother. RAD, which also became official in the DSM-III (American Psychiatric Association, 1980), describes the effects of pathogenic care on the child's ability to bond appropriately. These children are either hypervigilant, aggressive, and averse to comfort, or, in fewer cases, inhibited, ambivalently needy, and withdrawn. They are suspicious of caretakers—a suspiciousness that, sadly, they come by honestly. They are prone to dissociative states and in the fugue of mother loss, they do not readily perceive their primary caregiver.

A 4-year-old boy we'll call Sam showed all of these characteristics. He was hypervigilant and aggressively resistant to comforting. Even as he grew to trust his adoptive parents, he would wander away from his mother to take the hand of a stranger on the street. While on a camping trip with other residents and residential staff, Carl, whom we've already met, left the campsite with a family he'd met the night before. When he was retrieved 100 miles up the road, he had no explanation. He wasn't running away; he just didn't discern any difference between those who had cared for him for 3 years and people (obviously with some significant problems of their own) whom he didn't know at all. The DSM diagnosis misses perhaps the single most grievous symptom: the fear and rage they typically feel and unleash, characteristically, on their mothers. It was Carl's near-lethal attack on his adoptive mother that brought him into our treatment center. Sam nearly choked the life out of his only sibling and he set fire to his foster home at age 3. Neither of these boys could orient toward care. They were abandoned by their mothers and left alone to navigate a world apparently hostile to their existence. They had been handed off from adult to adult. It is very difficult to know how this constellation of neglect is actually experienced by an infant, but given their real vulnerability, it would be hard to imagine anything but stark, animal terror.

These boys suffered from both PTSD and RAD—and they suffered more. When we open the lens to look at the larger developmental picture, we can see that the experiences of the absent mother, attachment trauma, and the assaults that can accrue as a result (sexual, physical, and emotional) profoundly impact the child's ability to regulate affect, particularly the flood of the primary limbic emotions: fear, shame, and anger. Without any capacity for affect regulation, a child will have great difficulty relating to parents, other adults, or peers. When a child cannot emotionally regulate herself, she'll find it daunting to learn the rules—social or academic A child's readiness for interpersonal regulation and for learning is inborn. We are a social species.

However, for the inherency of attachment to unfold, a child needs at least one reliable, regulating, other—best, his own biological mother and father—and, optimally, a larger regulating environment. It is difficult to imagine that a child whose biological mother is present, attuned and attentive, would be subjected to the physical, sexual, or emotional assaults that can, and usually do, lead to a diagnosis of PTSD. Children can of course suffer from PTSD as the result of natural disasters, accident, surgery, or the circumstances of war. They can also suffer significant dysregulation from losing their mothers, without any form of abuse. But characteristically children like Carl and Sam are actually suffering neither from PTSD nor RAD, but from an unholy aggregate of both that will affect the course of their development throughout their lives.

In recognition of this reality, Bessel van der Kolk and other prominent researchers and clinicians have called for the new diagnosis of developmental trauma disorder (DTD). This diagnosis would subsume the diagnosis of PTSD in these children to emphasize the profound impact of early childhood trauma on development, *and* the diagnosis of RAD because disrupted attachment is central to developmental trauma. The diagnostic category of DTD is an attempt to more comprehensively reflect the dysregulation that results from the impact of these multiple horrors—abuse, interpersonal violence, attachment disruption, neglect, and all too often poverty—as well as to call attention to the differences between children and adults who experience trauma (van der Kolk, 2005). As the term suggests, developmental processes are at risk in multiple spheres of function in these children. It is not my intention here to enter into the contentious process of diagnostic validation for the DSM, only to say that we are constrained in our current thinking about these children and the adults they become by the use of two inadequate diagnoses, PTSD and RAD. DTD, in contrast, encompasses the profound and enduring effects of traumatic events and neglect on a child's developing brain and body, on his ability to self-regulate, to learn, and to relate to others.

A final caveat on this topic: As I wrestle with the issue of best diagnosis, I have to acknowledge a bind. Since beginning to work directly with the brain using neurofeedback, I have come to question whether our nosology of mental disorders helps or hinders our ability to understand what another is experiencing. I think it hinders us. With neurofeedback, the framework shifts to arousal and communication patterns in the brain and the treatment focuses on symptoms, most of which are shared across DSM categories. But the DSM is the ruling paradigm, so we need a diagnosis now that best describes the multiple impacts of childhood neglect and assault. As neurofeedback practitioners, we will learn to see through the diagnosis to discern the underlying patterns of arousal. It is the arousal embedded within the diagnosis that we are treating.

Core Features of Developmental Trauma

Attachment rupture, poverty, neglect, the absence of empathy, and emotion and sensory dysregulation are all central aspects of developmental trauma. I will explain each in detail here.

Attachment Rupture and the Motherless Child

Attachment rupture, the central disorganizing core of developmental trauma, can manifest in much less dramatic ways than described in the cases above, but in ways that can be equally devastating to the development of a regulated self. Research in attachment has identified several "attachment styles" that emerge in children as a result primarily of attachment experiences with their mothers. These styles are categorized as (1) secure attachment, (2) insecure attachment with anxious/avoidant and anxious/resistant subtypes, and (3) disorganized attachment (Ainsworth, Blehar, Waters, & Wall, 1978; Bowlby, 1988; Main & Solomon, 1986). The children and adults whom I describe in this book fall into the latter two groups.

It must be noted here that there are many children and adults with insecure attachments who do not seem to suffer psychopathology as a result. They adopt more or less workable attachment strategies and live their lives. In fact, in an issue of *Scientific American Mind* (Levine & Heller, 2011) there was an article on understanding your attachment profile in order to find a mate. With the exception of disorganized attachment, which looks frankly disturbed (the child who approaches his returning mother walking backwards, or the adult with no significant relationships), it may be difficult to diagnose an individual's attachment style as disordered. People relate to each other differently, and these differences are not pathological per se. There are, however, symptoms that do alert us to the devastation of attachment rupture, and they cluster, as we have seen, around problems in self-regulation. In the absence of a regulating mother, the child does not grow and develop around the being of another but alone, in the midst of ongoing, daily eruptions of his own powerful emotions. When these emotions are not regulated, they overtake and deform the development of the child.

My emphasis here is on the child's experience or perception of having no mother, of being motherless. Clearly babies can be successfully nurtured by their fathers, grandparents, adoptive parents, and other caregivers--which is why we don't often see these children or adults in our offices. More often we see the after-affects of the felt rupture between baby and mother, and, as proposed, it is this disorganizing attachment disruption that is the core of developmental trauma. The experience of motherlessness, of profound helplessness, leaves the completely vulnerable child in the throes of daily, unrelenting fear for his survival. All too often motherlessness allows, even invites, assaults on the child. The core trauma may not be the assault(s) itself, however terrible, but the absence of the mother, physically or emotionally, to prevent, address, or repair it.

A significant subset of these patients, particularly those with mothers who suffered from mental or physical illness, learn to blame themselves for their mother's condition or death. This patient organizes her sense of self and other around this belief, which is, as we will see, deeply etched in patterns in her brain. When it is the mother herself who attacks her child, the child has no body to turn in to, no way to escape. The whole of the universe has turned against this child. When she manages to survive physically, she must still fight for emotional and psychological survival, and, in all too many instances, for the rest of her life.

Children not held in the minds of their mothers are lost, forgotten. Being held in the mind of the mother is the original holding environment, an experience that most of my patients have never had. Several adults with whom I have worked have described being in constant state of free fall, backwards through a black hole. They are themselves black holes and so, often, are their mothers. It is less a metaphor than a transcription of state. One patient had a revealing dream early in her neurofeedback training. She dreamt that she was approaching her mother eagerly, but when she got to her, she saw that her mother was only a cardboard cutout. She walked by the cutout into empty, dark space. These are, I think, images of the energetic field of motherlessness, which leaves patients not just with the sense that they are alone, but that they don't exist. A patient said recently, "Before I came here, I didn't have a body." In Chapter 2 we explore the focal structures in the brain that underwrite the embodied sense of self. This patient did not experience herself in her mind or in her body. She had yet to discover that the hand she held up before her face belonged to her.

The effects of motherlessness coalesce into a background field of ambient fear, which exerts a powerful gravitational pull. Many of my patients with DTD have told me that they have not lived a day of their lives without fear. Fear is their default position, their universe. These patients typically experience only the faintest sense of personal boundary, a sense that would allow them to know clearly that "This is me, and that is you." They may feel as if they have no skin. When they can give voice to it, many report an agonizing feeling of diffusion, as if their nervous systems have no end, but move out infinitely into space. They have no felt experience of containment, which leaves them feeling unmoored, even wild. One young woman, whose mother suffered from paranoid schizophrenia, described herself as feral. In the chaos and absence that was her home, she was on her own; she was never raised. These are nervous systems with no experience of constraint; these are people with no experience of being held.

In a conversation we happened into about attachment, a veterinarian told me about an approach to gentling wild horses that captures what this patient wanted me to understand. It is a story about the need of the organism, whether young horse or young child, to feel a constraint on the central nervous systems (CNS) to be able to bond. Both, in their way, need to feel securely wrapped. The wild horse is backed into a small stall and the head is held by a halter chained to either side of the stall. The door is closed. The horse will fight this arrangement, often wild-eyed with terror and kicking to get free. Horses are prey animals, whose lives depend on their ability to run. In addition, they are genetically programmed to fear mountain lions whose attack begins when they jump on the horse's back. The goal, of course, is for this horse, so programmed, to accept a person on its back. The stall is slowly filled with grain until it covers the horse, over its back and up to its head. In rather short order, the horse surrenders to the weight and the containment of the grain. Its sympathetic arousal, its instinct toward fight or flight, is immobilized, which seems to allow a CNS disconnect between weight on its back and threat to its life. As the horse calms, the rider climbs over the top of the stall and settles her weight on its back, rubbing its head and ears, speaking softly, further quieting the fear response. In this new position of no fear, the horse accepts the rider. The chains are released, the door to the stall is opened slowly, the grain slides to the floor, and the horse and rider leave the stall, a bonded pair.

The unbonded child "lives" in a similar nervous system and relies on the same survival-oriented defenses of fight and flight to protect her even when there is no apparent threat. And when fight or flight is not possible—which is always the case for these babies and children—the only defense remaining is the freeze response. As Levine notes: "Traumatized people have a deep distrust of the arousal cycle, usually for good reason. This is because to a trauma victim, arousal has become coupled with the overwhelming experience of being immobilized by fear" (Levine, 1997, p. 128). A person who feels motherless and uncontained lives in a CNS that is frozen in fear.

Among the lesser troubles of one such girl, Lori, who wandered this trackless interior landscape, was difficulty reading. Lori came to me when she was 24 years old. As a premature newborn, she had been brought to an orphanage in a shoebox and was not expected to live. She was fed with an eyedropper. After many neurofeedback sessions to help her lower arousal, organize her brain and regulate herself, she reported to me that she could suddenly see pictures arising from the words. This happened for the first time when she was reading Toni Morrison's *The Bluest Eye* in her college class. I only learned of this problem after she protested, "Why do they make us read this stuff?!" This was the first book she had ever "seen." When I asked her how she had read before, without pictures forming, she said that she'd just tried to string the words together to make sense of them. This is how I imagine it was for her in all realms, trying to string things together to make sense out of her essentially uninhabited world. How would she learn to discern social realities, to trust others or, even more profoundly, to trust her own mind? In optimal or even good-enough circumstances, when a baby cries out, the cry alerts the mother to attend to the baby's needs and comfort him. The two establish a rhythm of reciprocity, heartbeat to heartbeat, and they soothe one another's distress. The mother of the child who will suffer developmental trauma perceives her child's needs as assaults and pushes away. The child's need is either ignored, subsumed, or punished. There is no alignment: no recognition, no soothing, no rocking, no singing, no rhythmic attunement. Without these sources of regulation and comfort, there is within the baby no sense of "mother/other" and no sense of "baby/self."

The rhythms of brain, mind, and relationship are profoundly disrupted and so too are the rhythms of the body. As a group, those with developmental trauma suffer inordinately from somatic problems, including sleep disorders, headaches, a wide range of gastrointestinal issues and for some problems with physical co-ordination, all of which typically worsen over time (Porges, 2011; van der Kolk, 2005). These physical manifestations are often experienced beneath clinical threshold, and the reaction to them can be easily exaggerated by baseline fear. Patients who remember their childhood ordeals through their bodies are routinely dismissed as hypochondriacs or "somaticizers," and of course, in most people with DTD, the body is where the memory is. As van der Kolk (1994) famously wrote, "The body keeps the score" (p. 253).

Poverty

Attachment catastrophe can happen in any home, but when these children and their families are also poor, there is no buffering of fear that material comforts, however thin, can offer. The environment within which this child lives offers no external source of safety and none of the inherent affirmation afforded by class status. As well as suffering from abuse and neglect at home, these children also routinely contend with abandonment by their fathers; poor, neglectful schools; violent neighborhoods and inadequate housing; homelessness and food insecurity: Guns, rats, and empty bellies. Children who grow up as members of despised or disenfranchised groups are highly susceptible to shame. According to the Minnesota Longitudinal Study of Risk and Adaptation from the Institute of Child Development (Carlson et al., 1975–present), after their first year of life, poor children will hear the word "no" three times more often than more privileged kids. Alan Sroufe, Professor Emeritus at the University of Minnesota and lead researcher in this study, underscores the added impact of poverty on disabling symptoms later in life (Sroufe et al., 2005). Although in this article he is focusing on the diagnosis of attention-deficit disorder (ADD), it is safe to assume that many of his subjects who qualify for a psychiatric diagnosis would meet criteria for developmental trauma. Sroufe (2012) summarized his data in an OP-Ed article in the *New York Times*: His team began to follow 180 children who were born into poverty in 1975. The researchers focused on many aspects of the children's development and particularly on their relationships with their caregivers, teachers, and peers.

By late adolescence, 50 percent of our sample qualified for some psychiatric diagnosis. Almost half displayed behavior problems at school on at least one occasion, and 24 percent dropped out by 12th grade. . . . Other large-scale epidemiological studies confirm such trends in the general population of disadvantaged children. Among all children, including all socioeconomic groups, the incidence of A.D.D. is estimated at 8 percent. What we found was that the environment of the child predicted development of A.D.D. problems. In stark contrast, measures of neurological anomalies at birth, I.Q. and infant temperament—including infant activity level—did not predict A.D.D. (Sroufe, 2012)

Although we may be encumbered here by diagnostic labels—there are many reasons that a child could find it hard to pay attention—what is clear in this very important study is that poverty counts. When children grow up poor within a more affluent community, they can feel saturated by the shame of overt or covert scorn. There is no comfort, at any turn, for these children. I once asked an adolescent patient with DID who was abandoned by her mother, brutally sexually abused by her father, and homeless much of her childhood if she had any good memories. I watched her slowly light up. She had two: the day her father bought her cotton candy and the times when she would play for hours with dolls and eat peanut butter. By the age of 8 she had learned how to break into the affluent homes across town and play with other children's toys.

The Adverse Childhood Events Study

The Adverse Childhood Events Study (ACE; Anda & Felitti, 2003) details the multiple impacts of attachment disruption and trauma that occur in childhood and endure in later life. Psychotherapists have always understood that events in childhood affect the well-being of adults, but this correlation is far from established in the medical community or the culture at large. The ACE study—overseen by Vincent Felitti and Robert Anda at Kaiser Permanente's Department of Preventative Medicine in San Diego, and in collaboration with the Centers for Disease Control and Prevention (CDC)—has sought to change that. Felitti, who ran an obesity treatment program in San Diego, was puzzled by a common outcome primarily seen in his female patients: They would be very successful in losing weight, and then many would regain it. He interviewed these patients and was startled to learn that most had been sexually abused as children and either consciously or unconsciously feared becoming sexually attractive. Their obesity was their protection. This insight eventually led to the study of over 17,000 middle-class men and women (in equal numbers), with an average age of 57, in an effort to discern the ongoing effects of early childhood trauma on health (Lanius, Vermetten, & Pain, 2010). The ACE score is determined by the number of "Yes" responses to the following questions:

Prior to your 18th birthday were you subject to any of the following circumstances:
- A. Abuse
  - 1) emotional: recurrent threats, humiliation
  - 2) physical: beating, not spanking
  - 3) contact sexual abuse
- B. Household dysfunction
  - 4) mother was treated violently
  - 5) household member was alcoholic or drug user
  - 6) household member was imprisoned
  - 7) household member was chronically depressed, suicidal, mentally ill or in psychiatric hospital
  - 8) not raised by both biological parents
- C. Neglect
  - 9) physical
  - 10) emotional (Felitti, 2010, pp. 78–79)

The number of discreet events experienced by an individual is only loosely represented by the responses of "often" or "very often," and yet the number of times a person answers yes to these ten categories—the ACE score—strongly predicts illness and premature death in adulthood. Psychiatric consequences are clear:

54% of current depression and 58% of suicide attempts in women can be attributed to adverse childhood events and . . . male children with an ACE Score 6 or more have a 46-fold increased likelihood of later becoming an injection drug user compared with a male child with an ACE Score 0. (2010, p. 82)

The ACE score also correlates with a wide range of medical problems, not seen as psychological, including liver disease, chronic obstructive pulmonary disease (COPD), coronary artery disease, and autoimmune disease. "Individuals with ACE Score 6 and higher had a lifespan almost two decades shorter than seen in those with an ACE Score 0 but otherwise similar characteristics" (2010, p. 84).

A recent study (Shalev et al., 2013) found that "compared with their counterparts, the children who experienced two or more kinds of violence exposure showed significantly more telomere erosion between age 5 baseline and age 10 follow-up" (p. 1). Telomeres are chromosomal structures that get shorter as we as we age. This study suggests that aging is already advanced in very young children who experience violence. The boy Sam had some gray hair at age 7.

Childhood trauma makes itself known in physical as well as mental problems, which is why patients who use neurofeedback may show striking physical as well as emotional and behavioral improvement. In the course of my work with neurofeedback, I have seen changes in eyesight, hearing, smell, taste, thyroid function, stability of blood sugar, constipation, irritable bowel syndrome (IBS), blood pressure, motion sickness, migraine, neuropathy and other chronic pain problems, and skin rashes, among other physical complaints, while training the brain to quiet anxiety or depression. The physical and the mental are inseparable. In Chapter 8 we explore the resolution of many physical complaints as well as body memory during the course of neurofeedback.

Neglect

Since the relatively recent embrace of PTSD, most of our therapeutic dialogue has focused on trauma, such as physical and sexual abuse, emotional assault, witnessed acts of violence, chronic humiliation, and the devastating effects they have on children throughout their lives. We have talked less about neglect. Perhaps this is because neglect, in its multiple manifestations, is pervasive and difficult to define. It is like pornography; the therapist should know it when he sees it. When the parent leaves the baby alone in her crib for days at a time, or fails to feed or change her regularly, we know to label that neglect. But maternal neglect can also occur when the mother is physically present but emotionally absent. This level of neglect can be difficult to document and its effects can be difficult to gage. In many cases it may be close to normative. This is the depressed mother who attends to the survival of her baby but who cannot mirror his facial expressions because her own are frozen. She cannot, from her own deadened place, enliven her baby. As attachment research has demonstrated (Bowlby, 1988; Ainsworth et al., 1978; Main & Solomon, 1986; Tronick, 2007), babies depend on this face-to-face, eye-to-eye, voice-to-voice, emotionally reciprocal interaction to know that they exist. The children of depressed mothers are at risk.

And what is the plight of the baby born to a mother who is herself suffering developmental trauma? What internalized experience will this mother draw on when she is with her baby? One researcher found that he could predict, with greater than 75% accuracy, the attachment style and status of a baby based on an interview with the mother during her pregnancy (Fonagy, Steele, & Steele, 1991). If the mother had suffered unrepaired attachment rupture, the great likelihood was that her baby would as well.

And then there are those children, estimated at 320,000 a year in the United States (Cook, Petersen, & Moore, 1990), who are born to mothers who are abusing drugs and alcohol. It is accepted that these substances affect brain development in utero, but even after the child is born, if the mother is drug- or alcohol-dependent or addicted, and her relationship is with the drug, not with her baby, this too will have a negative impact on attachment, as well as the brain development that is dependent on attachment. The mentally ill mother who is preoccupied with her own demons and delusions can love her baby but still wreak havoc on the baby's developing mind. Her terror-driven distortions become embedded in her child.

As one person with this history said to me, "It is motherlessness, but it is worse than that. She is in me; she is me; there is no me at all." Another woman, who was abandoned by her mother and father as a toddler, told me that she had known "at some level" (the cognitive level) that I was concerned for her, but that she was totally unable to feel my existence or her own. At best, this made for a highly attenuated therapy, one in which she was, as it were, stringing words together. When we talked about feelings, she literally could not understand what I was saying. No picture arose from my words and, since neither of us existed, she could not experience my being as engaged with hers.

These are some of the starker circumstances but in no way the only ones that qualify as neglect. One man came to me saying that all he could feel was anger. He said that he looked around and saw that others felt an array of feelings and seemed to be more "alive" than he. He was considered "the prick of the office," he told me; no one liked him. His marriage was a relationship of convenience. He'd grown up in an affluent family with an angry father who was mostly away on business and a mother who sought to comfort herself with bourbon. Every year during his school vacation he was hospitalized for 2 weeks with asthma. His parents would visit infrequently. He compared himself to Ted Kaczynski, the Unabomber (a man who seemed to have had much more caring parents than he), who was also hospitalized away from his parents. Kaczynski was kept in isolation with severe hives for 8 of his first 18 months. He suffered from a form of hospitalism (first described by René Spitz in 1945) and must have felt abandoned not only by his mother, but by the human race. His mother wrote in March 1943, "Baby home from hospital and is healthy but quite unresponsive after his experience" (Ferguson, 2009).

Sadly, my patient felt that his days in the hospital were the best days of his life, precisely because his parents did not visit him. He believed that his mother lay awake at night deciding how she could torment him. (The year after his surgery for esophageal cancer, his mother gave him a high-end coffee maker for his birthday.) He neglected and taunted his sons as he had been taunted and neglected, and initially saw nothing amiss in this behavior. My patient, like Ted Kaczynski, had internalized his mother's absence, and as we will see, both his mind and his brain had taken shape around it. He made little progress in a year of talk therapy for much the same reasons as the others. He did not know I was there. He did not emotionally comprehend me or what I was saying. Although he felt understood when I gave him the diagnosis of attachment disorder, mostly what he gained in therapy was a further opportunity to vent. Until we started to use neurofeedback, we could not develop an interpersonal rhythm. There was no spark, no resonance between us, and this resonance is essential to a therapy that works. As his therapist I was, essentially, trying to talk to his amygdala, the part of the brain that is shaping these perceptions, memories, actions, and fears. The nonverbal, subcortical amygdala cannot make sense of words. Talking, however, is what therapists are expected to do and what patients are expected to benefit from. (We explore the amygdala and the brain driven by fear in Chapter 2.)

In her important and influential book, *Cognitive Behavioral Treatment of Borderline Personality Disorder*, Marsha Linehan (1993) argues that the source of borderline personality disorder (BPD) is "the invalidating environment." She considers abuse in childhood to be an example of a particularly terrible invalidating environment and as part of the etiology of this disorder. She does not, however, contend—and her data do not support—that individuals have to be abused or traumatized as children to develop BPD. Unfortunately, she makes too little of the disorganizing and dysregulating effect of neglect. This omission is problematic because neglect clearly contributes to the high level of arousal and emotional instability that is the hallmark of BPD. Others argue that there is an absolute overlap between developmental trauma and borderline personality disorder and that BPD should be reclassified as complex PTSD or, more recently, developmental trauma (Herman, 1997; van der Kolk, 1994). Were Linehan to rename this disorder, however, she would call it *emotion regulation disorder* (personal communication, May 7, 2011). To my mind, this term would represent a quantum leap forward in our understanding of the core problem in those given this diagnosis. They cannot regulate their emotions to save their lives. One wonders where the mother is in the invalidating environment.

I would contend that the profound motherlessness that we have seen in developmental trauma, we see also in most people meeting criteria for BPD and, in fact, for all other personality disorders. In disturbances this severe, when there is no known history of physical, emotional, or sexual abuse, it is time to look for emotional if not physical neglect. This was the situation for a woman whose mother was a trauma "survivor" and who was both depressed and dissociative. My patient too has struggled with depression and dissociation, not because she was abused, per se, although she was, but because she could never locate her mother, even when they were in the same room. She eloquently described the disorganizing but discrete sense of diffusion of her nervous system: "Untouched skin holds nothing; no one. My nerves have no endings. They go forever out into space." Her mother was unable to hold her in any of the ways that Schore (1994) asserts develop a stable, evolving sense of self—not with her gaze, her voice, her touch, or her embrace. Her mother's neglect was a manifestation of her own internal distress (as, in some way, it always is). My patient sensed that her mother wanted to care for her but just could not.

Also included in this invalidating environment are the mothers who, for many reasons, just shouldn't be mothers. They have no desire and no gift. They are uninvolved with their children. Their adult children often have very few memories of their childhoods. A good deal of the relationship between an attached mother and child involves building memories. Once language develops, mother and child engage in an ongoing commentary on the life they share together that routinely includes the question, "Do you remember when we . . . ?" But much of this dilemma is preverbal: no mother there; no mother inside me; no one to remember, and no one to remember me. These patients cannot conceive that I hold them in my mind, and many have feared that I will not be present when they return for their next appointment. They believe that I will forget them. The children of uninvolved mothers often describe themselves either as "mistakes" or as "trophies." They too end up feeling hollow, hungry, and fearful. They too have the experience of the mother who turned away.

The experiences of neglect that leave the child and the adult with this felt experience of *no mother* vary widely, but regardless of the specifics, the effects of neglect on the developing brain are devastating. These effects may, in fact, be even more catastrophic than the effects of abuse. But, as we have seen, both happen in the vacuum of motherlessness. When physical, emotional, or psychological neglect goes unrecognized and unaddressed, this baby is truly alone in the world.

When the mother is present and aligns herself with her baby, the child develops from the fabric of her being. A known self develops. In developmental trauma, the self is fashioned around the motherless void. *Self* is, at best, a casting that can present itself socially, even sometimes beautifully, and perpetuate itself through time and space, an object propelled by its biology. Commonly in this group, however, there is little capacity to sustain the artifice of false self. It is as if the casting were carelessly or furiously smashed into fragments, a self shattered by assault or falling to pieces from the weight and weightlessness of neglect. These images suggest the toll from the seemingly benign to the seemingly untreatable.

Empathic Failure

Empathy and its absence is a hallmark issue for children and adults with histories of developmental trauma. Two kinds of problems arise: an impaired capacity to feel for the other and/or feeling for the other without end. The latter may not be true empathy as much as a truncated ability to see the other as the other, and as a result, feeling the pain of others as one's own. Lack of empathy is characteristic of those on the antisocial end of the spectrum, people like Carl whose empathic failure arises in the interpersonal void of no mother. Individuals who are overwhelmed by their feelings of empathy are those who are routinely overtaken by their feelings in general. This pattern suggests the experience of a mother who was unable to help her child discern and regulate feelings. Children without the experience of empathic caretaking have had too few experiences of empathy. As a result, not only will they not know how to be empathic, but they will fail to elicit empathy in another. Particularly for those kids who end up in the foster care or residential system, it is vital that they be able to evoke an empathic response. If they can't get someone to care about them, they are at great risk of living out their motherlessness throughout their lives.

Unrelenting ambient fear makes empathy impossible. It is like asking a person who is being mugged to feel kindred feelings for the attacker while being attacked. The unbonded, motherless child lives in the CNS of a prey animal, with predators all around her, both real and imagined and always anticipated. Empathy cannot develop, much less flower, in a being terrified of its own imminent extinction. Simply put, endogenous fear severely impairs the capacity for empathy, and empathy, even more than love, forms the connective tissue of human relationships. And, of course, empathy requires the experienced presence of the other. It requires some recognition that the other has a mind and a life separate from yours, but, at the same time, very much like yours. This is what is called "theory of mind," and it is routinely attenuated in those who have experienced developmental trauma. When there has been no mother to protect them, there is no representation, or only a distorted representation, of mothering in their psyches, their brains, and their bodies. Babies cannot survive without a mother, even when they appear to do just that, and motherlessness leaves them in a constant state of underlying or erupting terror. Neither their bodies nor their psyches experience the company, much less the comfort, of others. Their mandate is pure biology. It is to survive.

Affect Dysregulation

Without the original empathic, attuned presence, a child is left in the throes of her own affective storm. Affect regulation, which is the single most important accomplishment of the first 3 years of life, does not organize in those with developmental trauma. Affect regulation can be thought of as an evolutionary imperative. A crying baby alerts predators in the hungry, prehistoric forest, so the mother's capacity to soothe her child enhances survival. The baby's growing ability to self-regulate protects the mother as well, not only from the ravenous tiger but in day-to-day modern life. Colic is an example. When a baby develops colic, he is difficult, if not impossible, to soothe and the mother will become exhausted and disheartened, often feeling high levels of frustration and resentment. Colic or other physical problems that the mother cannot address can themselves cause attachment disruption. When a child persistently turns away from the mother for any reason, the mother often blames herself and then subtly (or not so subtly) rejects her child as she has been rejected. Adopted children who have encoded the loss of their biological mother as rejection and betrayal will push the adoptive mother away. (As a nurse colleague said in a workshop, gently chiding psychotherapists, "Sometimes it's the baby's fault!") In the modern jungle, there are still situations and environments in which the baby's life may literally depend on the mother's ability to emotionally regulate her child. The quality of the baby's life depends on it, absolutely.

Allan Schore has shone a floodlight on the relationship between affect regulation and the development of self (Schore, 1994, 2003). He has argued extensively and persuasively that "good-enough" emotional attunement between mother and child not only teaches the baby how to regulate herself by example, but, more important, that it builds structures in the brain that, over time, provide the child with the capacity to self-regulate. As we will discuss in more detail in Chapter 2, the part of the brain that Schore documents as most affected is the right hemisphere, particularly the right prefrontal or orbital cortex. These are the areas of the brain that are devoted to the regulation of affective states and the ones most affected by the absence of emotionally attuned mothering. Schore goes on to contend that the mother's attunement with her baby, and specifically the regulation of her baby's affective states, are prerequisites for the child to develop a felt sense of self and a recognition of the reality of the other.

When the mother is incapable of regulating her baby—when she cannot attune herself to the emerging rhythms of her dependent, defenseless infant—her baby is at risk of never knowing that she exists. If we are to believe Schore's argument, as I do, the development of a sense of self relies on the regulating, reliable, and felt presence of the other. Carl is the poster child for Schore's theory as well as for this new concept of developmental trauma. He had no mother, no ability to regulate himself, no ability to learn, and such a high pain threshold that he hardly perceived his own body. Carl had the biological imperative to live, but his sense of identity went no further than his name. He did not exist to himself, nor did others exist to him.

Clearly no two children's circumstances are the same, nor are they experienced the same way internally. The impacts of developmental trauma can be seen to occur along a spectrum, with Carl, or those even more disastrously antisocial (antisocial personality disorder; APD), at one end, to those who flail desperately in the vacant center of their beings hoping for human connection, at the other (BPD). People with histories of untreated developmental trauma are usually diagnosed with personality disorders in adulthood. Anyone who occupies a space on this continuum of dysregulation is unable to fully occupy their own interior, and each of them, to the extent they can feel, feels motherless.

Sensory Dysregulation

Schore and others (Schore, 1994, 2003; Siegel, 1999; Stern, 1985; Tronick, 2007) have focused most of their attention on the attunement of mother and infant through face-to-face reciprocity and the impact of this reciprocity on the development of the prefrontal cortex. The prefrontal cortex, as it slowly matures into our late 20s, develops the capacity to inhibit amygdala activity and allows for the regulation of affect. But we also know that before the acquisition of language-based learning, babies and small children learn through their senses and through the integration of sensory input. Sensory integration is the province of the parietal cortex and the cerebellum, structures at the back of the brain. As we will explore more fully in Chapter 2, the development of the infant's cerebellum depends mostly on the security, consistency, and rhythmicity of his parent's holding. When there is a history of significant neglect, the mother does not hold her infant with intentionality or a feeling of connection, when she holds him at all. (It is, unfortunately, increasingly common to see mothers holding their babies on their knees, or worse yet propped in infant seats, while relating entirely to their cell phones.) Many of my patients report no remembered or felt experience of being held or rocked—maternal activities that promote cerebellum development. Some have even told me that they feel an absence at the back of their heads where a loving hand should have cradled them. This is probably the first place in the brain that encodes the mother's presence. If she were there, we would never forget her. Her presence is held in procedural memory. And so is her absence.

We can understand many of the symptoms these patients have as symptoms of cerebellar dysfunction and poor sensory integration (Teicher et al., 2003). I described the young woman who had been orphaned at birth. She had multiple signs of disturbed sensory integration. She was painfully uncoordinated to the point of dropping things and walking into doorjambs. She hated seams in her clothes, and a wet sleeve would send her into paroxysmal rage. She could neither throw nor catch a ball. These troubling realities did little for her already shredded sense of self and self-esteem. When she swam, she always swam underwater, and when she took a bath she slid down until her ears were covered. She was trying to provide rest to a nervous system that felt under siege from an onslaught of sensory input that she could not process. She was averse to touch, as most of these patients are. One man, since joining Alcoholics Anonymous (AA), tried to calm his dangerous, rage-driven system through long-distance running. However, he would have to curtail this daily activity if he felt even one drop of rain. "I just freak out and the rage thing goes crazy," he told me. The light touch of the raindrops set off his hypervigilant nervous system, and he could not bear it. It is interesting to note that he talked about his rage as something that was not him—as "the rage thing"—while experiencing himself as rage itself.

Children and adults with DTD suffer profound deficits in both physical and emotional regulation. If their sensory systems are not organized well enough, they may also develop learning disabilities. You can't organize a sense of the world if you cannot organize sensory input. A person with sensory integration problems can feel things as sweet as a drop of rain as an assault. The world is often too loud and too bright. One woman with this history did not hear stereo sound, a fact that she serendipitously discovered after a session of brain wave training. Another had a half-second auditory processing delay, which always left her scrambling and often scrambled in school, in conversations with friends, and in therapy. These kinds of sensory integration problems make another catastrophic contribution to the high arousal and reactivity of these individuals' nervous systems.

Neuroscientists are investigating the role of the cerebellum in learning (Schmahmann, 1997; Bostan, Dum, & Strick, 2010). Procedural memory, which is held primarily in the cerebellum, may be the template for all other learning (Doyon, 1997). As noted above, it holds the memory of a mother's presence or her absence. The regulation of the cerebellum is literally in the mother's hands, in how she holds her baby and moves with him. Emerging neuroscience research seems to suggest that the cerebellum may be as critical to early self-regulation and self–other organization as the later developing prefrontal cortex (see Chapter 2). This may be the reason that we automatically know to rock babies rhythmically, swaying or rocking with them, to comfort them. As we have seen, most people who have suffered from developmental trauma have adverse reactions to being touched or held, and babies with these histories may not be soothed by rocking and cooing or much of anything, instead arching their backs as if to throw off the predator. As adults they will also shy away from touch and embrace. Others crave touch to ease the never-ending hunger for their absent mothers and will do almost anything to get it. Both courses come with personal and relational consequences and often self-recriminations, the voice of shame.

As we will explore in Chapter 2, emerging neuroscience (Buzsáki, 2006; Llinás, 2001) and the practice of neurofeedback suggest that the brain organizes itself rhythmically. It is clear that lack of organized sensory input is core to the dysrhythmia that these patients suffer (*dysrhythmia* simply means rhythmic disorganization). The orphaned girl who couldn't read was notorious for knocking over lamps and tripping on her shoelaces. Another woman, also with a history of significant developmental trauma, could not learn to clap in rhythm with others. She came in on the wrong beat more often than the right one. Both had histories of severe disturbance, requiring psychiatric hospitalizations. They experienced no flow and no rhythm. As we consider the brain in development trauma (Chapter 2), we will see that rhythm is not just a metaphor but an organizing principle of brain function. For now, it is clear that whatever language or diagnosis we use, these children and adults suffer from severe dysrhythmic dysregulation, often at all levels of their being, and all too often, for their entire lives.

The Meaning of Symptoms

The effects of early abuse and neglect endure. These effects can take many diagnostic trajectories, but it is never the diagnosis we are treating. We are always addressing the individual and her symptoms. I have argued so far that abuse and neglect arise in the absence of the mother and leave the infant afraid for her survival. Not only does someone with this history feel overwhelmed by terror or, perhaps more subtly, constantly pressed by fear, she also feels pervasive shame. Shame is the feeling of being bad, unworthy of being alive (Fisher, 1985). These states —they are more than transient feelings—give rise to anger, even to rage.

Fear, shame, and rage have chambers in the amygdala, and in this population they drive the sense of self–no self.

People living in the aftermath of these histories find it increasingly difficult to recognize a self that is other than the feelings they are having. They *are* fear, shame, and rage at the same time as they are being torn asunder by them. There is a compounding effect. Fear gives rise to more fear (we will look at the circuitry of this in Chapter 2), to anger at being scared, and to humiliation at being incessantly afraid—and often afraid of nothing. One woman told me at our first interview that she was "a borderline." I hadn't been able to conduct her intake with her because of her rapid descent into dissociation. She would dissociate if I used the word *dissociation*. When I questioned her use of the diagnostic term, she told me that this is what her therapists had told her *she was*. For 2 years it was typical of her to respond to almost any question I asked by quoting a therapist. She had no reference point for herself. She recognized that she was constantly flooded by fear, but she was terrified at the prospect that she might not always feel it. Without fear, she feared she would disappear.

All symptoms of developmental trauma relate directly to these negative, primary emotions that can obliterate, dysregulate, or deform the self. They are either manifestations of these emotions, such as dissociation, nightmares, or hyper-startle responses, or short-term and ultimately futile attempts to regulate them, such as cutting or substance abuse. They can also be ill-conceived attempts to either maintain or sever the relationship with the therapist. I'll talk more about this when I consider the problems in psychotherapy that arise with these patients and their therapists in Chapter 8.

People suffering from developmental trauma can either ignore self-care altogether or attempt to hold themselves together with an unholy devotion to it. One woman went weeks without brushing her teeth or taking a shower. Her hygiene obviously became an important focus of behavioral intervention, but this behavior was symptomatic of something more than inadequate self-care. It was for her yet another manifestation of no internalized mother. When she did shower, she felt torrents of shame about her body, which then spiraled into a vicious feedback loop, making the next shower even more difficult.

In contrast, the young woman who held onto life perilously for the first year in the orphanage was always immaculate about her appearance, as if trying to keep herself together with her sweater sets and her impeccable makeup. Two of my young patients got extensive tattoos (over my futile objections) as if to draw their story on their skin and perhaps to draw attention to their unrealized existence, in full color. Many of these patients engage in frank self-harm, and most often target the skin. They burn and they cut. They report that the pain gives them respite, however temporary, from numbness and derealization or from feelings of fear or shame so intense that they can no longer bear them, or rage so out of control that they fear they will act on it. As we will explore more in Chapter 2, numbness, dissociation, and derealization are symptoms of parasympathic fear, whereas symptoms such as outbursts, aggression, hyper-startle response, self-harm, and suicidality are signs of sympathetic overarousal. All too many of these patients suffer all of the above.

Symptom formation is a complex business, and the mind of the trauma survivor as well as that of the trauma therapist will have tales that justify or explain them. But at base, they are elaborations of fear. Rage is seeded by fear and shame, too, has fear embedded in it—in fact one of the worst fears that anyone can have. Shame means having to live beyond the pale. The expression "beyond the pale" relates to the custom of exiling the bad one outside the walls of the ghetto, the pale, keeping them cut off from family or tribe and vulnerable to the attack of barbarians (the other tribe) and wild animals. This is exactly how my patients feel and exactly what they fear. When a patient says that she just wants to "feel what normal people feel," it is a plea to return to the tribe of which she has never felt herself a member.

Most of us would do almost anything not to feel, even for a moment, the feelings these patients endure every minute of every day and every night. If cutting themselves, banging their heads, or drinking or throwing up until their throats burn quiets or even interrupts these states, they will do it. If the states are unrelenting and unbearable and the only way they can imagine escaping them is death, they are at very high risk of suicide. One boy I worked with told me that he was going to kill himself, essentially because he had broken the code of his ultra-Christian tribe by being "incurably homosexual." I asked him what he would do if his bet on nothingness after death didn't pay off. He told me that he would just commit suicide again. It could be argued that we were a bit outside the realm of cause and effect, but he clearly was not embracing my argument. His shame was too terrible to bear, and he had to have this plan to stay alive. When his landlord, a policeman, took the front door off his apartment for late payment of rent, the boy hung himself. He had been left utterly exposed and without refuge. Shame and terror took his life.

Perhaps to avoid that fate, patients more commonly turn to mind-altering drugs, both prescribed and not. Drugs of choice include alcohol, marijuana, heroin, methamphetamine, speed, cocaine, and crack. These drugs beckon the user by promising relief, and because of the way they are processed in the brain, they often make good on the promise, at least initially. The problems with these coping mechanisms are obvious. They ultimately don't work, most are illegal, and they can lead to permanent disability or death. And prescribed drugs offer little to quiet the affective storm. Most of my patients arrive in my office on multiple prescription medications, usually including the newer, "atypical" antipsychotics, mood stabilizers, antianxiety medications, antidepressants, and stimulants. In disturbed children the sequence of medications often begins with stimulants, then on to selective serotonin reuptake inhibitors (SSRIs), then atypical antipsychotics, and finally mood stabilizers, which are, in fact, anticonvulsants.

As this progression suggests, many psychiatrists find themselves medicating the effects of medication—which leads, inevitably, to the inadequately studied practice of polypharmacy. One woman who was still actively dissociating, clawing at her face, and hitting her head had a long history with pharmacology and came in taking Tegretol, Wellbutrin, Lamictal, Ativan, and Lexapro, as well as medications for IBS and high blood pressure. I suggested to one young man, nearly drowned by his biological mother as a baby, that he had to stop making his psychiatrist feel so crazy or he was likely to be prescribed even more antipsychotics. On a trip to visit his family, in an attempt to quiet his fear, he accidently overdosed on risperidone, which made him wildly psychotic. His sister rushed to the emergency room, where he was being held in restraints and dumped out a bag of 27 bottles of different medications. They were, he said, his safety blanket, but they hardly touched the pulse of fear that drove him. He used alcohol as well, to the point of blackouts, and still got no respite from his mother and his motherlessness. How does a person whose mother wants him dead psychically survive?

"Wantedness" seems to be communicated to babies, most likely beginning in utero. There is no question that this feeling of being wanted is a critical issue in a child's learning to self-regulate. The child establishes herself in the experience of being wanted by mother, father, family, and community. According to Robert Sapolsky (2005), a highly regarded researcher on the impact of stress, the steady decline in rates of violence in the United States correlates directly to the legalization of birth control and abortion. If your mother doesn't want you, no one will. At least, this seems to be the operating assumption, often unconscious, that can drive the desperation of attachment strategies. One woman, in a good marriage and with children she loved, recognized only after years of psychotherapy that she woke up every morning with the echoing question, "Who loves you, who loves you, who loves you?"

Sadly, but importantly, symptoms are never worse than the events that originally gave rise to them. Further, they are often literal communications about a state of mind that is either unknown to the patient, impossible to contain, impossible to express in words, or all of the above. We see this in the assaults on the skin, the point of contact between self and others or the point of no contact, of no skin. Burns, while temporarily interrupting amygdala-driven circuitry in the brain, also momentarily cauterize the feeling of no skin. Cutting, which also disrupts this circuitry, tears at the fiction of a skin boundary, and simultaneously, establishes its reality. I see head banging as an attempt to change state, to communicate the harrowing disorganization within the head, and, like cutting and burning, an attempt to rearrange the brain waves. Bingeing and purging can be seen as poorly disguised manifestations of unrelenting mother hunger, and they serve as a kind of single-pointed concentration and constant distraction from the pain of it, particularly the shame of it. These patients are attempting to keep shame at bay through controlling their intake and their body size to disguise their shameful and angry hunger. But as is true for these and most symptomatic behaviors in developmental trauma, no matter what the story is that gives them meaning, we can always trace them back to the chambers of the amygdala, firing out of control.

Transference

I explore transference and the possibilities of "transference cure" more fully in Chapter 8. Here, I want to focus briefly on how motherlessness and survival fear shape it. Transference expectations for those with developmental trauma often precede the actual meeting with the therapist, like hunger precedes the meal. These expectations are always influenced by multiple factors, most prominently, the patient's early relationships with his mother and father. It can be even more complex, nuanced, and dramatic in those with histories of developmental trauma. I have, however, observed some common themes, albeit with many individual variations.

Transference requires some template of mother and father, and for Carl and people like him, it can never develop. Neither Carl nor I ever emerged from the void of his childhood. With the exception of one day in jail when I was summoned by the authorities, who were very concerned about his depression, I never saw him suffering. He bounced out of this deeply sad and relational place into his sociopathic rendering in less than a day. He was, in a way, too dysregulated and disorganized to suffer. His feelings, such as they were, seemed best described as an increasing pressure and then the need to discharge it, most routinely by abusing others or himself. Relating to him was akin to relating to a volcano—very little connection, very little nuance, and constant smoldering threat.

When there is enough experience of parents, particularly of the mother, transference does develop, and it invariably reflects the profound absence, perceived or actual, of the mother. The core issue is an intense mother hunger, an unbearable and hopeless longing for a present, loving mother. Some patients have the combination of courage and desperation it takes to dive deep into these turbulent and muddy amniotic waters. If the therapist can embrace it, a patient with this history will attempt to construct their child's version of being mothered. This can come with requests to be held, nursed, and taken home. They want and need the experience of being tucked in and wrapped up. These needs feel deeply humiliating to them and add to the vicious feedback loop of shame. Asking the patient to analyze these feelings risks shaming him more, and skills training, when this defining need is acknowledged at all, can only teach the patient to learn to somehow bear this unbearable, insatiable hunger.

The drive toward reconstruction, or initial construction, of a tender and attuned mother–infant relationship is healthy. Being held in the mind and the arms of the mother is the way affect regulation begins in the human species. Therapists are, however, proscribed from holding, primarily due to a history of sexual exploitation in the field. (Given their histories and the nature of their need, sexual exploitation of these patients is tantamount to child sexual assault.) But as a result, patients who need to be held, cannot be. This basic human need will go unmet and all too often completely unaddressed because of the proscription on the therapist and the shame of the patient. In the residential center, most of the kids deserving this diagnosis would find ways to be restrained. They would provoke physical holds because they needed them, both to contain their aggression but more fundamentally to provide them with some experience of benevolent, attuned human contact and the gift of constraint to their nervous systems.

Some will express their need by denigrating it and by feeling determined to "just grow up"—somehow. As talk therapists we can, unfortunately, promote an illusion that understanding this need will suffice. Those such as Allan Schore (1994, 2003) who discuss the therapeutic limits of talk and the body's felt sense of maternal deprivation suggest that we can treat this deficit within the intersubjective experience between therapist and patient. Thankfully, this is at least partially true for many patients. But for many who have suffered developmental trauma and are left profoundly disorganized and dysregulated, the transference that would allow an intersubjective experience doesn't develop. They do not have the preexisting template—*me* and *mother*—that would allow them to experience intersubjectivity. When they do have the semblance of a template, the intersubjectivity can feel perilous, riddled with hypervigilant fear of abandonment and often ruptured by intense affect that can be difficult for either patient or therapist to contain.

As mentioned above, many patients find it nearly unbearable to be touched at all or even looked at, much less to return the gaze. Touch has been too threatening, too sexual, too injurious and even life-threatening to ever be trusted. In this situation, the therapist's job is the rehabilitation of touch. Loving touch protects and enriches our lives. One such boy whom I treated in foster care comes to mind. He hated being touched. He had been severely sexually and physically abused while his mother tried to manage the effects of her own trauma history with heroin. When we ended our sessions, I would cuff his shoulder lightly, and initially he would shudder me off. I would apologize, telling him that he would have to remind me because this felt natural for me to do. He never reminded me, there were more apologies, and slowly he began to accept my touch. When he left the program, he came to say good-bye. He gave me a bear hug. He went back to dealing heroin. He was not "cured." He was not even deterred. But he'd had the experience of nonsexual and nonviolent physical contact between him and another. He had learned that touch could be safe and even positive, and hopefully this made it easier for him to recognize nurturing touch and to seek it out in other relationships.

Particularly in the adolescent treatment center, I often found myself conducting therapy with a child who was looking either at the floor or around the perimeter. (With those who would not jump out, I had some of my best sessions driving in my car.) Several of my adult patients have described eye contact as physically painful and look away as if being asked to gaze at the sun. There was no way that I could help them regulate with gaze. Ultimately it may be prosody, the song of the therapist's voice, that most influences the patient's regulation. As it is with the mother, the prosody of the therapist's voice reveals her state. It is the therapist's steady state, her ability to attune to her patient but not be overwhelmed by her overwhelming affective states that makes therapy possible at all. A steady state of equanimity is not easily achieved in general, and it is particularly difficult when we are under the assault of shame, rage, and fear—theirs and ours.

Many patients will turn against their hunger for a mother. They are too ashamed of it to allow it to infuse the transference. If the hunger for the mother's body is experienced physically, it can feel overwhelming and dangerous, particularly when the patient knows it cannot be met. It is far from uncommon for this simple longing for a mother's body to be sexualized by the patient, the therapist, or both. This is almost to be expected for a patient with a history of child sexual abuse. It is easy to confuse the nature of these simple, deep yearnings. Some will attempt to rely on their partners or significant others to both understand and fill this need. The pitfalls to this approach are obvious. The partner cannot be the mother, and a relationship constructed around these needs is in constant jeopardy. Reenactment of the overwhelmed mother who eventually abandons her child is highly likely and constantly feared by the "child" of the dyad. Diverting this deep need to a partner can also imperil the success of the therapy. When this is the route taken, this need may never surface in the therapeutic relationship, where it can be at least partially addressed.

The term *transference* itself presents a problem. It can suggest that this feeling is not "real," when there is nothing more real than this unmet need for a mother. It is an embodied memory of absence that finds its expression in the transference. *No-mother* means internal chaos and predicts a chaotic transference. The hope against hope for a mother, for self-organization and self-regulation, is why these patients endure therapy at all.

No matter how this motherlessness is felt and expressed, I think it is best understood at the level of the CNS, as the primary infant need for affect regulation. We know our mothers across time through the regulation of our nervous systems. Our mothers are encoded not solely in our minds but in our brains and our bodies. Training the brain to regulate itself may well give the CNS its first experience of being "mothered." When the CNS begins to regulate, the person begins to feel mothered. Neurofeedback that teaches CNS regulation in the context of an attuned relationship with the therapist is the next best thing to having a mother who did this for you in the first place. It is exactly this premise that we explore throughout the rest of this book.

The Therapy

We will explore many of the issues that arise in psychotherapy with patients who have DTD more extensively in Chapter 8. Here, I want to briefly address the core themes, particularly those that relate directly to the presence of the other: affect regulation and self. The single most important factor in a successful therapy may be the patient's ability to care about his therapist. We have seen how complex this is for those with developmental trauma histories. When this is the patient, all of the therapy must bend toward regulation. There is no other goal. This is often considered Phase 1 or stabilization in trauma treatment. But it is more than stabilization: It is the laying down of a neuronal pathway for the experience of being mothered.

These patients live in a state of constant internal crisis that inevitably manifests in the therapy. Helping them regulate themselves often means emergency phone calls, crisis intervention, hospitalizations, medications, and steady nerves—the therapist's ability to self-regulate. All too often, however, the patient's terrified dysregulation and, at best, ambivalent attachment can trump the therapist's ability to regulate her. When this happens, the therapy fails. These abandoned patients live with fear of abandonment and expect betrayal. They are pumping out excess stress hormones: cortisol and adrenaline. This is not, as it were, the chemistry of trust, and it often predicts the reenactment of abandonment in the therapy or in reality by the therapist.

When the patient is angry, aggressive, threatening self-harm or harm to others (including the therapist), unable to bond, and hypervigilant and terrified, the therapy and the therapist are easily overrun. These dynamics are not rare. They are the primary reason that Linehan's therapy requires a consultation team (Linehan 1993). According to Linehan, therapists "vacillate among feeling alone, discouraged, hopeless and depressed, feeling angry and hostile at the patients . . . and feeling energetic, confident, encouraged and hopeful. . . . These patients as a whole engage in the three most stressful patient behaviors (suicide attempts, suicide threats, and hostility)" (1993, pp. 424–425). In dialectical behavior therapy (DBT), ideally at least, no therapist is left to deal with this alone, because it isn't possible. But most therapists do not have these teams to help them understand and deal with their own feelings of fear, anger, frustration, and discouragement—and, alternately, a powerful desire to protect and nurture when the patient fails at even basic self-regulation. In psychodynamic therapies, the therapist's response—including any resentment that he is being treated badly, helplessness at not being able to help, and even at times feelings of impotent rage in the face of these dysregulated emotions—constitute the core of negative countertransference.

When a patient with developmental trauma evokes protection and nurture in the therapist, it usually means that somewhere along the way someone has cared for him. This patient has learned to elicit empathy. Although these feelings can also cause problems in the therapy, they can be an early indication of a positive outcome. The therapist is called upon to recognize his feelings, whatever they are, so that he will act on them with consciousness. But if the therapist is unable to help the patient regulate her rage, fear, and shame, these affects will hijack the therapy. Ultimately, it won't matter how much self-awareness the therapist has or even how much empathy he is able to maintain for his patient. If he is unable to help his patient regulate intense emotions, the patient's dysregulation will triumph and the patient will lose, once again.

Although we talk about transference and countertransference as belonging to the patient and therapist, respectively, both are always *co-arising* and *co-constructed* at the place where the therapist's experience meets that of the patient. The therapist must be as conscious as possible of the dynamics she brings to this potentially combustible relationship. But self-awareness also depends on affect regulation, and these therapy experiences can challenge emotional regulation in even the most experienced and gifted therapists. Here is where neurofeedback is particularly valuable because it not only helps the patient, it helps the therapist as well. It off-loads most of the affect regulation to the training and makes it possible for the therapist to train himself. Perhaps more than anyone else, patients with developmental trauma need a regulating other as they learn, sometimes late in life, how to meet the developmental milestone of affect regulation.

These patients have often lost meaning, or, in the phrase Pavlov used to describe his dogs after the traumatizing flood of his lab, even the "instinct of purpose" (Pavlov, 1928). And they have often truly lost their minds. They cannot trust their own perceptions or those of others to help them establish or disestablish their reality. Plagued by dissociation, derealization, and depersonalization, they do not know if what they perceive is actually part of the shared reality. This is a shape-shifting world that is impossible to inhabit, but one that patients with developmental trauma must negotiate daily. The dysregulation that is often still felt emotionally can begin to manifest physically. As we saw in the ACE study, these patients, as a cohort, suffer more illnesses and die younger than others—which is far from surprising, when we consider that they are living in states of unrelenting stress. They are stuck in terror. They find it very hard to evolve, to move from rigidity to complexity. (In Chapter 2 I discuss mental illness as rigidity, repetition, and reactivity and, in contrast, mental health as flow, complexity, and stability.)

There is hope. It appears that although they have lost the mind's template for self, other, and relationship, even those people who have been deeply deprived, neglected, and injured in childhood, maintain the circuitries in the brain that underwrite their essential humanness. As we will see, when we activate these underlying circuitries, we also activate the individual's innate potential for relationship, and we ease the pain of history. This is a critically important hypothesis of this book: It suggests that when we reach this CNS, we will find this person.

As is true for most therapists, I was schooled in theories of mind, emotion, and behavior. As a meditation student I was trained to work with my mind. When I was in graduate school there was no focus on the brain, how it works, or how it gives rise to mind—and there is still very little. But the brain is the infrastructure of mind, and when we can access how it functions, we can change the mind that it gives birth to, even these very tortured minds. But before discussing neurofeedback, our access route, it is important to take a look at the brain, focusing particularly on what happens to the brain in developmental trauma to better understand how and why neurofeedback can help people with these devastating histories.

Chapter 2

The Brain in Developmental Trauma

*And men ought to know that from nothing else but
thence [the brain] come joys, delights, laughter
and sports, and sorrows, griefs, despondency, and
lamentations. And by this, an especial manner, we
acquire wisdom and knowledge, and see and hear,
and know what are foul and what are fair, what
are bad and what are good, what are sweet, and
what unsavory. . . . And by the same organ we
become mad and delirious, and fears and terrors
assail us. . . . All these things we endure from the
brain, when it is not healthy. . . . In these ways
I am of the opinion that the brain exercises the
greatest power in the man. This is the interpreter
of those things which emanate from the air, when it
[the brain] happens to be in a sound state. . . . To
consciousness the brain is messenger.*
—Hippocrates (400 B.C.E.)

We have discussed, in general terms, the mind of those who have suffered from developmental trauma, the vacant universe of *no self* and *no
other* and the unrelenting assault of fear. Now we turn to an exploration
of the brain as it is impacted by developmental trauma. When the mind

is suffering, the brain is suffering as well. The brain is devoted to its own regulation—it has to be—but it also learns its own errors and, unfortunately, practices these as well. This is very much the case with those who have experienced developmental trauma. Early childhood neglect and abuse significantly impact the brain's ability to regulate itself, which directly gives rise to the unbearable dysregulation of mind that we discussed in Chapter 1.

Developmental trauma dysregulates both structures and foundational rhythms in the brain. This chapter provides a user-friendly overview of the brain, focusing particularly on the brain structures most directly impacted by developmental trauma and on the rhythms that give rise to what I call the *fear-driven brain*. Once you have some fundamental (and cutting-edge) neuroscience under your belt, you'll be able to understand how neurofeedback can help organize the disorganized brains that these children and adults are left with.. Although it is beyond the scope of this book to address the immense complexity of the brain in any depth, the neurofeedback clinician does need to know her way around it, at least in an introductory way, to know which structure performs what function.

In neurofeedback, we are trying to discern what is happening in the brain that then gives rise to the patient's presenting problems. We begin here by considering those structures that have been identified as playing a role in developmental trauma, and then place this information in the context of the brain as a whole. As we will see, both through emerging neuroscience and through the phenomenology of neurofeedback, the brain regulates itself via the electrical domain of frequency and timing. Throughout the discussion of specific brain structures, keep this basic fact in mind. Although these structures are key to our understanding of the problems suffered in developmental trauma, they are all firing and misfiring in vast neural networks that connect them rhythmically with all other brain structures. In neurofeedback, we reward the brain to generate frequencies that allow it to develop new firing patterns at particular sites related to particular structures that will influence signals throughout the neural networks (see Chapter 3 for a discussion of this reward system). We'll get to the electrical networks or brain circuits later in this chapter.

For now suffice it to say that most problems involve vast neural networks and that within these networks there are identified focal structures. For example, obsessive–compulsive disorder (OCD) is known to be a problem of overactivation of the anterior cingulate. This structure misfires and its signals are transmitted over neural networks that connect the cingulate to other structures. OCD is also one of the common comorbidities of developmental trauma. It is no surprise to learn that the anterior cingulate plays a vital role in inhibiting the amygdala. In cases of developmental trauma it appears that just the opposite has happened: Hyperexcitable and habitual firing of the amygdala has overtaken and dysregulated the cingulate. Once we know that the anterior cingulate is overactive in OCD and is responsible for functional inhibition of the amygdala, we can think about beginning the training at the site closest to the anterior cingulate. These comorbidities might both yield to lowering arousal and activation at the same site. In brain terms, the comorbidity may be the same morbidity.

Figure 2.1 illustrates the standard 10–20 measuring system of the skull. In the case of the anterior cingulate, the site is "FZ." The letters and numbers that I insert are part of the 10–20 measuring system, or "map," used by neurologists and will make much more sense after Chapter 3. Every neurofeedback practitioner learns this system. I use these designations throughout this chapter to orient the practitioner to sites on the skull, relating to structures of concern. These are the sites to consider when training a person suffering from developmental trauma. (The reader may want to come back to this chapter when considering protocols to quiet reactivity and fear.)

As we will soon see, the circuitry of fear casts a wide net, but quieting the amygdala is essential when addressing fear. Further, developmental trauma manifests with multiple symptoms and disrupts development in many arenas of brain function. Neurofeedback practitioners need to have a general idea of which structure correlates with what problem, as they look for ways to reduce toxic fear and all of its ongoing fallout. Every topic that I touch on deserves at least a chapter, if not its own textbook, so this chapter can only introduce the reader to the key areas of the traumatized brain and how unrelenting terror deforms its function.

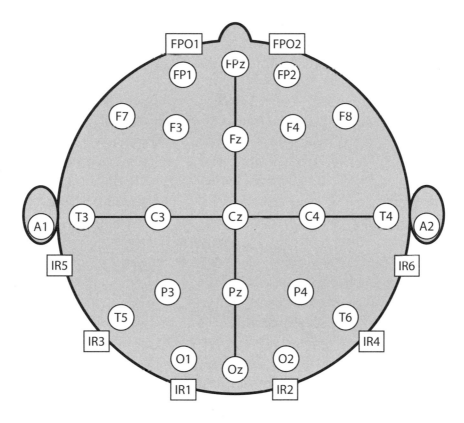

Figure 2.1.   The standard 10–20 measuring system of the skull.
FPO (Frontal Pole Orbital) and IR (Inion Ridge) are not in the
10–20 system but are used as sites for training in neurofeedback.
(Courtesy of Sam McClellan.)

The Autonomic Nervous System in Developmental Trauma

Human beings (and most other mammals) have two interdependent branches of the nervous system: the autonomic nervous system (ANS) and the central nervous system (CNS). The ANS is a system of neural pathways responsible for the homeostatic regulation of organs in the body, including the gut, the lungs, and the heart. The ANS has two branches: the parasympathetic nervous system (PNS) and the sympathetic nervous system (SNS). Simply put, the PNS allows the body to rest and digest, and the SNS primes the body for fight or flight. Optimally, these two systems modulate each other, which allows for an individual's ongoing flexibility of arousal in response to the demands of the environment.

When the environment is chronically overwhelming, however, it can happen that neither system is able to exercise influence over the other; they are both tapped out. This is often the case in those with developmental trauma. As babies and small children, they could not respond to the threat of absence or injury through activation of the SNS. They could not run and they could not fight. The PNS is often described as restoring homeostasis after sympathetic activation, but it can also go into overdrive in an attempt to reduce the futile sympathetic activation that occurs in helpless infants and young children. *Homeostasis* is an elusive experience and perhaps even an elusive concept for those who are systematically injured or mindlessly neglected as children. The treatment goal is not to *return* these systems to homeostasis but to establish a new experience of it.

When both systems go into overdrive, the person trying to manage these now warring influences is held in an unbearable suspension of his nervous system. When this occurs, the child has to rely on the most primitive defense that the organism has at its disposal, one that we have in common with reptiles: the freeze response. Freezing is seen as a hyperactivation of the PNS. In developmental trauma, this hyperactivation is dissociation. This child who cannot escape leaves her assaulted, neglected body. In animals, freezing is called *death-feigning*; they are trying to trick the predator into believing that they are already dead so that they will not be killed. It is probably the same strategy for the traumatized child.

One of my patients told me the following story that illustrates sympathetic arousal barely contained by a severely overactivated PNS. She had been admitted as a suicidal teenager to a local mental hospital. There were very few private rooms, and every patient, including her, wanted one. Every day she passed a boy her age who stood at the door to his private room in a catatonic state. In retrospect, she believed that her actions might have been fueled by his absent presence more than by her envy over his private room. Whatever her reasons, his standing there day after day overcame her fragile inhibitions and she ran down the corridor and tackled him. She expected him "to fall over like a dead tree." Instead, he came awake and began to pummel her with fists and feet and had to be pulled off her by the staff. His profound freeze response gave way quickly to sympathetic activation. He mobilized instantaneously, and his freeze response turned into a fight response. (She told me that his psychiatrist thanked her and swore her to secrecy—apparently disinclined to be seen as rewarding aggressive behavior.) It doesn't, however, always turn out in a positive way. It can happen that the ANS of a child forced into this over-the-top parasympathetic response shuts down the body so completely that vital functions just stop. In these thankfully rare circumstances, the child will die. This is a child literally scared to death.

This PNS shutdown is mediated by the vagal nerve. The tenth cranial nerve, the vagus nerve, extends from the brainstem down the front of the spinal cord to the colon. It is thought to be primarily parasympathetic in tone (80%), but it also has sympathetic capacities (20%). It speeds arousal information from the brain to all the major organ systems and information from these organs back to the brain. The most common somatic complaints in developmental trauma are vagally mediated: stomachaches, constipation and irritable bowel, trouble breathing and a racing and pounding heart or a heart that is pumping much too slowly (van der Kolk, 2009). Steven Porges made a significant contribution to the understanding of the vagus nerve, particularly in trauma, when he introduced the polyvagal theory (2011). Briefly, he suggests that there are different fiber bundles in the vagus that mediate different autonomic responses. The most recently evolved is what he calls the *social vagus*, and it supports the ability to be socially engaged with others and to live at ease in our own skins. These vagal pathways support self-regulation throughout the body as well as the all-important sense of membership in the tribe. The well-regulated body sends messages back to the brain that all is OK, helping in turn to regulate the brain.

The second bundle of fibers ready the system for fight or flight. The alarm message is received and the vagus activates the heart and lungs and shuts down the bowel. Porges believes that the social vagus is distinctly human and that the fight-and-flight response is shar~
mammals. The third bundle of fibers is reptilian and seems to have been

retained in our evolutionary development as one last strategy for survival, the freeze response—our inner crocodile. As Porges points, out this is a good approach for a cold-blooded reptile under threat, but it is problematic for humans. Under the sway of this primitive vagus, we are prone to passing out, fainting, and dizziness. Freezing when speaking in public and fainting at the sight of blood are vagal events. The vagus nerve is implicated not only in somatic complaints but in one of the most daunting of traumatic sequelae: dissociation. When there is no escape and no chance at self-defense, dissociation is the last option—and often a daily reality of children with developmental trauma histories.

As we will see, dissociation shows up in the electrical domain of the brain as excess slow wave activity, and can look, as it is meant to, like very low arousal. But it isn't. As we saw in both cases above, this ANS response has been driven by terror, which involves hyperactivation of sympathetic arousal, and when you approach this nervous system with neurofeedback, you will be training the nervous system to lower its arousal. We'll be talking a lot about this in subsequent chapters on the practice of neurofeedback.

The CNS in Developmental Trauma

We can observe the expression of trauma in the ANS, but the ANS is governed by the CNS, the brain and the spinal cord. The CNS and the ANS affect each other, but, of the two, the CNS wields ultimate authority. In traditional peripheral biofeedback, practitioners enter the brain–body loop through the body and focus on regulating the ANS. They teach people that they can gain control over sympathetic and parasympathetic activation through increasing or decreasing the temperature of their skin, changing skin conductivity (galvanic skin response), releasing tension in their muscles, reducing their heart rates, and slowing the rate at which they breathe. These practices, which are also the practices of most meditation traditions, can help quiet an overly activated nervous system.

However, peripheral biofeedback—deploying the ANS to modulate the CNS—is as difficult for most patients with developmental trauma as meditation. Neurofeedback for this population enters the same brain–

body loop, but it focuses instead on the CNS by teaching people to change dysfunctional patterns and rhythms in their brains. The CNS is "on fire" in developmental trauma, and it is our job as therapists to put the fire out. This following overview of the CNS provides an outline for the new neurofeedback practitioner. It is just a hint of the neuroscience that underlies the practice of neurofeedback, and hopefully, an encouragement to further study the system that we wish to influence.

The Brainstem and Hypothalamus

The brainstem and the hypothalamus are responsible for life-sustaining functions, including respiration, heartbeat, temperature regulation, the sleep–wake cycle, hunger, pain perception, core maternal instincts, and core consciousness. It is this part of the brain that is most involved in the ANS. These are vital functions that continue whether or not we are aware of them. The brainstem is also involved in connecting neuronal pathways from the front of the brain (later to develop) and the back. Signals from the frontal lobes, the most advanced brain region, go to the most primitive part: the brainstem. The brainstem does not communicate directly back to the frontal lobes, but instead sends its signals to the cerebellum, which in turn, sends signals forward to the frontal lobes, completing the communication front to back and back to front.

The hypothalamus, also an ancient structure, is, like the brainstem, fully functional at birth. It is involved in all aspects of visceral, hormonal, endocrine, and autonomic systems as well as in the regulation of thirst, hunger, and the experience of pleasure and rage. According to Joseph (1996), the author of the text *Neuropsychiatry, Neuropsychology, and Clinical Neuroscience* (a much more readable book than the title suggests and still relevant despite its age):

> [The hypothalamus] constitutes the most primitive, archaic, reflexive and purely biological aspect of the psyche. . . . Moreover, being involved in maintaining internal homeostasis via, for example, its ability to reward or punish the organism with feelings of pleasure or aversion, it tends to serve what Freud has described as "the pleasure principle," and best corresponds to what has been described as the "ID." (pp. 177–178)

Antonio Damasio (1999) hypothesizes that the brainstem, the hypothalamus, and the basal forebrain constitute the origins of self in the nonconscious brain:

> The deep roots of the self, including the elaborate self which encompasses identity and personhood, are to be found in the ensemble of brain devices which continuously and unconsciously maintain the body state within the narrow range and relative stability required for survival. . . . I call the state of activity within the ensemble of such devices the proto-self, the non-conscious forerunner for the levels of self which appear in our minds as the conscious protagonists of consciousness: core self and autobiographical self. (p. 22)

This thesis is important to neurofeedback providers for a number of reasons. First, it posits the absolute connection between the brain and the self, between the nonconscious, the unconscious, and the conscious. The second is that it underscores the central role of the hypothalamus in fear regulation, as is documented in work investigating the hypothalamic–pituitary–adrenal (HPA) axis. This regulatory system is highly susceptible to the very stress hormones that it attempts to regulate. It appears that this entire regulatory feedback loop is disrupted in developmental trauma, making it ever more difficult to regulate fear, the emotion of most salience to the organism's survival.

A third reason is that these primitive brain structures are seen as the least plastic and therefore should be the least affected by neurofeedback training, which appeals directly to the mechanisms of plasticity in the brain. I am not at all convinced that this is true. It seems to be that once the brain finds its pathway to regulation, it may in fact prioritize the nuclei that give rise to the proto-self. One woman with a history of neglect and humiliation talked about the effects of neurofeedback training at the back of her head in ways that strongly suggest this possibility. She said, "I am becoming the person I would have been if my family had not interfered." This statement is a neurofeedback koan and perhaps also a declaration of the proto-self—a manifestation of the regulation of these primitive brain regions. We do expect to see changes in the ANS when patients with developmental trauma train to reduce fear. We expect to see improvements in sleep, in heart rate, temperature regulation, breathing, digestion, and awareness of hunger and thirst, all of which can be significantly dysregulated in developmental trauma. (See Figure C.1.)

Bruce Perry (2003) wrote a case study that demonstrates how much these primitive structures factor in trauma and in the circuitry of fear:

> *D. is a 9[-year-old] boy. He was the victim of chronic and pervasive threat and abuse from his biological father. From age 2 until 6 he was physically and sexually abused by his father. This abuse induced severe physical injuries. At age 6 he was removed from the family. His mother acknowledged the pervasive abuse. At age 8, he was seriously injured in a fall. He suffered from severe brain injury such that he was in a coma for 8 months following the injury. He continues to be difficult to arouse, is non-verbal and no meaningful communication is noted. In the presence of his biological father, he began to scream and moan and his heart rate increased dramatically. Audiotapes of his father elicit a similar response. . . . .* This child's brain did not have the capacity to have conscious perception of the presence of his father. However, the auditory and olfactory sensory neuronal patterns which entered this boy's brain were associated, even at the level of his brain stem and midbrain (cerebellum), with past states of fear. . . . Exposure to his father elicited no cognitive, narrative memory; his agitation and increased heart rate were manifestations of affective and state memories. (p. 7, emphasis in original)

The Cerebellum

Neuroscientists are becoming increasingly interested in the cerebellum and its role in emotion, cognition, and general regulation of the brain. *Cerebellum* means "small brain" in Latin; it is also described as the silent brain, meaning that it does not generate its own brain waves. It may actually be neither small—80% of the brain's neurons are in the cerebellum (Herculano-Houzel, 2010)—nor silent. Sarang, Osipova, Bertand, and Jerbi (2013) contend that oscillatory networks with frequencies as high as 250 Hz in the cerebellum mediate perception, action, and cognition, which are not commonly thought to be cerebellar processes. There is less and less doubt, however, about its significance to the cerebrum, the big and "talkative" brain. Emerging literature (Schmahmann, 1997, 1998, 2000; Teicher, Anderson, & Polcari, 2012; Levin, 2009) suggests that the cerebellum plays a significant role in regulating the cerebrum, both cortically and sub-cortically. Redundancy in the brain is trumped by plasticity—and we do not yet understand how these circuits function. On the safe assumption that the brain wastes no space and no energetic investment, we have to conclude that the cerebellum is important to the core function of the brain. It is the seat of procedural learning and memory. This is the part of the brain that remembers how to ride a bike. It also remembers being held and rocked by the mother. It is as yet unclear exactly how the cerebellum communicates with the rest of the brain, but it seems clear that electrical signals are involved, even though they may not be generated by the cerebellum itself. Here is Levin's (2009) summary:

> We know from birth onwards, long before the cortex is ready to function, the cerebellum is already functioning (and it probably starts its activities even before birth). On this basis the core self is felt to be part of the cerebellum, and it could be expected to contain a repository of personal memories relating to self from the beginning of life. . . . The first emotions and the earliest rhythms of movement, sound, and life itself, one might expect to be exclusively recorded in the cerebellum. (p. 164)

Interestingly, Damasio (1999) excludes the cerebellum from the construction of the proto-self, but it may be that the cerebellum promotes rhythmicity in the proto-self. Levin (2009) goes on to say that parts of the cerebellum are "principally concerned with affective and autonomic regulation and emotionally relevant memory" (p. 174). There is a growing body of research that suggests the vulnerability of the cerebellum to neglect, to the absence of rhythmic connection to the mother, and to abuse that happens most often in the absence of the mother. In good-enough mother–infant interactions, these rhythms may encode the presence of the other, particularly for the infant but for the mother as well, and in this way lay down the beginnings of interpersonal memory.

In the 1950s, Harry Harlow, at the University of Wisconsin–Madison, conducted the now-famous studies of orphaned monkeys given either wire or terry-cloth-covered surrogate mothers to cling to. The monkeys who had been given the skeletal wire mothers grew up to be antisocial and highly aggressive, more so than those given the cloth mothers. W. A.

Mason of the Delta Primate Center in Louisiana, working with Harlow, reported on orphan monkeys whose cloth mothers swung from side to side, and he noted that they had somewhat better outcomes. These observations led them to speculate on the part that the cerebellum, particularly the central cerebellar structure called the *vermis*, might play in attachment and affect regulation.

Martin Teicher, the influential trauma researcher, has been investigating the functioning of the cerebellum in traumatized patients. He began his research by developing the Limbic Instability Checklist, a paper-and-pencil test that accurately discriminates between patients admitted to a mental health center who had been abused and those who had not. He gave patients a list of symptoms associated with temporal lobe instability. The number of symptoms they endorsed correlated with abuse and neglect in childhood. Those who were sexually abused as children had more symptoms of limbic instability than those who had not been abused at all. Teicher, Glod, Surrey, and Swett (1993) summarized their findings: "Patients who acknowledged both physical and sexual abuse had average scores [on the Limbic Instability Checklist] 113% higher than patients [in the study] reporting none" (p. 302). They then had some of these patients screened by Carl Anderson, an expert in the cerebellum. They had hypothesized abnormal cerebellar blood flow, and they found it. These findings suggest that the cerebellum is affected in adults who were abused as children.

Neurofeedback practitioners are beginning to explore the use of neurofeedback to regulate cerebellar functioning, and our observations suggest that training at the boney inion ridge—roughly atop the cerebellum—enhances regulation in people with developmental trauma. It is difficult to know what signals we are picking up and whether they are essentially "cerebellar" or occipital, much less to know if we are directly affecting the silent brain, but for many of my patients, training at this site has provided significant relief from affective storms, typically associated with the temporal lobes. For the present we can only report our observations of behavioral change and speculate on how it might relate to temporal lobe regulation. These sites are not on the 10–20 map (see Figure 2.1), but we will "find" them when we discuss placement and protocols in Chapter 7. (See also Figure C.1.)

The Cerebral Cortex

The cerebral cortex, commonly (if imprecisely) referred to as the cortex, is colloquially described as the thinking cap, as the part of the brain that most differentiates humans from their close primate cousins. At most places it is six cells deep. It makes up for thinness by its essentially fractal topography as it rumples up in multiple folds to fit the brain's enormous complexity within the small circumference of the skull. As much as one-third of the brain's surface is tucked into its folds, called *sulci*. Specific areas in the cortex have specific functions. As an example, Broca's area, in the frontal portion of the left hemisphere, is specific to speech production (F7). It seems to be the case that the corresponding structures on the opposite hemisphere contribute in some way to the function of their sister areas. Homologous areas are more connected to each other, through the cingulate, than to any other site in the brain. In the case of Broca's area, its unnamed homologous partner on the right (F8) adds prosody, the song of speech. The absence of prosody in the voice suggests developmental or acquired injury to the right hemisphere. The cerebral cortex is not, however, solely about thought. It is, first and foremost, about affect regulation—particularly the right prefrontal cortex, which exerts control over the more primitive and often very powerful subcortical brain structures, specifically the amygdala. We focus mostly on subcortical brain structures and functions in this book because they house the fear circuitry fundamental to understanding developmental trauma. In neurofeedback we place sensors on the scalp to pick up EEG readings. When we are able to affect subcortical functioning, it is likely that we are activating the inhibitory capacity of the cortex to quiet errant firing deep in the brain.

Hemispheres and Laterality

As we saw in the example of speech, different sides of the cortex have different functions. This division of function is called *laterality*. The two hemispheres are divided by the central sulcus, the groove down the middle of the brain, and they are connected through a large bundle of nerves called the *corpus callosum*—larger in women than in men (Joseph, 1996, p. 136)—and the structure that runs from the back to the front beneath the central sulcus, the *cingulate*. Functions in the brain are *contralateralized* with the right hemisphere (RH) governing the left side of the body, and the left hemisphere (LH) governing the right. If a person suffers a stroke in the LH, her speech, which is organized there, will be affected, as will movement or sensation on the right side of the body. Due to the RH homologous site, many of these patients can sing what they can't speak. There are some exceptions to this schema, but it holds pretty universally. It is almost as though we have two separate brains with very different functions that are wired together for optimal communication and effectiveness.

The RH is nonverbal, spatial, and relational. It is devoted to affect regulation, spatial processing, prosody and song, facial recognition, novelty, and recognizing the gestalt—seeing the forest through the trees. It is the first hemisphere to develop, during the first 18–30 months after birth, and it shuts down development when the LH comes online at about that time. Mothers universally "talk" to their babies with "motherese," a musical language specifically pitched for the nonverbal RH. We will focus most of our attention on the RH because of its regulation troubles in developmental trauma, but these patients thankfully also have a left hemisphere, and, in most cases, we will need to train both sides of the brain for optimal outcomes.

In most people, the LH is verbal, sequential, and rational. It is about *text*, whereas the right is about *context*. It is focused on the trees, not the forest. The LH comes online around age 2, as the baby moves from babble-song, relying a good deal on prosody to make his point, to words and then to sentences. Premature talking and particularly sentence construction signal that the RH has not fully developed and predict the likelihood of affect regulation problems (this is a common developmental course in Asperger's). It has long been called the dominant hemisphere because it is the hemisphere of language, a defining characteristic of human beings. The ability to use language to describe and manage emotion is, of course, one of the primary treatment goals in helping people with developmental trauma.

Schore and others (Ornstein, 1997; Siegel, 1999; van der Kolk, 2005) might argue about which hemisphere actually dominates, however. Schore writes, "The orbitofrontal region is expanded in the right hemisphere, the cerebral hemisphere that is differentially involved in the bilateral regulation of arousal, is closely associated with heart rate regulation and neuroendocrine control, and is responsible for maintaining important controls over autonomic activities. . . . the right frontotemporal cortex specifically exerts inhibitory control over intense emotional arousal" (1994, p. 226). With specific regard to trauma, van der Kolk describes the difficulty that trauma survivors experience with semantic [LH] memory: "Having listened to the narratives of traumatic experiences from hundreds of traumatized children and adults over many years, my colleagues and I keep hearing both adults and children describe how traumatic experiences are initially organized on a nonverbal [RH] level" (1994, p. 287). Every one of us makes our rational decisions based on the influence of nonrational emotions, and in developmental trauma this is the exact process that we see as the illness. These patients are driven by their emotions. They think what they feel; they behave what they feel; they are what they feel. There is little apparent LH influence. As van der Kolk's fMRI research demonstrates (Rauch et al., 1996), a person has no LH activation at all during a flashback. (See Figure C.2.) Not everyone agrees that all emotion is a RH event. Some researchers have argued that the LH is the seat of positive emotion (Henriques & Davidson, 1991; Davidson, 2004). Again Schore would disagree: "Attachment, empathy, and perhaps even love are capacities of the right hemisphere. I think of these as very positive emotions" (personal communication, June 10, 2005). These positive emotions are the ones, of course, that are most attenuated in this population, crowded out as they are by the survival affects of fear, shame, and rage. It may be the absence of these compelling affective storms that researchers such as Davidson are describing as positive affect. For now we don't need to enter this debate. In my experience with neurofeedback, when people quiet their highly aroused nervous systems, primarily through addressing the regulation of the RH, they experience increasing capacity for love, empathy, and attachment and, as a direct result, feel happier.

The LH does its best to give language to the felt sense, but in developmental trauma that narrative itself is overly determined by a malfunctioning, poorly regulated RH. The capacity to put feelings into words depends on some level of regulation in the RH. This is, of course, the very real limitation of therapies that depend on language. As mentioned in Chapter 1, my sense is that language-based therapies that work may actually be prosody-based therapies. The good-enough therapist's communication is a form of motherese. There may also be less possibility for subcortical disruption in the LH; the survival-oriented amygdala is in the RH. At the same time, laterality suggests a therapeutic course: regulation of the RH to quiet affect and regulation of the LH to promote thought, articulation, and the formulation of a new narrative of self.

Because it is involved with words and very directly with reading and writing, we can think of the LH as the learning hemisphere. We see a high level of learning disabilities in those with histories of developmental trauma, but in this population these are most often *nonverbal* learning disabilities such as problems with relational cueing, spatial processing, and sense of direction—all RH properties. Cause-and-effect thinking is also mediated by the experiences of the RH. Long before a baby learns to talk, she will be making predictions about what comes next, what action predicts what response. When there is no response, as is so often the case in situations involving maternal depression and neglect, there can be no reliable way to develop an accurate, reality-based sense of cause and effect. Abuse that is random, that cannot be predicted by what you do—the case for most children with developmental trauma—will also visit havoc on cause-and-effect thinking.

Approximately 8% of left-handed people and a even smaller percentage of right-handed people have switched laterality, which means that speech and all other LH functions are located in the RH, and vice versa (Szaflarski et al., 2002). Knowing which hemisphere is doing what in any given individual is obviously important when you are considering how to approach brain wave training. There is a fairly reliable shortcut to determine where language is located in left-handed people: When they write, the fingers of their left hand point to the dominant hemisphere. If speech is in the RH, then affect regulation is likely to be in the LH, a situation that is called *switched dominance*, and one we clearly want to know about when we are training the brain.

Developmental trauma is primarily encoded as a disorganization and dysregulation of the RH due to lack of maternal attunement and care during infancy and early childhood. In better circumstances, the mother's attunement builds these structures. I refer the reader to Allan Schore and the work of attachment researchers to delve more deeply into the relationship between maternal attunement and infant attachment (Schore, 1994, 2003; Siegel, 1999; Tronick, 2007). Suffice it to say here that the mother's self-regulation becomes the baby's self-regulation because it builds cortical structures in the young child that inhibit subcortical ones.

The RH amygdala, however, comes online between 5 and 6 months in utero, the same time that fetal movement begins. From that time on, at least, the fetus can feel fear, and this fear is the fear of the mother in her loud, chaotic environment, external or internal. The fetus can hear her pounding heart and the angry voices, and the fetus will register the blows the mother takes. All the fetus can do in this gestational period and in early postnatal times is to react. There is no safety in these wombs.

I worked with a young woman who was pregnant with her third child. The father of the child didn't want the baby and during one of their frequent fights, he punched my patient in the stomach. This kind of assault on the mother predicts attachment disruption. At about 5 months into her pregnancy, my patient described wild fetal movement, all elbows and heels. She said, "If I didn't know better, I would believe that this baby was aggressive toward me." Serendipitously, I began to train the mother prefrontally, using a protocol that seems to directly affect amygdala reactivity. When she was doing the first session with this protocol, she told me that the baby had rolled over and gone to sleep: "Calm mother; calm baby." The baby and the mother seemed to be enjoying the co-arising regulation, and it seems probable that the dramatic reduction in fear in the mother invited this in her baby. The external environment had changed very little, but the mother was now much less reactive to it, and so was her child. This experience in which both the mother and the fetus responded to quieting the mother's lifelong ambient fear may suggest that, at least in these cases, this kind of fetal movement relates to the transmission of the mother's fearful self quite directly to her child, brain to brain, body to body. It also suggests that neurofeedback may have a role to play in interrupting the intergenerational transmission of trauma. I discuss this case again in Chapter 9.

Our goal in training the brain in patients with developmental trauma is to activate focal structures, areas, and circuitries that could inhibit high amygdala arousal and the erratic or habitual firing in response to cues or triggers. The structures that emerge developmentally to inhibit the amygdala are the insula (F8), the anterior cingulate (FZ), and the prefrontal cortex (FP1 and FP2). What I have observed in training these sites—at least as we approximate them on the skull—is that fear does diminish in most people.

Lobes of the Brain

The brain has four lobes, each with specific but complementary functions (many of which are still being discovered) depending on whether they are located on the right or the left side. Because of the complex symptomology that occurs in developmental trauma and the equally complex responses that we might see while training these patients with neurofeedback, it is important to have a basic familiarity with what we do know about the functions of the lobes, beginning in the back of the head. Figure C.1 shows the lobes.

The Occipital Lobe

The large occipital lobe mainly governs vision. When there is damage to this part of the brain, a person can go blind. In a condition called *cortical blindness*, there is nothing wrong with the eyes themselves, but the brain cannot process the information that the eyes are bringing to the occipital lobe. It is a large lobe whose size is understood mostly in evolutionary terms. We are a species that relies, more than any other, on eyesight. Based on experiences people have described when training at occipital sites, it seems that this part of the brain may be involved in more than vision. During one week, two of my patients came in having suffered accidental blows to the head, and both complained of double vision. In both, the double vision corrected while they were training at the occipital lobe. The next week, they each reported that they had had no further problems with their eyesight and also that they felt less anxious. We explored this and in both cases realized that they specifically felt less anticipatory anxiety. They described themselves as feeling more "laid back." This may well be a part of the brain to consider training in developmental trauma, particularly when the trauma involves witnessing abuse of the mother or siblings or witnessing other horrors, such as violence on the streets or in war zones.

The Parietal Lobe

The parietal lobe is often called the *association cortex*, and it is the seat of sensory integration. Information from all senses, except smell, arrives here via the thalamus to be processed, integrated, and with help from subcortical structures, particularly the hippocampus and the amygdala, made meaningful. As noted in Chapter 1, babies learn the nature of their world through their senses. (We are learning through our senses at all ages, but in infancy it is the primary learning modality).

Most people with a history of developmental trauma experience some level of difficulty with the integration of sensory information, including hypersensitivity and reactivity to touch, sound, light, and often to smell. Smell has a structure of its own, right behind the middle of the forehead, called the olfactory bulb. The limbic system, the subcortical area of the brain that sits atop the brainstem and that we share with all mammals, was first termed the *rhinencephalon*—that is the "nose brain"—because it was studied in animals that rely on smell to activate this part of their brains. I mentioned the man who came to me essentially disabled by the roar and quiver of his nervous system that registered a drop of rain on his skin as so alarming that he had to take refuge. Sensory integration problems also contribute heavily to learning disabilities, a common problem in those with histories of developmental trauma. The parietal area, along with the temporal lobes, house auditory processing, and if this part of the brain does not organize properly, it can impair the ability to take in spoken information and learn from it. Disorganization here can cause a slight but significant hearing delay. I spoke of the young woman with DID who experienced this delay. She was always behind the information being presented and constantly needed to ask people to repeat themselves. Before I knew more about sensory integration in developmental trauma, I assumed that she just wasn't paying attention. We will encounter her again in Chapter 9.

The Temporal Lobe

There are of course also two temporal lobes, just as there two occipital and parietal lobes. Auditory processing, lexical memory, language, logical reasoning, reading, writing, and arithmetic are lateralized to the left temporal lobe. Prosody, emotional valance, facial recognition and memory, spatial orientation and memory, time sense, rhythm, ability to sing on key and remember tunes, as well as the ability to recognize familiar songs and to enjoy music are all right temporal functions. Schore (1994, 2003) would argue that the sense of self, and by necessity, the sense of other organize primarily in the right temporal lobe. Ability to regulate emotions is in great part a right temporal lobe capacity.

Instability in the temporal lobes, as we have seen, may well be a hallmark of developmental trauma. Trauma researchers are investigating the overlap between developmental trauma and temporal lobe epilepsy (TLE), particularly in the right temporal lobe, and many suspect it is great. Teicher reported that "children with . . . confirmed diagnosis of depressive signs and symptoms and a history of severe physical and sexual abuse (without head trauma) have a 72% incidence of abnormal EEG" (as cited in Lanius et al., 2010, p. 114). The hippocampus and the amygdala have a low threshold for excitation and kindling, which makes them increasingly more prone to seizure, whether clinical or (more often) subclinical. Developmental neuroscientist Rhawn Joseph (1996) talks about it this way:

> Severe and repeated emotional trauma can, in fact, give rise to a propensity to develop kindling [of the hippocampus and the amygdala] as well as abnormal neural networks. This would make these individuals more likely to develop psychotic and severe emotional and dissociative disorders and put them at risk for developing TLE. (p. 511)

In a paper on neuropsychiatric disorders, Shelley, Trimble, and Boutros (2008) begin to address this overlap: "Subclinical electroencephalographic [EEG] epileptiform discharges in neurobehavioral disorders are not uncommon. The clinical significance and behavioral, diagnostic, and therapeutic implications of these EEG cerebral dysrhythmias have not been fully examined. Currently the only connotation for distinctive epileptiform electroencephalographic patterns is epileptic seizures" (p. 7). *Dysrhythmia* simply means "out of rhythm," which in the brain means errant firing patterns, poorly differentiated networks, and poorly organized network oscillations. The focus on seizure-like instability and subclinical seizure in those people with developmental trauma histories is a fruitful course of research and, as we will see, it underpins some key points in understanding the efficacy of neurofeedback in treating developmental trauma and its many comorbidities. Although these authors do not specifically consider developmental trauma, they do include data on dysrhythmias in borderline personality disorder, one of the adult sequela. These data include diffuse EEG slowing; increased slow-wave activity, often bilateral in the frontal lobe, the temporal lobe, or in a frontotemporal distribution; and a high incidence of paroxysmal (large bursts) EEG.

As we will see in the next chapter, neurofeedback was originally developed to control seizure activity in the brain. Seizures amount to a tsunami in the brain, and research demonstrates (Wyrwicka & Sterman, 1968; Sterman, 2000; Egner & Sterman, 2006) that a person with epilepsy can learn to control these massive, disruptive events with neurofeedback. It is likely that it can also help those diagnosed with developmental trauma who suffer lesser but still profound paroxysmal events. This likelihood of successful treatment is, of course, one of the central premises of this book. Neurofeedback trains the brain to regulate itself, to inhibit overly slow or fast wave activity, and to quiet even small, but nonetheless influential paroxysmal activity, or dysrhythmias, in the brain. Temporal lobe instability may be close to ubiquitous in cases of developmental trauma and might even qualify as TLE in many of these same patients.

Other common sources of TLE include head injuries and middle ear infections. Blows to the head and ear infections are, of course, sadly common in the histories of abused and neglected children. It is important that the neurofeedback clinician assess for history or indicators of TLE, subclinical or clinical, and generally assess the functioning of the right temporal lobe. It is also important to know that injury to the right temporal lobe, whether developmental or acquired, can lead to hyper-religiosity or spirituality and hyper- or hyposexuality. As we will see, the right temporal lobe is a common focus in neurofeedback training for developmental trauma (T4, T6).

The Frontal Lobe

The frontal lobe and the prefrontal lobe are considered a single lobe with each area having specialized functions. The frontal lobe is engaged with planning, and the prefrontal lobe, or orbital area, with execution. The left prefrontal cortex is heavily involved with agency, with going out into the world. The right prefrontal cortex exercises control over the impulses of the amygdala. When the amygdala is out of control—or perhaps more to the point, too much in control, as is so often the case in this population—we may consider training this area of the brain to activate and strengthen its inhibitory prerogative. Jeffrey Alan Gray, who developed the biopsychological theory of personality, wrote, "As pertaining to emotional arousal, it has also been postulated that the orbital area exerts a major influence on the experience of anxiety" (Gray, 1987). This part of the brain, which is responsible for executive function, is often impaired in these patients due most likely to excess fear or lack of inhibition of the right amygdala. There is a great deal of interest presently in prefrontal structures, particularly in fMRI research on developmental trauma. I'll briefly touch on what's known about them and what contribution their dysregulation makes to the symptom picture in developmental trauma.

• *The orbitofrontal cortex* (OFC) lies directly behind the bridge of the nose and exercises judgment, particularly over the needs of the body. It is also the terminus for the signals from the amygdala to the prefrontal cortex. For survival purposes there are many more pathways from the amygdala to the OFC than from the OFC back to the amygdala. When a predator or truck is bearing down on us, it is vital to react immediately, not take time to think. As we have seen, the person suffering from developmental trauma anticipates predators, and as a result, tends to react before thinking, particularly in situations that the amygdala has deemed dangerous. Ledoux (1996) explains:

The medial prefrontal cortex [the OFC] is nicely situated to be able to regulate the outputs of the amygdala on the basis of events in the outside world as well as on the basis of the amygdala's interpretation of those events. . . . A rat [with lesions to this area] continued to act fearful in the presence of a conditioned fear stimulus long after rats without lesions had stopped acting afraid. (p. 248)

He goes on to describe the troubled human being: "Humans with orbital frontal damage become oblivious to social and emotional cues and some exhibit sociopathic behavior" (Ledoux, 1998, p. 278).

This is a neuroscientist's description of the boy Carl, whom we met in the Introduction, whose prefrontal damage was developmental in origin and who was also diagnosed with TLE. Schore (1994, 2003) emphasizes the right prefrontal cortex particularly in the regulation of the survival-oriented amygdala, which lies watchful in the right temporal lobe. The work of Schore and Ledoux led directly to the development of a new neurofeedback training site, called *FPO2*, which is used specifically to quiet the unrelenting amygdala rant typical of developmental trauma. We discuss FPO2 in detail in Chapter 7.

• *The dorsomedial prefrontal cortex* (DMPFC), along with many distant regions, becomes activated when people reflect on themselves. (The fact that this function is not localized to the DMPFC reminds us that although one area may be focal for an activity or function, it is always embedded in neural networks that connect to other areas of the brain.) This area is critical to the capacity for conceptual self-awareness (Fogel, 2009) and to our sense of personal biography. "The DMPFC, then, is related to thinking and making decisions specifically about one's own thoughts and to thoughts about one's own feelings" (Fogel, 2009, p. 96). Developmental injury to the DMPFC results in impairment of the conceptual self, the self as known to us cognitively: the self that produces coherent autobiographical narrative. As we saw, Carl lacked any ability to reflect on himself. He had a story, not a particularly coherent one, but he had no narrated self. The woman who, on our first meeting, identified herself as "a borderline" had no sense of a self that was hers as differentiated from one that was provided to her by diagnosis or her therapists. She had been relieved to receive a diagnosis, which may have been partly because it provided a narrative for her where there had been none. Better a pathological self than no self at all; better some recognition than none at all. [Others get locked into rigid, repetitive, denigrating self-concepts that are very difficult to interrupt.] These problems in the realization of self seem to relate primarily to these prefrontal structures and networks, including, as we will see, the anterior cingulate (FZ and FPO2).

- *The dorsolateral prefrontal cortex* (DLPFC) relates to working memory and "the ability to keep an emotion in mind so that it can be evaluated by higher cognitive centers in the prefrontal cortex responsible for decision-making and affect regulation" (Fogel, 2009, p. 69). Anyone who has survived early childhood neglect and abuse, or who has worked closely with someone who has, will recognize the breakdown of this structure and its malfunctioning neural networks. Impulse overtakes reflection, impulse that is riding the pulse of fear. These patients distinguish themselves for being unable to learn from experience and for their routinely poor judgment. (F5, F6, and FPO2)

- *The ventromedial prefrontal cortex* (VMPFC), which sits just below the DMPFC, relates primarily to awareness of being in the body—to, as Fogel puts it, "the embodied sense of self" (2009, p. 53). It has significant connections to the amygdala. Many patients with developmental trauma report the lack of a reliable, felt sense of their bodies or of themselves inhabiting their bodies. One woman described herself as a huge, grotesque walking head. These patients lack the very continuity of a sense of their own skin, or the sense of having skin at all—which suggests the lack of a reliable sense of self-other boundary, and again, the lack of self and other. The VMPFC receives messages from the body and is part of the network that processes pain. People with developmental trauma have significantly higher pain thresholds than those without these histories, suggesting that this network is providing some level of endogenous analgesia, similar to that described in soldiers wounded on the battlefield who are unaware of their injuries until the battle is done. One boy with developmental trauma felt only a slight twinge when his appendix ruptured. Only his sudden fever alerted staff to the emergency situation. The very mechanism that he had deployed to bear the pain of developmental trauma nearly killed him.

Interestingly, when the DMPFC is activated (reflecting on the self or conceptual self- awareness), the VMPFC (body awareness and embodied self-awareness) shuts off, and vice versa. According to Fogel (2009), and as many meditators will attest, it is impossible to inhabit both kinds of awareness at the same time. People with developmental trauma who are often, at best, holding together a diffuse and fragmented sense of self, will experience impairment in both types of self-awareness. They find it challenging to conceive of themselves at all, and when they pull together some sort of self-concept, it is usually infused with perseverative self-hatred (originally the hatred or perceived hatred of the mother). And perhaps needless to say, patients with developmental trauma have learned not to inhabit their neglected, defiled, and blamed bodies. This truncated embodiment can be seen as the primary dissociation of trauma survivors, and it seems to be the failure of this prefrontal structure, under the onslaught of abuse and neglect, that is responsible. If the brain structures that represent self in the mind fail to develop, there can be no self (FZ and FPO2).

The Insular Cortex

The insular cortex, among its many functions, serves interoception, the perception of information that arises from the interior of the body and contributes to the felt sense of being. It functions as well to inhibit the firing of the amygdala. As we follow the case I am building here, we can hypothesize that these functions are parallel, if not one in the same. Craig et al. (2000) noted: "Early emotional trauma that interferes with the experience-dependent maturation of the insula negatively impacts its role in generating an image of one's physical state (body image), a process that underlies the experiencing of basic emotions" (as cited in Schore, 2003, p. 202). Teicher also discusses the focal importance of the insula as "a complex structure in which visceral, somatosensory, motor, vestibular and auditory functions converge and generate subjective feelings such as pain and craving. The anterior insula, particularly on the right side, can recast these feelings as social emotions" (Teicher et al., 2010, pp. 118–119). It is difficult to imagine an integrated and embodied sense of self without a well functioning insula. As neurofeedback providers, we too want to enhance the capacity for a felt sense of self as well as to play a role in the inhibition of the amygdala, and we will be well guided in the development of protocols by knowing the locations of the brain structures involved, at least optimally, in this same endeavor (F8 and FT8).

The Cingulate

Developmental trauma seems to deeply impact cingulate function. This midline central structure runs from the middle of the forehead (FPZ) to the back of the head (PZ) beneath the central sulcus and above the corpus callosum. Circuitry connecting homologous sites in the LH and RH pass through the cingulate. It is divided into anterior and posterior regions, which have separate but complementary functions. The anterior cingulate cortex (ACC) functions to inhibit the firing of the amygdala. It is often referred to as the *transitional limbic cortex* because it lies at the transition between cortical and subcortical regions. Joseph (1996) describes the anterior cingulate as "a supra-modal area that is involved in the integration of motor, tactile, autonomic and emotional stimuli, as well as in the production of emotional sounds and the capacity to experience psychological 'pain and misery'" (p. 243). Carl, as you may remember, was unable to feel pain and misery. Failures in the ACC feature prominently in the symptoms of developmental trauma, including lack of inhibition of fear, perseveration, and the frequent comorbidity with OCD. Functional MRI studies of people with developmental trauma show very little blood flow in this part of the brain. Along with the OFC, this part of the brain is correlated with reflection on the self, the conceptual sense of self, and the embodied sense of self. Once again, no blood flow means little neuronal activation, which likely correlates directly to the sense of self as a black hole, as nonexistent (FZ).

The posterior cingulate, at the back of the head, mediates the person's recognition of her existence in space. The precuneus is located here, and it may hold a good deal of a person's autobiographical memory, and in that, her sense of identity. This area, too, is poorly infused with blood in fMRI studies of the default mode network in patients with developmental trauma. (Interestingly, the networks related to the default mode cycle below 1 Hz, at 0.1, or once every 10 seconds. More about this in Chapter 7.) The default mode shows up in the fMRI when the person in the scanner is essentially told that there is a pause in the action and she has no task to do. Blood flow equals activation. The default mode, also called the resting state networks, is dysregulated in people with developmental trauma. They do not rest; they go blank. (See Figure C.4.)

The Limbic System

We are constructing a simple model of a complex brain, where the intelligent cerebral cortex, developing slowly over time with the help of parents or significant others, inhibits and guides the primitive impulses of the subcortical brain, or as it is usually called, the *limbic system*. But as has to be true, the limbic system has an intelligence of its own. "The limbic system is thought to be the part of the CNS that maintains and guides the emotions and behavior necessary for self-preservation and survival of the species" (van der Kolk, 2007, p. 229). There are many subcortical structures in the brain and many of these are engaged in mediating the fear response. Here we focus on the hippocampus and the amygdala.

The Hippocampus

The hippocampus, which lies adjacent to the amygdala, is generally thought of as the brain's portal to memory. As is true for the amygdala, there are actually two hippocampi, one in each hemisphere, and each has a different role to play in memory. The RH hippocampus records memory in spatial and temporal fields and the LH holds verbal memory. The RH hippocampus is central to implicit, nonverbal memory—in a sense, to unremembered memory. When RH memory begins to return, it does so most often in felt experience and sometimes in pictures and then in a spatial context. These experiences are very difficult to render verbally. Those struggling to recover from the ravages of developmental trauma often say, "I don't know how to put this in words," or "There just aren't words for this." This occurs because there is no language, at least initially, for nonverbal memory. The LH hippocampus is involved in declarative or explicit memory, also called *semantic memory* (i.e., related to words), and gives us the ability to use words to communicate emotional states. Sustained stress and high levels of circulating cortisol and other stress hormones (i.e., glucocorticoids) lead to a smaller hippocampus, structurally, and as a result, to impaired memory. "A likely explanation is that the shrinkage in the hippocampus is due to the effects of heightened cortisol, which is known to be toxic to the hippocampus" (van der Kolk, 2007, p. 233). Teicher, Anderson, and Polcari (2012) argue that the stress axis in the brain, now called the *hypothalamus–pituitary–adrenal axis* (HPA), is more accurately understood as the *HHPA*, or the *hippocampus–hypothalamus–pituitary–adrenal axis*, due to the level of hippocampal involvement and impairment in stress.

Memory in those with developmental trauma remains a highly controversial issue, particularly the matter of repressed memory. Trauma experts think of repressed memory as RH memory that is implicit rather than explicit, coded early in life and primarily in the nonverbal hemisphere. As we discussed earlier, it is this hemisphere that is developing in the first 2 years, not the left, and it would therefore have to be the RH that houses memories from these years. I'll return, perhaps at my peril, to this intriguing and conflictual issue more fully in Chapters 7 and 8. It is likely that the RH hippocampus is implicated in anniversary reactions, notoriously difficult events in the lives of those with developmental trauma. Trauma triggers, also memory, seem to be held in the amygdala, and these can cause daily eruptions in those with active developmental trauma. (See T4 in Figure 2.1.)

The Amygdala

This small almond-size nuclei that lies deep in the temporal lobe is involved primarily in rage, shame, and fear reactions, but also more generally in establishing the emotional valance of incoming stimuli. The RH amygdala is devoted to survival and reacts to threats, both real and perceived. As is true of the hippocampus, the amygdala is highly prone to kindling, the term given to repetitive neuronal firing that gains amplitude with each repetition until it collapses. This pattern of activation makes each experience a prime for the next episode; that is, each kindling event lowers the threshold to future ones, making them more likely. This vulnerability may help us understand why developmental trauma usually gets worse over time and why the amygdala may react to increasingly tangential stimuli in its efforts to keep its owner alive.

One colleague likened it to a "stupid car alarm" that goes off with seemingly little provocation. She talked about a child in foster care who was severely abused by his father as his mother watched helplessly. This abuse would happen most frequently right after his father returned from work and began to drink. This boy was naturally afraid of men who were drinking. However, his foster parents didn't drink, yet each night after their return from work, he would become oppositional, aggressive, and clearly afraid. They finally understood that the trigger had become the sound of tires on the gravel driveway—first only when it was dark, then anytime, and then any noise that sounded even close to tires on gravel.

People living in the throes of high amygdala arousal have no sense of time passing or of a past at all. It is as if the abandonment, abuse, and neglect suffered as children were ongoing, even though they know cognitively that this is not true. It is impossible to know how these events are actually held in the brain, but these early threats to life are likely distributed in subcortical patterns of activation throughout the fear circuitry. van der Kolk (2007) explains:

> During exposure to the scripts of their traumatic experiences, these [developmental trauma] subjects demonstrated heightened activity in the right hemisphere—in the paralimbic belt, parts of the limbic system connected to the amygdala. Most active were the amygdala itself, the insular cortex, the posterior orbito-frontal cortex, the anterior cingulate cortex, and the anterior temporal cortex. . . . Perhaps most significantly, Broca's area "turned off." We believe that this reflects the tendency in PTSD to experience emotions as physical states rather than as verbally encoded experiences. (p. 233)

In a more general way, it might be these limbic firing patterns that give rise to the frequently reported "inner child" who is overtaken by fear, shame, and often cringing rage.

In service of survival, the amygdala does not readily update its files. What could kill or maim you as a baby can still kill or maim you. Many years ago, on a walk along a country road, my two dogs were shocked by an electric fence. For a year or more they made a 100-yard detour away from the fence. One dog did that for the rest of her life; the other slowly narrowed the arc until by year 3, she was back walking on the road near the fence. This impromptu science experiment suggested to me the importance of individual factors in susceptibility to trauma reactivity—a susceptibility that may be more genetic than experiential. Individuals with developmental trauma have grown up with the limbic CNS informing their feelings, beliefs, and actions. They are captured by an overactivated amygdala that has no effective regulators. The insula, the anterior cingulate, the prefrontal cortex, and perhaps the cerebellum are meant to exercise inhibitory influence. In developmental trauma, these inhibitory structures are either not available or are functioning poorly, leading to dysregulated behavior and cognition heavily determined by shame, rage, and fear—each of which has a "chamber" in the amygdala. Interestingly, the glucocorticoids that cause atrophy in the hippocampus have just the opposite effect in the amygdala. Too much cortisol for too long a time shrinks dendritic branches causing hippocampal damage while in the amygdala, the same cortisol exposure promotes increased dendritic branching, increasing neuronal connectivity and reactivity (Sapolsky, 2004). Of course, in developmental trauma we see the mind's version of this differential effect in the reactivity of patients to trauma triggers and to their characteristic lack of intact memory for the events. The brain seems to wire itself to react and to forget what it is reacting to.

In common parlance the amygdala has become synonymous with fear and although we have seen that fear, like memory, is a widely distributed survival function, the focal point of fear reactivity is the amygdala. Fear is, of course, central to our developing thesis. I agree with Ledoux when he says that "fear is a core emotion in psychopathology" (1998, p. 132). It seems, in fact, that fear may well be *the* core emotion in psychopathology, and there is no group for whom this is truer than for those who have suffered from developmental trauma. These individuals are also prone to intense shame reactions and to disorganizing rage. Fear and rage are activated to save the life of the organism.

At first look, shame, also an amygdala affect, may not seem so clearly protective, but it is. "It appears that shame, at least through evolution, has served to keep the individual's behavior in line with cultural norms that further 'survival of the tribe.' It may, in fact, be the emotion that underlies formation of a conscience" (Rothschild, 2000, p. 63). Izard

(1971) argues that "shame comes to play an adaptive central active role in the regulation of (impulsive) emotional expression, and therefore for more effective social interaction" (as cited in Schore, 1994, p. 210). Shame socializes and protects our connections to other human beings. Carl and others like him seem incapable of shame, and they have no conscience. Although this is a core feature of antisocial personality, it is not clear, at the level of the amygdala, how this transpires and how the absence of shame serves those who have suffered profound neglect. It may be that shame can manifest only in the interpersonal world of mother and child. Shame has a parasympathetic tone in its dampening and withdrawal effects, and it may be that those with histories like Carl's have had little experience with PNS effects. In the treatment of a person with APD it would be as necessary to activate shame as it is in borderline personality to deactivate it. Those who are described as borderline or narcissistic are characteristically swamped by shame and organize themselves to avoid it. Fear, anger, and shame all have adaptive, survival functions. In developmental trauma, however, these affects, rather than informing the sense of self, overcome it. And there is evidence that in their toxic forms, they contribute to illness both psychological and physical and in many cases to early death.

In neurofeedback training our target is the amygdala and we attempt to activate those parts of the brain that are involved in its regulation. Schore calls the right front quadrant of the brain "the greater amygdaloid area" (1994, p. 181). In the search to regulate the amygdala, this will be an area of particular interest to neurofeedback practitioners (T4, FT8, F8, FZ, and FPO2). In Chapter 7, I discuss several cases that demonstrate the effects of training the right prefrontal cortex and its impact on the release of fear based memory.

The Electrical Brain

There is a new paradigm of brain function emerging that could change the way we understand the brain as a whole. This paradigm leans away from the narrow (but lucrative) focus on the brain's biochemistry and toward its bioelectrical organization, which is precisely what neurofeedback targets. In his book *Rhythms of the Brain* (2006), György Buzsáki,

Professor of Neuroscience at Rutgers University, proposes that the brain organizes itself through oscillating rhythms generated within the brain, as manifest in the EEG. He describes the brain more in the language of physics than of either neurology or psychology. He asks this question, "What does it mean to conjecture that the brain is a pattern-forming, self-organizing, non-equilibrium system governed by non-linear dynamical laws?" (p. 17). He is applying complexity theory, the study of complex systems, to his understanding of this most complex of organs. This is not a discussion of brain structures or brain chemistry, per se, but of nonlinear complex patterns and rhythms as the governing principles in brain function.

Happily, perhaps, we don't need to learn quantum physics to understand how Buzsáki's theory supports the phenomenology of neurofeedback. Appealing to the brain's basic governing principle, its rhythms, might in fact be useful to helping it self-regulate. Buzsáki, in fact, uses early experiments in neurofeedback to advance his theory: "Whereas it takes several years of Zen meditation to reach the stage of slowing the frequency of alpha and the spreading of alpha oscillations forward to more frontal areas, approximately the same results can be accomplished by a week's training with alpha feedback" (2006, pp. 216–217).

There have been many advances in instrumentation and in the clinical applications of neurofeedback since the experiments he's citing from the late 1960s, but the principal remains the same. With feedback directly to its electrical domain, the brain can, and usually does, learn to regulate these rhythms. When we provide feedback to the brain we are, essentially, providing it with a mirror of its own function and "inviting" it to make more of some frequencies (*frequency* and *amplitude* are the parameters of rhythm) and less of others—that is, to oscillate differently. In neurofeedback, we seem to be nudging the brain to set up new oscillatory patterns that enhance both its natural complexity and its inherent and necessary bias toward self-regulation. In effect, we may be freeing up innate but "stuck" oscillatory properties in the brain and allowing new ones to propagate. These oscillations or rhythms underpin the currents and undercurrents of mind.

What we see in neurofeedback is not just the impact on targeted symptoms of the patient but on the evolving presence and dimensionality of the person training. Patients widen their focus, think new thoughts about old problems, and typically even their vocabulary expands and becomes more nuanced. They are able to escape the stubborn repetitions of their narrative. In this cosmology, we can think of rigidity as a core component of mental illness. In developmental trauma, this rigidity arises from the brain practicing fear; that is, wiring and rewiring fear circuitry. Our job is to help move the system from rigidity, repetition, and reactivity, to complexity, creativity, and stability by addressing these circuits.

A tight feedback loop, as it were, exists between mind and brain; they cannot be delinked, nor should we want to do so. We do, however, need to address them separately. Most psychotherapy theorists focus on the mind. Dan Siegel, one the most influential thinkers in the field of psychotherapy today, writes eloquently about the mind as a complex system: "We have stated from the beginning that the mind emanates from the activity of the brain, and thus it is fair to say that the mind itself is complex and has self-organizing properties" (1999, p. 215). Our focus, as neurofeedback practitioners, is primarily on the brain and how mind arises from the oscillatory patterns it produces. Siegel is focusing on the complexity of the mind, and I am focusing on complexity of the brain, and both are one with the body.

Clearly, addressing the mind helps people. Psychotherapy and meditation are changing the brain. It would have to be so or else they wouldn't work, and now fMRIs can document the actual changes in the brain. It has been my experience, however, and the central tenet of this book, that we can exercise more influence on the mind by addressing the brain than we can have on the brain by addressing the mind. This may in fact be the defining reality in disorders that we find intractable. We just can't appeal to this brain's self-organizing properties solely by engaging, however attuned we are, with this patient's mind, a common dilemma in work with those suffering from developmental trauma. Siegel (1999) talks about complexity as a feature in normal, healthy development:

Rather than viewing children as having stepwise increments in their abilities, we can view development as the emergence of patterns of increas-

ingly complex interactions between children and their environment. . . .
From a dynamical viewpoint, the system is maximizing its complexity and
therefore its stability by pushing behavior forward, applying old patterns
in slightly new situations. Every moment, in fact, is the emergence of a
unique pattern of activity in a world that is similar but never identical to
a past moment in time. (pp. 217–218)

In the 1962 film *The Miracle Worker*, from the play by William Gib-
son, we watch as Annie Sullivan repeatedly hands Helen Keller various
common objects and then finger-spells their names on her palm. For
months, Helen only mimics the signs, with no understanding of their
meaning. Then one day, following a heated argument in the breakfast
room, Helen makes the connection between the sign for water that
Annie is furiously finger-spelling into her palm and the water running
over her hands from the pump. Suddenly, the world opens to her. Creative learning, as opposed to memorization, may well consist of many
such "Helen Keller moments," the small and not-so-small eureka events
that open and prime the system for more.

But how do we organize this propagation of complexity? The work of
Buzsáki and Llinás (2001), as well as the rapid changes often seen in
neurofeedback, suggest that complexity in the brain plays out primarily
in its oscillatory and rhythmic domain. Biofeedback to the brainwaves
appeals to these rhythms and in this way to the "pattern-making" and
"self-organizing" properties of the brain. "Non-equilibrium" fundamentally means that the brain is an open system profoundly influenced by
its environment, the most important part of which is other human
beings and for the child, his mother and father. "Non-linear dynamical"
refers to the butterfly effect in which small local changes in one geo-
graphical region (the butterfly's flapping wing in Thailand) can have
large effects in a geography even at a great distance (a weather front in
Iowa). We see something akin to the butterfly effect routinely in neurofeedback training. We will see the strongest effects locally at the site
where we place the sensor, but it seems clear that this perturbation influences all parts of the brain, via its vast neural networks

What happens to this capacity to develop complexity and stability
under the assault of fear? The brain is affected at all levels. Basic homeo-

static rhythms are disrupted, including those related to sleep and wake-fulness, eating and appetite, reproductive cycles and body temperature —the rhythms of the brainstem and higher-order cognitive and atten-tional systems are undermined. Van der Kolk (2007) notes: "The organ-ism needs to be able to engage in routine tasks without getting distracted by irrelevant stimuli, and to be able to explore new options without getting disorganized . . . to be able to do all this, the organism needs to be able to learn from experience" (p. 215). One of Carl's most persistent and disturbing clinical features was his inability to learn from experi-ence. Fear had overwhelmed his system to such a degree that it morphed from its evolutionary trajectory as an open and complex system that is constantly learning and adapting, to a closed, repetitive, and rigid one that can neither learn nor adapt. When we consider oscillations as foun-dational to the system, we can imagine that Carl suffered a kind of oscil-latory constriction that we, as his clinicians, were unable to budge. In a sense Carl was all brain and very little mind. It was as if his nervous system, paralyzed by motherlessness and devoted solely to its own sur-vival, did not have the luxury to develop a psyche.

In Chapter 3, I describe the process of neurofeedback in some detail. In terms of oscillations, my sense is that neurofeedback allows more robust and interdependent oscillations to develop; that is, it moves the brain toward complexity and stability. When complexity and stability are the organizational reality of the brain, they are the organizational reality of the mind as well. Having practiced neurofeedback since the late 1990s, I greatly appreciate the advances in neuroscience that sup-port it. As is the course in science, the phenomenon precedes the theory that explains it. Our endeavor, however, is clinical, and as a clinician I explore clinical phenomenology through observations, patient reports, and my experiences training my own brain.

Circuitry

The paradigm shift that is emerging through the work of Buzsáki and others asks us to look at the electrical domain, at the way the brain fires. Les Fehmi, one of the pioneers of neurofeedback, talks about "the brain's 'spark,' its electrical properties, . . . not the 'soup,' its neurochemicals"

(Fehmi & Robbins, 2001, p. 56). These are co-dependent properties. Very simply put, a neuron builds up an electrical charge chemically and discharges it as electrical potential down the neuron's axon to the synaptic gap—the tiny space between the end of the axon and any adjacent neurons—where the electrical signal is again converted into neurotransmitters (neurochemicals) and picked up by receptor sites on the dendrites of those neighboring neurons (see Figure 2.2). Here the activity is converted back into an electrical signal, which is propagated again chemically. It takes thousands of neurons engaging in this process simultaneously or in synchrony to produce a brain wave. The number of times this happens in the frame of a second determines the frequencies at which the brain fires. As we will see, with neurofeedback for those suffering developmental trauma, we look for the frequencies that help quiet fearfulness and reactivity and reward the brain for making them.

There is no way to fully comprehend the complexity of the brain in any of its interdependent domains, structural, chemical, or electrical. That being said, I do want to provide a very basic sketch of its electrical domain, the "place" we visit as neurofeedback providers. In an article entitled "Faulty Circuits" in *Scientific American* (2010), Thomas Insel, Director of the National Institute of Mental Health, explored this emerging paradigm shift: "Brain regions that function together to carry out normal (and abnormal) mental operations can be thought of as analogous to electrical circuits. . . . The latest research shows that the malfunctioning of entire circuits may underlie many mental disorders" (p. 44). Although he doesn't mention neurofeedback as a way to regulate faulty circuits, his endorsement and acknowledgment of the paradigm shift to the electrical brain would seem to support a neurofeedback approach. (See Figure C.5.)

Donald Hebb, a Canadian psychologist, prepared the field for the discoveries it is now making. He focused his research on how the brain remembers by examining the process called *long-term potentiation* (LTP) (1949). He hypothesized that the more often a group of neurons fired together in response to a stimuli, either internal or external, the more they would be wired together—a theory that gave rise to the now well-known saying, "What fires together wires together." As we have seen, the

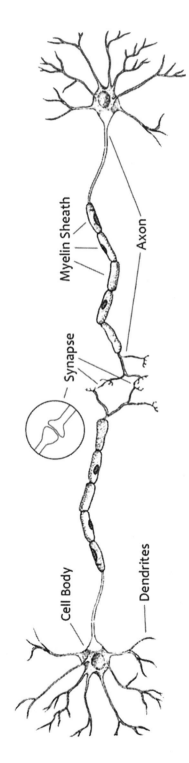

Figure 2.2. The neuron is the fundamental unit of brain function, but it takes ten thousand or more firing at the same time to build a wave form. (Courtesy of Sam McClellan.)

amygdala is a master of LTP. It does not forget, even if it does not remember. Neurofeedback prepares the brain for new learning as it relaxes the firing patterns that sustain fear and reactivity to fear.

Revisiting Medication

As suggested by Insel's (2010) article, the concept of circuitry gone awry is gaining both scientific and popular acceptance. The brain is an electrical–chemical organ. The two domains depend on each other absolutely. But since the discovery of Thorazine in 1950, we have focused almost exclusively on ways to manipulate the brain's chemistry, and as a result, tend to think of it primarily in terms of its synapses and its neurotransmitters, rather than in terms of the vast neural networks that sing with electricity.

There are a few significant problems with this overly determined focus on the chemical brain. The first is the most obvious, given that we have been ignoring the electrical domain of the brain with its oscillatory patterns and frequencies, and it is this domain, not the chemical one, that gives rise to the brain's self-organization and its plasticity. The chemical focus has allowed for the development of psychotropic medications, which have been very beneficial for many people. The reliance on psychotropic medications, however, has some problematic consequences. The Holy Grail of pharmacology is to find a medication that targets only the problem for which it is designed—and this seems as likely to occur as actually finding the Grail.

Medications always have side effects, some of them very serious. They will always, at the very least, negatively affect the liver, which works over time to discharge these substances from the body. Even if there were no side effects, the brain, the organ most devoted to learning, does not learn from medications. Once they are stopped, the symptoms often reappear and sometimes return with a vengeance. Medications often fog cognition, and those used routinely for disturbed children—mood stabilizers and atypical antipsychotics—make it very difficult for these children to attend to life or school lessons. None of these medications has been officially tested in children—it is illegal—but as we know they are widely used. And we have no way of knowing what the long-term effects will be. Researchers are beginning to express concern, for instance, about connections between long-term use of SRRIs and a once rare form of dementia, called *frontotemporal dementia* (neuropsychologist Ed Hamlin, personal communication, January 24, 2012). It has taken 20 years for these effects to begin to manifest. Frontotemporal dementia is particularly devastating because it affects the greater amygdaloid area, one of the parts of the brain that is of special concern to us in developmental trauma. Patients with this form of dementia lose the capacity to inhibit expression of their temporal lobe impulses and may become behaviorally, unwillingly antisocial. They are no longer able to subscribe to the complex rules that have governed their social behavior. This is the person who will disrobe in the grocery store or begin to shoplift or swear nonstop.

There are immediate effects as well. Andrea Meckley, a neurofeedback clinician, talked about the medication course reported by the parents of most of the children who come to her practice (personal communication, February 18, 2012). Most children are first prescribed stimulants since most are, to some degree or another, hyperactive. If stimulants don't work or don't work well enough, these children are then most frequently prescribed one or more of the SSRIs, because they are also anxious and depressed. SSRIs are known to decrease seizure thresholds, and in our population of kids and adults, we have seen why this can be a problem. If SSRIs don't work either alone or with stimulants, the next drug of choice is usually an atypical antipsychotic. These drugs can instigate seizure activity. As we saw in a case cited in Chapter 1, an overdose of risperidone can lead to a profound psychotic break. It seems possible that this episode of temporary insanity was some variant of seizure sustained by the drug. (One of the most significant effects of risperidone overdose is convulsions [Acri & Henretig, 1998].) When this regime fails, the child is then put on mood stabilizers, which are, when prescribed by a neurologist, called *anticonvulsants*. The routine use of anticonvulsants lends further weight to the argument I am presenting here: that at the level of the brain, mood lability is fundamentally a dysrhythmia of convulsive proportion.

Most of my patients arrive in my office on multiple medications. The ongoing positive outcomes that we see in neurofeedback aside for the moment, it seems to me that concerns about the psychotropic approach to the brain and to mental health warrant, at least, some well-considered reevaluation. It would be difficult to look at these issues were medications the only approach for the dysregulated brain. Figure 2.3 shows EEG readings of a 6-year-old before and after a medication trial indicating, in this child, significant dysregulation of the EEG.

Plasticity

It wasn't long ago that we were taught that the brain we are born with is essentially the one we die with, with few changes over the lifespan, particularly after the first 3 years of life. Research in the last 20 years has proven that this is not accurate, that in fact the brain is quite able to reshape itself. It is, in essence, plastic. Joseph (1996) describes this property of plasticity:

> Experience acts to organize neuronal interconnections and the establishment of not just synapses but vast neural networks subserving a variety of complex behaviors and perceptual activity. Indeed, the brain is exceedingly plastic and is capable of undergoing tremendous functional reorganization not just over the course of evolution, but within a few years, months, or even weeks of a single individual's lifetime. (p. 663)

Further, not only does the brain change its function based on its learning, but it also has the capacity to give birth to new neurons, a process called *neurogenesis*. This process was experimentally demonstrated in a study of London cab drivers (Maguire, Woollett, & Spiers, 2006). New cabbies are required to memorize the labyrinth that is the map of London, a course of study that usually takes a year or so. The hippocampus was scanned in a group of candidates before and after they completed their course. They all had larger hippocampi after the course than before it, either as a result of increased dendritic branching or the production of entirely new neurons, or perhaps both.

Schore (2003) writes about plasticity to provide hope for seemingly hopeless conditions such as developmental trauma: "Current brain research . . . indicates that the capacity for experience-dependent plastic

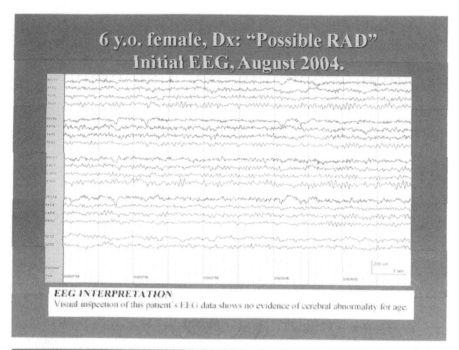

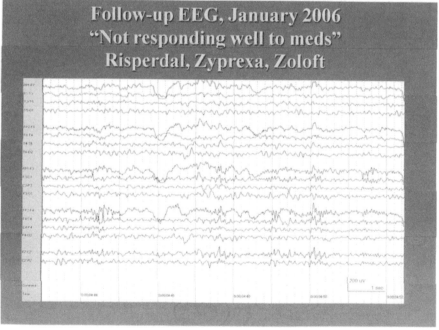

Figure 2.3.   EEG of a 6-year-old with a history of developmental trauma before and after medications. (Reprinted with permission of Jack Johnstone and QMetrix.)

changes in the nervous system remain throughout the life span. In fact, there is very specific evidence that the prefrontal limbic cortex, more than any other part of the cerebral cortex, retains the plastic capacities of early development" (p. 202). The question here is how do we optimize the brain's inherent potential for plasticity, particularly in those brains frozen by affective overload? The experiences of neurofeedback clinicians certainly supports the idea of brain plasticity and suggest, as does the work of Buzsáki (2006), that plasticity resides primarily in the ability of the brain to change its patterns of oscillation—its rhythms and self-organization. By providing new information to old, well-rehearsed rhythms stuck in repetition and reactivity, neurofeedback can encourage the brain's plasticity and maximize its latent capacities for self-organization.

It is important to note that I think of neurofeedback as brain wave training and not as therapy. It is a learning technology, and in my experience, it is much more effective when held within the embrace of a good therapy and a good therapist. But it is not therapy. I explore the fascinating interface between psychotherapy and neurofeedback extensively in Chapter 8, and in Chapter 9 take you through three case studies to illustrate how they work to enhance each other. That being said, were I called upon to work with child soldiers or orphans in an orphanage, or street kids in Baltimore, I would rely on neurofeedback as the major change agent, at least initially. Even more than a learning technology, I think neurofeedback is an interpersonal technology. It helps the brain activate its own intrinsic circuits of attachment, of dyadic self–other organization, by reducing the activation of fear, rage and shame, essentially by inhibiting the amygdala and its circuitry of fear. When you ease the grip of fear, a person emerges who, by his nature, wants to be in relationship. As we will see in subsequent chapters, quieting fear is what neurofeedback does. But first let's take a look at what it is and how it works.

Chapter 3

Neurofeedback

Changing Patterns in the Traumatized Brain

As I have mentioned along the way, when the history is one of neglect and abuse in childhood, the patient will be driven by powerful subcortical emotions, most predominantly fear, even when he may not look afraid or talk about fear. We have seen that implicit memory of trauma and neglect are held in the dysregulated amygdala and hippocampus of the RH, as well as in even "older" structures such as the hypothalamus, brainstem, and cerebellum, and that this memory is sustained as dysrhythmic, habitual patterns in electrical neural networks that hum with information and misinformation. With neurofeedback we attempt to intervene in the circuitry that promotes and sustains states of fear and traits of fearfulness, shame, and rage.

As we will see, neurofeedback experienced a rather dramatic birth in the field of epilepsy. It may turn out that most if not all people with active developmental trauma suffer temporal lobe seizures, either clinically or subclinically. The argument I am making is straightforward: Neurofeedback has a long track record of success with stabilizing the most destabilized brains (Wyrwicka & Sterman, 1968, ongoing to the present), those suffering intractable seizures. Judging from practitioner reports and from my own clinical experience, it has also proven successful in addressing the smaller but equally profound paroxysmal events in the brains of those with developmental trauma. A *paroxysm* is a sudden recurrence of a disease event or a fit or convulsion. These are unstable brains, destabilized by history, and neurofeedback seems to organize and quiet the paroxysmal dysrhythmias that arise in terror and that perpetuate terror. When this disruptive pattern starts to stabilize, we begin to see evidence not only of reduction in amygdala-driven emotions, the first of many nonlinear steps, but also more slowly but often quite dramatically, an emerging complexity in the person.

The case vignettes throughout the book describe this process. The brains of these patients learn to forgo habitual patterns, and the patients become less susceptible to a stress response and have many more choices in how they respond to a stressor when it occurs. Stress never lies with the events that we identify as stressful; it lies in our reaction to them. Neurofeedback raises the brain's threshold to stress and generally increases stress resilience as it increases stability. The former triggering stimuli no longer trigger. Several patients with developmental trauma have described an experience in which their brains begin to react to one of their triggers but that oddly, the reaction doesn't go anywhere. They are ready for the kindling buildup of yore and when it doesn't happen, they are surprised and also experience having many more choices in how they respond. They will, at first almost as an observer, be able to engage in new behaviors and new ways of thinking. As we will see, this is just the beginning of what's possible.

Appealing to the Traumatized Brain

The person who is suffering from developmental trauma lives in a system that has shut down in response to assault, abuse, and neglect and that is rigid with fear. Our job as psychotherapists is to help our patients move from repetition and rigidity toward discovery of innate self-regulating rhythmicity. As their brains learn to regulate themselves, they will move at all levels—physical, emotional, cognitive, and behavioral—toward complexity and stability. This is a demanding task for both patient and therapist when the amygdala is in charge, and difficult to achieve with talk therapy alone. It is actually not possible to "talk" to an amygdala that devotes itself to survival and has no sense of time—a subcortical structure deep in the nonverbal RH. As we have established, this is the epicenter of fear processing and production, and it is overwhelming and disassembling the very being of the person with developmental trauma. We have to reach it another way.

The Origins and Development of Neurofeedback

Neurofeedback had several nearly contemporaneous beginnings with different researchers interested in the brain, each approaching the study and meaning of its rhythms from quite a different perspective. There were many early investigators in the late 1950s and early 1960s, but three of the most influential may be Barry Sterman, Joe Kamiya, and Anna Wise.

Astronauts, Seizures, and Cats

It was research in medicine that first demonstrated that we could learn to control even the most violent storms in the brain. In the mid 1960s Barry Sterman, a sleep researcher at UCLA, agreed to conduct research that aimed to discover if people could learn to control induced seizures. This research was funded by NASA because astronauts on the earth-orbiting Mercury missions who were exposed to the fumes of rocket fuel were having seizures, symptoms of which included hallucinations. They reported seeing women from the South Sea Islands waving at them—a problem for the astronauts and for the space program.

Sterman began his exploration of this question with cats in his lab, some of which he had been using in his research on sleep. He had discovered the sensory–motor rhythm (SMR) in cats in his exploration of internal inhibition. He expected this brain wave activity to lead directly to sleep, but found instead that the cats were very relaxed (absence of muscle tension) and highly alert. Those of us who have spent time with cats will recognize this state of relaxed readiness as they await the movement of a potentially unfortunate mouse. They were peak-performing cats. This group learned to control penicillin-induced seizures more quickly and more robustly than the other feline subjects. Sterman was puzzled by this result until he realized that these were the same animals he had been training to produce a specific frequency, 12–15 Hz, in their EEGs. (He gave them a food reward when he saw this frequency.) These cats were clearly more seizure resistant. He called this frequency SMR because he was training across the sensory–motor strip (see Figure 3.1), the area of the brain between the parietal lobe—the sensory area—and the frontal lobe, the motor area. He went on to train the rest of the feline subjects, then monkeys, and then people with incurable seizure disorders, some of whom were on the wait list for psychosurgery at UCLA, all at 12–15 Hz at C3. (See Figure 2.1.) He was able to demonstrate an increase in seizure threshold in all subjects. None of the wait-list patients returned for surgery because they had learned to control their seizures entirely or sufficiently with the help of anticonvulsants, essentially by learning to make the same frequencies in their brains as their feline predecessors had learned to make in theirs. As their brains organized, they became socially more at ease and engaged and reported an enhanced capacity to learn.

This piece of history is important for a neurofeedback clinician to know, particularly one working with patients who have developmental trauma. As we have seen, there is a good deal of speculation about the likelihood, perhaps even the ubiquity, of temporal lobe seizure disorders

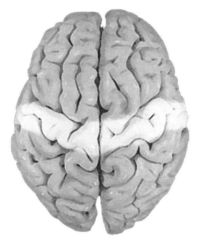

Figure 3.1.   The dorsal or top–down view of the sensory motor strip (lighter in this graphic). (Courtesy of Sam McClellan.)

in this population. This may be a signature brain problem associated with developmental trauma, and we have research evidence that people with epilepsy can learn to control seizures. The chronic emotional upheaval that characterizes these patients manifests the upheaval in their brains, and we know from this research on seizures that we can quiet it with neurofeedback.

This history is also important because, at least in this moment in time, all clinicians in this field will be told by someone at some point that they are producing nothing more than placebo effects due to relaxation in the chair, or to the razzmatazz of the equipment, or to the special attention they receive, etc. Of course, those who are working with patients with developmental trauma know that these conditions are hardly sufficient and could never, in and of themselves, predict positive outcomes. Sitting still rarely feels good, relaxing is unheard of, the equipment itself is, initially, either a negative or neutral factor for most traumatized people, and for those who felt "disappeared" as children, there is either never enough attention or threatening attention. And, to the point, there can be no placebo effect in cats.

Alpha Waves, Meditation, and Optimal Performance

Even before Sterman's groundbreaking work on seizures in the late 1960s, Joe Kamiya was exploring two questions about brain waves and states of mind at the University of Chicago. The first was whether humans could learn to make alpha waves, or 8–12 Hz, voluntarily, and secondly, whether these frequencies gave rise to the capacity for introspection. In 1958, during his fourth training session, Joe Bach, his graduate student, was able to produce alpha waves at will. Kamiya's feedback was decidedly low-tech: Depending on the frequencies his student produced, Kamiya said either "Correct" or "Wrong." At the time it was a basic science experiment. "We were just curious to see if people could control their brain rhythms. . . . We had no intention to help the ailments of mankind" (Robbins, 2000, p. 55). But, of course, he has in fact greatly helped the ails of humankind.

While Kamiya and Sterman were exploring the capacity for control of the EEG (in the field of neurofeedback "EEG" is used as a shorthand for *brain waves*), Anna Wise and her colleague Maxwell Cade (Wise, 1995) were interested in two other aspects of brain wave training: enhancing meditation and maximizing optimal performance. (Neurofeedback is used for these endeavors still.) Although those who live in chronic fear find it particularly difficult to meditate, people carrying the diagnosis of BPD and other adult manifestations of developmental trauma are now routinely instructed in mindfulness, one of the most important aspects of meditation. *Mindfulness* means calming the reactivity of the mind and acting from that state of mental quietude and attention. One of my patients with developmental trauma, an accomplished martial artist who had done sitting meditation for years, told me that she really learned to meditate only after neurofeedback and that it was for her like being on a fast track. She is much more able to practice both meditation and mindfulness on a daily basis, because the pulse of fear she's lived with since childhood is much less likely to arise, and if it does, to kindle and overtake her. A regulated brain gives rise to mindfulness; mindfulness in turn encourages a regulated brain.

I often teach meditation practices to my patients that focus on occupying "the present moment." I repeat the teaching I received from Thich Nhat Hanh, a Vietnamese Zen master, who said, "We fall back into the past and we leap ahead into the future and in that we lose our entire lives." Living in the present moment isn't easy for anyone, but it can be a particularly challenging concept and even more challenging practice for those whose amygdalas drag them into the past, sometimes at the slightest provocation, and who predict the future based on that past, not from the present they are actually living. And of course the present that they are in is overly determined by their pasts, not free of it. They are living out Faulkner's sad musing, "The past is never dead. It's not even past." The present moment is just right now, this second, nothing before, nothing after. The amygdala has no information to provide to the present moment; it has no imperative to activate. Skilled meditators can learn to use their practice to quiet fear eruptions, but again, as the Wise and Cade (1995) exploration suggests, it is easier to train the brain to do this and in doing so to gain an increasing capacity for mindfulness.

Fundamentally, the journey from dysregulated trauma survivor to well-regulated peak performer is the journey of brain regulation. Once you begin to use neurofeedback, you realize that this training is not just about quieting negative symptoms of trauma but about enhancing the potential of this person in all realms. When patients are released from the grip of fear, they naturally open to their full potential. The optimal performance brain is the same brain (physically, not functionally) as the traumatized brain, just regulated. Michael Tansey reported a 15-point gain in IQ in children training for learning disabilities (1991, p. 52), and Tanju Surmeli, a psychiatrist and researcher in Istanbul, has reported significant improvement in IQ (from 7 to 40 points) in children with mental retardation (personal communication January 5, 2013).

Even closer to home, Surmeli and Ertem (2009) report on positive effects using neurofeedback with antisocial personality disorder, another common sequela of developmental trauma—the one that Carl manifests. They reported the following results of a small but significant pilot study: "Twelve out of 13 antisocial personality subjects who received 80–120 sessions of NFB [neurofeedback] training showed significant improvement based on SA-45 questionnaires, MMPI, T.O.V.A. and qEEG . . . results and parent interviews" (p. 6). Their subjects (nine males and four females, ages 19–48) all answered "yes" to the following characterizations prior to neurofeedback training: aggression, failure to sustain consistent work or school obligations, insomnia, lack of remorse, loss of interest in life, lying, lack of insight, no interest in reading a book, and spending money excessively. After the training 12 of the 13 answered "no: to these same questions. In their conclusion, Surmeli and Ertem comment on a phenomenon we often observe in training: "After regulating brain activity in a short time, patients did not want to terminate, even though at first they did not want to take the treatment" (p. 6). These individuals were experiencing the intrinsic rewards of a better regulated brain and they stayed with it.

These practitioners were working with very different diagnosed disorders and report changes toward optimal performance. These results bring to mind the card of a colleague that reads, "Every brain deserves this chance." I agree completely, and no brain more so than the brain traumatized in childhood. In my own experience and that of my patients, neurofeedback enhances many of those aspects of treatment that are getting a lot of attention these days: affect regulation, trauma resolution, mindfulness, and the possibility of a life after trauma. We'll talk more about all of these effects, as well as about effects on the body and body memory, in Chapter 8. (You can read more about the fascinating history of neurofeedback in the Jim Robbins [2000] book, *A Symphony in the Brain.*)

What Is Brain Wave Training?

Neurofeedback is a computer–brain interface that uses sensors placed on specific areas of the scalp (corresponding to specific parts of the brain) to provide the brain with almost instantaneous feedback on frequencies in the EEG. It represents a new paradigm in brain science, and as is always true on the frontier, there are battles being waged over it. Unfortunately, the most common association people make between electricity and the brain is electric shock treatment, which induces the very activity in the brain that neurofeedback seeks to mitigate: a seizure. It is important to note here that in most systems, no electricity enters the brain in neurofeedback training. Instead, frequency information is picked up through sensors on the scalp and displayed on a computer screen as a scrolling EEG. Frequencies are selected to be rewarded or inhibited, based first on assessment and then on response and ongoing assessment, session to session. Neurofeedback is only information, but information to the part of us that can use it best, the brain. The power of neurofeedback suggests that we are talking in the brain's language. We will look at this process in more detail in Chapter 6.

As we explored in Chapter 2, therapists who use neurofeedback address dysrhythmias in the brain, and as we have seen, these dysrhythmias are profound in those who have been neglected and maliciously injured as children. Mental health, on the other hand, correlates highly with a well-regulated brain and may, in fact, be dependent on it. "One of the interesting findings . . . was that relatively good personality structure relates to a normal EEG" (Shelley et al., 2008, p. 11). Although this may indeed be more true than untrue, I have seen EEGs of many struggling people that looked pretty good. I am presently working with a man who was traumatized in adulthood and who is anxious and prone to temper outbursts and road rage. When he settles down to train his brain waves, at least on the metrics available to me using neurofeedback alone, he shows no apparent trace of these problems. I joke with him that he has the brain of a Buddha. Of course, beneath his reactivity this man does in fact have a "good personality structure." The point here is that a person can be symptomatic and still have a normal EEG, and we can still have a positive effect on her symptoms through training the EEG. The obverse can also be true. Not all abnormal EEGs show up as symptoms. That being said, I have yet to see a normal EEG in someone with developmental trauma.

How Neurofeedback Works

The matter of how neurofeedback works is a very big question that requires a Nobel prize-winning answer, which I don't have. Sterman (2000) discovered the complexity of neurofeedback in his earliest studies of seizure:

> The consensus arising from these findings is that most epileptic patients who show clinical improvement with EEG biofeedback also show contingent-related EEG changes and a shift towards EEG normalization. However, not all patients who respond to this treatment show expected EEG changes, and a few patients who show EEG changes experience little clinical improvement. (pp. 52–53)

David Kaiser (2013), a cognitive neuroscientist and neurofeedback researcher, reviewed the charts of over 100 children with ADHD who had had successful neurofeedback outcomes. Fifty percent of these children showed significant EEG changes, and 50% showed little change in their EEGs. In part in an attempt to conform to what we already know about learning, many neurofeedback researchers default to operant conditioning of the EEG as the explanation for how it works. (Operant conditioning is a type of learning in which a behavior is strengthened—meaning, it will occur more frequently—when it is followed by reinforcement/reward, and the behavior is weakened—it will happen less frequently—when followed by punishment.) As we will see, there are rewards (no punishments!), such as they are, for changing your EEG, but it is clear that we are quickly tapping into intrinsic rewards that sustain and propel the training process. We could see these intrinsic rewards as a proliferation of complexity and a move toward the self-regulation that is so prized by the brain. It feels good. These intrinsic reward systems in the brain may play by more complex rules.

Still, most would agree that there are elements of both classical and operant conditioning (classical conditioning is a process in which a previously neutral stimulus comes to evoke a specific response by being repeatedly paired with another stimulus that evokes the response), and most would also agree that these learning theories are inadequate to address the complex, pattern-making, nonlinear dynamical system that is the brain. We may in fact be using the EEG as a portal through which we leverage, perturbate, nudge more primary oscillatory processes represented by the EEG.

Although this kind of speculation is fascinating, it could well be wrong and, thankfully, it is not particularly clinically relevant. We don't know yet exactly how this process works, even though we observe that it does. But it is clinically relevant when you look at your rewarded frequency band (more on this in a moment) and notice that most often the changes in it are modest, even though you have spent 20 minutes rewarding it. And then you may observe that there is no clear correlation between the EEG change, in any given session, and the clinical outcome. You can have robust clinical changes without equally robust EEG changes. As a neurofeedback practitioner you will confront this confound on a daily basis, so I am taking note of it now. There is, as yet, no unified theory of how neurofeedback works. Even when this field matures, a unified theory of the brain may be as difficult to achieve as any unified field theory.

All neurofeedback requires a neurofeedback system or instrument, of which there are quite a few. Each of these systems incorporates the brain and the intellectual biases of its developer. This is inescapable and does caution the reader to use discernment in seeking training and purchasing equipment. At this stage, I recommend that therapists assess the regulation of the person who has designed a particular system and presumably, has used it, as well as his training in psychotherapy. Training the brain shifts the mind in subtle and not-so-subtle ways, and being familiar with matters of the mind is essential. Most of what I say here comes out of my experience with one of the most respected systems in

Figure 3.2.   A Miracle Occurs. (Copyright © Sidney Harris,
ScienceCartoonsPlus.com.)

the field: EEGer. The model that organizes my approach to training is called the arousal–regulation model, first proposed by Sue and Siegfried Othmer. No single model will ever address the brain's complexity, but this has been the most useful for me, particularly with developmental trauma.

Frequencies and Amplitudes

If you're anything like me, you have tried to avoid words like these and the particular rigors and arrogance of hard science. (This was much more true for me before my own neurofeedback training than it is now.) These terms and concepts are, however, key to the venture we are undertaking, even if we don't know exactly how. Fortunately, they don't end up being particularly daunting. Whenever we talk about circuitry, we are talking about frequency and amplitude. The frequencies at which the brain fires underwrite every feeling, thought, and deed, so frequency is important. *Frequency*, in our context, is the number of times a brain wave rises and falls in the period of 1 second. It is measured in Hertz (Hz), also called *cycles per second* (CPS). The brain operates in frequencies from 0 to 100 Hz and perhaps even higher. There are names attached to these frequencies, noted below, that are useful to know because they are so widely used, but in keeping records and talking to colleagues, you will always want to specify the actual numerical frequency range and not the name given to it. With that caveat, here are the names. (See Figure 3.3 for the wave formations of these frequencies.)

0–3 Hz	Delta
4–7 Hz	Theta
8–11 Hz	Alpha
12–15 Hz	SMR, also low beta
15–18 Hz	Beta
18–36 Hz	High beta
36–45 Hz	Gamma

These frequencies, as we will see, relate directly to arousal and to state.

Delta Frequency (0–3 Hz)

Delta brain waves are most often seen in sleep. It is a slow wave, rising and falling three or less times in a second. These wave forms happen when the brain is disengaged from external input and is in relationship primarily to itself. But delta is also seen in the waking brains of the vast majority of those who have experienced head injury and in most people

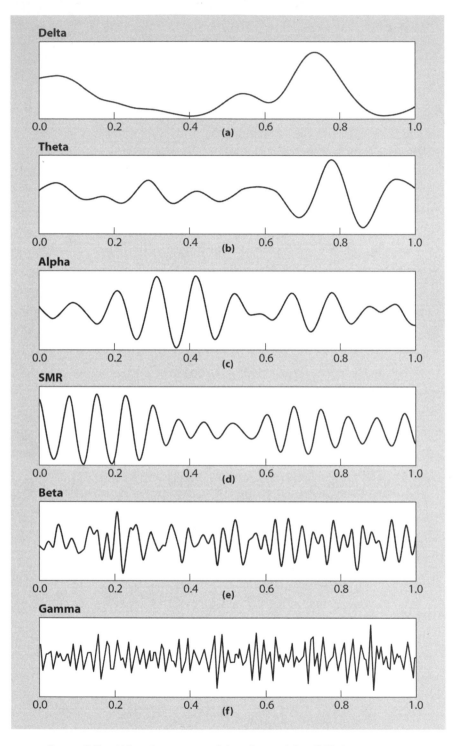

Figure 3.3.   Wave formations: delta, theta, alpha, SMR, beta, gamma.
(Kolb & Wishaw, 2001; reprinted with permission of Worth Publishers).

who have suffered early childhood abuse and neglect. There is a good deal of speculation about what this means in people with developmental trauma. Some speculate that it demonstrates the brain's tendency toward instability, because seizures tend to propagate subcortically in these slow rhythms. Others have suggested that it is a manifestation of a developmental or maturational lag; that these brains return to their earliest wave forms as a default position. The brains of babies cycle slowly, predominately in delta, until age 2 or so.

This frequency factoid becomes increasingly important, particularly when we discuss alpha-theta training in Chapters 7 and 8. Seeing delta frequencies in patients with developmental trauma suggests to me the likely presence of developmental brain injury. At the very least this frequency in a patient is an indicator that this brain at this sensor location is not appropriately interactive with the external environment and perhaps lost in its own repetitive internal brain dialogue. A system meant to be "open" to its environment is closed and necessarily self-referential. In most cases, we want our patients with developmental trauma to reduce the prominence of delta overtime, which is the purpose of inhibits. As we will see, we train the brain not only to produce more of certain frequencies (i.e., what we reward), we also ask it to make less of other frequencies, such as delta or theta (i.e., what we inhibit).

This need to reduce delta waves is particularly important when we are dealing with dissociative phenomenon. A young patient with DID decided to focus one session entirely on reducing her slow wave activity (in this case, 0–6 Hz). Her slow wave amplitude was high (we'll get to amplitude in a moment), often over 70 microvolts (µV). Ideally, the amplitude of these waves is less than 10 µV. I actively coached her in her efforts, and she brought her amplitude down to 12 µV. She said, "It is as if sparklers are going off in my brain. I don't think I have ever seen this room or you so clearly." And later she told me that her friends remarked on her clarity and her mental quickness. She diminished the influence of slow wave activity by, in this case, being rewarded to make less of it.

She arrived in a subsequent session in one of her male alters and said that she didn't want to do that slow wave down-training. As would always be the case, I agreed to her request and asked her why. Her answer stunned me. "I think it will make me [the alter] disappear." She was not being theoretical. Her concern suggests that she had a sense or had some-how known that her fragmented others resided in these slow waves. I don't know how she knew, but she was probably right. In Freud's hierar-chy, delta is the brain state that correlates to the unconscious.

Theta Frequency (4–7 Hz)

We pass through theta as we fall asleep, when we are drowsy and filled with hypnogogic images. Theta is considered a highly creative state, unlinked from the constraints of logic and daily demand. With practice its images are retrievable by the more conscious mind. It is reported that when Einstein felt stumped—when he had been wracking his brain without a breakthrough—he would take a nap, most likely to induce this theta state. He could then solve the problem that had per-plexed his fully awake mind. Theta is the state induced by most hypno-sis, and it also relates to some of the deepest states of meditation.

The patient with DID just mentioned had excess low theta at about 4 and 5 Hz as well as excess delta as part of the slow wave dysfunction. This profile is typical in developmental trauma, at least at the temporal lobes. Children are predominately in theta from ages 2 to 5, a time of magical thinking and normative hallucination, or perhaps daylight hyp-nogogic events. This can be seen in such common phenomena as imaginary friends. My 3-year-old daughter insisted that she saw an elephant in the woods . . . in Massachusetts. She was unshakable in her finding.

There is an approach to training called alpha–theta that rewards the brain to visit these deeper theta reaches while maintaining intermittent access to alpha, ideally allowing the trainee to remember what she expe-rienced and bring it into conscious awareness. Alpha–theta training is done in a reclining position with eyes closed. Body position affects brain wave production. We naturally make more slow waves as we recline, which is why most of us need to lie down to go to sleep. As we will see in Chapters 7 and 8, alpha–theta training can be very helpful in working with developmental trauma as well as with addiction, a sadly common comorbidity in adolescents and adults. Clinical experience has demon-strated that alpha–theta training facilitates access to traumatic memories otherwise unknown to the patient.

One of my patients, a woman who had been diagnosed with BPD and who was at perpetual risk of suicide, was a textbook example of the best alpha–theta outcome, and her results convinced me of its efficacy. She described being on the ceiling looking down at her father molesting her as a baby, confirming her worst suspicions. This alone would have impressed me some, but not all that much, as she had been speculating about this for a long time, without any prior source of validation. It could have been autosuggestion. I became convinced when she also reported seeing clearly that her father had not done other things that she feared he had. She became free of these haunts within 20 alpha–theta sessions, stabilized emotionally, and became newly compassionate and capable with her father. Not every case of alpha–theta training goes like this; in fact, there are always individual differences, but it is instructive nonetheless. (An important side note here. I can easily be criticized for making too much out of a single case, and it is a healthy caution. However, it must be remembered that a good deal of what we know about the brain comes from single-case studies of injured brains.)

The question that we explore more fully in Chapter 7 is whether early childhood trauma, and perhaps even later-occurring shocks, are encoded in theta and even delta frequencies and therefore not easily accessible to a brain–mind operating in higher frequencies most of the time. In Freud's system, theta might correlate to the subconscious. Theta frequencies are in overproduction at the very time in life when we are learning the social rules and may, in this light, also relate to the concept of superego, which is either overwhelming or absent in developmental trauma.

Alpha Frequency (8–11 Hz)

In normative terms, by the time a child reaches age 6, the dominant frequency in the brain is closest to alpha and by age 10 it will be around 10 Hz. Alpha is resplendent in the relaxation literature and associated with calm, perhaps even being "laid back" (note the postural reference). It may be difficult to put these two images together: that of a 6-year-old and that of relaxation—the very last thing that most 6-year-olds have in mind. Clearly the predominance of alpha frequencies (and for that matter, any frequency) can be experienced differently by different people, and there are very different environmental imperatives for children and adults. In children the frequency of alpha establishes what will become the dominant frequency for the adult. The dominant frequency is the background rhythm of the brain, or the sampling rate the brain uses in its interface with the outside world. It is also used to modulate activation. It is typically measured at PZ. In adults, a reading lower than 9 Hz or above 12 Hz usually signals problems. Ideally the adult dominant frequency is between 9 and 11 Hz.

Interestingly, alpha frequencies are not necessarily relaxing for adults either. For some, training to produce alpha can lead to heaviness and lethargy, and in others, to increased levels of reactivity and anxiety. The latter pattern is the most common in those with developmental trauma. Even alpha reinforcement (reward) can be too arousing for their overly aroused nervous systems. This is yet another conundrum for the field and a question yet to be answered about how the brain works. As mentioned above, alpha is also considered a bridging frequency between delta and theta, up into beta wakefulness. When people have trouble remembering their dreams, they are not spending enough time in alpha as they transition out of sleep. If you are awakened by an alarm, you are likely to bolt from delta right into beta, and dreams, theta-stuff, disappear. Increased alpha may correspond to lighter states in meditation.

Alpha and all higher frequencies would relate to Freud's conscious mind. We are awake in alpha but usually not all that active.

SMR (12–15 Hz)

The term *SMR* has been in use since Sterman's naming of it in the late 1960s. To the best of my knowledge, unlike the other categories, it is not presently used by neurologists. In the Greek classification, it is considered to be high alpha or low beta. The SMR state is characterized as calm and alert, like Sterman's cats. In neurofeedback, it can be used mistakenly to refer to any eyes-open training aimed at lowering arousal at C4. This is a case in point about why it is important to use the numerical frequencies. When the field was young, there were three placements: C3, C4, and CZ (you'll understand more about placement in the next section, "Applying the Sensors") and two frequencies to train, 12–15 (SMR) to lower arousal, usually on the right (C4), and 15–18 Hz (beta) to raise arousal, usually on the left (C3). I mentioned that alpha is not always calming and the same can be said of SMR, even more so, particularly with people who are dealing with trauma. It is rarely quieting for people who have endured this primary insult. In fact, this is a pretty safe beginning assumption until an individual's brain teaches you otherwise.

My chronically suicidal "borderline" patient reported feeling a sense of dread after training at 12–15 Hz. By then the neurofeedback system had evolved, and we had a full range of frequency filters—which meant that we could train at any frequency from 1 to 45 Hz. At 13–16 Hz the dread dissolved and she reported, "My whole brain is smiling." SMR was too low for her, but this is not a typical reaction. In cases of developmental trauma, 12–15 Hz is usually too high.

I met with a colleague, a trauma survivor in a country of trauma survivors. He was chain-smoking, speaking rapidly, jumpy and anxious. When I asked him if he was training himself, he said he that he'd given up, that it didn't work for him. He had done over 100 sessions at 12–15 Hz. The frequency was much too high for him and actually drove his nervous system into higher arousal and more dysfunction, rather than less of both. He had been a believer in SMR, and he'd made a classic mistake by pinning his training on theory rather than on observation of his own experience. When he trained at a much lower frequency, he was able to relax deeply. His assistants told me they had never seen him so at ease. This is just a cautionary tale. Although the RH normatively cycles at 12–15 Hz, or there about, it does not mean that it will necessarily benefit from training at that frequency. We find that out from an individual's response. We'll look into this issue more in Chapter 7 when we discuss protocols.

Beta Frequency (15–18 Hz)

Beta is the presumed cycling speed of the LH; it cycles faster than the RH primarily to support speech. Our brains are making primarily beta waves while we are reading, writing, or doing math. If you are not cycling in beta, you will have trouble with demanding cognitive tasks, and if you produce too much beta, it will be difficult to access the lower frequencies implicated in creative problem solving. In working with developmental trauma the problem generally is one of very high arousal. It is very easy to tip these nervous systems into overarousal with an outpouring of reactive shame, anger, and terror—the last thing you want to do. So when working with these patients it is the general rule to tread lightly on the LH and when LH training is indicated, a frequency band lower than 15–18 may feel better. In neurofeedback training what feels good is good. (Interestingly, the unnamed bandwidth of 18–22 Hz is elevated in almost everyone taking benzodiazepines [Tan, Uchida, Matsuura, Nishihara, & Kojima, 2003; van Lier, Drinkenburg, van Eeten, & Coenen, 2004]. It is called the *benzo bump*. This finding is a little counterintuitive, considering that these drugs are prescribed for anxiety.)

High Beta Frequency (22–36 Hz)

We have seen that as we raise frequencies, we raise arousal, all with mental state correlations. High beta has less of a mental signature. It is usually regarded as reflecting muscle tension and is almost always inhibited in standard neurofeedback setups. The goal for the trainee is to lower the amplitude of these wave forms both by relaxing their muscles and by watching the screen. A young Russian adoptee showed me her prowess during my visit to her residential center. She was able to reduce her amplitudes of fast wave, in the 30s, to 6 in the course of a few minutes without my being able to discern any effort on her part to relax her body. After the training she looked more relaxed and reported feeling so. She was on her way to becoming one of their success stories, and she was delighted with her ability to control frequencies in her brain.

This is not a trivial ability when you have lived believing that you had no control over anything—yourself or anyone else. All trauma survivors appear to carry memory in their bodies. One would surmise that we would commonly see excessive high beta in their EEGs, but we don't. This young girl showed high amplitudes of high beta, and not that much excess slow wave, at least by the time I met her. Frank Putnam reports that most of his patients with developmental trauma show excess high beta (personal communication, June 6, 2008). Although it makes sense that this should be true, I don't see it all that often. When I do, I will focus on it, as this girl did, and also teach breathing and relaxation exercises specifically aimed at relaxing the body.

I haven't yet been able to parse out profiles of patients with developmental trauma who show excess slow wave, except in the case of dissociation, from those who show excess high beta or fast wave. Perhaps this high beta–low slow wave profile suggests less vulnerability to seizure. These patients may complain of clenched jaws and fists. They may arch and hyperextend their backs and hold their shoulders high. Survivors of developmental trauma often have very high arches (a neurologist told me that high arches correlate with neurological instability), and posture is always an issue. It may just be how developmental trauma history has "taught" this patient to carry the reality of inescapable abuse and even more inescapable neglect. Most of my patients have little trouble with high beta, but every one of them has had excessive slow wave and some have high amplitudes of both.

Gamma Frequency (36–45 Hz)

When I began neurofeedback in 1996, there was little if any mention of the gamma band, but in the last few years interest in it has increased. It seems to be implicated in the full body nature of the "aha moment" that makes us almost shiver with delight. This may be a frequency implicit in the moment of deep insight, so important to the therapeutic process. It seems to be in this instance a frequency of mind–body communication. Its place in our work with the effects of developmental trauma is only now being explored, and we'll talk about a protocol that focuses on gamma in Chapter 7.

Frequency is one measure of a wave form and amplitude is the other. Every wave is measured by frequency (how fast) and by amplitude (how high) in microvolts (μV), as mentioned previously. When we are training, we are rewarding the brain to make more amplitude (bigger amounts) of a desired frequency and lowering the amplitude of other frequencies that are just causing trouble. The take-home message here is that we are using increases in amplitude to strengthen the frequencies that, in this population, lead to less fear and reactivity, and we are inhibiting those that contribute to it.

Rewards and Inhibits

We are working with two central parameters in neurofeedback training: rewards and inhibits. (It's no wonder that behaviorists take to this approach more readily than psychodynamic therapists.) Through a video game or movie that is synchronized with the patient's EEG, we reward the brain to produce a frequency band that stabilizes and quiets it. Until we try it, it is not always clear what that frequency band will be. I call this the *Goldilocks approach to neurofeedback*: "This frequency is too arousing [by symptom report]; this is too tiring; oh, this is just right." At the same time as we are rewarding the brain to make more amplitude of, let's say 10–13 Hz, we are also rewarding it to inhibit its bad firing habits, usually 0–6 Hz in patients with developmental trauma, because, as noted, they characteristically have excess slow wave. And we use the standard 22–36 Hz inhibit to ease them out of tense holding patterns in their bodies. We reward the brain to inhibit any excursions into paroxysmal activity—that is, any bursts of any frequency—because bursting EEG signals indicate a dysregulated EEG—and against the spike and wave formation that is seizure. All of this is accomplished by asking the brain to inhibit slow wave activity, where these troubling events occur. It is actually easier for most patients to exercise inhibition (i.e., to lower the amplitude) than to increase the reward, most probably because the brain devotes 80% of its energy to inhibition. It may be much less familiar to a brain, particularly one rigidified with fear, to make something new—that is, higher amplitudes of a wave form. Our results are tied much more to the reward band, and the results will reflect this brain's comfort or discomfort with the frequency that was rewarded. The affect regulation effects of brain wave training seem to derive primarily from the frequencies we reward. We'll look more closely at neurofeedback protocols specific to developmental trauma in Chapter 7, but for now, it will suffice to understand that reward frequencies, inhibit frequencies, and sensor placement on the scalp comprise a neurofeedback protocol.

Most neurofeedback systems have one computer and two monitors, one with scrolling EEG, primarily for the trainer to watch, and the other with a video game linked to the EEG for the trainee. The sensors placed on the head pick up the EEG signal, which is amplified 10,000 times so that it is large enough to display on the computer. In my system, the raw or unfiltered EEG is scrolling at the top. The reward frequency—usually but not always 3 Hz bandwidths (e.g., 10–13 Hz or 16–19 Hz)—is filtered out of the raw EEG and displayed separately. The inhibit frequencies are also displayed separately but usually with broader bandwidths. As we have seen, the inhibit bands that I use most commonly with trauma survivors are 0–6 Hz and 22–36 Hz. The challenge is set. The trainee is asked to sit quietly in the chair and focus on the feedback, usually provided by a video game that he is playing entirely by changing frequencies in the brain. The brain is asked to make more of the selected reward frequency and to make less of other frequencies that relate to dysfunction.

Some patients ask for instructions and are very focused on success, whereas others, particularly those who are struggling with dissociation, often don't ask at all. The instructions—essentially, "Relax and let your brain do the work"—are for the mind; the feedback is for the brain. I will ask patients not to try and very quickly they will see, when feedback stops, that trying is counterproductive. I will remind those training with me that we cannot "try to meditate," we just meditate. The same is true when training the brain. The patient's job is to bring her brain for training and to let the brain do the rest of the work of the session. When the patient is successful, she scores points in a video game, with parameters set up to correspond to the chosen frequency bands, and in most cases, the trainee will begin to feel some effect during the training.

In one game, as an example, the trainee engages in a space race. There are three rocket ships on the trainee's screen. The one on the left of the screen, often displayed in purple, signifies slow waves (inhibits); the one in the middle, usually blue, represents the frequencies we want them to make more of (reward); and the rocket on the right, often yellow, corresponds to high beta (another inhibit). When patients are meeting the frequency parameters that the practitioner has set, the center rocket will edge or race ahead of the others, and they will score points and, in this game, capture space gems. Although this is a decidedly different process than meditation, many people have described their states as similar to what they feel, or want to feel, after successful meditation. In this population if the training is accurate in relation to the needs of the person's nervous system, he might feel noticeably calmer and less reactive. It could also be said that it is the brain's job to bring the patient for training. I say this now only to suggest to the new practitioner what seems to be a neurofeedback law: If the protocol is right, the patient will want to come for training; if not, he won't.

The Setup

We have talked about the critical importance of attachment and attachment disruption to the development of the brain and its owner. Every aspect of neurofeedback, as I practice it, is intended to enhance attachment, from the fundamentals of quieting fear to the way the feedback system is arranged in the office. I set up the system so that I can see my screen and also be face to face with my patient. The practitioner needs to follow how the patient is responding, and the first glimpses of this response are often seen in facial expressions or in body reactions. It is also important that patients know that I am in this with them, and that they can see my face too. In this sense, the trainer is very much a part of the feedback loop. I never leave the room, and I check on how they are doing frequently, particularly when it is unclear to me. They see my eyes and my face and hear my encouraging voice intermittently throughout the session. My hope is to provide them with the regulating other at the same time as their brains are learning regulation from the feedback.

If face-to-face connection is dysregulating, then I keep my attention on my screen, taking only quick looks to make sure that all is well. Attention to these dynamics is important because you don't want your patient to feel abandoned to the impersonal and unfeeling other, the computer. Over time, if the computer is experienced as a friend of the nervous system, it too will become part of the therapeutic alliance. When the reward frequency is wrong and causes dysregulation, people may want to flee the training—and sometimes the therapist as well. We discuss the intricacies of negative training experiences more fully in Chapter 8. The point here is to align all aspects of your practice of neurofeedback with attachment in mind. This includes attention to how you touch your patient's head.

Applying the Sensors

Touch is a complicated issue in psychotherapy, and neurofeedback requires touch. The therapist must be mindful every time she applies the sensors to a patient's head. Touching the head is intimate, if not sacred. We have seen that touch is often negative for abandoned children. Even as adults they may not tolerate it well. Obviously, it is important to talk about this issue before you begin and to adjust your approach as needed by the individual. But touch cannot be finessed, and in actual practice, it is usually quickly tolerated and, in my experience, rarely misinterpreted. You may in fact have a unique opportunity, in pasting the sensors on and then taking them off and cleaning the paste off the head, to rehabilitate touch for some patients, to remind them or, or introduce them to, nurturing touch.

New practitioners are often instructed to strive for low impedance levels; that is, to get the best connection between sensor and skull that they can. Impedances below 20 kohms (1 kohm = 1,000 ohms) are considered important to the quality of the signal and presumably to the accuracy of the feedback. The higher the impedance, the lower the quality of the connection. When good impedance and mindful touch are in conflict, which they can be, I opt for the quality of the touch and, short of a clearly bad EEG display, trust the brain to sort out signal from "noise"—in this case, brain wave from artifact, introduced through a less than optimal connection between sensor and scalp. Training effects strongly suggest that the brain is able to do this.

New practitioners will have learned the 10–20 system, a way of measuring the head that is standard in neurology. There is also a 10–10 system, with sites closer together on the head. It is not unusual to look to the 10–10 when you are refining or using another's recommended protocol. In order to maintain connection with my patient, I measure now with my fingers or visual approximation. As a new practitioner, though, you'll need to practice accurate measurement with measuring tapes and reference to the head screen on your software. This is best done, as are all aspects of neurofeedback at the beginning, with friends or family who will forgive you your mistakes, before beginning with your patients. Over time, placement will become fairly automatic, and this facility allows you to be more mindful when you touch your patient's head.

The 10–20 and the 10–10 Systems

In the 10–20 and 10–10 systems, the letter denotes the area on the head where the sensor is placed and the number denotes which side of the head (which brain hemisphere). Even numbers are on the right. For example, "C4" refers to a central or sensory motor strip on the right side of the head. Odd numbers are on the left. For example, "P3" refers to a parietal placement on the left side of the head, and "FZ" means a frontal lobe placement on the midline (the letter Z always signifies the midline). "CZ," often called the *vertex*, is on the central strip (C) on the midline between the two hemispheres (Z) and at the place where the cingulate—front-to-back structure—and the corpus callosum—side-to-side structure—cross each other. "CZ" also relates directly to the thalamic cortical juncture, the central communication hub between the cortical and subcortical brain regions. Given the sensitive placement of "CZ," the vertex is likely to be a significant site to consider. "FP" means *frontal pole*, in effect, the forehead. F stands for the frontal lobe, C for the central or sensory–motor strip, T for the temporal lobe, P for the parietal lobe, and O for the occipital lobe.

The most common sensor placements involve three sites referred to as *active*, *referential*, and *ground*—although there can be many more. What is typically called a *monopolar* placement has one active electrode on the scalp, a second referential electrode on the ear on the same side of the head as the active electrode (called *ipsilateral* placement) and the third, "ground" electrode on the other ear. The ear is denoted by the letter A. "A1" is the left ear; "A2" the right. A bipolar placement consists of two active electrodes on the same hemisphere that are in reference to each other, also with a ground, such as T4–P4. In neurofeedback, the signal picked up by the active electrode is subtracted from the reference electrode. We are always subtracting the signal in one site from the signal in the second site. The signal that we see displayed on the screen represents the difference between the EEG activity measured at the two different sites on which the electrodes were placed. (In some instances, we may instead choose to look at the sum of the EEG activity at those sites, but this is less common, particularly in developmental trauma.) In a monopolar placement, the signal reflects the EEG activity at that site in comparison to some common reference site such as the ear. In a monopolar placement, the assumption is that we are subtracting nothing from the site we are training because, theoretically, no EEG should be measurable at the ear. In this population, however, people may show EEG readings at the ear that are actually reflecting activity coming from the temporal lobe.

Bipolar placements may have an advantage over monopolar ones—at least they should, theoretically—because the brain is all about communication, and training two sites in relationship to each other should promote communication between these sites and perhaps proximal ones as well.

Interhemispheric placement refers to a bipolar setup but with electrodes placed on both hemispheres, such as C5 and C6. As mentioned in Chapter 2, we have discovered useful placements off the 10–20 map, along the inion ridge at the back of the head and at FPO1 and FPO2 at the front (on the forehead at the juncture of the nose and the eye).

The subtraction in T4–P4, or any other bipolar or interhemispheric protocol, matters. The assumption here is that there is an optimal firing time, or *phase*, between two sites in the brain. Two sites that are distant from each other should fire at slightly different times. When two sites fire in optimal phase with each other, the brain is well organized. When two sites that should fire at different times, fire too close in time to each other, this is called *hypercoherence*—there is too much coherence. That is, there is not enough differentiation of function between sites so that they are, in effect, talking at the same time, and not well, to each other. Most of the people we see in our offices will have hypercoherence problems. The most severe example of hypercoherence is, of course, a seizure. Subtraction of one site from the other encourages a shift in phase relationship that signals the movement of the brain out of hypercoherence toward more normal, and even optimal, levels of communication. To get the reward, the brain is required to better differentiate functions at the different sites and to optimize timing differences between them. The more the trainee pushes these two sites out of phase, the less problematically hypercoherent, or hyperconnected, their brain will be—and the more functional.

When you are training two sites in reference to each other, you can also utilize what is called *two-channel training*. I just want to make a brief reference to it here because it is the way, when you are trained to do so, that you will implement coherence training. There are at least two channels to record EEG on every amplifier; more on some. To do two-channel training, you simply use a lead and sensor from Channel A and a lead and sensor from Channel B in the amplifier and tell the computer how they should relate to each other; that is, whether you want less or more coherence at given sites. You rarely want more coherence in this population, which, as we have discussed, can be seen as seizure prone. When we are more interested in arousal than in coherence specifically, we will typically use only one of the available channels. When you set up two channels, it allows the participants to see the signal at each site separately rather than as one signal subtracted (or added) to the other, as is the case with single channel bipolar or interhemispheric protocols. A lot can change in the brain with changes in coherence. The following story from my own experience will illustrate the point.

A Tale of Coherence

When I began training, hypercoherence was the default position of my brain. It was prone to seizure, to migraine, and, as is often the case in these instabilities, to hypoglycemia. I had one experience that involved training my brain in an area that was deemed hypocoherent, or too much out of phase (as opposed to too hypercoherent, or too much in phase) as seen on the quantitative EEG (qEEG) or EEG brain map. (We'll discuss the qEEG, or "Q" for short, more fully in Chapter 6 on assessment.) These two sites in my brain were firing at too great a lag time for optimal communication and may have resulted in slower than desired reading speed. Instead of rewarding the brain toward less coherence, we were training it to be more coherent just at these two sites. We were using a two-channel setup so that the trainer could discern changes in the EEGs, independently for both sites. When we began, the EEGs looked completely unlike each other, confirming the Q findings. But after about 10 minutes the EEGs seemed to be rising and falling in an almost identical pattern. We had moved from hypo- to hypercoherence in very short order. These sites quickly conformed to the trend of my brain toward hypercoherence. I felt fine for several hours and then had the single worst hypoglycemic attack of my life. I ate my way through my pantry to try to ease the life-threatening panic I felt. The local phenomenon of hypocoherence quickly flipped to hypercoherence and affected the brain (and me) much more globally.

There are several important points to be made here. (1) You can only know about coherence problems through the diagnostic information provided by the qEEG. (2) Hypocoherence can quickly change to hypercoherence, particularly, I assume, in brains prone to hyper connectivity. (3) We are always affecting coherence relationships, whether we are using one-channel bipolar or interhemispheric placements or two-channel placements. (4) Clinically, perhaps the most important take-home message is that neurofeedback can be powerful and sometimes can exacerbate preexisting tendencies in the brain. (5) When this happens, it can be scary. It helps both the practitioner and the patient to think of these events not as negative side effects but as data on the preferences of this particular brain, data that we will use to titrate training the next time.

Needless to say, I was not drawn to try that particular protocol again and would be even less inclined had this happened to one of my patients instead of to me. It is important to predict the possibility of negative effects in the process of informed consent (Chapter 5). Doing so will enhance the therapeutic alliance around training if the going gets tough and help the patient stay with the process, even as you change the training in response to a negative reaction. (6) But, all that being said, it is most important to remember that in neurofeedback, we are always working in the realm of plasticity. If the brain can throw itself into a hypoglycemic fit because of training, it can also learn, with different and better information (protocol), to correct this vulnerability and move itself toward stability. We'll cover all these points in more detail in Chapters 6 and 7.

The Arousal–Regulation Model

As I said before, no single neurofeedback model can accommodate the complexity of brain function, but to proceed with training, the trainer has to adopt one model, at least, one model at a time. All models of brain function are more useful than they are accurate or true. The two primary organizing models used in most neurofeedback approaches are *coherence* or co-modulation or synchrony (for our purposes, all pretty close to the same thing) and *arousal*. We took a brief look at coherence and its potential for good and bad, and now we turn to arousal as the dominant paradigm. It is the model I use most frequently and the one that seems the most economical, at least so far, in my practice. In Chapter 7 we discuss another emerging model, often called ILF, short for *infra-low frequency* training, which may be effective with yet other trainable mechanisms in the brain and that may be of particular help in developmental trauma, as well as approaches that do not rely on leveraging arousal but which also seem quite helpful in trauma resolution. But for now, we have enough on our plate with the arousal–regulation model.

Put simply, this model suggests that there is a vital connection, if not absolute correlation, between arousal and regulation. This is, of course, the correlation we have been exploring in developmental trauma, where high arousal of the nervous system leads inevitably to dysregulation or where fundamental dysregulation has led to high levels of arousal. Further, the arousal–regulation model attempts to explain how a brain functions optimally without specific regard to diagnosis. Optimal functioning can be defined as the brain's ability to shift flexibly between states of arousal, depending on the tasks before it. In broad strokes, we want a brain that wakes up alert and ready for the day, a brain that is influenced but not overtaken by external or internal events, and a brain that turns itself down when it is time for sleep. In people with developmental trauma even this basic level of self-regulation is unavailable because the brain has been driven into states of high arousal and repeating patterns related to survival. People with this level of trauma develop much less state flexibility. They are hypervigilant, hyperfocused, and quick to erupt into states driven by limbic emotions.

As we saw in Chapter 2, all arousal is driven by the frequencies at which the brain fires. Our goal with patients who have developmental trauma is always to find the frequencies that help them feel calmer, less afraid, and less reactive. As we consider this model, it is important to remember that the brain's two hemispheres normatively cycle at different speeds. In the arousal model, we expect to lower arousal through training on the RH (affect regulation), raise arousal by training on the LH (verbal), and stabilize arousal by training the RH and the LH together.

Diagnosis

We can be guided somewhat in neurofeedback by DSM diagnosis. Most diagnoses make an implicit and sometimes explicit assumption about arousal. Developmental trauma and the conditions that it gives rise to—BPD, DID, APD—call for lowering arousal as the primary path to regulation. A history of developmental trauma predicts overarousal, usually quite severe and uncontrollable. Most people, however, who find their way to neurofeedback do so because they have tried almost everything else available and have along the way picked up multiple diagnoses. Many "blind" scientists have already diagnosed this patient. Our patients come in with a diagnosis of ADHD or ADD, given by someone trying to describe their impulsivity or their difficulty paying attention. They may have been given the increasingly popular diagnosis of bipolar disorder to account for their mood lability, or even trendier (until it was removed from the DSM-5; American Psychiatric Association, 2013), Asperger syndrome to explain their alexithymia. (*Alexithymia* means an inability to describe or articulate feelings, and for some it means trouble recognizing that they even have feelings.) And, it seems that most people in clinical settings describe themselves as depressed.

Diagnosis, when it is accurate, tells us the likely tilt of an individual's nervous system, but beyond that it's not much of a guide. A person who comes in with an Axis I diagnosis (e.g., PTSD, major depressive disorder, pervasive developmental disorder [PDD], autism spectrum disorder), an Axis II diagnosis (any personality disorder), or with developmental trauma will be overaroused. That, at least, is the working hypothesis because it is true for 99% of people with these labels affixed to them. As we will see, we have to inquire deeply, beyond these labels, to find the set point of the nervous system that gives rise to them. This is the art of assessment that I explore in Chapter 6. We are not training in relation to the diagnosis but in relation to the *individual* with the diagnosis. We are, in a sense, freed from the capriciousness of diagnostic categories while needing to become even more cognizant of the interplay of symptoms. We rely heavily on clinical history, assessment, and observation to arrive at the first training protocol, but thereafter we rely almost exclusively on patient report, supplemented by the reports of others— parents, spouse, partner, teachers, and friends—and on our own interactions with the patient.

There is a fundamental conundrum in neurofeedback. We are asking the person most affected by his dysregulated brain to notice and articulate any changes that he feels. Sometimes this is readily done—people feel or observe changes even after the first session. We will talk more about the predictive value of first-session effects and effects observed during training in Chapter 6. If the effects are less clear-cut, or if the person is by the very nature of his brain rendered a poor reporter of internal shifts, then we can only judge by the reports of others and/or our own clinical judgment. (The body keeps the score for the most part in the RH. In adults, poor ability to report suggests impaired interoception, the flow of information from the body to the brain–mind, and in and of itself suggests a RH focus. But more about this later.) The better you know your patient, obviously, the better able you are to see what may be subtle shifts in arousal that will indicate whether to stay the course or to change it. As you become more accustomed to neurofeedback, you will find that your clinical intuition will help to inform your training approach.

As I hope is now clear, there is no protocol for developmental trauma, only a protocol for someone who suffers from developmental trauma, and the two of you will find it together. In Chapter 8, I explore how training affects the relationship between patient and therapist as well as the impact of training outcomes on the transference. Transference too sits atop these same frequencies.

Arousal

In this model, a patient's arousal is categorized as *overarousal, underarousal, instability of arousal*, and/or a combination of under- and overarousal. Although developmental trauma almost always falls in the overarousal category, people with these histories can also have symptoms of underarousal and instability of arousal. In Chapter 6, I take the reader through my approach to assessment, which is also, in effect, my approach to "learning to think neurofeedback."

Examples of overarousal include agitated depression, nightmares, restless sleep, hyper-startle response, and constipation. Examples of underarousal could include sugar craving, nonrestorative sleep, lethargy, and certain types of depression. Instability of arousal could include bipolar disorder, migraine, and panic attacks. (Interestingly, the well-known neurologist Oliver Sacks categorizes migraine as a disorder closely allied with many other disorders, including epilepsy, narcolepsy, "angst attacks," fainting, vagal attacks, acute affective cycles, bipolar cycles, catatonia, catalepsy, Klein–Levin attacks, protracted vegetative reactions, and even spasmodic asthma, croup, and angina [1985, p. 195].) If any of these disorders show up in assessment, the neurofeedback practitioner would primarily think about instability of arousal as the common thread. Practitioners would also look for indicators of high arousal that could be the common driver. Mixed arousal, the most common pattern, would include significant symptoms of both under- and overarousal. In developmental trauma, I train to lower arousal and see if that takes care of other problems attendant to the disorder, such as difficulty paying attention or sensory overload. It often does.

As we have seen, frequency drives arousal. In this model, as a rule, we continue to drop the reward frequencies until the patient begins to show signs of a quieting nervous system. Some patients with developmental trauma will train at very low frequencies before they experience any relief. We are looking for the best frequency to leverage the nervous system, and at times this can be as low as 0–3 Hz—delta?! I can almost hear the protest.

As we talked about, seizures tend to propagate in low frequencies, and these are event-prone brains. Most of these patients are already making too much slow wave activity. Training this low—training the brain to produce delta—would be dangerous, theoretically. This is where I find the idea of *leverage* useful. I doubt that the brain is actually making delta when we need to use rewards this low. Instead, I think that we are constraining this nervous system where it needs constraint. For some brains, this is just what it takes to "wake them up" to the reality around them.

We are also employing inhibits, usually 0–6 Hz in this population, to guard against any paroxysmal bursts. The inhibits will stop all rewards if the brain tries to take off in this direction. This approach can lead to an overlapping of inhibits and rewards, which is, at least initially, confusing. In this example we would have a 0–3 Hz reward and a 0–6 Hz inhibit. One of the most common questions I get from new practitioners is how that can work. How can you train to reward and inhibit the same frequencies at the same time? My first answer is that this is the brain; it knows how to use information, to extract signal from noise, and meaning from meaninglessness. It is also the case that we are all making slow brain waves all of the time, including 0–3 Hz. It is dysregulated slow wave that creates the problem, not well-organized, background slow wave.

As we have seen, one of the unanswered questions in neurofeedback is how we see these changes in regulation and arousal that are very specific to the reward frequency but often see very little change in the reward amplitude. We just don't know. We got to this approach pragmatically. Higher-frequency reward just wouldn't calm some of these patients, particularly highly aroused, traumatized children, so we just kept dropping frequencies until we saw the nervous system respond. Theory would not have gotten us here. In neurofeedback, once we see that something works, particularly something that theory suggests wouldn't, we have to make meaning of it—that is, develop a theory that makes this outcome plausible. I will be forgiven, then, if this is what I am doing here. It comes down to pragmatics. Training this low often works very well, and when it is right for this brain, there is no harm in doing so.

Tracking Arousal

Most emotional symptoms are subjective. It is exactly this subjective experience that we influence in neurofeedback training, but it is often the hardest for the patient to track. Fear, the ubiquitous symptom, may be exacerbated by a change in how that fear is experienced. Initially at least, many of these patients will be afraid of losing fear, so they may not report fear reduction. (We'll discuss the implications of this paradox in the next chapter.) Of course, reduction of fear is the exact outcome we are looking for, and we need accurate feedback from the patient to know if we are accomplishing this goal.

Those patients who also suffer alexithymia will be hard-pressed to articulate the often-subtle shifts in feeling states. In these cases, particularly, the neurofeedback clinician will track the most objective indicators, which are often found in the body. We look for clues in the patient's physiology: disrupted sleep patterns, nightmares, and constipation are examples of objective markers of overarousal. Constipation is very common in overaroused people. Remember the parasympathetic axiom, "rest and digest." The bowel of a person in predominately sympathetic arousal is constricted to allow for the fight or the flight without leaving a trail. The vagus nerve communicates between bowel and brain. Regulation of the bowel will predict regulation in the brain, and vice versa.

Arousal in Young Children

Babies and young children, before the age when they can be diagnosed, can struggle mightily with high arousal. In most of these children, their arousal is directly linked to their parents' arousal, particularly their mother's, and when this is the case, we will want to train the parents, even though the child may be the identified patient. (According to a social worker from the Department of Children and Families in Massachusetts, babies as young as 1 year old are being prescribed antipsychotic medications to sedate them, primarily so that their frustrated and dysregulated parents won't abuse them! How can this be justified when neurofeedback exists?) But in those instances when it is the child's arousal and not the parents', as is seen in many adoptions, loss of a parent to illness or death, birth trauma, medical trauma, accident, natural disaster, or from unknown causes, then we will want to train the child. It is, I think, vital to do so. The overaroused baby will find it very challenging, if not impossible, to absorb the mother's regulation, no matter how good it is. As a result, the baby will find it difficult to make a secure attachment and if left to this course, will develop without really knowing that she has a mother.

A local practitioner told me about an 18-month-old girl who cried a lot, who could not be comforted, and who did not seek out her parents. Her mother was beside herself with shame, anger, discouragement, and guilt. She was in her own therapy to manage all that this child brought up for her. It was clear to everybody else that she was a good, though rejected, mother. The practitioner trained the baby. After the sixth session, this little girl spontaneously crawled into her mother's lap and snuggled into her.

I trained a baby at 5 months who had been born with the cord around his neck and had suffered anoxia, or oxygen deprivation—very bad for the brain. For 5 months he had not slept more than 1 hour at a stretch, he screamed every time his mother gave him to someone else to hold, and he had a pronounced tremor. This baby was not letting his mother out of his sight after his near-death birth experience. His mother was exhausted and worried and scared. She knew about neurofeedback from her own experience, so she brought him to me. These were the days when we had only 12–15 Hz to calm the nervous system, so I rewarded this baby to produce 12–15 Hz. After seven sessions, he was sleeping for 5-hour stretches, waking to nurse, and then falling back to sleep. The tremor disappeared, and he could be held by others without displaying terror and protest.

These neurofeedback interventions could well have been lifesaving. There is no question that they promoted attachment and greatly improved the quality of these lives. As a side note, it is interesting that babies who produce primarily slow brain waves can be calmed by rewarding frequencies much higher than any they have made yet in any abundance.

I work almost exclusively with adolescents and adults, not with babies, but the same arousal and attachment dynamics seem to be at play. We are quieting arousal by training the RH to inhibit subcortical excesses, and when we do so, the brain recognizes its bias toward attachment. One of my patients, a very bright, extremely overaroused young executive, noticed the changes in herself but even more in her 20-

month-old daughter. She had always turned away from her mother and toward her father. When this mother quieted her nervous system, she reported that her daughter started coming to her spontaneously. Her parenting behaviors had become less rigid, but it was more than this. She was becoming approachable and inviting and more rhythmically attuned to her child. It was natural and easy for them to be together.

I am frequently asked how many sessions this approach will take, and I can't answer the question. There are many variables, but no matter what, it is rarely a quick process. It can take a long time to develop an RH. But there will be changes for most people from early on, enough to keep us and them invested in training.

In his editorial on neurofeedback, Frank Duffy, the Director of Clinical Neurophysiology Laboratory and Developmental Neurophysiology Laboratory at Children's Hospital in Boston, came to this conclusion: "The literature, which lacks any negative study of substance, suggests that EBT [neurofeedback] should play a major therapeutic role in many different areas. In my opinion, if any medication had demonstrated such a wide spectrum of efficacy it would be universally accepted and widely used" (2000, pp. v–vi). Of course, I couldn't agree more. Our specific focus is to reduce ambient or acute fear and to enhance self-regulation. This possibility has profound implications for a person who has lived in fear her entire life. In Chapter 4 we consider some of the most important implications.

Chapter 4

Trauma Identity

Arousal, State, and Trait

*"I have never been more myself and never known
less who I am."*
—Young adult patient with developmental
trauma, after several months of intensive
neurofeedback training

We have had glimpses of the havoc developmental trauma creates in
the brain, and as a result, in the mind of those who suffer it. I have asked
you to entertain the relatively new paradigm of a brain that organizes
itself rhythmically and the neurofeedback process that allows us access
to these rhythms. We have considered the plasticity of the brain that is
inherent in these rhythms. I am proposing that we are harnessing the
brain's plasticity and its complexity by this direct appeal. To borrow van
der Kolk's (2007) wonderful phrase, we are "befriending the nervous
system" where it lives in the CNS and the ANS, in the brain.

Neurofeedback is the working interface between brain and mind.
When this simple fact captures the wider scientific imagination, as it
will, there will be many books written about what arises in the mind
when you provide feedback to the brain. I address how this process

unfolds in most people with developmental trauma whom I have trained. It is a complex picture wrought with every possible individual variation. We are going to talk about identity as it is tied to arousal, affect, state and trait; how all of these formulations of self ride on arousal; and what happens when you begin to dislodge the cornerstone of fear.

Clearly, identity is a multifaceted construction that depends on many important, interlocking variables; family, peers, genetics, epigenetics, class, culture, race, religion, intelligence, and luck are just some of the contributors that are not addressed in this chapter. It is the thesis here that the cascade from abuse and neglect to brain dysregulation is central not only to developmental trauma in childhood but to many variously named disorders in adults. As we have seen, when you grow up in an abusive, neglectful, unpredictable, scary environment, there are often few remembered discrete events, and there is no coherent self to stand back and observe or report. As Schore (1994, 2003) has taught us, a sense of self requires affect regulation. In developmental trauma, identity is inseparable from affect. In terms of identity, these individuals suffer their own Cartesian error—in essence: "I am what I feel." This is what I have come to call *trauma identity*.

Profile of Trauma Identity

Fear is the death before death. Patients with developmental trauma survive, but they don't live. They cannot trust their minds or even their sensations. Just stop for a moment and imagine that right now, you cannot trust what you are perceiving: You don't quite know if you recognize this room, or the meaning you should take from the voices across the street. It isn't a conceptual error but a perceptual warp. Most people with developmental trauma know what is real; they just don't know what is safe.

One woman described driving during one of her episodes of depersonalization: "It is suddenly as if there is no one driving. It feels like the car is moving on ice in four dimensions. I know somehow that I will be able to get it from Point A to Point B, but it is a kind of faith." It is not unusual for these patients to describe themselves as untethered from a shared reality, and they often are. This woman also talked about watch-

ing a dog romping in the yard across from her window and the challenging search to place the event in time or space. She described trying to
find herself and this dog in a present time that seemed safe enough for
such innocent abandon. It was unknown to her. The problem, often
called *derealization*, felt to her like a desperate struggle to update and
ground herself in a simple, present, nonthreatening reality. Her amygdala, however, kept reasserting itself, insisting on the absolute necessity
of fear. She could not inhabit this sweet moment. As she trained and
quieted the subcortical eruptions, she described the time when a "yellow
sickly charge in the air disappeared" (tornado skies?) and the dog came
into the present with her. Both were safe. She experienced herself in
present time and present space.

Among its many enduring effects, neglect in childhood can lead to
severely compromised proprioceptive feedback—feedback that is essential to knowing where we are in space, where our bodies end. Ed Hamlin
explains:

> Proprioception is an extremely complex brain operation that requires
> much organization and automization to work properly. . . . Chewing gum
> and walking really is a significant feat as we manipulate what we are
> chewing without biting our cheek or tongue and also navigate what could
> be varying terrain. Visual proprioception, . . . which keeps us oriented
> toward danger or opportunity, is in the right temporoparietal area in con-
> junction with the cerebellum. This is an area clearly impacted by early
> trauma. (personal communication, April 27, 2012)

There can be no feeling of being grounded, literally or metaphorically
without a well functioning proprioceptive system. These patients are not
getting clear or dependable feedback from their bodies. Body workers
who work with patients who have trauma histories often focus attention
on ankles, which are usually weak and prone to injury. Every turn or
sprain kills proprioceptive cells in the tissue, making it even more challenging for these patients to feel grounded, connected to the earth. Problems in proprioception are linked most closely to neglect, to the absence
of the mother's body (Elizabeth Warner, Senior Supervisor at the Trauma
Center, personal communication, May 30, 2012). It is not uncommon

for patients with developmental trauma to look at others to see what they are wearing in an effort to confirm their sense that it is cold or even that they are cold, or to see what others are feeling to feel something themselves. The information from the body has never been reliable and emotions have been invalidated. It is no wonder that these patients can experience themselves as psychotic.

These profoundly uncontained fear-driven nervous systems can all too easily speed off the rails. Arlene Nock, a psychiatrist in Troy, New York, introduced me to the concept of *traumatic psychosis* to describe these states and to differentiate them from true psychosis, such as occurs in schizophrenia. I think this is an important distinction, particularly for those whose baseline fear makes them feel unhinged. The felt experience is one of fragmentation terror, and no matter what the diagnosis— trauma psychosis or psychosis—there is always heightened, dysregulated arousal.

Trauma identity is usually accompanied by a posture of immobility. Typically, children and adults with developmental trauma will have slightly arched backs; they will hold their shoulders high and rolled forward to protect vital organs; they will walk as if retracted from the lower half of their bodies; and they will stand with locked knees. This posture sends a report to the brain that all is not well. This is a body immobilized even as it moves. I am beginning to alert my patients to this phenomenon by demonstrating to them how easy it is for me to push them off balance when their knees are locked and how nearly impossible it is to do when they bend their knees just slightly. The first is the freeze stance, the posture of immobility and hopelessness. The second is a fight or flight stance, a posture of mobility. This postural shift can be difficult to learn after years of sustaining a habitual freeze mode. It is counterintuitive to body memory and the imperative for survival. Changing this aspect of the feedback loop has to become a mindfulness practice, attended to by both the patient and the therapist.

The brain and the body are not separable. The regulated brain begins to regulate the body and seems to quiet vagally mediated distress. One woman in her mid-60s, steeped in an early history of neglect and possible sexual trauma, reported that for the first time in her life she was not constipated. Her body temperature was newly regulated and she was able to sleep. Fluctuations in body temperature are common in developmental trauma and the fact that these fluctuations are normalized by brain wave training suggests again that we may be reaching primary regulators of arousal in the brainstem and the hypothalamus.

Before we discuss the changes that an individual can feel while training her brain, it is important to consider a moral hazard objection to the neurofeedback thesis. If our thesis is correct, or even mostly correct, then the brain is the problem. Every violent act erupts first in the dysregulated brain. People with these devastating childhood histories may not be responsible for their acts. But of course, they have to be. There is no one else to hold responsible. But the thesis leads us directly to the thorny and increasingly scientific question of free will, another topic to be pondered, but beyond the scope of this book.

Neuronal Origins of Trauma Identity

Fear sets the tone of trauma identity in the body and in the mind. I explore a way to think about what happens to the self that is engulfed in fear when the brain learns to interrupt incessant, reactive fear circuits. Neurofeedback offers us a new template for understanding how identity can form and re-form in the seemingly impersonal realm of brain wave frequencies.

The Role of Glial Cells

Before I begin my exploration of the neuronal origins of trauma identity, I need to discuss non-neuronal brain cells that undoubtedly contribute to this picture. It seems increasingly clear that the metabolic rhythms of glial cells give rise to the electrical rhythmic properties of neurons. Although my proposed progression from neurons to identity doesn't include glia, also called *white matter*, it is implied (neurons are gray matter). As we saw in Chapter 2, the default mode or resting state network cycles at 0.1, or once every 10 seconds. This is a vital brain property that gives rise to the quintessential human capacity of self-reflection and makes its contribution to a sense of self. The resting state network is severely disrupted in developmental trauma. Recall the research from Lanius's lab (Bluhm et al., 2009) fMRI study of adults with developmental trauma, which showed very little blood flow in those parts of the brain that give rise to self-awareness, autobiography, a sense of the body, and a sense of self in the body. (See Figure C.4.) Neurons fire at frequencies that range from 1 to 100 Hz (alternating current or AC). Glia cells fluctuate far more slowly, below 1 Hz (so called direct current or DC).

The word *glia* means glue. It had been decided long ago that the main function of glia was to provide myelination and fat storage (brain food) for neurons. But there seems to be more going on at this level of organization than was known. In short, glia also appear to respond to feedback. We discuss the possibilities of training cerebellar activation in Chapter 7, but for now suffice it to say that the cerebellum is chock full of glia. It is particularly salient for the neurofeedback practitioner to reflect on glia now because there are approaches to training the brain that seem to appeal to these very slow rhythms, called *slow cortical potentials* (SCP) or infra-slow frequencies (ISF), and that show good clinical effects. Even more intriguing is the theory, again built on felt experiences of many people, that it is this DC realm—this very slow metabolic rise and fall—that gives rise to the field of being. What we know is that these slow foundational rhythms have meaning to the brain, that they give rise to neuronal activation, and that they too can be trained. For this memoir of state, trait, and identity, it's best to keep the role of glia in mind even as we focus our attention on neurons.

Here I attempt to sketch an entirely nonlinear process in a hopelessly linear way. I connect arousal at the level of neuronal activation to affect, affect to state, the persistence of state-to-state dependence, the repetition of state to more enduring traits, and the contribution of traits to what we think of as personality. Each component in this evolving, nonlinear process contributes to our sense of who we are: to our identity (see Figure 4.1). As if this weren't challenging or intriguing enough, I then try to illustrate what happens when we equip the brain to do some reverse engineering.

Arousal

With the caveat about glia, we can say that who we are, or more accurately, who we think we are, begins with neuronal firing. Individual neurons have no say. It takes tens of thousands of neurons firing together

Figure 4.1.   After a 4-month period of neurofeedback training, this
10-year-old boy's drawings of his family reflect his increasing neurological
development and his developing sense of self.

to register as a brain wave. The speed and rhythm at which these neurons fire determine arousal levels. I use *arousal* to describe the level of activation or the neurological set point of the CNS as a whole. In developmental trauma fear structures and networks are in overdrive, firing too often, too much, too fast, too repetitively, and too influentially. High arousal correlates with an overactivation of the amygdala and other brain structures involved in fear and the underactivation of those structures meant to inhibit them. This brain finds itself, as we have seen, in a state of disequilibrium characterized by heightened reactivity to stimuli, even apparently benign ones. These inflexible and unstable nervous systems are routinely overtaken by subcortical neuronal storms that give rise to affect dysregulation. When arousal becomes emotion, it becomes a quality of the mind and it is felt: Arousal becomes affect.

Affect

Fear, anger, and shame—the emotions of most concern to us like all emotions and the states they give rise to, have frequencies underpinning them. High levels of subcortical arousal translate to dysregulated and even wild emotional states. The people trying to live in these nervous systems will be volatile, agitated, unreasonable, angry, shame-filled, shaming, and afraid, some even paranoid. They have no mechanisms in their brains to soften the scream of the amygdala. In his book, *Waking the Tiger*, Peter Levine (1997) quotes one of his traumatized patients:

> I don't know of one thing that I don't fear. . . . I fear anger . . . my own and everyone else's, even when anger is not present. I fear rejection and/or abandonment. I fear success and failure. I get pain in my chest, and tingling and numbness in my arms and legs every day. . . . I have headaches. I feel nervous all the time. I have shortness of breath, racing heart, disorientation, and panic. I am always cold, and I have dry mouth. I have trouble swallowing. I feel overwhelmed, confused, lost, helpless and hopeless daily. I have uncontrollable outbursts of rage and depression. (pp. 47–48)

This is the narrative of affect in trauma, and it becomes the narrative of state.

State

Levine's patient speaks for most people with developmental trauma. They are afraid most if not all of the time and usually ashamed and angry as well. The amygdala-driven affects determine their states and their experience of themselves and of the world. *State* can be understood metaphorically as weather, ever-changing, and *trait*, which we will discuss soon, can be seen as climate, prevailing, fixed. Patients with developmental trauma endure recurrent storms in the repetitious assaults of fear. State subsumes the discrete experience of emotion. Acute fear folds into the background ambient state of fear. Emotions are not experienced as arising and falling away, the reality of all emotion, but as phenomena that are more enduring and more self-defining. The person is no longer just capable of anger or of getting angry; he is increasingly defined, by self and others, as angry.

I witnessed a dramatic example of the interface between arousal, affect, and state just weeks after my initial workshop in neurofeedback. I was seeing a professor who suffered from unipolar depression and whose sister had committed suicide in the midst of a bipolar episode. We had been pursuing this issue in the only way I knew how: through talk therapy. She was uninterested in medications. She arrived that day sobbing, and said, "I am falling into this depression so fast that it terrifies me." She couldn't teach her classes, she couldn't sleep, she couldn't think. She was a popular, high-functioning professional, suddenly profoundly disabled.

She asked to try neurofeedback, which I was quite reluctant to do. I felt too inexperienced—a vital caution for anyone new to this approach. We both knew, however, that we'd done what talking could do. It wasn't what she needed. This was a brain that had toppled over its own edge. I trained her in the way I'd been taught. Unlike almost everyone with developmental trauma, she needed to raise her arousal. Over the next 30 minutes, I watched her state change. By the end of the first 30-minute neurofeedback session, she was no longer depressed and had experienced a complete change in her worldview. She was no longer hopeless. She knew she could teach, and the terror was over. By addressing under-arousal in the firing of her brain, we dissolved her urgent and compelling affect, thereby changing her state. She had an auditory dream that night about neurofeedback. She heard a voice saying, "The path to the enigma is now clear." She had 23 sessions of neurofeedback, about 11 hours in all, and never had another episode of depression. I did a 12-year follow-up with her, and she said, "Sometimes, not often, I can wake up a little blue, but it's nothing that a cup of coffee or meditation can't take care of."

It is important to stress that most depressions will take longer to resolve, and some may not resolve, even with neurofeedback, at least as we know it today. Developmental trauma can take even longer. But this vignette illustrates the direct connection between arousal, affect, and state. This woman never identified with her states, probably because they were so clearly episodic. There was an "I" who was falling into depression; she wasn't self-defined by depression. The state did not reify into trait because she had long refractory periods in which she had a self that was not depressed, she had loving parents, and she was not under unrelenting assault by her amygdala.

These resources and respites are not available to those with histories of developmental trauma. They have few, if any, refractory periods. They are driven by intense sympathetic and parasympathetic arousal, which leaves them immobilized, frozen, and helpless. These patients either feel afraid all the time or never—the difference perhaps between BPD and APD—and sometimes the difference between women and men who have survived these childhoods. Women are more often overrun by feelings; men are more often overtaken by no feeling; but, of course both men and women could experience either. Whatever the manifestation, adults with developmental trauma, being bereft of self and of discrete emotions, are not just *dependent* on their state, they are *defined* by it.

As a side note, it is well known that the diagnosis of BPD is given to women at rates 3 times higher than it is given to men (Skodol & Bender 2003). There have been many rich discussions in my clinical circle of this diagnostic trend in terms of gender politics, but it might be better understood in terms of brain structure. BPD is essentially a high-amplitude affect regulation problem. Women have more corpus callosum connecting right and left hemispheres than do men (Joseph, 1996, p. 68), which suggests that structurally, they have more access to their emotions than men do. Whether they are regulated or dysregulated, most women will be more influenced by affect than most men. In all of us, arousal gives rise to affect, affect to state, and state to reinforcing narrative—and all that, in this population, coalesces into trait and then identity. We believe our states, particularly urgent ones. It would be very difficult not to, when the state is determined by the felt threat to survival.

State and Narrative

As we saw with the professor, the state we find ourselves in recruits a narrative that supports and provides meaning to that state. When we are angry, we create a narrative that supports our anger—"That jerk cut me off and I have every right to be furious/flip him the bird/cut him off/kill him." The degree of reaction depends on the chain of evoked intensity from arousal to affect and to state. The man who was agonized by the ping of a raindrop reported driving people off the road who were going too slowly or who had challenged him aggressively. We can kill—thankfully, he didn't—when we think we are going to be killed, and he, like most patients with developmental trauma, always believed that. He understood himself as the victim and the other as the aggressor: the compelling narrative of the felt state.

Narrative arises from state, serves it, and reinforces it. Obviously, psychotherapy attempts to address this narrative, but LH talk is of little relevance to an erupting RH. The narrative is the verbal (LH) mind's best shot at justifying or understanding the state that arises from subcortical terror driving the non-verbal RH. But the narrative comes from the mouth of the child, from the imprint of early experience. There had been no update for him. This man was not the tall, strong, smart adult that he actually was. Instead he constructed himself from arousal and affect, and he felt that he was a powerless victim or potential victim, no matter what the circumstances—exactly what his amygdala dictated.

Helplessness rules state and ultimately becomes a trait in developmental trauma. Levine (1997) thinks of this hopeless, helpless state as an expression of immobility or freezing: "Helplessness is closely related to the primitive, universal, biological response to overwhelming threat—the freeze response" (p. 142). As a child, this man had vivid nightmares of annihilation and rocked himself to sleep to the sound of his brother's head banging in the bed across the room. He was bullied and became a bully. He drank heavily. His chronic rages, the most dramatic and potentially destructive human storm, overtook his states and over time became a trait of his and a source of his identity. He was a man defined by the arousal of survival fear and rage. Although he never talked about it, he was organized around an ontological shame, the central experience of "no." He, like many others, looked for himself in the DSM, and over the course of our work together he tried on many different identities to make sense of his states, of himself.

There is another characteristic of the trauma narrative that reveals the push of the nervous system beneath it. The story of a trauma survivor has no arc. There is no beginning because there is no end. It is a narrative of piling on: " . . . and then and then and then." There is not only no arc or structure to the narrative, there is hardly any pause. You will hear changes in the content of the narrative with training and, simultaneously, changes in the narrative form. We are listening in to the self, organizing. The narrative of state begins with "I feel . . . "; the narrative of trait begins, "I am. . . . "

State Dependence

This reinforcing scenario of intense affect and the narrative that it recruits is called state dependence. Because states are so believable, we are all, to some degree, state-dependent. We know, for instance, that it can be expensive to go grocery shopping when we are hungry. Although we're not actually starving and everything we buy is plentiful, we act as if we are starved and food is in short supply. We buy more food and easier food and more calorie-laden food when we shop on an empty stomach. This is state dependence. Relying on coffee to wake ourselves up in the morning and a glass of wine to quiet ourselves at night are state-dependent acts: The action is contingent on state. The term *state dependence*, however, is most often used as an indication of severe psychopathology. Patients diagnosed with BPD, for example, are usually described as state-dependent. When states are permanently urgent, managing them will require (or feel *as if* they require) urgent action. Patients will be riveted to their state and, over time, defined by it. They will do just about anything required to manage it, and all too often they may feel driven to alarming acts, primarily as attempts to influence the impossible, wild firing beneath their awareness. Urgent, fear-driven states cannot be reasoned with, nor can people in them easily learn new tasks. Developmentally traumatized patients get caught in an unreliable but compelling sense of self and worldview that depends entirely on the state in which they find themselves. They identify with their state and tend to rely on state-bound information preferentially over other incoming information. If it doesn't serve survival, it won't be learned. There isn't time enough. Death or oblivion awaits.

Traits

These urgent states, rehearsed over time without interruption or intervention, become traits. When emotional storms are no longer passing weather, hard enough for the patient and those in his world to endure, they will become the climate, the prevailing pattern that underlies any sense of identity. The more practiced a state, the deeper the "rut" in the brain. This circuitry has fired together and wired together for years, and each time it happens, the circuitry gets stronger. These states so dominate these individuals that they become hallmarks of who they are. This identification happens early in the course of developmental trauma, and it gets folded in to each developmental stage until, as adults, we see profoundly dysregulated women and men known to themselves only by what they feel (or don't feel). What was originally an unregulated affect and state promoted by the kindling amygdala becomes a prominent trait. It feels hardwired.

To pursue the weather–climate analogy, after nearly unremitting storms, the climate of the traumatized person has changed. The storms have reached tornado proportion and represent not only how they feel or how they behave, but now, who they *are*. This chaos that began with erupting neurons is a marker of these patients' sense of themselves, of their personality, and even of their identity. This unbearable alignment of affective storm and sense of self is what I am referring to as *trauma identity*, fragmented, unregulated, and driven by fear.

The traits common to personality disorders relate directly to the terror arising from neglect and abuse as a child. Ambient fear is the background condition of being. Fear narrows focus and attention. Dysregulated arousal leads to dysregulated, volatile mood. Fear drives cognition.

Patients with developmental trauma are angry, ashamed, and terrified. These are the traits of developmental trauma.

Personality

The defining characteristic of people given the diagnosis of a personality disorder is their identification with affect, of being what they feel. It is very important to understand that these severe disorders are affect regulation disorders, even when there is little awareness of feelings, as is the case for those with APD. The police saw Carl as fearless, and his therapists saw him as shameless, when in reality he was the creation of shame, fear, and rage. He was, tragically, nothing but these affects. Personality disorders can be seen as reified, continuously rehearsed limbic emotions. When we remember that the problem is arousal in the brain and affect ruling the state of mind, not something "other," then the therapeutic task becomes less daunting. Neurofeedback, I think, challenges the very concept of DSM categories, but none more uniquely than Axis II personality disorders. That being said, people who are what they feel have the most challenged and sometimes the most challenging nervous systems.

This model proposes that what we think of as personality is a collection of traits that, in turn, prime the person for particular states. When we say, "This is just who I am," we are affirming the felt sense of self that is our personality in a statement that implies stasis. We are all, in this sense, caught up in the necessary illusion of an unchanging self. As a Buddhist colleague quipped, "If you have a personality, you have a personality disorder." As we have seen, in developmental trauma and subsequent Axis II conditions, the personality is inseparable from the pervasive affects of shame, anger and terror.

Identity

As discussed earlier, identity is a complex affair and may not be distinguishable from personality. I don't want to get caught up in semantics, but it seems to me that identity is deeper and more ineffable than personality. It doesn't really matter here, the important message is that identity, or the way we experience and know ourselves, rests on firing patterns deep in the brain. When we change these patterns, everything we know as ourselves is up for grabs. Many of my patients have struggled to describe this experience. Most often they say something like, "Who is this person?", referring to something they said or did that they could not have conceived themselves saying or doing. One woman, who was timid in her job as a manager, found herself being assertive in a meeting with those she supervised. She watched this unknown self in disbelief while she also observing her known fear of what her supervisees would think. At a neurological level she expected terrible blowback to her asserting herself, even to taking up space at all, and she was quite surprised by the feedback she got. Many told her that it was a relief to them; they'd been waiting for someone to step up. No one reacted badly. This kind of assertion is a common development with these patients in the process of neurofeedback training. This is assertion not freighted with aggression. It has no charge in it, no threat. Another patient with developmental trauma told me about looking at a building and seeing that it was "safe." She described it as the first time in her life that she had a feeling that the world was safe.

One of the most rewarding aspects of doing neurofeedback is witnessing this level of change in how people know themselves. When these changes do happen—a potentiality of any nervous system—these patients feel simultaneously familiar and entirely unknown to themselves (see Figure 4.1). As you can imagine, these changes, particularly when they happen quickly, present us with new clinical challenges, which I address in Chapter 8.

Reverse Engineering

"You are wasting your time! I don't exist." An adult patient with developmental trauma issued me this confounding challenge. She was putting words to her experience of "no-self" that she and many of her more conscious fellow sufferers recognize. She felt a cowering terror and a towering shame, interrupted by explosions of rage. The question before us is what will happen to this patient's identity of profoundly dysregulated affect when we train the brain to regulate itself? This is what I mean by *reverse engineering*. The answer to this question changed forever the way I see developmental trauma and is really the reason for this book.

When we train the brain to change its frequency-based arousal, we change affect, or felt arousal. When affect changes, state changes. The storms become less intense and less frequent. There are breaks in the clouds. As the brain becomes less aroused and states more easily regulated, the narrative begins to change. As the storms recede, the climate changes. Traits, the hallmark of personality and of personality disorders that seem to be "who we are," begin to give way. One of my patients was seen, and saw herself, as a very angry person. In one instance, a car stopped too close to her in a crosswalk, and she slammed her fist down and dented the hood. When she talked about it, she felt entitled to her reaction: "Anyone would react this way." It was very difficult for her to see this incident in a different perspective until her brain could process threat differently. Like the man above, and most patients with developmental trauma, she believed that she was the victim of malignant intent. She lived in this pattern of reactivity. In the frenzy of overwhelming shame, another of my patients, a woman who had grown up profoundly deprived and abused, would have to fight with herself not to key an expensive car that blocked easy access to hers. She knew better, but it was, of course, neither a cognitive nor a moral appraisal that drove her. It was the paroxysmal force of unregulated shame and rage. As her training organized her brain waves, such impulses (e.g., keying cars), which had been state-syntonic, became not only dystonic but unimaginable. Both of these women were able to regulate the neuronal firing pattern that gave rise to sudden, violent outbursts that had, in turn, defined their very sense of being.

Not only do these patients suffer the original insults, they suffer them again each time they lose control. They are retraumatized by their own reactivity. It is almost as if they can feel the circuitry wiring itself more tightly. Those who can still feel may then feel deeply humiliated, angry, and terrified at being out of control. They are caught in a terrible affective feedback loop. The woman who dented the car described her nervous system "unfolding" as she trained. At the beginning of training, when outbursts would occur, she described them as more intense but of shorter duration. She reported feeling surprised at this; it didn't feel like her. She experienced more of herself outside of her affective state, so she was able to ride the rocket propulsion of rage, and although a bit helpless to its intensity, she was able to observe it. She was even more taken aback by how quickly and completely it resolved. Before training she would have felt the tsunami continue to flood her with multiple affective aftershocks. Now the event just ended. It was over when it was over, an experience she had never had before. She was probably reporting the absence of kindling in response to strong emotion. Len Ochs, one of the pioneers of neurofeedback, described this pattern in his patients as well. He also saw it as a sign that this pattern was on its way out (personal communication, February 4, 1999).

The person with epilepsy who trains to get her seizures under control is engaged in a similar, if not identical, process. So what's happening here? Before training, the provocative firing in injured tissue is picked up by adjacent healthy neurons and propagated. The more neurons that get swept up in this event, the larger the event will be, and if the neuronal synchrony travels across the corpus callosum, the result will be a grand mal seizure. With training, the healthy neurons surrounding the injured site begin to stabilize and no longer participate in the brain's small but influential error. The tissue continues to fire its errant signal, but no other neurons heed it, so it becomes an isolated event without consequence to the rest of the brain. I think of this like a demagogue trying to whip up a crowd to feel, think, say, and do outrageous things. If the crowd refuses to participate, he (or she) would no longer be a demagogue. He would be who he is—a mad man standing on a corner and snubbed, pitied, or arrested in his attempt to stir up fear and rage.

Over the course of training, the woman who felt so angry so often that she identified herself as an angry person felt less and less easily provoked. After beginning neurofeedback, she no longer experienced herself as angry, nor did others. Early on she noticed that she could drive on the highway in the rain without bracing, formerly a signature to her of her baseline high arousal. Her shoulders dropped below her ears. She could make small talk. As is true for most patients with developmental trauma who train, her CNS became noticeably less reactive.

In a similar way, the woman who could barely control her urges to key offending cars noted that the impulse was suddenly "just gone." She didn't need to control it because it was no longer arising. In her case, she became aware of her "shadow side," to use her term, her history-based antisocial bent, as she emerged from the burning carapace of overwhelming affect. Her temper quieted, as did shame and fear, and in the process, she found herself developing an observing ego, increased empathy—informed partly by her dawning awareness that others also experienced much of what she had experienced—she was gaining a theory of mind—and a relational, prosocial, and moral self. She described a deepening sense of internal coherence that she'd never felt before. She stopped dissociating and was able to describe the way it felt: "It's like I feel the impulse [to react] begin [often literally felt at the temporal lobe], but my brain just can't go there." The healthy, regulated neurons stemmed the tide and instead of following that well-worn fear circuitry, settled into rest. The temporal lobes did not ignite into what Daniel Amen (2001) calls the *ring of fire*.

Another adult with developmental trauma arrived at my office after almost two decades of both psychodynamic and DBT therapies. She was dissociative and working mightily, but unsuccessfully, to manage daily flashbacks. She was organized solely around her traumatic experiences. What little identity she had was a trauma identity. As she started to feel the grip loosen, she expressed a core fear that, in my experience, arises uniquely in brain wave training: "Who will I be when I am no longer afraid? Fear is what I am." This profound question predicts the crisis of identity that you will encounter when you work with these patients using neurofeedback.

Identity that ascends from the dysregulation of high arousal to intensely felt affect, to state and to trait, also begins, over time, to change. One of the ways to recognize that this shift is happening is when your patients begin to talk about themselves in the terms of their brains and in the language of arousal. It is not only that they are picking up on the idiom of neurofeedback; they are beginning to feel the ebb and flow of arousal. They begin to feel emotion as emotion, arising and falling away. Typically they stop using their diagnostic label but instead describe how aroused they feel or how regulated or dysregulated. The reorganizing CNS produces a new narrative. A new, tender sense of self begins to organize. These patients will become, in a sense, less their brain and more their mind. They will have a chance to think and to experience the nascent ability to reflect. Psychologically, self-reflection requires some level of affect regulation—in essence, some peace. Neurologically, it requires well-regulated structures doing what they are meant to do. Simply put, the therapeutic work with neurofeedback involves, first, the regulation of affect through quieting arousal and then helping the patient to integrate a newly organizing, emerging sense of self.

I want to alert you to this particular aspect of therapy with neurofeedback to help you avoid a mistake I made. Remember the man who came to me because the only feeling he had was anger? One day, after 30 or so sessions, he arrived in my office quite shaken. He had seen a squirrel run over on the highway. He had seen this kind of sight before, but he had never felt anything. We talked about these unfamiliar feelings of compassion and sadness, and about his emerging recognition of the innocence and slaughter in the world around him. In a very real sense, he found this world with the help of brain wave training. He felt empathy in response to suffering. But, I think primarily because I had not prepared him, he was frightened of such intense feelings. He was becoming unfrozen and prosocial, and he did not know this person. In the interplay of old, well-worn, and somewhat fixed patterns with new emerging ones, he wasn't sure he wanted to feel so much of the suffering of the world. He was mad at me for allowing this, and he left treatment.

Preparation for these changes is essential and because each individual is unique, the course of the changes can never be accurately predicted. A woman raised by her dissociative mother in terrible poverty beautifully described this transitional process of shifting identity in terms of the hunger of motherlessness: "My empty self flicks on and off with my full self—my getting-full self." I discuss how I have come to address this profound transition, from Schore's (1994, 2003) sense of "no mother–no self" to the inhabitation of self and, for some, to the realization of no-self in the Buddhist sense, in Chapter 8.

Healing Paradox

I have come to believe that healing developmental trauma requires brain wave training. I see most therapy, as we practice it today, as working around, rather than with, the amygdala. Our patients learn to manage their primordial fear to a greater or lesser degree, but they are never free from it. Our record of treatment failure makes it equally clear that this work-around approach leaves the amygdala in charge. I am not saying that patients with developmental trauma cannot do well with standard therapy; clearly, many do and they can even be quite functional. These patients who function well, atop these volcanic circuits, are those whom Linehan (1993) calls "apparently competent." But I think if we don't go right to the source, the subcortical kindling of fear, most of these patients are still held hostage by ambient fear. We can help them quiet their reactivity through insight or through teaching new behaviors, but we cannot, without neurofeedback, help them quiet the persistent pulse of fear.

Yet, as we have discussed above, the reduction of fear that neurofeedback makes possible is both welcomed and terrifying. As she began to experience herself as less afraid, one patient described a separate terror: nothing short of her own annihilation. This response gives rise to a central healing paradox in the practice of neurofeedback. How do we address fear in people who define themselves by it? We talk about this important issue more in Chapters 6 and 8, but here is the short version.

Our goal as neurofeedback clinicians, as well as clinicians, with these patients is singular: to reduce or ultimately to quiet limbic reactivity. But when we reduce fear, we challenge fear-based identity, the only known self. Many will cling to fear as if it were life itself. It is. It is who they are. Fear has also been the primary and often the only validation of a routinely invalidated traumatic past. It is a memory trace to a forgotten or overwhelmingly remembered childhood, and we are going to erase it. Fear is also experienced as a kind of early warning system. These patients will mistake their affective arousal as evidence that arousal is required. Any hope of a nurturing relationship has been conceived in need. Confusion and loss can set in as patients' need for the mother, and the therapist, diminishes. They can deeply fear that they will lose not only themselves but the newly emerging other. Depending on where they are in the process of unfolding fear, they are more or less able to see that these reactions arise directly from well-learned patterns of reactivity in the fear circuitry, rehearsed for a lifetime, and are not to be believed.

As we swim in the deep and turbulent waters of affect and identity, it is reassuring to know that we have no choice. There is no other path; we must reduce fear. We also must ease fear of no fear. It is especially important for neurofeedback practitioners to recognize and understand the dilemma that "the cure" creates and to help their patients recognize and understand it as well. I bring everything I can to bear at this juncture. We are attempting to disengage the amygdala, and in response it gets alarmed and reacts. It creates the narrative of its own necessity and its inevitable dominance. We keep training and talking about changes. We address lack of change with neurofeedback, not with psychotherapy. We ease the brain into this, while integrating neurofeedback training with whatever therapy we are doing and by teaching fundamental relaxation techniques such as attention to the breath, body scans and for those who can do it, meditation. Unfortunately, there will be many rounds in this shedding of fear as both the brain and the mind gravitate back toward their familiar and compelling patterns, initially, if left to their own devices. The brain has to be nudged out of this reactive position, and as it is, the mind comes with it.

What Is Possible?

In this ridiculously linear model, what seems to happen is that neuronal firing and, most likely, glial activity slowly but surely regulate in response to the training challenge. Errant provocations such as those that manifest as dissociation are ignored by the increasingly regulated brain, both subcortically and cortically. Arousal decreases and patients become more flexible and more tuned to the present than the past. This emerging nervous system can now participate in a full range of affective states, but increasingly, calm prevails. These patients find themselves making state transitions much more flexibly and smoothly and often surprise themselves by experiencing happy, even peaceful, states that they report are completely new to them. With lowered arousal they are less claimed by their states and, as a result, are increasingly less state-dependent. The narrative shifts from the past to the present.

The patient who arrived 5 years ago trying to manage her arousal and dissociation by clawing at her face, hitting her head, and holding ice packs lives in a very different narrative today, and a very different sense of self. She no longer has flashbacks, no longer dissociates, never engages in self-harm, has discontinued her psychiatric medications, and sleeps free from nightmares. But the change that I am describing as a change in identity is more profound and less measurable than the absence of symptoms. She is learning to trust her mind, and she has gained a sense of her own agency.

Increasingly, these patients are able to see states for what they are: temporary. When we are no longer state-bound, the traits to which arousal and engrained state gave rise begin to, well, vanish. A patient told me that she had experienced these states as living organisms. She felt certain that as she withdrew energy from them (i.e., reduced her fear), she would experience their deaths. She had been raised by a terror-stricken and dissociative mother, and she came by her original diagnosis of DID honestly. It surprised her that nothing bad actually happened. This primary reorganization of the CNS allows, even demands organization or reorganization in the sense of self. A video from Melbourne, Australia shows a young adolescent before and after neurofeedback. He was so out of control, he was about to be sent to juvenile detention. Watching a video of himself battering a door with a pole, he said, "I can't believe I was ever like that. Even if I tried, I couldn't be like that again." You can watch this video on YouTube (http://www.youtube.com/watch?v=8uRFRkfBlTs).

Neurofeedback is not a quick fix, but unlike any other approach, at least any other approach I have tried, it may well be a fix. I don't think, however, that anyone can learn and change at this level with brain regulation alone. If that were the nature of being human, we could just hook people up to neurofeedback systems and let them train. Neurofeedback enhances affect regulation and attention, and surprising things happen that we never see with therapy alone. But human beings need other human beings, and this is probably never truer than for those with histories of developmental trauma as they begin to coalesce a new, fragile, tentative, but increasingly stable identity. I can think of no greater privilege than to attend this labor and assist this birth.

PART II
PRACTICING NEUROFEEDBACK

Chapter 5

Introducing Neurofeedback to Your Patients

I have been providing neurofeedback in conjunction with psychotherapy for over 16 years, more than half of my professional career. I was originally trained in psychodynamic therapy and still work primarily dynamically, although I have also been trained in DBT and, as fate would have it, was the first to implement DBT in an inpatient setting. DBT author Marsha Linehan and I have argued the merits of our approaches —she obviously behavioral and I, psychodynamic—over many years, usually long-distance between Massachusetts and Seattle. Neither of us could convince the other. When I started using neurofeedback, she told me that I had to admit that I was now a behaviorist, or as she said, "a radical behaviorist." I was now, after all, discussing brain behaviors, conditioning, and learning. For me, however, neurofeedback signaled the *collapse* of distinction between schools.

The core problem is in the brain, and yet no school of therapy, even those considered evidence-based, directly focuses on the brain's plasticity and our access to it. All psychotherapy, when it helps, must in some manner enhance the mind's capacity to regulate the brain. We are all too often arguing over what manner we use—psychodynamic, body-oriented, analytic, or cognitive–behavioral—when what we need to discuss is how we best help the brain to regain or gain its regulation. As a psychodynamic therapist, I use many DBT approaches, particularly in the early stabilization stages of neurofeedback, and particularly with those who are so overrun by intense emotion that they have little sense of their own minds. As we progress in neurofeedback training, I am working with my patients in the therapy to understand and address the habits of emotion, thought, and behavior that arise from dysregulation and that can in turn excite it. With the possible exception of somatic therapies, no single approach to therapy seems inherently better as a companion therapy for neurofeedback.

Regardless of school or approach, the one point that is essential for neurofeedback practitioners is that they understand the core issue of affect regulation and that they understand and prepare their patients for the contributions of brain wave training. The treatment of developmental trauma involves regulation of the brain, the body, and the mind. Everything bends toward regulation. A skeptic could always argue that it is the therapy and not the neurofeedback that accounts for the change. I would have done so at one point in my career. Most of my patients, however, arrive after years of therapy (including therapy with me) still suffering core dysregulation, and they experience the regulation organizing within them as they train in neurofeedback as something entirely new. Again, more about this topic in Chapter 8.

I work primarily with people I would now diagnose as having developmental trauma. When I learned what neurofeedback had to offer, through my own initial and ongoing experience with it and after my first professional training, I wanted it for my patients. In previous chapters, you read about some of my patients who happily went along with my new approach in its early days, but not everyone received this paradigm change with such enthusiasm. I'll share some stories illustrative of different responses and reactions to help you anticipate those of your patients. I'll talk about the issues that can arise in introducing neurofeedback to a patient you are already seeing, and to someone new. There are different issues as well between those who are coming to you for therapy and those who seek you out for brain wave training. And there are, of course, myriad individual differences across these categories.

Introducing Current Patients to Neurofeedback

As we have discussed at some length, neurofeedback represents a major paradigm shift, and this is not only true for the field of psychotherapy, it is also true for our patients. As you may remember, it was nearly impossible for me to embrace this approach until I tried it. I had no paradigm for it and no experience of it. I often joke with my audience at neurofeedback workshops that they are far ahead of me in their ability to grasp neurofeedback through talks. I doubt I could have done that, at least not when I began. Initially, I had to experience it to get it.

In my psychotherapy practice, most of my focus was on the lasting effects of early experience, particularly on relationships with parents. But even before I had any inkling of neurofeedback, I knew the limitations of this kind of inquiry. Even when we understood the historical root, we still had to deal with the chronic undoing of powerful affect. I found the same to be true with DBT. No matter how skilled they became, these patients were still struggling with intense states of fear, anger, and shame. One of these patients, a woman in her late 40s, came to me after 20 years, most of it in DBT. She credits that treatment with keeping her alive and out of the hospital, but she nevertheless arrived dissociated and profoundly disabled. She was caught in a tight, looping narrative of early trauma, alternating between dissociation and flashbacks. For over a year, she left every session crying, something she reported having done every week for two decades.

Most of my patients now come to me primarily for neurofeedback, and we'll discuss those issues in a bit. When I was new to this approach and my patients even newer, the task was more complex. I was asking them to reconsider all of the work we had done; at the very least, to recast it. It felt to some as if I were reducing the rich complexity of their history and individuality, much of which we had co-constructed over years of work together, to the firing patterns of their brains. They felt abandoned to the new paradigm that had caught my attention.

One patient insisted that the computers not enter her space in the consulting room. Although this had the feel of sibling rivalry at the time, it turned out to be sage advice. If you are bringing neurofeedback into an established setting and established relationship, the computers can feel like intruders. If at all possible keep them out of your consultation room. If that's not possible, consider using laptops that can be stowed out of sight. I did as she asked, but in the end this patient could not manage the shift and eventually felt she had to leave. Although I felt no disavowal of our relationship or our therapy, I may have communicated exactly that. I was, of course, impressed with what more could happen for people when they trained their brains. But she and two others felt misunderstood, and, I think, scared of the seemingly sudden change in my views.

And for my part, in my excitement, I was somewhat of a true believer, which didn't help them or, in fact, anybody. Some patients may not want to follow this path, and this is just as it is. As much as I wanted to stay with them in therapy as they wished it to be, I felt myself in an ethical bind. I knew the possibilities with neurofeedback, the limitations of psychotherapy, and the dangers of medication and found it increasingly difficult to practice psychotherapy alone, or, as had been the case for years, to endorse the use of medications. This could be my problem. Many of my highly ethical colleagues have been able to maintain separate practices without feeling this pinch.

The first conversation about neurofeedback is important. When I was beginning, I didn't do it all that well. Timing is everything, and at that point, my enthusiasm trumped my timing. It's a cautionary tale. This may be less of an issue for those of you who have learned about this approach and adopted it without personal experience. I had a sense of urgency in wanting to give my patients what I had been given. You need a partnership to pursue neurofeedback. It is unlikely that adults will benefit from training if they don't want to do it, particularly if they are afraid of it or associate the arrival of neurofeedback with the loss of you. Some of your patients may not be able to make the transition with you. As we saw in Chapter 4, others may be ahead of you, already knowing that the problem is literally in their heads.

Introducing Patients to Their Brains

Most patients are as unaware of their brains as are most therapists, so the first step is to make the introduction. If they are interested, I show patients a three-dimensional model of the brain, pointing out the different structures that could be implicated in the problems they are trying to manage. And then I essentially take them through the high points of this book. I am likely to tell them that at least some of their difficulty lies in the way their brain has learned to fire, that the primary dysregulation is in this realm, and that whatever the brain has learned to do wrong, it can learn to do right (well, almost everything). This is the basic introduction to the concept of brain plasticity, and we'll see soon how important this understanding is for both clinician and patient. The idea that dysregulation lies in the brain can be validating or invalidating for patients, depending on the individual variables we just discussed. In my view as a neurofeedback clinician, the problems my patients suffered were evidence of nonoptimal brain regulation; as a psychotherapist the same issues were understandable feelings with historical meanings that we had to address. Both, of course, were true.

One of my patients suffered from towering rages, and her primary response to my telling her about neurofeedback was anger and fear. I was upending our entire history together. We had extensively explored her childhood with a narcissistic, angry, and unavailable mother and made sense of her rages in that context. We had combed the transference to understand how her childhood issues played out with us and with others. We adopted behavioral anger management strategies. But none of this did much to alleviate her rage. And of course, it was the narrative of rage that dictated her mostly negative transference and negative life experiences.

With my new study of the brain, I came to recognize that the seminal event for her, at least in terms of the uncontrollable rages, was less her mother and family and more a right prefrontal head injury when she was thrown off a horse and landed hard on her forehead when she was 8 years old. (She had been unconscious for several minutes, but it is important to note that serious consequences can occur even when there is no loss of consciousness.) We had focused our earlier inquiry into this event on the fact that she had disobeyed and angered her mother by not wearing a helmet. (Hopefully, this is ringing some bells for you as well.)

When we reviewed her history in this light, she recognized something that she hadn't previously: She had changed after the accident, and it was then that the rages began. This injury had undermined, or perhaps for her, further undermined, the development of her prefrontal cortex and with it, her capacity to inhibit the raging amygdala. This perspective wasn't entirely a relief to her. In fact, she felt that the paradigmatic rug had been pulled out from under her and with it, a very real sense of meaning. Even though she had a significant decrease in rages, both in their frequency and amplitude, as it were, she could never align herself with this approach. She felt abandoned to it and for her it seemed devoid of meaning. Even though she made very real progress, she left to engage in more traditional talk therapy—where she felt she could better pursue meaning.

The issue of meaning, particularly meaning in suffering, is too big to take on here, yet also too important to ignore. For most of us it is our story that provides meaning and a sense of continuity and coherence. In this sense the practice of neurofeedback may be more like the practice of meditation: both practices are, in great part, uninterested in story. They focus instead on the quality of mind and on an end to suffering. I am not dismissing in any way the importance of our stories, especially as they lend understanding and contribute to self and self-regulation. All too often, however, they do just the opposite. When the stories inflame emotional pain rather than illuminate it, and when this pain leads to dysregulation, they aren't helpful. When this happens, we are very likely to identify with the story. The narrative of arousal can become us. Many books have been written about story in meditation—as one teacher called it, our attachment to autobiography—and there are likely to be many books on this very issue in the practice of neurofeedback. But for now, I just want to alert you to it.

The take-home from my early missteps is to stay with your patient and to introduce the possibility of neurofeedback training gently. Don't try to convince anyone to do neurofeedback, just keep the offer on the table. I have to confess that this level of therapeutic abstinence or detachment was often difficult for me once I recognized the centrality of dysregulated affect in these troubles and how well neurofeedback addressed it. This was clearly the case with this rage-filled patient. In such cases, I don't think we have much choice. I kept it on the table with her as much as she could tolerate but did not push the issue until there was another round of turbulence. I then felt it was necessary to insist on training as a prerequisite for ongoing work. Ironically, my understanding the role of her brain's disrupted functioning made it considerably easier for me to bear the brunt of her rages, but it also made it increasingly pointless to do so. But she had, as it were, grown up under very different therapeutic assumptions and due in great part to her wild affect, she found this new approach to affect regulation difficult to embrace.

In the beginning, when times got rough with this patient and others, I just wanted to return to what I knew and do what felt safe for both of us: talk therapy. And, as it would happen, this woman, with her very dicey, bruised brain, had one of the worst neurofeedback reactions I have ever witnessed. When I trained her over the site of the old injury (FP2), she exploded with teeth-bared rage. Needless to say, we were both deeply rattled. I felt terrible for precipitating the event and frightened, and she felt out of control, enraged, and distrustful. We returned to therapy because, at least for me at the time, it felt like a safe if futile harbor. It wouldn't take long for me to remember why I'd insisted on training. Even with this scary event I was able to remember two things: my own compelling experience with training (I wasn't taking this on faith) and the reality of brain plasticity. I also had an experienced mentor who eased my apprehension by helping me understand what had happened. (I'll talk more about the importance of mentors before I leave this chapter.) She never had another experience like this (I did not return to the same site) and slowly she gained control. We'll also discuss the possibility (and, for some, even the inevitability) of rough times when we discuss the somewhat complex issue of informed consent later in this chapter.

If most of my patients had reacted to neurofeedback in these ways, I might well have given up on it. However, this was not the case. Some of my patients already felt that their problem was in their brains and for them training the brain was an overdue and welcomed shift. Those who felt hopeless and stigmatized, such as the "borderline" woman we discussed in Chapter 4, embraced it. When these patients learned that the problem was in their brains and not in their character, they thought about themselves differently. Almost every one of them felt less stigmatized, which meant less bathed in shame. I think of shame as an anaerobic emotion, a feeling that dies when exposed to air. But when shame is activated, our common strategy is to hide. No one easily talks about it. Talking about shame threatens exposure and more shame. Patients with developmental trauma live in this internal shame environment, so reducing stigma by locating the problem in the brain can be quite positive, in and of itself. It gives these patients room to breathe and, with therapeutic help, to reconsider themselves. It engenders hope.

Expectations of Training

Hope, Emily Dickinson's "thing with feathers," is a unique issue in neurofeedback and best to address right from the beginning. Neurofeedback clearly offers hope for significant change. In most people most of the time, it will ease the symptoms of errant patterns that habitually replicate themselves. But because this is so much about the highly individual brain and not the diagnosis or, in a sense, even the individual, we can make no guarantees. It is best to gently downplay expectations if they are high and to raise them carefully when they are low. This is another aspect of the Goldilocks approach: the middle path. False hope is as unbearable as no hope, if not more so, and there is no need to risk it. Neurofeedback will demonstrate its own efficacy. Managing expectations requires knowing what they are, so this is an important question to ask in the initial neurofeedback assessment. We'll discuss this issue more fully in the next chapter.

Because neurofeedback is still relatively new after more than 50 years, most people won't know what to expect. If they are the first in their family or circle to use neurofeedback, their expectations will be influenced mostly by yours. In my experience, I have found it difficult to discern a placebo effect. There have been times that I have made an error in protocols, and when I recognize this, I have been known to suggest that we may have opened a new window of possibility. Most of the time, if the patient is feeling good as we end the session (if at all possible, I won't end until then), she will feel optimistic too. In a sense, I may be doing what I can do to induce a positive placebo effect, but if the training direction wasn't right for patients, their brains won't cooperate—unless this error does, in fact, turn out to be beneficial. This can happen. It is how some protocol discoveries have been made. (I'll talk more about mistakes in Chapter 7.) So I am not worried about suggestibility, per se (even though, as a whole, trauma survivors tend to be a suggestible group), but about the possibility of raising expectations.

Every brain has its own course. Some are sensitive, some are reactive, some are stodgy and slow to respond, and some take to training like ducks to water. You have no way to predict this course, and yet prediction is important to help provide a context for the experience. I predict the gamut of possibilities: There may be no change, there may initially be an activation of symptoms, and there could be an easing of symptoms. One might experience improvement in one area but an exacerbation in another. The patient could sleep well that night, sleep as he always does, or sleep poorly. The prediction at the beginning is for possible positive change, possible negative change, no change, or all of the above. I explain that whatever happens, it is the brain giving me information about what it needs and doesn't need. It is a wonderful inherency in the brain that what it likes in training is almost always what it needs; what feels good is good. Patient responses provide data on their brain's plasticity. I will learn if I have pushed the arousal too far in one direction or the other, if it felt as if nothing happened, or if it felt right. These responses are the basis of our conversation with the brain and we will use what it tells us to adjust protocols as we proceed.

All this being said, the effects from the first session have to be considered novel effects, and as such, may not predict the response to this protocol even the second time you use it. You'll want your patient to know this upfront, again to manage expectations and even confusion and disappointment if initial positive changes aren't replicated. When this happens, I suggest what I think is true: that somewhere their brain knows how to do this, and it will find its way there in its own time and fashion. (I discuss novel effects more in Chapter 6.) Initial changes, whether positive or negative, will not hold for long after just one session or even after several. If we stop training after only a few sessions, the brain will default to its known rhythmic patterns, to its familiar habits.

I discuss all of these points with my patients, if they are willing to have this conversation with me. I also make a simple but important contract:

1. From now on we can best understand that any changes, positive or negative, relate to the training. Please do your best to keep track of anything that seems different in how you feel, in what you do, in what you say, and in how you relate to others. That being said, of course, neurofeedback might not turn out to be the best explanation, but until we can rule it out, let's agree it is. You have to make your best effort to tell me what you are experiencing physically, emotionally, and behaviorally.
2. I will use that information to evaluate ongoing training and protocol selection but we are in this journey of regulation together.

The point of the "contract" is simply to remind people that neurofeedback training is likely to play a major role in their state of mind and body. As we have discussed, training the brain can quickly change states, and states supply justifying narratives. Once in the grip of state, it can be challenging to remember that neurofeedback has played a role. If you haven't discussed brain plasticity in the electrical domain, now is the time, for both you and your patient. By anticipating the possibilities, you provide a context for the unknown and the unpredicted. Even with such a broad brush, you cannot anticipate everything.

One woman, raised in a harsh maternal environment, came to try neurofeedback after it had helped quiet her brother's anxiety. She experienced significant anxiety herself and wanted to see if neurofeedback could help her, as it had him. One of the significant but not central points in her narrative was that she'd undergone a traumatic eye surgery as a small child. She felt good when she left our session, calmer and brighter than she'd remembered feeling in a long time, but later that afternoon she felt a dramatic pulling in her eye—"just like it was before the surgery"! It resolved quickly, and although the positive effects endured, she was too frightened by that sensation or body memory to return to do more.

When this kind of disconcerting experience occurs, it is particularly important for the practitioner to trust that the brain is indeed plastic. If you don't remember this (and even sometimes when you do), you too can get frightened when things like this happen. It is also the case that effects like this rarely repeat; they are novel. I had no way of predicting this response, although now, were someone to come to see me with this history, I would share this story so that if it happened to them, it would scare them less. This is the value of prediction, and since placebo effect seems weak in neurofeedback, I think there is little downside.

Introducing New Patients to Neurofeedback

When someone comes to me for psychotherapy, I talk with them about my use of neurofeedback as part of my approach and tell them briefly what it is and why I use it. But again, timing is everything. It will become clear if therapy alone is not sufficient and neurofeedback can be further discussed at that juncture. There is no point in trying to override the wishes of an adult. Children, particularly those with developmental trauma, routinely reject treatment of any kind. Since they are almost entirely subsumed by their dysregulated nervous systems, the goal with these kids is to get them to train. Sammy, the 4-year-old who was considered the most disturbed child in Massachusetts, trained on his fifth day in foster care. He was feral, dissociative, nonverbal, and terrified. He fought the electrodes and completed only a few minutes of neurofeedback as a result. This boy who was wracked by night terrors then slept through the night. It saved his placement. His brain was much more receptive to training than he was. But after this experience he never fought again over training. It must have just felt good to him, intrinsically.

Most people who come to see me now are looking for neurofeedback. Many arrive saying explicitly that they do not want to do psychotherapy, usually adding that it didn't work for them. Although I never do neurofeedback alone, if the problem is affect regulation I devote most of our time in the beginning to brain wave training. No meaningful therapy can occur when affect is significantly dysregulated.

One woman in her 40s told me at her first session that she'd tried therapy many times, that it didn't work, and that she only wanted neurofeedback. She told me that she had ADHD and, as a result, found it difficult to pay attention. Her clinical assessment quickly revealed that there was a lot more going on for her than ADHD. She had grown up in dire poverty—she'd found their pet bird frozen to death in her house when she came home from second grade one winter afternoon—with alcoholic parents who fought viciously. Both of her parents were trauma survivors; her father a veteran and her mother neglected and abused as a child. This woman had been emotionally, sexually, and physically abused by both parents and her brother from a very young age. Despite these overwhelmingly negative experiences, she had a professional, if slightly edgy, presentation. She was diffusely distressed, hopeless, and angry. She dressed modestly in slacks and sweaters and generally used little makeup. Then one day she arrived dressed in a sheer white blouse and short skirt, wearing dark-blue eye shadow and deep red lipstick. She acted more aloof and at the same time, seductive. It was if she were holding a cigarette in a cigarette holder between her dark red fingertips. She seemed completely unaware of the stark contrast in her presentation.

This event and clinical assessment confirmed that she and I were dealing with DID, not ADHD. As the training quieted her core fear—a nonlinear process and, for her, an erratic one—she became actively engaged in therapy. This is the common course for those with developmental trauma. They have little if any idea of the relationship that is therapy, either because they didn't have the experience of a good-enough therapist or because the therapist never fully materialized for them. It is most often the latter because at that point in time, there was no patient and no therapist. Once the CNS begins to regulate, you will begin to exist to these patients and they will want to talk. They have, each one, a terrible and necessary story to tell. Even more importantly, they will come to know that they have someone to tell it to.

As suggested, it is always important to find out why someone is coming for neurofeedback. This is the time to discover their expectations and adjust them as needed. Suggest that the outcomes could be modest. This advice falls in the category of "Do what I say, not what I do." Even after 16 years, I am excited about neurofeedback and can still find it difficult to lower expectations, at least *my* expectations, particularly with people who are feeling pretty hopeless. It is like every other aspect of your work with patients: finding the right moment and the right tone for each person in your care. So, when new patients arrive wanting psychotherapy, I would advise keeping neurofeedback in play as needed, and when they come for neurofeedback, keep the therapeutic frame with the understanding that therapy will be—and is—happening.

Taking Measure: Cognitive Performance Tests and Brain Maps

In Chapter 6, I take you through the clinical assessment as I use it and discuss how it informs my practice of neurofeedback. Before a full assessment is undertaken and prior to training, many practitioners use assessment instruments not only as a way to introduce clients to their brains, but as a way to evaluate the tenor of their nervous systems.

Cognitive performance tests (CPTs), like the Test of Variables of Attention (T.O.V.A.™) and the Integrated Visual and Auditory Continuous Performance Test (IVA) that are used for medication titration in ADHD, can yield useful information in this regard. In these tests, both visual and auditory, the patient has to react to the target when it is flashed on the computer screen, or to a tone, by pressing a button and refraining from reacting to the nontarget. These tests reveal the functioning of the nervous system in four domains: attention, impulsivity, speed of response, and consistency of response. As you might expect, those with developmental trauma tend to have difficulties in all of these areas.

Many clinicians will administer one of these tests initially and then every 20 sessions or so throughout the training process. Improvement in the patient should be reflected in improvement in the T.O.V.A. or IVA scores, which can provide objective measures of progress. They also take very little time to administer. One of my patients actually felt serene after doing the T.O.V.A., but to date she is unique in that reaction.

Many practitioners in this field use quantitative EEGs, also called, qEEGs, or more briefly, "Qs." The Q provides a snapshot of the brain interacting electrically at 19 sites simultaneously. The quantitative part comes when the patient's Q is compared to a normative database that contains information from hundreds to thousands of brains considered normal, matched for age but not for sex. *Normal* here means the absence of brain injury, seizure disorder, or a diagnosis of psychopathology. The raw EEG is also reviewed. In general, what a Q reveals best are coherence abnormalities and the distribution of frequencies around the brain. The Q report will also offer suggestions for training protocols. To minimize expense and to get a less involved, if somewhat less accurate picture, clinicians can opt for a mini-Q, which is essentially a comparison of this brain to itself with a series of measurements at different sites taken sequentially during the same sitting.

I suggest, particularly as you are getting started in this field, that you adopt some method to assess your patients' EEGs and the reactivity of their nervous systems. I used all of these measures mentioned above when I began and when they were available. Now, I tell my patients about these assessment measures, but I don't routinely use them. In my experience, clinical assessment has yielded more reliable protocols than those derived from brain maps. For some in this field, this stance is controversial if not heretical, but I have come by it honestly. I have many friends in the Q field, and they have all provided me with a Q at some time in the course of my rather long tenure. These maps are fascinating to see and often revealing. In my case, I learned that I had subclinical seizure activity at both temporal lobes and that they fired off independently of one another. This finding explained a lot about troubles I had experienced. As a young adult I had been diagnosed with temporal lobe epilepsy and had used anticonvulsants for some time then.

There is an instructive story here. In my early 20s, I was diagnosed at a highly regarded neurology clinic in New York. After 3 hours in a teeming waiting room, I met with a young, kind, and thoughtful neurologist who took the time to review my complaints and my history. He was confident in his diagnosis. I was, he told me, schizophrenic and presently in remission. The diagnosis sent me reeling. Fortunately, at this clinic, every patient was also evaluated by a psychiatrist. Unfortunately, it was several weeks before I had this second appointment. She was older and wiser and told me, after an equally exhaustive assessment and with even more confidence, that I was not schizophrenic, that I had epilepsy. They were both competent doctors, and they were looking at the same set of clinical data. I had temporal lobe epilepsy (TLE) and I could feel pretty crazy, like people with developmental trauma do.

When this Q report came in three decades later, it was suggested to me that I use medication again until my brain gained its own regulation. I did. In this instance, the findings were very helpful, but more in the arena of medication than in that of training. I took anticonvulsants to hold my brain stable until it could provide that stability through its own evolving regulation. This is the best use of psychotropic medications, judicious and transitional, because they can help the brain while it is learning to help itself. In my case, as in many others who use medications to this end, I was able to discontinue the medication within several months. It can be important and often quite validating to see the map of what is happening in the troubled brain. But in each instance, when I followed the Q protocol recommendations for my own training, they weren't helpful. I trained my own brain by addressing symptoms, and it is this approach that I describe much more fully in Chapters 6 and 7.

There is no easy way to understand why a Q recommendation fails. The brain is too complex, and the desire to quantify it is, understandably, great. The Q feels to me like looking at the sky through Galileo's telescope when we need something even more advanced than the Hubble. We are, I think, at the kinematics stage in qEEG—that is, describing what we see happening but not yet knowing what forces are actually at play. Our understanding is Newtonian when it needs to be quantum.

Even for those clinicians who routinely use Qs to design protocols, symptoms always trump the Q. You have to follow the lead of the brain. That being said, the Q offers us the best understanding to date of the temporal or frequency domain of brain functioning. I always recommend a Q when there is a history of head injury, brain injury, or seizure, or when my patient is not responding to training in ways that I would expect. Mark Steinberg, a very experienced neurofeedback clinician in California, cited his "one-third rule" on Qs: He sends one-third of his patients for Qs, and he finds one-third of these reports clinically useful (personal communication, July 15, 2002). If there were no cost and easy availability, I might well send every patient for a Q. But given my experience thus far, the cost–benefit ratio and the very real limitations of any measurement system to grasp the quantum phenomenon that is the brain, I use them sparingly.

Referring a patient for a Q is another time to check on expectations and also to counsel the patient on the limitations of the map. I have had patients become alarmed at unexpected Q findings, and I think it is just common sense to prepare them. Here I do what I say and keep expectations low. Prior to training, I will also review any other evaluations the patient has had that might shed light on this brain, including neuropsychological testing, neurological workups, clinical EEGs, occupational therapy reports, and educational assessments.

After introducing patients to the electrical nature of their brains, to the theory underwriting neurofeedback, and if they wish, to the considerable body of research on neurofeedback (see Hammond, 2013), I will show them the system—in my case, EEGer—and describe what will happen in a typical session, much as described in Chapter 3. I leave a lot of time for questions. If a patient asks you a question you can't answer—a high probability when you are beginning this practice—acknowledge that you don't know and then find the answer. Most neurofeedback software companies have list servers on which your question will be answered by one of your forebearers in the field. If they have not already done so, encourage your patients to research neurofeedback on their own and to ask you any question that comes up when they do.

Informed Consent

Before we plunge into the somewhat complex issue of informed consent in the context of neurofeedback training, it's important to review the basic principles. Informed consent has four components: (1) adequate disclosure of information, (2) the freedom of the patient to make a choice, (3) the patient's ability to understand the information, and (4) his capacity to make decisions. Now let's take each principle and apply it to doing neurofeedback training for patients with developmental trauma.

(An important side note before we begin: Pay attention to your prepositions! I cringe when I hear my colleagues say that they are doing neurofeedback *on* or *to* their patient. This is a powerful learning technology, and the last thing we want is to do it *to* someone or *on* them. The words that reflect the reality of our venture in neurofeedback, at least as I use it, are *for* or *with*. Neurofeedback requires a partnership *with* your patients, and you provide it *for* them.)

Adequate Disclosure of Information

Adequate disclosure of information legally encompasses four areas: diagnosis, the nature and purpose of the treatment, the risks of treatment, and treatment alternatives.

Diagnosis

As I discussed in Chapter 2, there are significant problems with the DSM classification system of psychiatric diagnosis. Emerging neuroscience, brain imaging technologies, and the practice of neurofeedback all challenge the accuracy and usefulness of this nosology. We now have unprecedented access to the brain and growing understanding about how it contributes to problems that are seen as mental or emotional or behavioral, but still do not know how brain function relates to a specific disorder, or indeed if there are such discrete disorders. DSM diagnostic categories are what we have, and we have no choice presently but to use them.

Since neurofeedback is, for now, often the treatment of last resort, most of your patients will come with a diagnosis (or two) in hand. Although developmental trauma is the best descriptor of what has befallen these patients and their developing brains, it is not yet an official diagnosis. However, the single most important aspect of a mental health "diagnosis" is that it accurately describes the condition of the patient to the patient, or her parents, and as we have seen for this group, *developmental trauma* does this best. If the patient understands the likely effects of developmental trauma on her brain, this understanding will more than satisfy the criteria of diagnosis for adequate disclosure, even if developmental trauma isn't officially recognized by the DSM. No other diagnosis currently in play describes more accurately what these patients are experiencing.

Nature and Purpose of the Treatment

The purpose of neurofeedback is easily explained: regulation of dysregulating affect. The first four chapters of this book contain speculations on the nature of this approach. We don't know actually how

neurofeedback works, but we have some compelling directions to
explore. In terms of informed consent, your patient needs to know that
neurofeedback training involves computer-generated biofeedback to the
firing patterns in the brain. Through an auditory signal and either a
video game or a movie, your brain will get feedback when it is making
more of the desired frequencies and less of the undesired. Experience
has repeatedly demonstrated that people and other mammals can learn
to change these patterns. It is noninvasive and does not rely on drugs. I
have to say that I have some ambivalence about referring to neurofeedback as a treatment at all. It is a powerful way to help the brain watch
itself and learn what it already knows somewhere: its own regulation.

The Risks of Treatment

As we have seen, there can be negative effects with the use of neurofeedback, and they can be hard to predict. I don't think of these as side
effects but as effects that provide an informational exchange between the
patient's brain, the patient, and the therapist. It is important to inform
your patient of the possibility of temporary negative effects, particularly
if you assess this brain as unstable, as it is in those with mood swings,
panic attacks, IBS, or migraine, regardless of DSM diagnosis. It is very
important that your patients (1) know that negative effects are possible,
(2) understand that you will address these also with neurofeedback, and
(3) agree to this training with the understanding that this could happen.
It is important for them and for your alliance. Overall, I think that the
most negative outcome in neurofeedback is no response, which can happen. As discussed briefly above, anticipate all possibilities and discuss
them fully with your patient. Discuss, as well, that there is very little way
to predict. Each brain will respond uniquely, but rarely obliquely. In this
regard brain wave training could be understood as a vanguard approach
to personalized medicine.

Treatment Alternatives

At this point in time, most of your patients will come to you after trying most other treatment alternatives—psychotherapy, often many different approaches, and medications, so they are usually well aware of
alternatives. The discussion in this practice may have more to do with

how you will be using complementary treatments along with brain wave training.

Medications can be useful, as they were for me, to help the brain while it learns to regulate itself. Some patients may not be able to forgo medications, but in most cases they will reduce or eliminate their reliance on them over time. Other treatments that I think complement neurofeedback, which many patients may not have considered, include somatic approaches, eye movement desensitization and reprocessing (EMDR), Emotional Freedom Technique (EFT), and trauma-informed body work.

The Freedom of the Patient to Make a Choice

Neurofeedback does not work for everyone, and the patient is always encouraged to make his own decisions about continuing it. The rule of thumb is if you have not any seen changes in 20 sessions, it is likely to be a difficult CNS to budge. That being said, it is not uncommon for the practitioner to notice changes that patients don't notice, either because they are rapidly folding them into their experience of themselves (typical of children) or because the very problem they have makes it hard for them to track or report progress. Patients with RH deficits may not notice changes because of impaired interoception, lack of body awareness, lack of affect regulation, and/or lack of awareness of feelings at all. Sometimes, when they cannot report change, the only way you can know that something is happening is that they return for training. One of my patients asserted regularly, for almost 2 years, that training wasn't helping her, and yet always wanted training. I was also seeing marked changes in her that she was still too overwhelmed to experience. She stayed with it, but if she had decided to end neurofeedback, of course, she would have had every right to do so. If you have used a CPT measure, this might be a good time to retest. It can be reassuring to such patients, and perhaps to yourself as well, to see objective indicators of change.

The Patient's Ability to Understand the Information

As in all matters, this ability varies widely, and it is the clinician's job to make neurofeedback as comprehensible as possible for each patient.

Many people who arrive at my office are impatient with explanations, at least initially. They just want to feel better. A young corporate executive was referred to me by her physician for severe IBS and intractable rectal pain. I made it clear to her on the phone that treating physical illnesses was beyond my scope of practice, but that I could address the anxiety she had over the symptoms. I expected that quieting her arousal would positively affect these physical symptoms, even if only her reactivity to them. In her case, the rectal pain cleared up in three sessions, but it was only after she felt less aroused in general that she was able to be curious about what we were doing. Trauma does not allow curiosity. It promotes urgency, questionable judgment, and lack of trust in one's mind. These patients will ask when they are able to understand. In the interim, you might want to provide them with a frequently asked question (FAQ) sheet (see Appendix B) to take home that includes informative websites.

The Patient's Ability to Make Decisions

Developmental trauma impairs the development of the prefrontal cortex and RH. The prefrontal cortex is the part of the brain devoted to executive function and thus to decision-making. One of the common presenting problems is difficulty in this very area of decision-making. So with this population we begin with some level of impairment in this realm, but rarely so significant as to render the individuals incapable of making a decision about training their brains. We would expect, in fact, that quieting arousal (RH usually) and training for the activation of prefrontal circuits would make it much more possible for them to make decisions over time.

When we add neurofeedback to the psychotherapy regime, clinical experience predicts that we will see significant changes 85–90% of the time, and we will see indications of those changes within the first 20 sessions or sooner. We have no way to know at the assessment stage whether this patient will fall in the 90% or the 10%. To further complicate your informed consent task, there is only one recent study with individuals who have experienced developmental trauma that demonstrates the efficacy of neurofeedback (see Kluetsch et al., 2013), so you can't rely on research into this disorder. But once you have explained basic mechanisms that apply across disorders, such as arousal or fear circuitries, you will be giving your patient the means to make an informed decision.

That being said, it is almost impossible to predict the course an individual will take, and this uncertainty is extremely important to discuss. As part of my informed consent process with patients who have DID, I have discussed the possibility that they will lose discrete alters, that regulation can be a challenge for those who have only known dysregulation, and that they may be less attracted to drama and to relationships dependent on drama. With a patient I knew well, I suggested it was possible that she would lose tolerance for her abusive partner who was also her main source of financial support. This, in fact, came to pass. One of my young patients who had spent most of her childhood in institutions became uninterested in the pastimes of her peers—"getting wasted," racing cars, and numbing out with video games. As she was leaving her session one morning, she asked me the poignant and heartfelt question, "Who will I marry?" She was outgrowing her group and had some understandable fears about how this shift would affect her in important areas.

With neurofeedback we can encounter changes that range from impact on target symptoms to changes in food preference, responses to alcohol and drugs, and, as we've been discussing throughout, changes in sense of self. And none of this might happen. There is a possibility of no change or slow change; change that is too rapid or that is disorienting. Until there are published studies on trauma and neurofeedback, we must represent this approach as "experimental." (See Afterword for more on obstacles to research). And even when these studies materialize, with any given individual we can really guarantee nothing but our own best-informed effort. In light of these realities we need to default to a legal consent form.

Scope of Practice

All of medicine and treatment in general have formed around Descartes' tragic error: his notion of the split between mind and body. Scope of practice codifies Cartesian principles. We have doctors for the mind and doctors for the body. Clinicians who use neurofeedback in their treatment of developmental trauma are, in some manner, doctors of the mind, and their training will qualify them to recognize subtle or not-so-subtle changes in mentation, emotion, and behavior and their significance. They will have had little if any training in illness or afflictions of the body. Mental health licensure relates to advanced training in matters of the mind, and we are forbidden, as we should be, from promoting any treatment of what are thought to be solely physical disorders. We are not trained. However, in reality there is no mind–brain–body separation, and when we train the brain, we train the body. Scope of practice and licensure dictate that neurofeedback practitioners trained in mental health will always be treating mental health complaints, but as we address dysregulation in the mental body, we will also address dysregulation in the physical body. As I have alluded to earlier, we will often find ourselves tracking changes in the brain by changes in bowel function. We cannot, however, claim that we are treating constipation.

As neurofeedback becomes more widely accepted, it is likely that doctors and others trained in physical illness will adopt it. Scope of practice may be even more salient in this situation because most medical people have very little training in the psychological consequences of trauma, either physical or mental, and they have no training in manifestations of emotional deprivation that give rise to transference, distorted sense of self, or in erratic behavior from mood dysregulation. Given the power of this technology and to be in a conversation with the brain, you really need to know these things. I would actively discourage anyone from practicing neurofeedback who does not have mental health training and an advanced degree in their field. Observe your limits. If you don't have the training you need, affiliate with someone who does, and know that you will inevitably tread on domains outside your legal scope of practice because in the brain, it's all about regulation.

A patient with a history of profound emotional neglect, two serious suicide attempts, and multiple hospitalizations wanted to try neurofeedback to address a lifelong, intractable depression. After the first session, he noted a lifting in his spirits, an increase in his energy, and the quite common "clean windshield effect" whereby colors were more vivid and the world in general more dimensional, more alive. I altered the protocol slightly, believing—falsely, as it turned out—that raising his arousal (C3 at 15–18 Hz) had yielded these results. We had done 6 minutes of left-side training the first time. At 7 minutes, in the second session, he went into a full-blown neuropathy attack, resulting in severe pain in his feet and legs. I stopped left-side training—I had raised his arousal too much —and trained him for 20 minutes on the right to quiet things down (C4 at 10–13 Hz). Clearly, "treating" neuropathy was beyond my scope of practice, but for him it turned out to be a signature symptom of arousal. The neuropathy attack, which usually lasted 3 days, was over within a half an hour. His highly reactive nervous system manifested in psychological symptoms such as anxiety and depression, behaviorally in impulsivity and overspending, and physically in neuropathy: one mind–body.

Touch

Neurofeedback requires touch, and providers need to discuss the reality of this with their patients, who, as adults must consent, of course, to the touching of their heads. You may have to work with this issue of touch in creative ways with terrorized children or with other torture survivors, many of whom have endured electric shock. In both cases they will quickly learn that this use of touch and of electrodes is positive. For a person who has endured assaults to the head—a very common problem in those with developmental trauma—touch to the head can evoke intense and complex feelings of fear, shame, gratitude, relief, or all of the above. At the beginning of training, particularly, pay close attention to how you touch your patient's head and how she responds to it. It may be important with some patients to discuss this issue more than once. All of this being said, in my experience, this kind of touch has not presented an obstacle.

Trust

As we know, trust is not the long suit for trauma survivors. You are going to be, by agreement, rearranging the patterns in their brains. Engaging in this endeavor puts a heavy demand on trust. Some patients will fear mind control specifically, whereas others will be afraid of the power presumably in the hands of the other. These fears arise in the heightened arousal we are attempting to change, but until these concerns can be sufficiently eased in therapeutic conversation, we cannot go ahead with training. In these circumstances the first goal is to grow the therapeutic alliance. Patients will need, or at the very least profit from, neurofeedback (we all would), but it has to come in their time and within the boundaries of a trusted relationship. This presents us with a bit of a Catch-22 situation that we and our patients have to negotiate together.

Transference

As we have discussed earlier, the paradigm shift affects the transference. As I introduce training to those with whom there is already a transference relationship, I acknowledge the changes and discuss the tradeoffs between time with me in conversation and time with me and the training. These are very real concerns and will become less of an issue if they are acknowledged and discussed. These issues are less likely to concern those who come to us primarily for neurofeedback; however, they can arise as these patients begin to experience the reality of our presence. It may seem somewhat reductionist, but in the realm of the brain, transference can be understood as the drive of the dysregulated CNS to find regulation. Abandonment is a core issue in this population—it long outlasts discrete trauma as an issue—and you are likely to encounter fears of abandonment, either to the training itself or to a more global and looming fear: the loss of you should they gain self-regulation. We'll talk more about this in Chapter 8. For now, my point is that it is a concern to be understood and tracked from the first session.

Speed of Change

We have already established that we can't know how quickly change will happen, but for many it can be fairly quickly, particularly when compared to psychotherapy alone. It is important to predict this, as well as to caution that it can also be a slow and cumulative process. (I think neurofeedback is always cumulative.) One young girl decided not to train when I suggested that this would ease her constant state of worry.

She was alarmed because she thought of her worries as early warning signs that helped her predict inevitable danger. She felt that she wouldn't be safe if she were no longer scared. My patients with DID have expressed considerable fear over losing alters. Neurofeedback seemed tantamount to an offer to excise vital aspects of themselves. These possibilities are frightening enough when they are encountered slowly and incompletely in psychotherapy; they can be terrifying if they happen in something close to overnight. It can also be disruptive if the change is slower than anticipated. Often, the patient with developmental trauma worries that this approach, like everything else, will not work for him or her. And, of course, it might not. All of these issues should be talked through at the beginning.

Neurofeedback for Another Therapist's Patient

The problems pertaining to developmental trauma are notoriously treatment resistant. As neurofeedback becomes more widely recognized and as your colleagues see the results you are getting, it is likely that you will be approached to provide brain wave training for patients struggling in their standard treatments. Due to the complexity of developmental trauma in adults, including the complexity of the transference, I would be cautious about assuming this adjunctive role. There would be three active "treaters" in the picture: you, the primary therapist, and the training. The transference implications are daunting. Further, when self-regulation is the goal, it is difficult to decide whether psychotherapy or neurofeedback is actually the ancillary treatment. If you know the referring therapist well, and he (1) has an understanding of neurofeedback, (2) understands the subtle and not-so-subtle indicators of change related to neurofeedback, and (3) is prepared for the possibility that the patient might end up wanting to see you, then it could work. But more often than not, this arrangement will create problems between you and your referring colleagues and may well disrupt regulation more than enhance it. This is a caution and not a rule. For those dealing with developmental trauma, receiving neurofeedback and psychotherapy from an attachment-oriented therapist is the best option.

Self-Training

It is astonishing and dismaying to me how many people in this field have never trained their brains or have trained only briefly. To me this is a basic requirement for neurofeedback providers. It is more important than knowing how to read a Q or learning how to track numerical EEG values. There is no better way to understand the impact of neurofeedback than to provide it for yourself. There is what may be an urban legend about one of the more influential figures in the field. He was resistant to trying this technology for himself. When colleagues finally convinced him to do so, he reported that an allergic reaction to the connective paste had sent him to the doctor, and according to the story, he never tried it again. It seems likely that he trained his arousal too high and didn't recognize this for what it was—a gateway to discovery about arousal and state—but instead found a way to excuse himself from further personal exploration. He was captured by his uncomfortable, probably unfamiliar state and his paradigm about how neurofeedback should be done. I very much want the field to adopt the standard adhered to by psychoanalysts: You have to do it, to provide it.

The Devoted Other

This anecdote well captures the problem of state and its convincing narrative. To avoid the trap of believing self-justifying states, you need to engage with another person, whom a colleague has called a "devoted other," someone whose feedback you will privilege over your own. The best candidate for this vital assignment is someone who not only knows you well but who has done neurofeedback and understands it. And once you begin, you have to observe the same contract with yourself that you ask your patients to make.

1. *Everything relates to the training until you can rule it out.* I listen as carefully as I can to shifts in tone or vocabulary describing internal states. It was, at first, very easy for me to inadvertently jack up my arousal. I started to recognize a shift in my internal dialogue from "We are all bozos on the bus" to thinking "They are jerks" or worse. The difference in narrative—the change from *we* to *them* and from inclusion to

insult—was arousal. This level of tracking requires a capacity for self-awareness that was itself made possible by regulating affect. I would check my own perceptions about myself, essentially asking my devoted others about how they experienced my arousal, and most of the time heeding their feedback. My partner is one of my devoted others. I arrived home one afternoon, took a cursory look around the house, and said, somewhat demonstratively, "We need to clean this place!" It was due a cleaning, but it was my arousal that alerted him to ask, "Did you do left-side training today?" I had, and I could see with this feedback, that I had done a little too much!

2. *Keep track of protocols and effects.* Even when my colleagues train themselves, many don't keep notes. We are all state-dependent creatures, and therefore we will forget where we were and what a given training did. We need to keep track of our responses, our states, any deep shifts we may experience, positive or negative, at each session. This is the most important way to teach ourselves to "think neurofeedback." Your experiences may well make an important contribution to the ever-expanding conversation about neurofeedback among its practitioners. And, as noted for our patients, it's not just about changes in symptoms. As mentioned before, neurofeedback is a cumulative practice and part of keeping a running account is to keep track of the accumulation. Brain wave training is optimally a journey of deep personal unfolding, and you have access to the instrument that makes it uniquely possible. Take the time to train regularly and to note its effects. Be as interested (even more interested) in yourself as you are in your patients.

3. *Try different protocols when you and your devoted other don't like what you are feeling.* As you experience being able to change your felt sense of self as well as your acid reflux or sugar craving, you will know the reality of brain plasticity like few others do. Perhaps the fundamental rule in training yourself is to attend to your experience without believing it. This is a meditation instruction, and it falls along the continuum of "easier said than done," particularly when you are also recovering from developmental trauma. When I went to Bessel van der Kolk's Trauma Center to train the staff, I asked for anyone with a history of childhood trauma to talk with me before we did our first session. Bessel said, "This is a trauma center; everyone here has been traumatized." If you are deal-

ing with these issues, don't train alone. The whole point is to come increasingly into relationship, and you, like your patients, will need the devoted other to deeply engage with you as you change your brain.

Mentoring

Most practitioners get into neurofeedback after a 3- or 4-day initial course. It is profoundly not enough. Not only should you train yourself and friends for several months before you begin with patients, you will also need to find a mentor or two to guide you through your first year of training both yourself and others. You will be able to find mentors most readily among those clinicians who also use your neurofeedback system. A very gifted young practitioner happened to mention to me that she was severely hypoglycemic. It had not occurred to her to train herself until I mentioned it in our mentoring session. If you can arrange this type of relationship with someone nearby, that's best. You will have a chance then for close, personal supervision. But in most cases, you will receive your mentoring by phone, Skype, and/or e-mail. I only use the phone, not e-mail, because mentoring is an inquiry about subtle states in both the patient and the therapist, and these cannot be well represented in e-mail. The clues we need usually surface in the interchange between practitioners. Look for someone with a background in working with developmental trauma and neurofeedback, but if you can't find that person, then someone who is deeply and broadly experienced in neuro-feedback and affect regulation. As with my young mentee, your mentor can serve as one of your devoted others, to some degree. As you begin this practice and are introducing your patients to their brains, make sure you have also introduced yourself to yours.

Chapter 6

"Thinking Neurofeedback"

The Art and Science of Clinical Assessment

One of the many strengths of neurofeedback as part of the therapeutic endeavor is the requirement for a fresh assessment at every session. The process of neurofeedback is reminiscent of the saying "You never step into the same stream twice." It has to be the case that when neurofeedback is working, we are never training the same brain twice. In psychotherapy with developmental trauma, it can feel, though, as if we are stepping into the same standing and turbulent pool over and over again. By definition and diagnosis, this nervous system has little fluidity or flexibility; it has no flow. When your patient responds to training, you know that flow, however erratic, has begun. Assessing this course, session by session, is the key to protocol design and to successful neurofeedback.

Assessment in neurofeedback is, in effect, an ongoing conversation with our patient's brain, learning to hear what it is trying to tell us, and learning how to respond. In short, it is learning to "think neurofeedback." All of us have been trained in one way or another to assess our patient's state of mind. When you add neurofeedback, you are adding an assessment of the state of your patient's brain before, during, and after every session.

As a part of the assessment, I talk with my patients about how they might feel were a symptom or characteristic to disappear. People can like these symptoms and in fact prosper with them. As I have said, they may even identify themselves, consciously or unconsciously, through them. In as much as the symptoms are manifestations of dysregulation, they are likely to be affected as the brain becomes increasingly organized and stable. This discussion is a vital part of the process of informed consent in neurofeedback, as discussed in Chapter 5.

An assessment of my state of mind after my first weekend training might have been dire (Introduction). People were worried. I was hypomanic, I had pressured speech, I was not sleeping, and I had a level 8 migraine headache. These symptoms meant that we had trained my brain in a frequency range that was too high for me, and it had raised my arousal too high. We needed to reassess and revise protocols and to lower the frequency of the reward, which was not possible at that point in time (there were only two reward bands available then, and I was already using the one that was supposed to calm me down). But as you may remember, another layer down, I felt an abiding sense of calm, of oneness, and of quieted fear. I experienced both my overaroused emotional mind but also some foundational change in the lived-in habitual reactivity of my brain.

Listening to the Brain

Mind and brain are interdependent, emerging properties, and in that sense they are not distinct and yet not the same. When I assess a patient after a neurofeedback session, I listen for two reports that may or may not align: the report from the mind and the report from the brain. A simple example of these dual reports would be the patient who tells me that she is as anxious as ever and then later on, often in a response to my "sleuthing the ANS," reports that she has had no constipation, a chronic problem, since the last session. I am sure that her subjective experience (her mind) is as reported—she feels no change—but I also know that positive change in the brain is occurring: in this case, that there is evidence of parasympathetic activity in the regulation of the bowel, where there had been sympathetic dominance before. The system is quieting down and finding its way toward balance. Although she cannot yet feel the changes subjectively, I know that we are on the right track and I will make protocol decisions accordingly. In the mind–brain dichotomy, the mind will offer you subjective indicators more often than objective ones (it is its nature), and the body–brain will provide the clearer objective indications. Trust the latter.

Sammy, the 4-year-old boy who was described by his workers in the Department of Youth and Families to be the most severely disturbed child they had seen, was overtaken by night terrors, and then slept through the night after his first neurofeedback session. This response signaled a dramatic change in his nervous system, but he was still feral in the morning. Due to his age and his profound deprivation, Sammy was little more than his brain, wildly firing behind his dark, glazed eyes. He was yet to develop the capacity for mind. For him, developing a mind would depend on neurofeedback organizing his brain, as the good mother soothes and organizes her baby's overwhelming affect. No adoptive or foster parents, no matter how devoted or how skilled, could withstand the unrelenting onslaught that was Sammy. Had neurofeedback not worked, he would have been institutionalized and probably, like Carl, deemed untreatable. Quieting the reactivity of his nervous system, would allow him to propagate self and other, the very foundation of mind.

I find that this is a useful if false dichotomy in thinking about particular patients. Are their difficulties primarily brain problems or problems in the way they have learned to think or reinforced to act? After years of assessment and work with this population, I think it is safe to say that patients with developmental trauma are always more brain than mind. As we discussed in Chapter 3, the goal is to nudge the brain out of its rigid, reactive, and repeating patterns and toward its own inherent complexity. As you do, you will see the blossoming of a complex mind.

Sammy and his foster parents lived in a cabin next door to me. He came to them as an emergency placement in late November, and he gobbled his hoarded Thanksgiving meal under the table, glowering and grunting. In January, he sat at the table and in February, he offered to share some of his food. As most of you know, even much less disturbed children with developmental trauma can have great difficulty making eye contact. It is a signature symptom. In May, 7 months after he started neurofeedback, Sammy ran over to me and jumped into my arms. I was wearing polarized sunglasses. He leaned back and protested, "Seboin, I can't see your eyes!" He was training two to three times a week.

Thinking Neurofeedback

Part of the clinical appeal of the qEEG is that you can feel as if you have been given a certified training path. In the nearly infinite field of possible protocols, this can be comforting. As I discussed in Chapter 5, Qs can offer you exactly this clarity at times, but not yet routinely. Some people use systems that rely on a single protocol, a one-size-fits-all approach, banking on appealing to the brain's nonlinear dynamical "wish" to self-regulate, without protocols that specifically target CNS arousal or the functioning of different brain areas. We are all, of course, banking on this inherent bias of the brain toward self-regulation, and all versions of neurofeedback tap into the nonlinear, dynamical, pattern-making nature of the brain. I follow the arousal model as it applies to activation of brain regions because I typically get robust clinical outcomes when I do.

I need to make a momentary detour here. I often hear confusion among practitioners over the terms *arousal* and *activation*. They are not the same. We activate the brain area and its associated networks beneath wherever we place the electrodes. The frequency at which we set the reward will determine the level of arousal. For example, I use C4–P4 when there is a complaint of reflux, gastrointestinal problems, or constipation. Since it works, this placement must be activating some circuitry that informs the vagus. The placement matters. We won't get the same response if we train frontally, for example. We have activated something at a certain frequency. The frequency matters. If I train too high for this individual, the reflux could get worse. When you adopt the arousal–regulation model you will learn how to listen to the brain and to follow the path prescribed by symptoms. This is learning to *think neurofeedback*. The whole premise seems preposterous: We affect major brain circuits and the states to which they give rise with three silver sensors and a beep. But that is exactly what happens, and it is exactly what we are tracking when we *think neurofeedback*. Thinking neurofeedback can be broken down into four major components:

1. *Once you begin neurofeedback, no matter what the symptom or report, you must first consider the impact of the training.* This may seem self-evident, but it is often a core challenge when you have been trained, as most of us have been, without reference to the brain. There is a tendency to default to a more familiar paradigm to understand the change or lack of change that we are seeing. For example, a patient might tell you about a crying meltdown with her spouse a day or so after training. She might cite this as evidence of her innate badness, or of her spouse's narcissism —any number of things that will characteristically constitute a reprise of themes already well known and well rehearsed. As a psychotherapist, you might well understand her mood as a result of the fight or of her ambivalence about her relationship. You will think about how she thinks about the incident.

As a neurofeedback clinician, however, you will primarily assess her meltdown in terms of her arousal, and as we discussed in Chapter 5, attribute her arousal first to training, with only a glancing regard to the details of the conflict. Once we begin training, our emphasis is on the brain's response more than it is on our patient's interpretation of her response. Of course, the circumstances have information in them, but you are primarily focusing on the training effect on emotion regulation, not on the story, per se. When there is no change or change that seems too slow, psychodynamic therapists can default to a familiar construction and think of this as resistance. When we do, we have subtly shifted our emphasis from brain function to the more familiar constructs of mind. It may be possible for a person to resist training, but I doubt it. What interest, other than habit, would any brain have in undermining its own regulation? Symptoms are either manifestations of dysregulation, failed attempts to regulate, or both. The patient may have a poorly informed and overly determined identification with these symptoms, but her brain doesn't.

2. *Follow the fear.* When you adopt the arousal model, you assess for shifts in arousal and with patients with developmental trauma, this means primarily shifts toward quieting terror and its ensuing chaos. As a general rule, when arousal is too high, you will reward the brain to

produce lower frequencies. We discuss how low you can train a brain in the next chapter on protocols. The arousal-based answer to how low you can train is, I warn you, controversial. I'll address the controversy briefly as well. There are plenty of people with developmental trauma who will say that they like the feeling of being "jacked up." Although they are strung out along their last nerve, they may drink copious amounts of coffee. It serves their hypervigilance, and as we have discussed earlier, it is the only state they know. When this overaroused state is syntonic, your patient is unlikely to agree that he needs to lower his arousal. Don't be swayed. Your job for these patients is to quiet the habitual firing of fear circuits. These are never underactivated or underaroused in people with developmental trauma.

3. *Follow the brain's preference.* Every response after a training session is data from the brain. When we are training to quiet arousal, if our patient begins to have trouble with word recall or with waking up frequently, then we have new protocol decisions to consider. It bears repeating that there are no side effects in neurofeedback training, only negative or positive effects, and these constitute direct communication from the brain about what it prefers. When you are thinking neurofeedback, you'll follow the brain's lead. What it prefers is what it should get.

4. *Think plasticity.* When you begin to think neurofeedback, you will think brain plasticity. If you and your patient like where the brain has gone, you will train more sessions at this protocol. If you don't, you can train the brain to "back out" of its momentary dysregulation. These decisions are based on patient report, on what you observe, and on objective body-based indicators. Training those with developmental trauma can be a long process. When it is, it can be encouraging to remember Schore's (2003) statement on plasticity: "Current brain research . . . indicates that the capacity for experience-dependent plastic changes in the nervous system remain throughout the life span. In fact, there is very specific evidence that the prefrontal limbic cortex, more than any other part of the cerebral cortex, retains the plastic capacities of early development" (p. 202). With patients who have suffered developmental trauma, it is likely that we will train prefrontally, and it is important to remember that we are always directly tapping into the brain's plasticity, not just prefrontally, but everywhere.

The Assessment Process

Most neurofeedback practitioners develop their own approaches to assessment. This is my description of my process, but by no means the last word. As you will see when you review the sample assessment questionnaire in the Appendix A (the tables in this chapter reproduce the parts of each section of this form most salient to developmental trauma), there are many more aspects of assessment than we can discuss here. I am choosing to focus on the symptoms that provide the most information about the nervous system and the various adult manifestations of developmental trauma. The original assessment is, of course, done before you begin to train, and we discuss that first. But ongoing, session-by-session assessment is essential, and I talk about that process as well. At the beginning, we are essentially proceeding on an educated guess, knowing that the brain's responses will soon guide us. It is also important to note that the first training can yield novel effects (as can be the case after the first training with a new placement). You can't always count on seeing these results after the second training even with exactly the same protocol. I have seen this often enough to consider the effects of the first training session as provisional, awaiting confirmation from the second.

Initial Assessment

The initial assessment consists of the review of any prior testing that the patient has undergone and a thorough clinical history with a particular emphasis on: significant, unrepaired attachment breaks; experiences of neglect; early childhood trauma; head injury; seizures; and the effects of medications and other drugs. Take the time to get to know your patient while giving him or her time to know you. Don't rush this initial period, even when your patients are impatient to get started. It is a time to learn not only their history but to get a sense of their level of baseline arousal, their ability to relate to you, and the idiosyncrasies of their brains. Short of any real emergencies, take the time before you train each patient to get a well-informed sense of the brain you will be encountering.

I intertwine the clinical history-taking with the neurofeedback assessment. This process generally takes 2–3 hours, sometimes less and sometimes longer depending on the complexity of the patient's presenting symptoms, her experiences in life, and her willingness and/or capacity to talk about them. The assessment questionnaire has a clinical history section and seven distinct categories of symptoms and/or diagnoses that relate to arousal and structure. Anyone doing neurofeedback should know how to take a clinical history, so I don't discuss that topic here.

To begin, the assessment questionnaire is laid out with attention to the brain's laterality (my form, in Appendix A, is based on the original arousal–regulation model authored by Sue and Siegfried Othmer). Symptoms that typically indicate underarousal are on the left side of the form and typically signify the need to raise arousal by training at a higher frequency on the LH. We consider different LH and RH placements and why you might use them when we discuss protocol selection in Chapter 7.

The symptoms suggesting overarousal and the common need for RH training are on the right, and symptoms that suggest underarousal and the need for LH training are on the left. Symptoms suggesting either instability or the need to train both hemispheres are in the middle of the page. Instabilities usually benefit the most from interhemispheric train-ing. Although I find this form very helpful in guiding my protocol decisions, much of the language we use can mislead us. Every symptom a patient checks off has to be assessed in the context of his history and in the light of all other endorsed symptoms. I'll give examples of this process as we go through the first category: attention symptoms.

Assessing Attention

It is important to remember that much of the clinical work and recent research in neurofeedback has been in ADD and ADHD. The focus in the field has therefore been on attention much more than it has been on affect regulation. When there is early childhood trauma and neglect, it is useful to consider attention in relation to emotional dysregulation. It can be very difficult to pay attention to math problems when one is braced against imminent threat. With patients who have developmental trauma, some of the typical indications for LH training may actually confirm the need to address the RH. Let's explore how this works. Table 6.1 catego-

Table 6.1. Attention Symptoms in Relation to Arousal Level and Training Approach		
Underarousal: Train the LH	**Instability: Train both hemispheres**	**Overarousal: Train the RH**
• ADD • Inattention (internal) • Daydreaming • Poor concentration • Lack of motivation	• ADHD • Hyperactivity after sugar • Hyperactivity after sedatives • Overwhelmed by stimuli • Difficulty making decisions • Disorganized	• Impulsivity • Distractibility (external) • Stimulus seeking • Thrill seeking • Competing thoughts, too many thoughts

rizes the attention-related symptoms covered in the assessment questionnaire in Appendix A and notes how they will inform protocol selection.

I have worked with very few people with developmental trauma who endorse ADD, but I have had many check all the other symptoms in the left-hand column and, quite commonly, ADHD. When you have understood the problem in terms of developmental trauma, you may need to make some important translations. When a patient checks "inattention," I ask if she can describe what makes paying attention difficult. Invariably, it will boil down to the unbearable distraction of unmanageable affect, as is also the case when patients endorse "poor concentration" and "lack of motivation." But don't assume this is so. When a patient endorses "daydreaming," I investigate the nature of it, listening for, but not imposing, the possibility of dissociative process. If these translations seem right to you and your patient, then all of these typically left-side symptoms move to the right, and you would expect them to be addressed, at least in good measure, by RH training.

All of the symptoms in the right-hand column clearly indicate overarousal and are actually very reliable indicators for RH training. There is no quiet in this nervous system. When you are eliciting the symptom profile, ask your patient if he has ever had these symptoms, even if they are no longer a problem. If a patient used to be a thrill seeker as a kid, but has grown out of it, you will still want to take note. When she endorses a symptom, ask for an example of what the patient means, to make sure the symptom has a similar valence for both of you. Roller-coaster rides indicate thrill-seeking behavior; so is playing "chicken" in a car at midnight. You are trying to understand the background of this patient's nervous system, and details matter. Any symptom that is in the background of the CNS could become foreground and recur during training.

A 44-year-old patient with developmental trauma had an episode of sleepwalking, which she hadn't had since age 10. As we will see shortly, sleepwalking is a signature symptom of unstable arousal and poor state transitions in sleep. The training didn't cause it; it found it. If the symptom has remained important to the brain, it will recur, but usually briefly—a swan song. Even if you never see it again, knowing the former symptom helps you to understand the tilt of this particular nervous system. In this case you might begin to wonder what part instability plays in the clinical picture. If it is going to play a large role, other symptoms of instability will be endorsed. The most common of these in patients with developmental trauma are "overwhelmed by stimuli," "hard to make decisions," and "disorganized." How could it be otherwise? When you have completed this category, you will begin to get a glimpse of the arousal puzzle. As often noted previously, most patients with developmental trauma will need RH and interhemispheric training—except of course for the few who won't. The brain will let you know.

Assessing Sleep

Sleep is, of course, a critical problem for many who have suffered from developmental trauma. They can't fall asleep or stay asleep, some because they are afraid to yield to unconsciousness, some because they fear the onset of yet another night of nightmares, some who associate sleep with abuse and others with less focal issues, but who have been left fundamentally neurologically disorganized. In sleep, as in waking, we all need an optimal level of arousal for the task. If arousal is too low, we may snore or develop sleep apnea because muscle tone at the back of the mouth and throat is too low. Table 6.2 summarizes symptoms of sleep issues to guide us as we gather more information to determine our initial protocol(s).

Table 6.2. Sleep Symptoms in Relation to Arousal Level and Training Approach		
Underarousal: **Train the LH**	**Instability:** **Train both hemispheres**	**Overarousal:** **Train the RH**
• Night sweats • Frequent waking, without agitation • Sleeping lightly • Sleeping too much • Sleep apnea (nonobstructive) • Snoring • Not rested after sleep • Waking early • Difficulty falling asleep; mind quiet	• Night terrors • Nocturnal myoclonus (jerking or moving while asleep) • Sleepwalking • Sleep talking • Narcolepsy (falling asleep frequently or suddenly) • Too busy to sleep (manic quality) • Night sweats • Bed-wetting (enuresis) • Sleep paralysis when awakening; still dreaming when awake	• Difficulty falling asleep; busy mind • Hot flashes during sleep • Physically restless sleep • Bruxism (teeth grinding) • Nightmares or vivid dreams • Restless leg syndrome • Clenching jaw • Waking with agitation • Vigilant sleep

For most patients with developmental trauma, problems with sleep fall almost entirely in the right-hand column. Their sleep is also over-aroused. You would expect these symptoms, like all other symptoms of overarousal, to slowly but clearly remit. Neurofeedback is considered very effective for regulating sleep and when it is going to work, you will typically see these changes early in the process. Sometimes, however, and more so with this population, normalizing sleep may take many sessions and, in a few cases, sleep remains elusive. I am one of those cases. My original goal when I went for my weekend training marathon was to sleep normally. I was a vigilant sleeper. I could startle awake when my partner entered the room, even when he did so very quietly. The vigilance is long gone, but I still sleep poorly, a bad habit that persists in some stubborn or as yet untouched oscillatory realm. By contrast, my 96-year-old friend who trained to quiet neuropathic pain reported "sleeping like a baby" for the first time in her life from the first session on.

Sleep is an excellent indicator of the flexibility of the CNS. When training helps patients normalize their sleep and does so quickly, it predicts that the training will go well. These individuals are receptive to training. Sammy, whose nights were consumed by night terrors, slept for 12 hours every night after his first session. Even though neurofeedback has not normalized my sleep—nothing has—it is no worse, and I am no longer reactive to being awake when I should be asleep. As in all things, the magnitude and significance of any problem diminish when we are no longer reactive to it.

Brain instability often manifests in what are seen as the most disruptive sleep problems. Sleep talking and sleepwalking, common in these childhoods, are symptoms of failure in the neurological mechanism that facilitates sleep paralysis, which stops us from acting out what we are dreaming. Sammy didn't sleep. He crawled on the floor of his foster parents' bedroom calling out "No! No! No!" for hours, terrified and unconscious. They could not wake him and he had no apparent memory for these events when he would awake at 5:00 A.M., sometimes collapsed over his hands and knees. We could hardly call that sleep.

The brain is most vulnerable to seizure or other unstable firing patterns when we are negotiating the state change from waking to sleeping and from sleeping to waking. Seizure patients are most prone to seizure during these transitions, and patients with developmental trauma can also come up against their own instability particularly as they are falling asleep, when they begin to orient toward waking usually around 3:00 A.M., and again as they begin to wake up in the morning. As mentioned, they can fail to engage normal sleep paralysis and they can also have trouble pulling out of it when it is engaged. Three of my patients reported experiences in which they were awake for several minutes but unable to move. Their brains did not release them immediately from sleep paralysis, even though they felt fully awake. This is quite frightening when it happens, and as seems true for sleep terrors, sleepwalking, and excitable sleep talking, it has the deep imprint of trauma memory. Over time with training, the nervous system learns to negotiate these state changes more smoothly, and these symptoms fade.

People who report that they don't dream or that they don't remember their dreams may well begin to remember them. As we are waking up, we are transitioning from delta to theta to alpha and then to alert beta states. When we make this transition slowly and smoothly, uninterrupted by a suitably named alarm clock, or any other claim made by the waking world, we are much more likely to remember dreams. Maintaining yourself long enough in alpha will allow you to hold onto the images and to take them with you into beta. Interestingly, one of the changes people will report while training is their ability to rely on their internal clocks and to wake up without alarms. We could see this as a brain attuned to its own natural sleep–wake rhythms.

Dreams and Nightmares. Nightmares are a signature symptom in PTSD and often in developmental trauma as well. One of my patients futilely fought sleep, even while drugging herself to attain it, because she was so afraid of her nightmares. Her nightmare content was repetitive and rarely elucidating. They were night events of more gratuitous suffering and as such became a target symptom of heightened arousal. After several months of training her to lower her arousal, they went away. This is the expected course, but as is always true, it doesn't always happen. One patient with an appalling history of daily, sadistic violence has trained for over a hundred sessions. She had become much more emotionally regulated and cognitively well organized, but she still had nightmares and vivid dreams. Her nightmares, however, overflowed with important content; they were anything but gratuitous. They gave us further insight into what had happened and how she has dealt with it. When she was not having nightmares, she was having vivid dreams also resplendent with meaning, and more often than not, beautiful. Since she is no longer afraid of these dreams, they are losing their nightmare status. I consider nightmares an objective indicator of arousal and, as such, watch for this pattern to change. For this patient, the nightmares and vivid dreams were essential to her recovery and when I realized that, we took them off the list of target symptoms. They eventually subsided.

Dream content, even when the dreams are not vivid, can change in response to neurofeedback. A woman dealing with significant attachment problems was plagued by anxious dreams in which she could never reach the party she was calling. She came to understand the meaning of these dreams, but analyzing them did not stop them. Understanding them was not sufficient to change them or the core anxiety that gave rise to them. As we would expect, these dreams slowly evaporated as she calmed her CNS.

I ask practitioners, particularly those who are working with children, to take special note of dream content. If it turns violent, it can mean that you have trained your patient's arousal up too high, even if you are not yet seeing this overarousal manifest behaviorally. I still believe that dreams are the "royal road to the unconscious," as Freud put it, and that they also inform us, perhaps more reliably, about states of arousal. With these patients it is helpful to address their dreams with arousal in mind. For patients like Carl, there seems to be no unconscious to travel toward. The unconscious is also an interpersonal construction, which begins to develop in the interaction of mother and child. It is an aspect of self. Although this topic is far beyond the scope of this book, it is an observation that suggests that as we help organize a nervous system to underwrite a sense of self, we will also witness more dimensionality in our patients. They begin to develop not only a sense of self that is deeper and richer than the thin biological imperative they have been living out, but also a sense of their own unconscious mind.

Dreams too will become more meaningful and often more complex. It will be clear when the content is meaningful and the dreams themselves useful and when they are just more random violent noise. It has been through my experience with dreams that I have come to one of my primary tenets in neurofeedback: Whatever is productive is good, even when painful. (In Chapter 7 we discuss training experiences that brought this principle home to me.) Whatever is stagnant, looping, or repetitive is not productive. When emotion moves, it is positive even when that emotion is sadness or grief. I never target either feeling with training, unless it gets stuck. I support flow.

Sleep Hygiene. Adult patients with developmental trauma, as a group, practice poor sleep hygiene. Unable to fall asleep readily, many watch TV in bed. The sleep–wake cycle is foundational to the brain's rhythmic regulation, so working toward establishing this circadian rhythm is important. Of course, the content of TV programs that many of these patients choose is violent and disturbing, in its own right. "Law and

Order: Special Victims Unit" seems to be a particular favorite. My patients have told me that they feel understood and assured of the justice that few, if any, actually received. But this is not the fare of lullabies. The challenges for sleep may not be in the content alone. Ed Hamlin wrote: "LCD screens are loaded toward the blue end of the light spectrum (often used to activate a depressed person's brain). Blue light tells the brain to shut off its melatonin production and start waking up. . . . TV can have an impact on our sleep, quantity and quality" (Ed Hamlin, personal communication, March 17, 2013).

Some individuals disrupt their sleep by drinking too much caffeine or drinking it too late in the day. Few of these patients get adequate exercise, and those who do exercise are often doing that too, without regulation, for regulation. Compulsive exercise, like compulsive food restriction, provides a single point of focus. With the mind preoccupied like this, there is little room for self-reflection. When assessing for sleep problems, you'll want to cover the whole terrain of good sleep hygiene and work with your patient to work with you toward regulation of this basic sleep–wake rhythm. The questions about sleep in Table 6.2 and in the assessment questionnaire in Appendix A are self-evident except for the last one: "Do you dream in color?" This is my personal research question based on the completely unsupported notion that dreaming in color would correlate positively with a well-organized brain. To date, I have no data that clearly support this idea, but I am collecting it.

Assessing Emotional and Behavioral Symptoms

Everyone, it seems, is depressed, and it appears, even when they are not, they are on antidepressants. I am reminded of a scene from a 1980s movie in which a man begins to panic in a Hollywood restaurant and asks if anyone has a Valium. All of the diners reach into their pockets or handbags. Today it would be SSRIs. Almost everyone who comes to consult with me is on an SSRI, or has been on at least one at some point in their lives, for depression but also for anxiety. The first two symptoms in this category, anxiety and depression, can be tricky to understand and assign accurately to the arousal spectrum, and they can never be understood from the terms themselves. See Table 6.3 for an overview of the following discussion.

Table 6.3.   Emotional and Behavioral Symptoms in Relation to Arousal Level and Training Approach

Underarousal: Train the LH	Instability: Train both hemispheres	Overarousal: Train the RH
• Anxiety (worry) • Depression (blue, low) • Helpless and hopeless • Irritability • Passivity • Feelings easily hurt • Obsessive thoughts • Withdrawal when stressed • Guilt • "Wish I were dead" • Grumpy • Thinks little of self • Performance anxiety • Rumination • Shyness • Whiney • Fidgety • Seasonal affective disorder • Jealousy/envy • Listless	• Binge eating • Anorexia • Bulimia • Bipolar episodes • Panic attacks • Encopresis (soiling) • Irritable bowel syndrome (IBS) • Dissociative identity disorder (DID) • Borderline personality disorder (BPD) • Posttraumatic stress disorder (PTSD) • Developmental trauma • Rages • Anti-social personality disorder	• Anxiety (fear) • Depression—agitated • Anger • Aggressive; initiates conflict • Lacks remorse • Agitation • Paranoia • Suicide plans or actions • Shame • Compulsive behavior • Self-hatred • Suicide plans or actions • Dissociative • Lacks empathy • No cause and effect • Exhaustion • Controlling; manipulative • Poor understanding of emotions • Holds a grudge • Lack of body awareness • Loud, unmodulated voice • Humorless • Poor eye contact • Poor social awareness • Road rage • Hair pulling or twirling • Involuntary movement • Nail biting, nervous habits • Attachment disruption/disorder • Autistic symptoms

Anxiety. Anxiety is a very different experience for different people, and we want to pursue what this symptom means for each patient, as precisely as we can. Patients with developmental trauma often endorse symptoms on both the left and right sides of the questionnaire. There is no question that they are afraid, and people who are afraid will worry. For most of these patients, the tendency to worry will give way with RH training and be exacerbated by training on the left, particularly at the higher frequencies typically used to raise arousal. People with these childhoods need to quiet ambient fear, and all symptoms have to be understood in their personal historical context. To further discern the nature of anxiety, I want to assess patients' felt sense of threat and their reaction to it. A patient's vulnerability to threat, actual and perceived will give you good information about sudden activation of subcortical switches. In almost all cases, patients will feel overcome by amygdala-driven affects. Perhaps the most disabling and distorting of these, as we have discussed, is shame. The most common reaction is fear and many of these patients are driven as well by anger. These affects underlie most, if not all, of the symptoms listed in the right column.

Depression. Depression in this population rarely signifies under-arousal, but most patients with developmental trauma think of themselves as helpless and hopeless, descriptors that suggest underarousal. The words are troublesome. There is a robust literature in the trauma field on "learned helplessness," and most of these patients have felt so badly for so long that they indeed feel helpless. So these terms can be red herrings and lead the practitioner to train on the LH. Raising arousal is rarely helpful to those who live in chronic overarousal, so again it is vital to consider every symptom in the context of clinical history. People are rarely hospitalized for underaroused depressions, although of course, if it is crippling enough, this can occur. People are more typically hospitalized for agitated depression, the kind that leads to desperate acts such as self-harm or suicide. Emotional underarousal may not feel good but it is rarely dangerous. Overarousal can be dangerous and I begin training with that point in mind. I err on the side of lowering arousal.

Exhaustion. There is a difference between *tired* and *exhausted*. If semantically only a matter of degree, in the CNS, exhaustion typically signals collapse. Beneath everything else, patients with developmental trauma suffer exhaustion at the core, from holding themselves together and from falling apart. When the allostatic load (essentially the accumulation of stress over time [McEwen & Stellar, 1993]) is too great, stress topples the patient into feeling exhausted, far beyond tired. Exhaustion can be mistaken for underarousal, but it is in fact a signature of over-the-top high arousal and is best, typically, addressed with RH training.

Anger versus Irritability. Distinguishing irritability, a symptom of underarousal, from anger, a symptom of overarousal, can be challenging if you rely on vocabulary alone. I make the distinction by asking patients what would happen if the feeling were amped up, exaggerated. Would it feel like they would implode or explode? Often this helps to clarify. When it still isn't clear, I ask if they were 4 years old, would they be whiney or throwing a tantrum. Usually one of these questions will make it clear which they are feeling. Again, it is rarely the case that a person who meets criteria for developmental trauma will be underaroused, even when he endorses symptoms of underarousal. In fact, it is not uncommon for those in this population to endorse all or most of the emotional–behavioral symptoms on the right side of Table 6.3. When you see lots of checkmarks on the right side of the questionnaire, it is time to reconsider the meaning of any endorsed symptoms on the left side. If this page in the questionnaire has a lot of checkmarks and notations, it will be a graphic representation of overarousal. It will look like this and it is.

Instability. Many of the checkmarks will fall in the middle column of the table as well. As you probably know by now, I think that every one of these problems and diagnoses is the direct or indirect result of fear. But they are also indications of an unstable brain. If these are the most prominent or most threatening symptoms, address arousal with an inter-hemispheric protocol to help the brain gain stability as you look for the frequency that will quiet this particular nervous system.

Panic. It is important to note that a history of panic attacks strongly suggests going slowly as you seek to reduce and stabilize arousal. With the neurofeedback challenge, the brain is in a dynamic process with itself, exploring changes in its patterns and returning to the patterns it knows. If you reduce arousal too quickly, you can provoke a panic attack, either during training or more likely a few hours afterwards, as the brain attempts to find its way back to known territory.

I once inadvertently trained a patient into a panic attack, and I probably don't have to convince you that you don't want to do this. With unstable brains, particularly those prone to panic, train slowly. This is always the case with panic in the profile but all the more so with jacked-up nervous systems like those we see in developmental trauma. When there are no symptoms endorsed in the middle column of Table 6.3—diagnoses don't count for this calculation—I think it is safe to assume that however deranged, there is fundamental stability in the system, and this person will be more likely to experience responses without reactions or push-backs from the CNS. These individuals are rigid, not instable.

Carl called me when he got out on probation after one thoughtless, cruel act or another. He wanted to try training. He worked with a colleague of mine, Catherine Rule (who also did most of Sammy's early training) and when she did a T.O.V.A. with him, it looked completely average. He was captured by his high arousal, but it was a stable high arousal. He called me again after several sessions, newly amazed at himself. He had lost it with the case manager overseeing his probation (nothing new), realized it (completely new), recognized that his behavior may have had an impact on this person (!), and called him to apologize. "I've never done this." Unfortunately for him, the police didn't recognize these subtle changes, and they found many reasons to lock him up again. For Carl it was all a matter of time, and due to his default state of anti-social impulsivity, his time ran out. Although in very competent neurofeedback hands, he was doing brain wave training without therapy, and it is clear that particularly in this population, this is not optimal. These patients need the containment, constraint, guidance, and understanding of the therapist, the devoted other, to take them through the process, to help them recognize the changes, validate them, and to use their new brains.

With developmental trauma we assume the need for RH and inter-hemispheric training and the need to lower arousal, until the individual's brain tells us otherwise. This focus on lowering arousal is where we begin and, of course, it will change over time. As it does there is often a need to address other aspects of this person's dilemma. Your patient will be better able to guide the training when he is less urgent and terrified. You are likely to witness an increase in emotional vocabulary and in nuanced understanding and description. But in the beginning and throughout your training course, the first area to consider is how you are affecting emotion regulation. When quieting the nervous system leads to lethargy or to crying over nothing, or even more objectively to scrambled syntax or to frequent waking, then it may be time to consider training that raises arousal.

One of my patients with Asperger's, childhood sexual abuse, and a severe eating disorder needed RH training, but every 7 or 8 weeks (we did twice-weekly trainings), she would complain about problems with syntax. She would report, for example, "The word I say is the one that is coming four words further out in the sentence." We were able to correct this timing error with a minute of LH training. If we did more than a minute, her speech would be appropriately sequential but also loud and pressured. She would interrupt her fellow students and dominate the class. For a girl learning the basics of social skills, this behavior was not helpful.

Another young woman, with a conviction for attempted murder at age 12, quieted her adult rage with RH training. She quelled the rages within 10 sessions and was doing well with the exception of a new problem that had cropped up during training: waking frequently. We could not rule out neurofeedback as the culprit in this problem (it wasn't her cat or inconsiderate neighbors), so I trained her at C3 for 1 minute for this blip of underarousal. Interestingly, she was hesitant to do this training. I should have listened to her. She left a message on my answering machine saying that it was one of her worst nights ever—"worse than my worst cocaine trip." I got her back in that day and trained again at C4 just to ease her arousal and she was again calm. (This experience and many others have led me to respect my patient's hunches about what protocol they need. These hunches are data.) She was clearly highly reactive to LH training at that site and at that frequency for that amount of time. This was all we really knew. Had she agreed, we might have explored both frequency and site, but, quite understandably, she refused any further LH training. I addressed the need to lift her arousal by slightly increasing the frequency of the reward on the right, and she began to sleep through the night again.

It is, of course, impossible to anticipate every individual response to training, much less what this response might mean for that person. This is the reason to work within a psychotherapy context and to work closely with a mentor for at least the first year, while you are also engaged in ongoing training of your own brain. These practices will help you better understand what is going on in your patient's head. The clinical vignettes above underscore the need to monitor affect regulation, to remind you of plasticity, and to encourage you to "think neurofeedback."

Most of the symptoms in this category are subjective and are difficult to track if your patient has little access to her emotional state or lacks the words to describe it. Objective measures such as nervous habits, road rage, and eye contact will be easier to follow and to quantify. And there are almost always some more objective symptoms in other categories, such as constipation or sugar craving. If you follow the most objective symptoms, the brain will design its own protocol. Listen to what it wants. Look for it. Sense it. Even at times, smell it. One of my patients, a poorly attached raging man, had a problem common to children with developmental trauma: an acrid body odor. His hygiene was impeccable, and the odor he exuded went away only when we adequately addressed his fear (FPO2)

Cognitive Symptoms

Cognitive symptoms are, for the most part, objective indicators. Nonverbal learning disabilities are common in developmental trauma. These are essentially learning problems of the RH, beginning with lack of cause-and-effect understanding. Bright, verbal people with developmental trauma will learn to compensate for difficulties in nonverbal learning, so it can elude evaluation. Given the early disorganization of sensory processing, RH learning disability has to be ruled out. When neurofeedback organizes brain functioning, as it should, patients will report positive changes in social and spatial abilities. Table 6.4 categorizes the cognitive symptoms covered in the assessment questionnaire in Appendix A to further elucidate how this brain organizes or disorganizes itself, to add to our understanding of arousal, and to help us hone our protocol selection(s).

Sense of Direction. One of the symptoms that clearly captures RH disorganization is the lack of spatial orientation, and its resolution is an excellent illustration of how neurofeedback can organize the disorganized brain. The young woman with Asperger's had significantly impaired spatial relationships, but even more daunting for her was her inability to form a map in her head even of her own neighborhood. She

Table 6.4. Cognitive Symptoms in Relation to Arousal Level and Training Approach		
Underarousal: Train the LH	**Instability: Train both hemispheres**	**Overarousal: Train the RH**
• Dyslexia • Indecision • Poor word fluency • Poor sequential processing • Poor sequential planning • Poor reading comprehension • Difficulty decoding words • Poor arithmetic calculation		• Nonverbal learning disability • Poor visual–spatial skills • Poor spelling • Poor tracking during reading • Poor sense of self in space • Lack of prosody; loud voice • Poor handwriting • Poor drawing • Poor sense of direction • Poor fine motor skills • Left and right not automatic • Poor math concepts

could not conceptualize the space around her. After many neurofeed-back sessions, while riding a bus to school, the map of the area suddenly dropped into her head. The following weekend, she was able to find her way to a party in Boston, a city in which its natives can get lost. She had had what I call a "Helen Keller quantum learning event." Once she got it, she had it.

There are many people who do not automatically know right from left—I have heard estimates of 25% of the population. One of my patients described her utter confusion and self-consciousness when she went out square dancing with her friends. Although this isn't a signature symptom of developmental trauma, it is a symptom of something poorly organized in the brain, and for most patients, it will change.

Handwriting. Handwriting is interesting to track. People with DID can switch handwriting from a back slant to a forward slant, from cursive to printing in mid sentence. Poor handwriting is characteristic of poor RH organization. This does not mean that every doctor in the US has developmental trauma, but that most people with developmental trauma will have ugly, poorly formed handwriting, and many will have great difficulty drawing. In Chapter 4 (Figure 4.1), we saw the drawings that a boy completed over the 4-month course of neurofeedback develop form and complexity. This is a two-dimensional representation of the increasing organization and complexity of his nervous system on the page.

Prosody. Lack of prosody (the song of speech) and even more frequently a loud voice are signature symptoms of overarousal and fairly easy to evaluate. In fact, the volume of the voice may be more important in assessment than the content of the narrative. A loud voice often signals the background scream of the CNS.

Cognitive symptoms in the left-hand column of Table 6.4 are objective and reliably lateral, so if they are endorsed in this category, we know that we will need to train the patient on the LH at some point, most likely not until the patient's arousal has calmed down.

Pain Symptoms

When assessing for pain, take note of the qualifiers. *Burning, stabbing, throbbing,* and *shooting* sound different and are different from *aching.* Table 6.5 categorizes the pain symptoms covered in the assessment questionnaire in Appendix A; this information adds to our growing understanding of the arousal of the patient's CNS and gives us more insight into which protocols we might use. The symptoms on the right describe a nervous system under attack—overarousal; and aching signifies a collapse in tone—underarousal. Pain is not a signature symptom in developmental trauma, in part because a high pain threshold is characteristic of this population. Interestingly, a person can have a high pain threshold and still be emotionally reactive to pain; you will see this often. They are both indications for RH training. Patients with developmental trauma are likely to have more symptoms of everything than their low ACE (Adverse Childhood Events study) score counterparts, and whether or not they are signature symptoms for developmental trauma, you will want to follow them as clear markers of arousal.

Neurological and Motor Symptoms

When we assess for neurological and motor symptoms, we are collecting data on frank, documented, or in some cases, suspected injury. *TBI*

Table 6.5. Pain Symptoms in Relation to Arousal Level and Training Approach		
Underarousal: **Train the LH**	**Instability:** **Train both** **hemispheres**	**Overarousal:** **Train the RH**
• Chronic pain with depression • Chronic aching pain • Tension headache • Low pain threshold	• Fibromyalgia • Reflex sympathetic dystrophy (RSD) • Trigeminal neuralgia • Migraine • Headaches • Jaw tension • Motion sickness	• Chronic burning pain • Chronic throbbing pain • Chronic stabbing pain • Chronic shooting pain • Emotional reactivity to pain • Sciatic pain • High pain threshold • Peripheral neuropathy

stands for *traumatic brain injury*. We are not diagnosing, only assessing, and clearly any symptoms endorsed in this table are very important indicators of where the trouble may lie. As mentioned earlier, when a patient has suffered head injury, brain injury, or seizure, I will get a qEEG if at all possible.

Earlier, I hypothesized that there may be a continuum or an overlap between TLE and developmental trauma, even when there is no diagnosis of seizure disorder. A psychiatrist at the adolescent residential program was the first to suggest this link to me. Much to the delight of line staff, he had every new patient undergo a sleep-deprived EEG. This required keeping a new, traumatized, sometimes paranoid and always dysregulated teenager up all night without stimulants. This psychiatrist was trying to catch the brain's display of dysrhythmia in state transitions. He was the first psychiatrist I knew to make reference to the EEG; he was looking for information from the EEG to help inform his medication choices, particularly for the use of anticonvulsants/mood stabilizers. Unfortunately, clinical EEGs have a high degree of false negatives, and short of serious dysfunction, will be deemed normal. The dysfunction will show up in the EEG, but most neurologists and psychiatrists are not trained to see it. In fact, a neurologist told me that they were trained to see past it, so as not to unnecessarily alarm their patients. Of course, the premise here is that every symptom has at its root in neurological dysfunction, neuronal dysrhythmia, and that we will address it by appealing to the EEG. Table 6.6 categorizes the neurological and motor symptoms covered in the assessment questionnaire in Appendix A as we come closer to deciding the initial protocol.

Autoimmune, ANS, and Endocrine Symptoms

Throughout training we are primarily assessing ANS symptoms as information from the body that we are reaching the brain. The ACE score data (see Chapter 1) prove that stress matters in immune function, and there are few more fundamentally stressed than patients with developmental trauma. Table 6.7 categorizes the autoimmune, endocrine, and ANS symptoms covered in the assessment questionnaire in Appendix A in terms of arousal and treatment focus.

Table 6.6. Neurological and Motor Symptoms in Relation to Arousal Level and Training Approach		
Underarousal: Train the LH	**Instability: Train both hemispheres**	**Overarousal: Train the RH**
• LH seizures • LH stroke • LH injury (TBI) • Right body paralysis or paresis	• Generalized seizures • Absence (petit mal) seizures • Temporal lobe epilepsy • Tonic–clonic (grand mal) seizures • TBI with brainstem injury • Vertigo • Tinnitus • Motion sickness • Tics	• RH seizures • RH stroke • RH injury (TBI) • Left-body paralysis or paresis • Spasticity • Tremor • Poor balance • Poor coordination • Involuntary regurgitation • Hiccups • Nervous habits/laugh
Note. TBI = traumatic brain injury.		

Autoimmune Symptoms. Dube et al. (2009) note: "Childhood traumatic stress increased the likelihood of hospitalization with a diagnosed autoimmune disease decades into adulthood. These findings are consistent with recent biological studies on the impact of early life stress on subsequent inflammatory responses" (p. 243). None of these symptoms or illnesses is a signature symptom in this population, but developmental trauma does seem to increase the likelihood of most diseases and may be particularly predictive of autoimmune diseases. These are conditions in which the body's immune system has, simply put, turned against itself. One has to wonder if there is a memory or perception embedded in this disorder: the mother turned against her own flesh and blood.

ANS Symptoms: Multiple Chemical Sensitivities, Chronic Fatigue, Allostatic Load, and Constipation. Multiple chemical sensitivities (MCS) suggest an overwrought, overaroused, and unstable nervous system. One patient with developmental trauma was reactive to the smell of freshly mowed grass and to the smell of newspaper ink, along with the

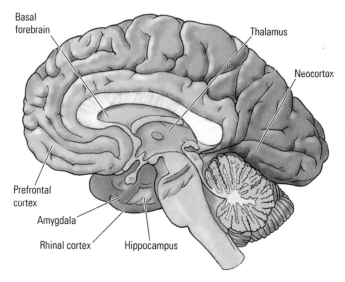

C.1. Medial view showing brain stem and cerebellum. The hypothalamus is not designated but it sits at the top of the brain stem. (Kolb & Whishaw, 2001; reprinted with permission of Worth Publishers.)

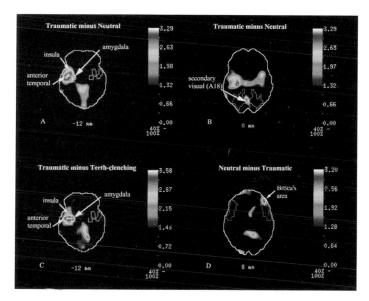

C.2. PET scan showing the activation of the right hemisphere amygdala (non-verbal and sub-cortical) and the lack of activation in the left frontal cortex (verbal and cortical) during a script-driven flashback in 8 subjects with developmental trauma disorder. (Rauch et al., 1996; copyright © 1996 American Medical Association. All rights reserved.)

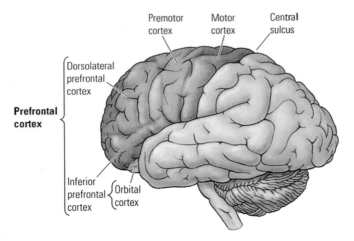

C.3. The prefrontal cortex. (Kolb & Whishaw, 2001; reprinted with permission of Worth Publishers.)

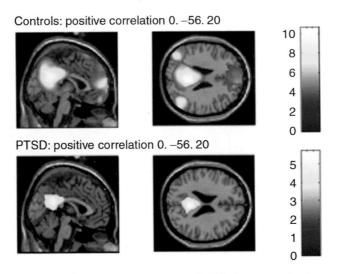

C.4. An fMRI representation of default networks involved in representation of the self in "controls" and in patients with developmental trauma. Red and yellow demonstrate the activation of self-reflection in controls and the failure of activation in those with developmental trauma. (© 2009, Robyn L. Bluhm et al.; reprinted with permission of *The Journal of Psychiatry and Neuroscience*.)

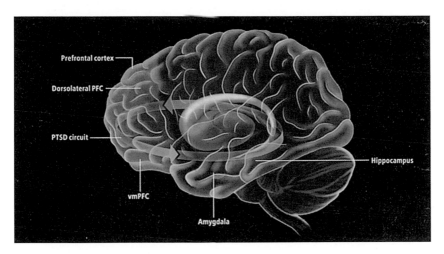

C.5. The circuitry of fear. (Reprinted with permission of Precision Graphics, PrecisionGraphics.com.)

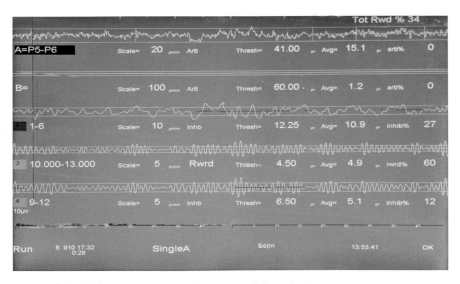

C.6. EEG training screen. (Courtesy of the author.)

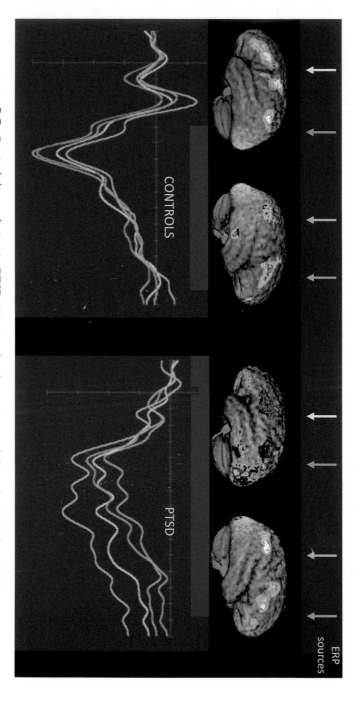

C.7. Cortical disregulation in PTSD. (Reprinted with permission of Alexander McFarlane, MD.)

Table 6.7.	Autoimmune, ANS, and Endocrine Symptoms in Relation to Arousal Level and Training Approach	
Underarousal: Train the LH	**Instability: Train both hemispheres**	**Overarousal: Train the RH**
• Immune deficiency • Low thyroid function • PMS—low arousal: Irritability, insomnia, sugar craving, pain, cramps • Intolerance of alcohol or other sedatives	• Hypertension • Hypotension • Incontinence • Postpartum depression • Severe mood swings with PMS • Migraine with PMS • Chronic fatigue syndrome • Irritable bowel syndrome • Autoimmune disorders: Type 1 diabetes, lupus, rheumatoid arthritis, Crohn's disease, multiple sclerosis • Asthma • Intolerant of coffee/ alcohol/many medications • Multiple chemical sensitivities	• Menopausal hot flashes • Irregular periods • Skin allergies; eczema • PMS—high arousal: Mania, rage, agitation, racing thoughts • Heart palpitations • Pounding; racing heart • Constipation • Intolerance of coffee and other stimulants

Note. ANS = autonomic nervous system; PMS = premenstrual syndrome.

more common aversion to perfumes. She lived in a nervous system that was hyperreactive to these apparently minor stresses. Her "safe place" as a young child was behind a chair, the only piece of furniture in the living room. She had no refuge from her abusive, disturbed parents and her raging older brother; no comforts, no margin of error. Even with neurofeedback she remained somewhat sensitive, but I remember the day, two years or so into treatment, when she told me that she was no longer bothered by newly cut grass, that she in fact now enjoyed the smell.

In the arousal model, chronic fatigue is seen as the collapse of the Type A nervous system. This is a person who has either insufficient information about his need to rest or who has habitually over ridden it. This person may have valiantly pushed through his life until there is just one too many stressors for the system to manage. It has been pushed beyond it allostatic capacity and in response, it collapses. *Allostatic load*, as noted earlier, refers to wear and tear of stress on the body, either from too much stress (these children) and/or to inefficient stress management (these adults) as a result of early unrelenting stress in childhood.

As discussed earlier, chronic constipation is a reliable sign of chronic overarousal, and IBS suggests CNS instability. As we discussed in Chapter 2, the brain–bowel connection is bidirectional via the vagus. You will find yourself following bowel symptoms as an important guide in developing your protocols, and you will get support from Stephen Porges (2011) when you do:

> Clinical disciplines rarely acknowledge the proximal functions of visceral state. Clinicians seldom monitor the expressions of vagal withdrawal or sympathetic activation in their patients. Such a shift in autonomic state would be manifested in several physical and psychiatric states including flat affect, difficulties in auditory processing, hyperacusis (everything is too loud), tachycardia, and constipation. (p. 262)

Acknowledging and tracking the ANS responses as primary indicators of CNS regulation are central to your work as a neurofeedback clinician.

Endocrine Symptoms: Postpartum Depression. A patient with developmental trauma had postpartum depressions after the birth of her first two children, severe enough to require hospitalization. She is the woman doing neurofeedback while pregnant with her third child, who was assaulted by her partner, early in her second trimester. Her doctor recommended an SSRI as a prophylactic in her last trimester, but she refused, saying, "I am betting on the neurofeedback." She reported feeling deeply connected to this baby in utero—a new experience for her—and she had no depression after the birth. I cover this amazing case more fully in Chapter 9.

Additional Initial Assessment Issues

Below are a few other factors to consider during the assessment process.

Sensory Integration Issues

As discussed in Chapter 2, most patients with developmental trauma have sensory integration issues, so we assess for these as well. Sensory processing problems can include auditory delays and more generalized difficulty in organizing incoming data from the senses. To the extent that a brain struggles and fails to organize and make sense of the information from the senses, sensory processing can underlie a fragmentary view of the world. Even if you don't initially know what the condition is, if it begins with the prefix *hyper* (e.g., hyperacusis—too loud!), it is likely to be a sign of overarousal. (Hypersexuality and hyperreligiosity usually indicate a need for right temporal lobe training (a common focus with this group), and hypergraphia (i.e., writing compulsively or at great length) suggests a left temporal focus.

Neurofeedback and Creativity

I have wondered if Dostoyevsky or van Gogh would have sought training. It is almost impossible to imagine either of them choosing to be free of the symptoms that seemed deeply entangled with their art (both seemed to have been afflicted with TLE). The connection between suffering and creativity is an age-old question, but usually not a real choice with which people have to contend. With neurofeedback, it could be. One of my patients, a gifted poet, stopped writing for a period; another began writing good poetry; an artist known for her primitive style gained the third dimension in her paintings (before training she had only seen the world in two dimensions); and many of my patients have taken up abandoned instruments and played them better than they had in the past. For the young woman who stopped writing, her poetry was an attempt to manage her overwhelming emotional pain. As the pain subsided, so did her poetry. She missed it, but she no longer felt compelled to write. Who, other than this person herself could judge whether this was a good or bad outcome? In each instance, it was the outcome dictated by her nervous system.

The work of Gruzelier, Egner, and Vernon (2006), on optimizing performance in musicians and dancers using neurofeedback training, demonstrates a positive training impact not only on proficiency but also on creativity in interpretation. It may be the case that to the extent that the art serves to regulate arousal, the artist will feel the impact of neurofeedback regulation. As suggested by the case of one young poet, if a person writes or paints as if life depends on it, he will write or paint less and/or differently when living in less peril. Clearly, if there is something that functions well for the patient within the dysfunction, the two of you have a deep and important discussion to engage in. So far, my experience suggests that we can, indeed, be creative without suffering from our brain's dysregulation.

Neurofeedback and Sexuality

Most patients with developmental trauma have a history of sexual trauma, but even if they don't, their arousal will take a toll on their ability to engage in and enjoy a reciprocal sexual relationship. In terms of the arousal model, the problems to assess for range from erectile dysfunction, to loss of libido, and problems with orgasm. One of my most severely abused patients said, "It is a tragedy when you are robbed of your sexuality. It's a separate crime." In developmental trauma, we can expect to ease these symptoms when we help patients lower their baseline arousal. Many of my sexually abused clients have told me that they have regained or newly gained a sense of themselves as sexual beings, and many have begun to enjoy sex for the first time. If questions about sex and sexuality aren't appropriate to ask initially, then don't. There is a high probability that patients will organize in this domain as well, as they learn to quiet their fear, and they will tell you about it then.

Medications

In this phase and in an ongoing way keep a list of medications that your patient is presently taking. In the initial assessment it is also important to do a thorough review of how patients have responded to medications they have used in the past. You will want to research what happens when someone is on too high a dose, and you and your patient should be aware of the side effects of all medications she is taking. Look for these as you train. I have boldly stated that you should always suspect neurofeedback first, whatever the report. The only standard exception is when your patient is on psychotropic medication. When this is the case, first suspect the medication. As the CNS becomes more efficient and medications are used more efficiently, your patient will require medication adjustment, and this, of course, requires the active participation of the prescriber. Psychiatrists are beginning to embrace this paradigm shift and most will work with you. Remember your scope of practice: Unless you are a psychiatrist or other licensed prescriber, you don't have the authority to recommend medication changes. You do, however, have a responsibility to discuss medications with your patient. If you are a psychiatrist or other prescriber, you will now have more than medication to offer your patients. The assessment of medications should include your patient's attitude toward being on them and/or the family's attitude. Some patients are heavily reliant not only on the medications but on the idea of being on medication.

Early Development

You will want to know about any problems or anomalies in development. Talking early, as an example, suggests the premature shutdown of RH development by the early onset of LH development (the hemispheres normally develop sequentially and in cycles, each for about 2 years). So early talking, particularly talking in full sentences before age 2, is not a good sign for affect regulation.

It is common for people with developmental trauma to have histories of early ear infections. These can be hard even for attentive parents to detect and when they don't, their efforts to soothe their baby through rocking become a torture. From the child's perspective, the parent is hurting him or her. We are looking for any event or behavior on the part of the mother or the child that is likely to have impinged on attachment. You will find many other questions devoted to early development in the History portion of the assessment questionnaire in Appendix A.

Drug Use and Addiction

A good history of recreational drug use will help you understand the steps your patient has taken to try to regulate him- or herself. The most common drugs of choice, in my experience, are alcohol and marijuana, both of which usually sedate. When they don't sedate but instead make a person angrier or more paranoid, the drug is having a paradoxical effect. But people always turn to these drugs to quiet themselves, even when this is not the primary effect of using them. There is some discussion in the field about training people who are actively using substances. These drugs will have effects on the EEG, which you'll see. Both drugs induce alpha rhythms, which is probably the reason they are used: so patients can experience a fleeting bit of something faintly like relaxation.

Cocaine and methamphetamine speed up the nervous system; all too many patients with developmental trauma use these drugs. They use them, however, not to raise arousal, but to escape arousal or the terror of boredom. In this population, use of these drugs does not suggest an underaroused CNS.

It is clear that most, if not all, addicts have suffered developmental trauma. The ACE study reveals that an increase in alcoholism correlates directly with the number of endorsed ACE questions, with a 500% greater risk of alcoholism for those with ACE scores of 4 or more compared to those with a score of 0. The debate in neurofeedback is not whether we can help people overcome their addictions but whether we can help them while they are actively using. I think most practitioners would recommend, at least in the best of all possible worlds, that patients with addictions begin with detoxing in a facility and then participate actively in a 12-step program, while they are also training. That being said, such an orderly process is rare in the life of an addict.

A man with an ACE score of 5 was slowly able to wean himself from alcohol, but he had many relapses in the process. He came for a session during one of them—he was drunk. I trained him, not knowing what would happen. He was sober at the end of 20 minutes! He had been drinking because he was anxious about a date. I don't know why he sobered up so dramatically or if that response is replicable. But we were training to reduce fearful arousal, and he became less afraid and quite sober. He left the office to meet his date. We'll talk about training for addictions in the next chapter, particularly when we review the alpha–theta protocol.

Head Injury

This developmental trauma population seems to share a significant history of head injury. Their brains may have been subject to everything from anoxia, fetal alcohol and drug exposure, beatings, falls, comas, starvation, infection, high fevers, overdoses, and frank brain injury from concussion, car accidents, and whiplash. You need to know. Most experienced neurofeedback clinicians will ask about head injury many times in the course of an assessment, and I recommend this too. I ask my patients if they have ever been unconscious. Most people believe that unless they have been unconscious, they have not had a significant injury. You can start there and let them know that this is far from true. Shearing or bruising of the brain may not lead to loss of consciousness, and these injuries are not detectable even with magnetic resonance imaging (MRI). You might ask patients if they have ever been in an emergency room, had a sports injury, or broken their nose. Pester them a bit. Brain injury can manifest in idiosyncratic training responses that will stump you if you don't know about it.

Assessing Front to Back–Back to Front

In the arousal model we have mostly considered laterality in the brain: the LH and RH. We don't yet have a well-developed neurofeedback model for the brain's front to back–back to front relationships. The further back in the brain we go, to the brainstem, hypothalamus, and cerebellum, the more primitive the structure and the more basic the function; the further forward we go, the more advanced and distinctly human structures that support executive function. We know that prefrontal communication goes directly to the brainstem, and that all messages sent forward to the prefrontal cortex are sent by the cerebellum. The primitive and the highly evolved are in constant communication. It appears that the cerebellum plays a prominent role not only in physical balance but in emotional balance (see Chapter 2). As we will see in the discussion of a protocol called *Beta Reset*™ (Chapter 7), the practice of neurofeedback also suggests that this is true. The cerebellum exerts considerable influence on the temporal lobes, the "hot spots" in developmental trauma, perhaps even more than do the prefrontal lobes. As we discussed in Chapter 2, a poorly organized cerebellum may well be the first brain problem for the unheld child.

Allan Schore (1994, 2003) has made the case that prefrontal development is impaired in the infant to the extent that it is impaired in the mother or primary caretaker. You should assess for difficulties in making decisions and/or problems with motivation—both important aspects of executive function that are commonly problematic for those with developmental trauma. If these issues are not resolved with RH training, or training at the back of the head, you will likely end up with prefrontal training at some point. When the prefrontal cortex is working well, it structurally regulates amygdala-driven emotions in the RH and promotes agency in the LH, allowing us to go out and explore the world.

Keeping Track of the EEG

I spoke briefly about the use of qEEGs and mini-Qs earlier and in Chapter 5. You will learn about both in much more depth, and with the complexity they deserve, as you continue with your own education in the field. Whether you decide to use brain maps or not, you will want to follow the EEG as you appeal to it. The EEGer software has samples of what EEGs look like under various conditions. If you use this software, you can see what too much theta or alpha looks like in the raw, unfiltered EEG. You can see a seizure pattern. You can learn to recognize an artifact, which is anything in the EEG that doesn't come from the EEG, such as the effect of chewing gum or a cell phone ringing. But as you begin with neurofeedback, you are likely to be fairly EEG illiterate. When you see a pattern that just doesn't look right to you, but your patient is OK, you can watch the EEG on the review screen after your session to see if this activity is an artifact. If the signal ripples through all frequency bands, it is likely to be a significant event. This is an important time to contact a mentor or EEG consultant. You can send him or her a digital clip of this EEG data for assessment and training guidance. In the end, however, we would expect errant patterns to resolve through training, and if you use the arousal model, you will still determine protocols primarily related to assessed level of arousal.

When you see a strange EEG reading, ask your patient what she is experiencing and thinking. The most common problem I see with patients who have developmental trauma is a sudden increase in the amplitude of slow wave activity. Often this pattern correlates with a fear memory that is arising. You have two choices at this point: Either stop and talk about what is coming up or continue training. I have done both. Particularly with an experienced patient, I have also often continued to train and to talk. We are able then to watch how the brain responds to the conversation. If talking creates more slow wave at 2 Hz or above (below 2 Hz is typically considered an artifact and could arise from the moving jaw), it suggests that the brain is becoming more dysregulated. This could be a momentary and even important dysregulation. But if my patient is becoming dysregulated as well (there is not always a correlation), I will work with him or her to focus on the breath and on changing brain parameters, and I will consider changing reward frequencies if I think I am contributing at all to an increase in fear. Whether to talk or train is one of the core issues addressed in Chapter 8 on the integration of neurofeedback and psychotherapy. And like so much else in both neurofeedback and psychotherapy, it depends.

Dominant Frequency

The dominant frequency is the background firing rate of brain function, the gating rhythm of the brain off task. It is standard practice to measure the dominant frequency during your first assessment. In adults, a slow dominant frequency—low alpha, say, 8 Hz measured at PZ—suggests the possibility of learning problems; a higher than normal frequency, above 11 Hz, suggests a driven brain. You will want to track if neurofeedback changes the dominant frequency. It should move closer to the middle range of 9–11 Hz. The presence of this range should correlate with better organization and function.

Typically there is excess slow wave, as low as 2 Hz, particularly at the temporal lobe in people with developmental trauma. You will learn how to read this in your training to become a neurofeedback practitioner; expect it. Those who do not have excess slow wave will often have excess amounts of high beta, considered mostly a representation of muscle tension. As you have learned, you will set your inhibit wherever there is excess slow wave and/or excess fast wave to encourage the brain to stop doing this. In my experience, slow wave averages of 50 μV or even higher are not uncommon in this population, even in adults. These readings can indicate dissociative processes. If there is excess slow wave, particularly delta–slow theta, at a particular site, you can conclude that the brain, at least at this site, is not communicating adequately with the outside world; it is mainly talking to itself. Record the amplitudes of inhibit and reward frequencies at the beginning and end of each session. Then you can be as puzzled as the rest of us when you see little movement in the amplitude of the reward band and yet see robust clinical change.

Artifact

When I was trained initially, I learned that there could be no slow wave in a waking brain—that when we saw that frequency, what we were seeing was an artifact. The meaning of *slow wave* is still not resolved, particularly at 2 Hz and below. It could be, however, that even if it is an artifact, it has meaning to the brain. There is no doubt that we routinely see high amplitudes, particularly at 2 Hz, in clinical EEG training and that reducing these amplitudes seems to have clinical impact. When I train people with developmental trauma histories who show high-amplitude slow wave, I use a broad inhibit, usually 0–6; I am drawing my conclusions from the prominence of 2 Hz and its inclusion in the parameters of the inhibit, not on inhibiting 2 Hz alone. These very slow high-amplitude waves do drop in amplitude. This drop in slow wave activity (including the frequency and intensity of artifacts) signals that the brain is waking up and reorganizing.

Assessment in the Chair

When you do neurofeedback, you are always assessing for change. Obviously, you watch for changes during the actual training session as well to see if you can get feedback on your patient's experience at that point. Look for changes in facial expression, heart rate, posture, body tension, or in dissociation as you are also watching the number values of the EEG. At the beginning, if all of this these factors seem too much to track, just watch your patient, and on the EEGer, use the F11 key to change training thresholds. As an important side note, the default on the EEGer system will provide feedback on the reward frequencies 75% of the time, on the inhibited slow wave frequencies 25% of the time, and on fast wave inhibits about 15% of the time in eyes-open training. You can change these thresholds to make them harder or easier depending on the needs of your patient.

Patients with developmental trauma judge themselves through these external measures and are prone to seeing themselves as failures. I make the reward, rewarding—that is, not too difficult for them to achieve. I haven't seen any clear indication that the brain learns more slowly if the rewards and inhibits are "too easy." I have, however, had to work with people's issues of self-esteem and accomplishment—which are not relevant to this particular challenge and divert attention from the brain task at hand—if the rewards and inhibits are too hard.

You can look at numbers later. Ask what she is experiencing if you see something in the patient's expression or posture, and if you don't, remind your patient that you want to hear her subjective experience. If, on the quest to quiet fear, I inadvertently take the brain to too low a frequency, the patient may report one or both of the most common indicators: nausea and neck pain. A boy with a history of anoxic brain injury started to cry after I made a shift to further lower his arousal. Before that, he had been in a sunny mood, and he returned to it when I shifted the frequency higher. I'd trained his brain at a frequency too low for him. Usually a shift up a notch in frequency, as little at $1/8$ Hz for some people, will alleviate these reactions.

Unfortunately, the patient's response in the chair does not reliably predict his response even 2 hours later. Your protocol will be determined ultimately by how well your patient functions the rest of the day and that night, the next day and night, and the day and night after that. I think we have the best sense of how the brain responds to a particular protocol 2 or 3 days after training as the brain assimilates what it has learned. Because of this time lag, I ask patients to keep a log of their responses or to call me and let me know what they are experiencing. Few comply. Colleagues of mine send tracking forms on the Internet for their patients to fill out, but they too have trouble with compliance. (Perhaps we need an app for this!) Each session begins with a review of the days since the last training. Training effects can unfold for many days, even weeks, and perhaps longer after training, a fact to keep in mind as you are assessing. A response coming a week or 2 and sometimes even longer after training could indeed relate to the session.

Assessment: Session to Session

Some clinicians have asked me if I get bored doing neurofeedback. I have felt scared, worried, impatient, confounded, relieved, fascinated, and even at times elated doing neurofeedback, but never bored. I look forward to seeing my patents and to their reports. It is always, at the very least, interesting. Many therapists have talked to me about their feelings of burnout, primarily due to the lack of change in their patients. I certainly felt that way before I started doing this work. But if I have learned only one thing since adopting neurofeedback, it is that people can change only to the extent that they can change their brains. As neurofeedback clinicians, we are in the privileged position of participant observers in that process, and we expect to see change.

It is helpful to keep your assessment questionnaire with you throughout your work with a patient. Due to the profound impact of state, patients may not remember how they felt or the symptoms they had at an earlier time. And you may forget too. When you look back over your notes, you will want to know what you were thinking and, of course, what your patient was thinking, feeling, or doing that prompted the protocol decisions you have made. I often quote my patients verbatim in my records to keep track of their arousal, their self-regulation, and their perception of self and other as they all unfold over time; as they evolve. The assessment questionnaire also functions as a cheat sheet: We can use the left-side indicators to reveal if and when we have taken the patient's arousal too low.

At the end of each session, I use my notes to remind myself about symptoms to follow in the next session. I choose these symptoms, as described above. I find out the most important information with the single question, "Did you say, feel, or do anything that surprised you?" I often learn vital information serendipitously (and sometimes later than I would have wished). Listen particularly for what comes after the patient says something to the effect, "I doubt this has anything to do with neurofeedback. . . " It will always have something to do with neurofeed-back. Some data may seem trivial, but they are not trivial to the aroused nervous system. One patient reported that her ice cream had freezer burn on it, which had never happened before; her ice cream *never* went uneaten. She'd just forgotten about it; she had no craving. A man I worked with reported that he found himself inexplicably driving at the speed limit—a novelty for him. Another patient mentioned that it was much easier for her to pack for a business trip. Listen for all of it and think neurofeedback. These reports have meaning. They are missives from the CNS.

Life happens and, as I said at the opening of the chapter, at times it will be difficult to discern whether the sleeplessness of the night before was due to the training or to the patient's anxiety about a life event, a job interview, or a paper due. You can only figure this out in conversation with the brain. You will be assessing all domains—physical, emotional, and behavioral—to do so. One symptom marker is not enough information to answer this question. In this hypothetical example, we would need to know sleep history (i.e., is insomnia common or unusual?) and how anxious this patient was feeling and if this was typical, or better or worse than her norm. I ask my patients to use the Subjective Units of Distress Scale (SUDS) with 0, the least anxious (angry, restless, etc.) and 10, the most.

There will always be additional information to elicit, such as bowel activity or degree of patience or a quieter or louder voice, which will allow you to form your hypothesis and to plan your next protocol. Most patients will first think about almost any other explanation for the changes they feel. Until they become experienced with their brains, they have no reason to do otherwise. Who would expect that training could change thresholds to allergic reactions or to sciatic pain? They may instead talk, quite reasonably, about the pollen count or their visit to the chiropractor. And, of course, these factors could be the reasons for changes. As practitioners, though, we have to cast a broader net. There is one central principle guiding neurofeedback with people with developmental trauma: These patients suffer from extreme affect dysregulation, erupting in fear or rage and or imploding into shame. We are assessing for the arousal that underpins and undermines this patient's ability to regulate intense feelings, and we are assessing for arousal in all domains. We are always monitoring for intensity and reactivity. If our patient is not quieting, we'll need to consider changing protocols (more on this in the next chapter).

There is ongoing discussion in the field about how long to train at a given frequency and site. When I began neurofeedback training the technology wasn't available to allow me to make changes, much less changes during the session, so this was a decision that we didn't have to make in the early days of EEG biofeedback. But we do have to make it now. You will be trained to be conservative, which translates to not moving sensors or frequencies without a clear rationale. It is easy to feel impatient for change in this practice, but we should never make protocol changes out of impatience. However, when we see a negative effect from what we are doing, such as the patient's heart beginning to pound or neck beginning to ache, or when a patient reports feeling more anxious while training, we need to assess, then and there, and in many cases change the frequency.

These decisions will come more easily as you become more experienced and learn to use your clinical intuition in the service of neurofeedback. I have been working with neurofeedback for over 16 years, and I will make rapid changes, particularly in frequency, when I see an effect that is negative. Patients will often describe getting tired or sleepy particularly when the training is asking the CNS to quiet itself. In most cases this sleepiness is an indication of a shift in arousal and not a reason to change reward frequency. Sleepiness or feeling tired will usually lift within an hour after training. If either persists into the next day, it may well indicate that the frequency was too low. My decisions are often quick but rarely impatient. When you do make protocol changes or additions, be sure to make note of them in your paper record (the computer will too), and just as importantly, document the thinking that led to the decision. It will all be wrapped into your ongoing assessment.

When Training Plateaus

At times neurofeedback just doesn't seem to budge the brain you have before you. You should have a good idea if this is the case within 20 sessions. If the patient continues to come for training despite seemingly meager results, I assume that the neurofeedback is helping them. Consider the possibility that they are experiencing some subtle, wordless unfolding. It is rare that neurofeedback does nothing at all. When this does happen and it is feasible financially for the patient, I recommend a Q. More frequently, however, a particular protocol can just stop working; it seems to plateau. When it does, the first thing I do, again in reference to quieting arousal, is to lower the frequency of the reward. I train at this lower frequency and then assess the changes at the next session. I typically change the frequency I am rewarding before I change the site. There will be exceptions. New protocols come out of this ongoing dynamic interplay between the brain, its observers, and the feedback. A protocol is only right if it feels right to the patient and/or to the therapist and devoted other. Neurofeedback is a collaborative process, and ongoing assessment and protocol design require some level of consensus on how the patient is doing.

Perhaps the most important area to investigate and address in nonresponders and in those who plateau in their training is what they eat. There is a question on the assessment questionnaire about eating habits, and you'll want to investigate this question in some depth. In the Introduction to her bestselling book *Primal Body, Primal Mind*, Nora Gedgaudas (2009), a neurofeedback practitioner as well as a nutritionist, alerts her colleagues and her patients:

> Some [patients] experience inexplicable backslides or have difficulty getting their brains to move at all. . . . Typically there seems to be an issue with diet, food sensitivity, endocrine dysfunction, severe nutritional deficiencies or a combination of conditions. . . . It is abundantly clear that all the brain training in the world . . . cannot create a nutrient where there is none or remove a problematic substance that does not belong. (p. xxii)

The most common culprits seem to be trans fats, sugar, and gluten. My colleague, psychiatrist Arlene Nock, told me that she'd kept a "Happy Meal" (burger, bun, and fries) in its original wrapping in her desk drawer for a year to illustrate the negative effects of fast food to her patients. The paper had decayed but the "food" hadn't. It was hardened and completely intact. Bacteria were no match for trans fats. In essence, this fat that is so common in our diet and particularly in fast foods is nearly impossible to break down. Our brains need fat to function, but they simply cannot use trans fat—it is not digestible. The impact of food on the brain is its own endlessly controversial topic. Suffice it to say that there is a direct and powerful connection between what we eat and drink and how our brains function. Mold exposure and allergies to dust, household chemicals, and other substances can also inhibit or stall the brain's innate flexibility.

Once the brain learns how to regulate itself, it will remember it. That being said, events can derail it. For example, the brain undergoes enormous change at puberty, and sometimes these new hormones, themselves powerful neurotransmitters, can destabilize even the most well-regulated brain (note your average teenager). Viruses can also play havoc with the information system that is the brain. And a new trauma, not rare for these patients, may reset the brain into its original "trauma mode," which means dysregulation. The good news is that the brain remembers fairly quickly what it seems to have forgotten, and it usually takes only a few sessions for the patient to regain stability. One patient, who had resolved the impact of early childhood sexual abuse after 60 neurofeedback sessions, returned to see me 2 years after we had ended. She was disturbed by old symptoms that returned after her dog was run over. We trained for three sessions and she felt her self again, quite literally.

Ending Training

How do you know when training is over? There are clinical answers to this question, the most obvious being when the presenting symptoms are either much more manageable or are gone. As we have seen, however, neurofeedback does not address symptoms alone, but symptoms as the portal to the riches of self-regulation and the developing self. It is hard, at least for me, to decide when that practice is over. The journey of self (and perhaps even for some, the journey of no-self) doesn't end. A therapist described her experience with neurofeedback as the journey from Schore's (1994) "no-self/no other" to a clear organization of self and other, and then, with startling speed, to the Buddhist sense of no-self.

Her description suggests that we can travel far beyond the clinical realm. There are practical constraints, of course, in the clinical setting, but it is important to ponder the possibilities. In this regard, neurofeedback may be best compared to meditation. When is meditation practice over?

I have highlighted aspects of the clinical assessment process with patients who have histories of developmental trauma. There are many ways to go about this endeavor. Take note of how patients stand and sit, the tenor of their voice, their eye contact, even the energetic field that surrounds them. I have often imagined Pig Pen when I am with these patients. I feel for changes in this developmental trauma field. There is less debris, less fallout, less drama. Of course, these changes depend on the training protocols we employ. In the next chapter, we explore protocol selection and design, remembering as we do that all protocols are individual and all are based on assessment, on learning to listen to the brain and to think neurofeedback.

Chapter 7

Neurofeedback Protocols for Developmental Trauma

Based on our initial assessment process, we will begin to make protocol decisions. In this chapter I discuss the specific protocols I use most often in developmental trauma, but I have to begin with two caveats. The first is that there is no protocol for developmental trauma. We will, in most cases, find a protocol that quiets fear in the individual who has suffered this history, and it is amazing to see what unfolds then. But what unfolds in this process is entirely individual. *Personalized medicine*, a term used mostly in reference to using the individual genome to guide intervention, applies equally to neurofeedback. We are never treating the diagnosis; we are treating its manifestations, or more precisely the manifestations of early history in this individual nervous system. In a moment of frustration I said to a patient struggling to give a name to her "condition," "You don't have a disease—you have a childhood." So although we have protocols that may work for most, they won't help everybody.

This brings me to the second caveat: Not only is there no specific neurofeedback protocol for treating developmental trauma, there is no developmental trauma disorder. Neither the medicine nor the disease exists. As I have said before, the DSM does not recognize developmental trauma as a diagnosis. In a way, this is as it should be. All mental disorders are brain-based, and most, if not all, arise from perturbations in the brain's rhythms that make regulation of arousal a demanding proposition, truly beyond our will alone. (Will itself requires regulation.) The field has medicalized and categorized disruptions in the brain's rhythmic regulation and attempted to quantify them as discreet DSM diagnoses, but the practice of neurofeedback quickly disabuses us of this taxonomy.

At least in those with developmental trauma histories, I think it is safe to say that all morbidity and comorbidity are expressions of early, profound brain dysregulation. These individuals often experience problems with appetite, eating, and body image, and if those symptoms grab the attention of the clinician, these patients will be given a preemptive diagnosis of eating disorder. Body sensations and representations are located primarily in the RH, and the press of fear and shame is ubiquitous in those with eating disorders. Eating disorders correlate with high ACE scores, which of course correlate with histories of developmental trauma. Eating disorders represent an intense effort at self-regulation in persistent states of heightened arousal.

As we have seen in Chapter 2, the anterior cingulate is disorganized in developmental trauma. Hyperreactivity of the anterior cingulate is also the brain signature of OCD, another common comorbidity, as is substance abuse. There are, to be sure, people who are "grabbed" by substances, and because of the lock these substances put on the brain, can't get free of them without help. But if we look again at the ACE study from Chapter 1, we see data that link early childhood assault and neglect to substance abuse and addiction. Most people who are in trouble with alcohol and drugs are trying to medicate and escape their reactive amygdalas. Personality disorders are also far from discreet. They are best understood as affect regulation disorders as well, ones so well practiced and reinforced over time that they overtake the personality.

I no longer see these as distinct disorders or comorbidities but as different manifestations of the same overwrought, dysregulated nervous system. With neurofeedback, we are attempting to tweak the dysrhythmias into rhythmic flow. Our protocols are designed first to quiet fear in this person, as it manifests in her, not to treat a disorder. In the process we would expect the patient to develop more regulated eating habits because she feels hunger and satiation, to quiet obsessive thoughts and compulsive behaviors, and to become uninterested in substances, whether prescribed, legal, or illegal. When the brain learns its own regulation, these symptoms and behaviors drop away because they no longer serve their primary purpose. When the neurofeedback protocols are on track, training will establish rhythmic flow, movement, even dance. It is about emergence. The process is best felt as a verb. Diagnoses are coffin-nail nouns.

We are seeing patients who although best understood in terms of their developmental trauma histories, are given a myriad of diagnoses. But as a neurofeedback practitioner, the first step is to recognize the impact of early neglect and abuse and to keep this history in mind as you consider protocols. As we have seen, that explains a lot. The protocols that I share in this chapter all have their roots in an understanding of brain development. Many different practitioners have pioneered them, and more approaches will arise as we more fully understand the brain.

Every protocol I describe here I have tried, most of them for myself. I provide the rationale for each protocol as well, but it is vital to understand that this rationale only has meaning as long as your patient is responding to that particular protocol. If patients don't like the protocol or if they have no reliable sense of themselves, and if the "devoted other" (often you) doesn't like it, then it's wrong, no matter how good the theory. Felt experience trumps theory.

Given how individual neurofeedback is to each brain, the following protocol guidelines are just that. There is no dogma here. What works, works, and sometimes, it can be discovered quite serendipitously. I discovered that placement at O1–O2 (occipital region) was helpful for anxiety when training to address acute double vision in two of my patients with developmental trauma. When they gave their reports the following week, they both described less anxiety, and specifically, less anticipatory anxiety. They had become, as it were, "more laid back," and it was much harder for them to "get ahead of themselves."

Although I will always start on the RH with developmental trauma, a colleague told me about a very disturbed young adoptee that he trained, to great benefit, on the LH with a frequency intended to raise arousal. Colleagues in Australia are trying to parse the responses of their traumatized refugee population, some of whom have also needed to raise their arousal with LH training, and it has quieted their reactivity. We are, in the end, guided by our conversation with the brain, learning to listen attentively to what it wants. Sometimes this conversation is quite straightforward and the responses are clear. The patient is a good responder, sensitive to neurofeedback, and able to report. Were that it was always so. But this is the human brain we are talking about, and in many cases, there are conflicting indicators. It is impossible to even begin to cover all the permutations of training the brain—just the number of possible protocols approaches infinite—but I nevertheless provide the guidelines that I use as a way for the new practitioner to begin to think neurofeedback. (You will know for sure that this is happening when you begin to assign protocols to strangers on the street!) Over time, your patients too will learn to think neurofeedback. They will begin to use the language of arousal and regulation and will discuss their amygdalas instead of their mental illness. As one patient noted recently, reflecting on what she had just said, "This has a distinctly almond shape to it!"

Initial Placements

As you may remember from Chapter 3, a protocol consists of (1) the frequencies you choose to reward and to inhibit and (2) the locations where you place the sensors on the scalp. Many people begin their training on the sensory motor strip, which Barry Sterman has dubbed the "keyboard of the brain" in conversations we have had (see Figure 3.1, p. 81)

The C4 Placement

Although I recommend other protocols, C4 is often a good place to begin to get a feeling for the frequency reward that this brain appreciates. Unless there has been an injury near this site, it tends to be less reactive than either temporal or frontal lobe placement. You are likely to train both temporally and frontally over time—as we have seen, Schore (1994, 2003) has found considerable data indicating that these locations are important in developmental trauma—but C4–A2 usually offers us safe harbor as we explore reward frequencies.

I always choose C4 or C4–P4 (right parietal) to begin with people who express their dysregulation primarily in the soma. For many with severe childhood histories, the psychosomatic becomes the somatopsychic. These patients look less mentally ill and more physically eroded. The ACE study data support this observation. High ACE scores relate not only to emotional, cognitive, and behavioral dysregulation but to physical breakdown as well. It is a sign of collapse under allostatic load. The digestive system may be the most sensitive system to unrelenting stress. I use C4–P4 when there are issues with the digestive tract such as reflux, hiccups, or constipation, and look for the frequency that will increase parasympathetic tone and calm the nervous system.

The T3–T4 Placement

It is common for patients with developmental trauma to show signs of CNS instability, such as panic attacks, IBS, or migraine (interhemispheric symptoms), and when I see these symptoms, my initial training is at T3–T4. This protocol was developed out of frustration. In a conversation with Sue Othmer (1999) she described "chasing" migraines. When she would train on the right, the headache would move to the left. When she trained on the left to "grab" it there, it would move back to the right. She developed this protocol in an attempt to capture and restrain this volatility.

T3–T4 can also be useful when the patient is highly reactive generally; when there are many symptoms endorsed, right and left; or when you get a clinical sense (sometimes your own low-level dread) that this nervous system is not only highly aroused, it is highly unstable. I tried this placement on myself, and it stopped migraines that I had lived with since late adolescence. I was duly impressed and started to use it widely for my patients. They all became more stable, but at some point they (and I also) became more rigid and less fluid. Watch for rigidity, coolness, or anger as indications that you have done enough of this protocol. There is a thin line between stability and rigidity. When it is clear that T3–T4 offers stability that other protocols can't, I'll continue to use it, usually for less than 6 minutes, and then continue with other RH protocols.

The T4–P4 Placement

Most of the literature on affect regulation and a good deal of what's written on interoception focus on the RH. The subcortical drivers are nestled along the midline, deep in the temporal lobes. Even when my patients have somatic markers, which most do, I most often begin training at T4–P4. I still, of course, keep track of the body, but my focus is on emotion regulation, and the fear structures are, for the most part, in the temporal lobe. But as a reminder of how important it is to follow the brain and not the theory, let me tell you about one patient's response to temporal lobe training.

She was a clear candidate. She came for neurofeedback to try to quiet eruptions of murderous rage and her fear that she would act on it. I started at C4 and found the frequency that was right for her. She calmed down and was over the rage crisis in three sessions. Then, as I should, I went to the right temporal lobe to more specifically address her long-standing emotional volatility. She became more dysregulated—angry, bothered, and resistant—and changes in frequency didn't make it better. She couldn't tolerate the placement. Were she to have had a Q, I imagine we would have seen evidence of injury—her mother weaned her by hitting her across the head when she asked for the bottle—but the map wasn't available to her. I listened to her brain, returned to C4, and she regained her emerging sense of calm. I trained another patient at C4–P4, but it wasn't helpful to her, regardless of frequency. I changed her to T4–P4 at the same frequency and she told me at the next session that I had changed her life, "literally."

In the initial stages of training, we are looking for the right frequency at the right placement, hoping to find a default protocol. Most patients with developmental trauma will need to train at various sites to deal with their so-called comorbidities. For example, we are unlikely to advance a person's reading speed or help him or her with word finding using RH training. Before we go to the left to address those complaints, it is comforting to have established a protocol to which the brain has already responded well. We will have that protocol to fall back on, should we trip across dysregulation as we explore additional protocols. That being said, in some this default protocol either does not develop or is not helpful when we return to it. The brain is changing, and we need to flex with the changes. As an example, if a bipolar person (this can be another common comorbidity) is in the manic phase, we would train to quiet arousal, but when she is in the depressed phase, we would train (carefully) to increase arousal. We need to meet the brain where it is. Clearly, if neurofeedback is helping, the brain and the protocols will become more predictable over time.

Initial Reward Frequencies

Determining initial reward frequencies are essentially an educated guess, based on the patients' history, clinical assessment, and the information we pick up just sitting with them. Unfortunately, there is no rule for a beginning frequency except that dictated by developmental trauma itself. These are among the most overaroused nervous systems you are likely to encounter. Because I know this, I tend to begin at 10.5–13.5 Hz to 9–12 Hz. Most adult patients will tolerate somewhere in this frequency range, at least at the beginning, and most will train comfortably lower than this, even much lower. There are also patients who will need to train higher, as we saw in the case of my suicidal "borderline" patient. When she reported feeling dread after training, I hooked her back up and raised the frequency. Her report: "My whole brain is smiling." In people who calibrate in fear tones, *dread* usually means that the frequency is too low. You can almost hear the thud in the word. Don't despair if these translations don't come immediately to you. Your clinical intuition will inform your protocol choices increasingly over time.

These patients are prone to emergencies—another factor that we must consider. In situations in which the presentation is unclear, I will err on the side of lowering arousal too far (except in patients with instabilities) rather than of raising arousal, particularly if the patient and I are facing a clinical emergency. So we make our best informed initial protocol choice focused on the level of arousal, and for some, the level of emergency. As we would in all therapies, we continue to assess all surrounding contingencies such as the level of therapeutic alliance, family environment, and safety.

Medications are also a factor in our decision about initial frequency reward and sometimes placement as well. There are very few under-aroused people on atypical or "second-generation" antipsychotics. These medications would suggest beginning with a lower, rather than higher, frequency reward. SSRIs are the first drug of choice for anxiety, so even though they are called antidepressants, most who use them suffer from over- rather than underarousal. If the patient has done well with anti-convulsants (mood stabilizers), this is an indication for stability training at either T3–T4 or C5–C6. My colleague, Ed Hamlin, has worked with many people with severe bipolar disorder, usually genetic and not trau-matic in origin. With this group, he found that C3–C4 was not enough to stabilize them, but that they were usually too reactive at T3–T4. His experience was that interhemispheric training was the right course, so he tried C5–C6, which was more predictable and less dramatic. Although he is unlikely to call it this, he was employing the Goldilocks principle to find a new protocol.

We have the entire frequency spectrum from 0 to 45 Hz to consider in protocol decisions. With developmental trauma, we are training with one goal—to reduce arousal—and to do this we take the reward fre-quency as low as it needs to go. For some, this can mean training as low as 0–3 Hz, a bandwidth that targets 1.5 Hz (the midpoint), and, as we will see, practitioners are exploring frequencies below 1 Hz. In this case, we are using this bandwidth to leverage arousal, not to "up-train" slow wave frequencies. And we see no increases in slow wave—which are also inhibiting (see the next section, on inhibits)—even when we seem to be training the brain to make it, but we do expect to see a reduction of fear. We are always exercising some homeostatic mechanism in the brain no matter where we train or what we ask it to do. When we make the right request, the brain will propagate new patterns manifesting in new but apparently inherent capacities—emotional, physical, and cognitive. How-ever, I don't begin training at very low frequencies. We get there only at the brain's request.

It is important to note that we will be biased toward using the proto-cols that have been helpful to other patients and, even more likely, those that have been helpful to us. It may be an informed bias, but it is not a reliable one. I tend to hear the RH's wild arousal calling to me. If you have trained yourself successfully for attention, you may lean toward LH brightening. Our brains have had powerful learning experiences, and we will want to pass these on, quite naturally, to those with whom we work. But as we are deciding protocols, it is important to listen to our patient's brain, to discern his needs from ours.

A man in his mid-60s came to me to see if we could calm his "states of terror." Steeped in understanding and treating developmental trauma, I heard these descriptors and trained him to lower arousal. He noticed something, but he was not calmed. He does not have a history of developmental trauma, but that, in itself, would not rule out RH training. Overarousal is overarousal. Except in him it wasn't. Patients with developmental trauma have trouble functioning because they are terrified. This man felt terrified because he couldn't function. He did much better when we raised his arousal on the LH, which allowed him to rise to the occasion, not to be cowed by it.

Initial Inhibit Frequencies

Initial inhibit frequencies depend less on intuition than do initial reward frequencies and more on the spectral display of frequencies dancing along the bottom of your screen (EEGer). Typically, you will see an abundance of slow wave activity, usually below 6 Hz. Because these brains are either seizure-prone or seizure-like, and because seizures propagate in slow wave activity, I begin with a 0–6 Hz inhibit. I use a standard 22–36 Hz inhibit for excess fast wave, which is less characteristic of this population. The fear of these patients seems to be coded in the slow waves. That's where we'll see amplitude increases if the patient begins to dissociate or has a run of fearful thoughts or memories. As we'll discuss shortly, alpha–theta training is predicated on the notion that the demons live down deep—as do, with fear quieted, the angels.

The spectral frequency display will show you which frequencies are bursting or erratic, either confirming your decision or leading you to inhibit somewhere else. You will learn about this part of the process in your initial seminars. Many systems use 4–7 Hz as the default inhibit because excess theta is implicated in ADD/ADHD. In developmental trauma, however, I would expect the excesses in theta–delta, 0–6 Hz. A note of caution here: Some new practitioners will see this bursting activity and use the word *spike*. In neurology, a spike is a signature of epileptiform activity (see Figure 7.1), so unless you are seeing a seizure—typically, a spike followed by a wave—don't use *spike* when you mean *burst*.

Clinicians can use the spectral creatively. Some look for the lowest frequency with the lowest amplitude in the display and train it to become more robust and to contribute equally. Others try to shift dominant frequency, shown in the EEGer spectral as an orange bar. There is a good deal of information in those dancing bars. Whatever way you use it, judge the outcome first by how it affects arousal and organization, not by the brain's impressive gymnastics. A mother called to consult on her son, who has Asperger's, and who had been doing neurofeedback for several months. He'd played a game in which you try to take a cursor all the way across the screen to drop and stack chips in a column at the far right. As the brain is learning, chips or bricks will fall, mostly randomly,

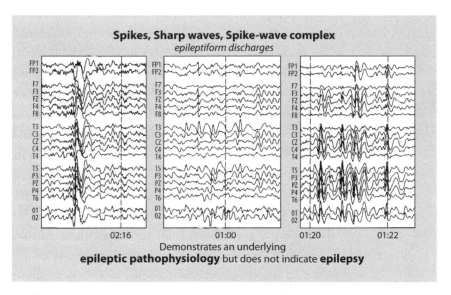

Figure 7.1.   Epileptiform activity in a patient with developmental trauma. (Reprinted with permission of Andrea Meckley, MA.)

in columns along the way, stacking up in piles of different depths on the path to the goal at the far right, signaling where the brain dropped its focus on the task. She told me that her son had learned to drop the little bricks in designs of his choice—mental Legos! This amazing feat apparently impressed his neurofeedback practitioner, who concluded that there was nothing more to be done—the boy had proved his control over his brain. The mother, however, was still seeing most of his worst Asperger's symptoms. This boy who had gained this extraordinary agility could still not regulate his emotions or his behavior. He needed a protocol adjustment. Although he had control over his brain in the game, his highly aroused CNS still had control of him.

Protocol Changes

Beginners are usually trained to stay the course with a given protocol over a session. This is the only way that you will know whether a specific protocol was helpful. But in actual practice you can't always do this, and it isn't always advisable. If someone's heart begins to pound or thoughts begin to race while training, it means that we are inadvertently driving the CNS (and the ANS) and we need to quiet it with a change in frequency. A pounding heart is a sign of sympathetic arousal and racing thoughts, of cortical overarousal, and both suggest lowering the reward frequency.

You will develop a deeper understanding of your patient's nervous system with each training, and with this, a richer context to inform these decisions. Nothing that I say here can substitute for your paying attention to, and getting to know, your patient. I do respond to signs of heightened arousal in these patients during the session, if they make either the patient or me uncomfortable, and in this population, this will usually, but not always, mean lowering the frequency. I watch my patient's face and body for signs of relaxation or distress. A deep sigh usually means that the nervous system is letting go. It is as if you are hearing the quantum shift. The arousal has dropped down a notch. If you have shifted in the right direction and lowered the frequency reward sufficiently, you should see symptoms begin to abate. Neck pain, lower back pain, and/or nausea have been for me the most reliable indicators during the session that the reward frequency may be too low. We are changing the body's tone. I check for these symptoms as I lower the frequency reward to address sympathetic overactivation.

Our decisions will prove out, or not, over the next 2 hours to 3 days. If the frequency was too high, you will see increases in arousal symptoms (right column in the tables in Chapter 6); if it is too low, an increase in symptoms of underarousal (left column); if destabilizing, more symptoms of instability (middle column); and if it is just right—you'll know. Overshooting is not uncommon and generally not to be feared. We are in the conversation and the brain will respond with plasticity. There are moments, however, such as those with my rage-filled client, when training effects take on emergency proportions, almost always because arousal is too high. This is a state that can give rise to a dangerous narrative that can be acted upon, and you will want to address it immediately. Once you find the protocol that quiets fear and also allows cognitive clarity, this will be your default protocol for that particular patient, and you will train here as long as the effects continue and remain positive. As mentioned above, once you have established this protocol, in most cases, you'll have your footing and can begin to explore other protocols that could benefit function. Most training for high arousal is on the RH, but there is usually a need for LH training as well. As a general rule, if you have trained below 10–13 Hz on the right, you'll want to train below 14–17 Hz on the left. Let the brain and the assessment sheet guide you.

Time and Timing

My typical session, depending on the number of protocols I am using, will last about 20 minutes. It could be less (e.g., when there has been a history of head injury) and it could be more, up to 30 minutes (indicated if training effects are not holding). In this universe, it is possible that less is more; it is also possible that more is more.

Unless I know a patient well and have an established protocol, I don't train before either one of us is going to be away for any length of time. Of course, this too is a rule to be broken, particularly if there is an emergency that you feel training could address. Time allocation is a major issue when we are integrating neurofeedback with psychotherapy, and like everything else, it has to be addressed for the individual. Characteristically, I devote a good deal of our time initially to training, solely because affect regulation is vital to the success of talk therapy. As time goes on, my patients make the choice to train or to talk. Many can do both at the same time, with no apparent effect on outcome. But, as we discussed in Chapter 4, state—or perhaps more accurately, belief in state—influences all of our decisions. I will weigh in for training and at times insist on it, when I see evidence of reactivity or overarousal.

Additional Protocols in Developmental Trauma

We have focused primarily on finding the correct frequency for RH training at C4, C4–P4, T4–P4, and interhemispheric training at T3–T4 or C5–C6, and these will take us a long way. However, there are additional RH protocols to explore, as well as training on the midline. All of these trainings rely on changing the arousal curve. We will also explore several approaches that affect arousal but that do not rely on this model. Whatever you try, remember the goal is to quiet fear. Were there time and space, I could devote a chapter to each of these protocols, but given the scope of this book, I offer just a bit of the history and rationale for each one.

Right Temporal Focus and FP02

Allan Schore's (1994, 2003) work would suggest training at FP2 to address impaired prefrontal development and to enhance its capacity to regulate the amygdala. Use it with caution. I have seen some heightened reactivity with this protocol, in my experience, independent of reward frequency. It is as if we have poked at the unregulated amygdala and riled it up. This will not always be the case, and because the theory is so compelling, it is well worth exploring with your patient. But in response to these effects, I have relied on T4–FT8 (10–10 system) with its presumptive "appeal" to the insula, the seat of interoception in the brain, and a structure that inhibits the amygdala. If facial recognition and/or interpretation of facial expressions is impaired, I will focus some atten-

tion on T6 as well, either at T4–T6 or at T6 alone. T6 sits atop the fusi-
form gyrus, the part of the brain most specifically engaged with these
functions. Fear blindness—a lack of registration of fear in the other—is
often associated with antisocial personality and would be most directly
addressed at this site. As always, no matter what site or frequency, assess
first for the impact on arousal.

In 1999, drawing primarily on Ledoux's (1996) work as well as on
traditions in body and energy work, I decided to put an electrode at a
site I called *FPO2* (frontal pole–orbital on the right). Typically I train
here quite low, often beginning at 4–7 Hz (inhibit 0–6) and going lower,
and infrequently, higher to find the frequency that quiets fear. For most
people, FPO2 induces feelings of well-being and increased self-control.
This site is off the standard 10–20 system and sits at the juncture of the
right brow bone and the top of the nose, in the inner corner of the eye
socket (the site is included on the EGGer software). Most people will feel
a slight notch in the underside of the bone, and many will feel some
tenderness at this spot. This is the FPO2 placement (see Figure 7.2).
Ledoux (1998) describes the importance of this site:

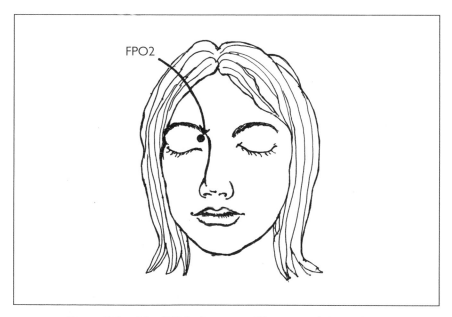

Figure 7.2.   The FPO2 placement. (Courtesy of the author.)

> The medial prefrontal cortex . . . receives signals from the sensory regions of the cortex and from the amygdala, and sends connections back to the amygdala, as well as to many of the areas to which the amygdala projects. The medial prefrontal cortex is thus nicely situated to be able to regulate the outputs of the amygdala on the basis of events in the outside world as well as on the basis of the amygdala's interpretation of those events. (p. 248)

One of my patients also made a significant contribution to the development of this protocol. She was descending into a full-blown PTSD episode and asked me to put pressure at the inner corner of her right eye. When I did, she ascended out of the flashback state and back into present time, within minutes. As she did, the arch in her back released and her tonic posture relaxed. Pressure on this point seemed to "short-circuit" the episode, but it did not help to forestall future ones. FPO2 was born to address the fear kindling of the RH amygdala, and the following case vignettes provide hints of its importance as a protocol for those suffering from developmental trauma. In these cases, FPO2 was usually combined with other protocols that preceded it, but this site, as you will see, seems to yield distinct results. The last vignette also offers a caution. FPO2 usually quiets fear, but at times it provokes fear memory. This is not necessarily a bad thing, but you will want to know how to work with trauma memories clinically if you intend to use this protocol.

FPO2 Case Vignettes

The day after we first used FPO2 training, my then 17-year-old patient with developmental trauma, anorexia and bulimia, and Asperger's reported the following: "I feel as if I am in a totally different brain, like someone turned off the static. I dropped down to a place I'd forgotten existed. Feelings of desperation about getting through the day are gone. It's like being washed." She went on to tell me about wanting to begin a binge, but seeing how it would affect her father, she stopped herself. She told me, "I had my first experience of moral compunction." (This case study is detailed in Chapter 9.)

We have spoken about the young woman, diagnosed with borderline personality disorder, who came to me because she was afraid she would kill someone. Her rage diminished greatly with several sessions at C4, and she felt it vanish after training at FPO2. She endorsed this site in her own idiom: "This is better than the best drug I've ever had. Everyone should have this training."

A 48-year-old woman, diagnosed with DID and developmental trauma, reported that she was feeling a memory beginning to emerge. "Felt memory" is the most common route for the return of traumatic material. I could watch it arise in her body and in her face. It came to her slowly. She remembered standing in a crib, wailing as her mother hit her repeatedly across the head with a plastic toy bat. We spent that session and several more processing what she had experienced. Later that first day she had a routine appointment with her physical therapist. He asked her with some alarm what had happened to her head. She had a ridge across the top of her skull!

A colleague reported an overwhelming sense of smell. She could smell everything at twice its normal intensity, and she was on vacation in the Caribbean where every flower and vine competed for her olfactory attention. I had a similar experience. Shortly after FPO2 training, I was driving down a highway when I suddenly smelled hamburger. It kept getting stronger until I came to a Burger King about 2 miles from where I first caught wind of it. The smell went away shortly after I passed it. My sense of smell was more like that of a wolf in the wild than a woman on her way to Cape Cod. The olfactory bulb lies directly behind FPO2 and we can activate it at this site.

Another colleague, who was helping me test the efficacy and effects of this site soon after I first found it, gave this fascinating report. As a 12-year-old, she had jumped over a fence and landed on a spike that went through her foot. She had tried every approach she knew since then to address the unrelenting pain in that foot, to no avail. After a brief training at FPO2, the pain went away. This was in 1999. I have checked in with her periodically to ask if the pain had returned, and as of our last talk, 10 years or so later, it hadn't. She believes that this training addressed chronic inflammation, and if so, it further suggests that we are quieting amygdala reactivity, as seen in fMRI studies of chronic pain (e.g., Neugebauer, Li, Bird, & Han, [2004]).

Perhaps the single most significant outcome in terms of developmental trauma was for a multiparous pregnant woman with a diagnosis of BPD and a history of multiple hospitalizations, including two for severe postpartum depression who we have met earlier in this book. We observed "in- session" effects on fetal movement during FPO2 training that we didn't see with training at other RH sites. Fetal movement that the mother had described as "somersaults" and as "almost aggressive," quieted. (Fetal movement begins at the same time that the amygdala comes online in utero.) The mother reported, "Calm mother, calm baby." She suffered no postpartum depression and the baby was an exceptionally well-regulated infant and toddler. This result suggests that there may be an important role for neurofeedback training, perhaps specifically at FPO2, in the prevention of intergenerational transmission of trauma. (You can read more about this case, session by session, in Chapter 9.)

The last vignette is that of a 35-year-old woman who, along with a history of severe sadistic sexual and physical abuse and maternal neglect, also had suffered a RH stroke (transient ischemic attack; TIA), migraines, and a seizure disorder. Prior to using FPO2, she had gained significant stability in all arenas with central and temporal training on both hemispheres. I would not have trained her at FPO2 until she had gained this stability—an important cautionary point when considering the use of this protocol. As we will see, she had a powerful response even with the level of regulation she had achieved.

She had only sparse recall of her life up to age 13. Given her history and her stability, she seemed a good candidate for FPO2 training. Within a minute, her face began to twitch, often a precursor of migraine or seizure. We ended the training immediately. The twitching stopped, but she did not like how she felt. It may have been that this protocol had precipitated the beginning of a seizure. She did not develop one, but in the next 2 weeks she remembered many significant and traumatic events from that missing time period. These memories returned through dreams and spontaneous recall. She was overwhelmed with the magnitude of memory, and we spent many therapy sessions on the material that arose after the brief activation of the amygdala. It seems we had set off a process in her brain that activated encoded traumatic memory and the possible eruption of seizure—an electric brew of instability and terror. She did not, however, suffer abreaction and she did not feel retraumatized. Before using this vignette here, I asked her if she would ever consider FPO2 training again. She said that it had been very rough, but that she would definitely do it again, saying, "It gave me my life back." (Consult FPO2 protocol guide in Appendix for more information.)

Frontal and Prefrontal Training

As you may remember from Chapter 2, the frontal areas of the brain are devoted to planning and execution (executive function). Emotion serves motion, and motion that is not in response to habit, instinct, or emergency requires planning. RH frontal sites are also very much involved in regulation of the amygdala. Without this capacity, events are processed as emergencies, even when they're not, which makes planning subjectively irrelevant. Under threat, we don't make plans, we take action. Training at these sites, either unipolar or in a bipolar montage with T4, can be helpful in quieting reactivity. FZ may be the most useful frontal site. It sits atop the dorsomedial prefrontal cortex (DMPFC)—the center of conceptual self-awareness—and beneath that, the ventromedial prefrontal cortex (VMPFC)—embodied self-awareness—and seems to speak to them. As the fMRI literature in OCD (Fitzgerald et al., 2005) and clinical neurofeedback experience would suggest, training at FZ can address obsessive and compulsive symptoms. Studies of peak performers (Baumeister, Reinecke, Leisen, & Weiss, 2008; Doppelmayr, Finkenzeller, & Sauseng, 2008) as well as EEG studies related to anxiety (Inanaga, 1998; Suetsugi et al., 2000) reveal interesting, somewhat counterintuitive findings on frequency at FZ. These studies show that peak performers make higher than average theta amplitudes at FZ. As a result of these findings, I begin training at 5–8 Hz, ready to move the reward band up or down, more often down, depending on the individual response. Practitioners have also used F3–F4 to quiet reactivity in this region. F4 has been colloquially referred to as "the valium spot."

Parietal Training

Particularly for those patients who are reactive to frontal and prefrontal training, I recommend going to the back of the head. Training at PZ,

8–11 Hz or lower, usually quiets anxiety without risking reactivity. Since 8–11 Hz is the normative (i.e., dominant) frequency band at PZ, we have a good rationale for beginning here. I also can go to the temporal–parietal–occipital (TPO) junction, using an interhemispheric protocol. This is the tristate area in the brain. I explored this placement first with a woman who suffered from severe IBS and who relied on self-harm to manage her affect storms. I wanted to try to quiet her vagal reactivity. All of these symptoms quieted considerably, but did not entirely go away. In the terms of polyvagal theory (Porges, 2011), I wanted to quiet the reptilian and limbic pathways to allow more social vagal activity. Like O1–O2, it seems to help people who are filled with anticipatory anxiety (hypervigilance in this population) to "lay back" just a little, to be less reactive.

One young woman, an adolescent adoptee who was teetering at the brink of psychosis, told me after training that she just didn't react to provocations like she had previously. She actually no longer experienced the same events as provocative. Like so many of my patients, she didn't quite recognize herself in her lack of reactivity. P4–A2 can also be used primarily to calm sensory reactivity and perhaps the vagus. Dr. Angelo Bolea (personal communication, April 29, 1998) used this placement initially with patients hospitalized with schizophrenia and considered to be untreatable, and the treatment brought them out of seclusion rooms and then out of the hospital.

P5–A1 has been remarkably effective in quieting negative self-talk. P5 seems to address repetitive patterns at Wernicke's area, the part of the brain that processes verbal intake (the parent's critical voice taunts and echoes here). Following Bolea's lead, I train here, usually starting at 12–15 Hz, and watch for effects not only on the internalized voice but on arousal.

As you enter and explore this field, you are likely to encounter many apparently divergent protocols to address the same issue. Practitioners are using infra-low frequency (ILF) training, as well as training slow cortical potentials (SCP), rewarding at below 1 Hz. Others are relying on Z-score training, which addresses amplitude excesses and insufficiencies. People use inhibit strategies; that is, they train the brain to reduce

certain frequencies without a specific reward frequency. Some researchers are focusing on training event-related potentials (ERPs), which are
the wave-form responses to stimuli. We know from McFarlane's work
(1993) that ERPs are poorly organized in traumatized patients, so this
approach to training may yield significant benefit (see Figure C.8). Les
Fehmi, coauthor of *The Open Focus Brain* (Fehmi & Robbins, 2007),
trains these patients to make synchronous alpha. The number of possible
protocols may approach infinite, but our clinical time is anything but. As
a result, we often find ourselves relying on what has worked for us most
reliably. I have tried the following protocols after conversations with
their authors. I am interested in the birth story of protocols, and if these
seem coherent and the training effects notable, then I try them.

Beta Reset™

This protocol has a compelling birth story. It arises from research on the
regulating influence of the cerebellum, on glial communication, and on
the importance of gamma frequency (40 Hz) in mind–body communication and the sudden experience of insight, which we call the "aha
moment." Jeremy Schmahmann at Harvard University and Massachusetts General Hospital is one of the prime movers in researching the
cerebellum. "While the [research] was fraught with problems," Schmahmann (1999) says, "it looks like there is indeed a motor cerebellum and
a cognitive cerebellum." It seems likely that "the cerebellum is doing
most of the brain's fine-tuned coordination, not just for our muscles but
for our senses, memories, emotions, thoughts, and attention." Another
researcher who is also interested in the cerebellum, Carl Anderson,
teamed up with Martin Teicher (as cited in Teicher, Glod, Surrey, &
Swett, 1993) to consider the effects of early trauma on the cerebellum,
particularly on its central structure, the vermis. They concluded: "Overall, studies on the effects of early stress . . . led to the novel hypothesis
that early stress exerts deleterious effects on the cerebellar vermis. . . .
These findings fit with a growing body of research indicating that the
cerebellum may play a much greater role in mental health than hitherto
realized" (as cited in Teicher et al., 1993, p. 241).

Jaclyn Gisburne read this research (Fink et al., 1996; Hagmann et al.,
2008; Teicher et al., 1993) and integrated it with emerging literature on

the active role of glia (Fields, 2010; Koob, 2009) and on the special properties of gamma (Sheth, Sandkuhler, & Bhattacharya, 2009; Kounois & Beeman, 2009). She started to work as close to the cerebellum as she could, placing sensors at the inion ridge (IR) and on the parietal lobe (two-channel, interhemispheric training). With beta reset we seem to be training the brain to reach toward gamma in 90-second increments beginning at 16–19 Hz up to 38–42 Hz (40 Hz). The "aha" moments in life are registered in gamma, and these moments always signify a new coordination of information, a novel rearrangement that shivers down the spine. With its quick steps up into gamma, beta reset keeps making new demands on the brain, and this focus on novelty may be one of its key features. People who have suffered trauma are caught in repetition and reactivity that makes it difficult to learn new things, particularly new gestalts, new ways of thinking. But our brains are wired for novelty; it is an inherent property in learning. With beta reset, the brain has just settled into a frequency band when it is asked to reach for another, and then again until it reaches gamma. After 90 seconds at 38–42 Hz, we return to 16–19 Hz to bring the brain back closer to where it lives.

I have used this protocol extensively with patients who have developmental trauma, and many report a subtle but noticeable change in their sense of self. All report less reactivity and more fluidity. Many describe becoming more organized and tell me about finally clearing their garages or their overtopped desks. As their nervous systems become more organized, so do they. Although there is a robust signal at the ridge, we can only speculate on its source and destination. We don't know if we are reaching the cerebellum, and if we are, how we are, but the results with this placement suggest that whatever circuits we are tapping into can play a critical role in self-regulation.

Alpha Down

This protocol was developed in a collaboration between Ruth Lanius and Thomas Ros. Ros had been well schooled in neurofeedback by one of its most important researchers, John Gruzelier, in London, England, but he knew very little about trauma before he met Ruth Lanius in London, Ontario, Canada. Lanius, who is one of the foremost fMRI researchers in the field of developmental trauma, was just beginning to explore neurofeedback. Their initial research demonstrated that just one 30-minute session of down-training alpha (she used 8–12 Hz) at PZ impacted the connectivity of the structures prominent in the salience and default networks in the brain (Ros et al., 2013). The default network underwrites self-reflection and the salience network responds to stimuli prequalified as worthy of attention. Both networks are responsive to changes in alpha. The default network, also called the *resting state* network, is at play when the mind is off-task, and it is typically self-referential. Recall the slides (Figure C.4) that show the liveliness of this network in non-traumatized controls and the lack of any activity in those with severe developmental trauma. This network consolidates, stabilizes, and sets the context for future information processing. It is the coherent self, going forward. Its paucity in individuals with developmental trauma illustrates the disrupted, diminished sense of self sadly typical for these patients.

The salience or alertness network facilitates switching between other large-scale networks that allow working memory and attention in response to meaningful stimuli. In developmental trauma this is often the hypervigilance network. In her initial studies (Ros, et al., 2013 of changes after neurofeedback, Lanius saw less recruitment of the left amygdala after training than before. The left amygdala is very much a part of the salience network in developmental trauma but not in non-traumatized populations. (You might be thinking, maybe we should train to address the LH amygdala—and I am thinking just that, perhaps at FPO1.) The salience network is also involved in communication between the anterior and the posterior insula, which modulate autonomic reactivity to stimuli, and it serves to couple activity between the anterior cingulate (FZ) and mid-cingulate (CZ), facilitating rapid access to the motor system. Lanius and Ros (in press) hypothesized that reducing alpha would increase connectivity in both networks. Unlike most clinicians, they could test their hypothesis with pre and post fMRI, and Qs. Their hypothesis was correct.

Clinically, Kluetsch et al. (2013) saw significant change in people suffering from chronic developmental trauma. They reported fewer intrusive thoughts and more abiding calm. They described themselves as clearer, and those with dissociative symptoms reported that they were gone. One of her patients reported that the voices in her head had ceased and that there were no more "parts." She described suddenly being in her body. But, as we might suspect, she was now dealing with intense feelings that had been kept at bay, presumably by these obfuscating repetitive patterns, which we often call defenses. She was able to use her therapy to address these feelings, and both doctor and patient learned to do this training in small doses. This patient also represented this process in the sketch in Figure 7.3.

Alpha–Theta

We have discussed at some length how we can help people produce frequencies that quiet arousal and enhance regulation. But frequencies also encode information related to global domains such as capacity, memory, and creativity. The frequency most studied in this regard is theta (4–7 Hz). We can train people to drop into the realm of theta with an approach called alpha–theta. Here we discuss when this protocol is recommended and when it may not be.

Alpha–theta, or deep state training, is probably the most celebrated protocol in the fields of PTSD, addiction, and, interestingly, peak performance. This is a protocol with many authors, the most influential among them being Elmer and Alyce Green and Eugene Peniston. The Greens, then at the Menninger Clinic in Topeka, Kansas (Green & Green, 1989), were exploring theta training as a portal to expanded consciousness. One of the Greens' workshop students, Eugene Peniston, took their work with "normals" and designed what was to become the Peniston–Kulkosky or alpha–theta protocol. His goal was to provide his patients with access to the often unremembered trauma (coded in theta) while holding the nervous system in a state of calm (alpha).

Peniston worked at the VA Medical Center in Fort Lyon, Colorado, with men suffering from severe PTSD and crippling addiction to alcohol. Their first study (Peniston & Kulkosky, 1989) was with alcoholics who had been hospitalized four or more times due to relapse. All participants were given an EEG, the Beck Depression Inventory (BDI), the Minnesota Multiphasic Personality Inventory (MMPI), and the Millon Clinical Multiaxial Inventory (MCMI). They all had blood taken to measure levels of stress hormones. Ten of the 30 study participants were not alcoholic and

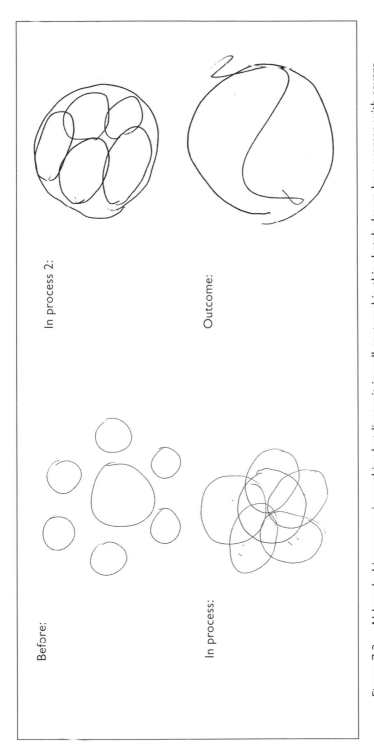

Before:

In process:

In process 2:

Outcome:

Figure 7.3. Although this process is anything but linear, it is well captured in this sketch drawn by a woman with severe dissociative disorder. Self-representations before, during, and after neurofeedback. (Reprinted with permission of Teresa Kinney.)

were only given these measurements; 20 were relapsed alcoholics. Ten alcoholic controls were provided with standard therapies (i.e., talk sessions and a 12-step programs) and 10 of the 20 relapsed alcoholics were trained with alpha–theta every day for a month in addition to standard therapy.

All of those given standard treatment were rehospitalized within 18 months. In the alpha–theta group, eight stopped drinking completely, one drank once but got sick (dubbed the *Peniston flu*) and didn't drink again, and one continued to drink but the alcohol didn't make him drunk. These patients showed increased power in both alpha and theta frequencies, stabilization of beta-endorphin levels, clear and positive changes on both personality inventories, and a marked reduction in depression as measured by the BDI. These results were maintained, without further hospitalization, on 3-year follow-up. Experts in addiction have told me that they expect a 75–80% relapse rate.

Of course, most of these vets had a comorbidity: the Vietnam war. These were the men (there were only men in these initial studies) whose condition had called for a new diagnosis: PTSD. In 1991, Peniston and Kulkosky published the results of a second study on the use of alpha–theta to resolve symptoms of PTSD. By the end of the month-long study, again the alpha–theta group showed marked improvement in clinical scales and in symptoms. They too normalized their MMPI and MCMI scores (see Figure 7.4). Nightmares, flashbacks, and manifestations of hypervigilance were significantly reduced, and they used less psychotropic medication after training. In a follow-up 2½ years later, 12 of the 15 alpha–theta veterans were living normal lives, whereas all 14 in the control group were still suffering from PTSD.

There has only been one follow-up study of alpha–theta and that has been with addictions. Although published results don't reference developmental trauma, it is likely that a good number of these men and women did in fact have these histories, a hunch confirmed in personal correspondence with two of the study's investigators. The study was spearheaded by Bill Scott who learned this approach from his boss and mentor, Eugene Peniston. He and his colleagues conducted this research at an addictions treatment center, called Cri-Help, in Los Angeles (Scott, Kaiser, Othmer, & Sideroff, 2005). The outcomes were similar to those of

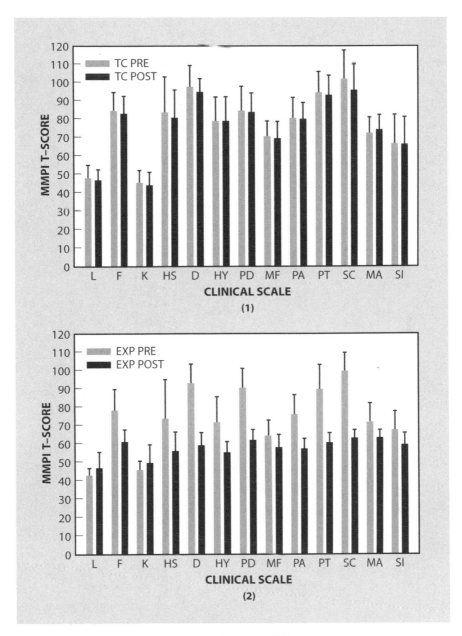

Figure 7.4.   Pre- and post-MMPI in PTSD veterans receiving
thirty 30-minute alpha–theta sessions compared to controls in treatment
as usual after one month. (Peniston & Kulkosky, 1991;
courtesy of *Medical Psychotherapy*.)

Peniston and Kulkosky (1991). Scott et al. had 121 volunteers, 49 women and 72 men, ranging in age from 19 to 53. The primary drugs of choice were heroin, 31%; crack cocaine, 28%; methamphetamine, 26%; alcohol, 6%; and other controlled substances, 9%. Ninety-four percent of this population were polydrug abusers. Anyone with a diagnosis of psychosis, personality disorder, or seizure disorder was excluded. At 12-month follow-up, of those who could be contacted, 36 of 47 neurofeedback subjects were abstinent (71%) and 12 of 27 (44%) of the controls. The researchers also found substantial changes in MMPI scores. These outcomes suggest that alpha–theta training can further quiet reactivity and ease craving for substances that have been used to bear overwhelming fear-driven states.

As therapists working with trauma, it's clear that we should be interested in alpha–theta training. With the exception of FPO2 (which Siegfried Othmer once called the *poor man's alpha–theta*), all of the training described to this point is done primarily with eyes open. Most of the day's important tasks are done with our eyes open, so it is important for most training to be done that way too. When we close our eyes, we change the environment of our brains. We make more alpha (higher amplitude) almost immediately. Some people with developmental trauma will become more hypervigilant with their eyes closed, and you might see this in the EEG as a lack of change in alpha amplitudes.

Ed Hamlin elaborated on the issue of alpha abnormalities in developmental trauma: "Not only do I see a lack of typical eyes-closed alpha [amplitude increase] [the largest state change in the waking EEG], but with the [developmental trauma] population we see alpha amplitude very often *drop* when the eyes are closed. It happens so often we've considered it as a possible marker variable" (personal communication, December 10, 2012). Having lost the use of their primary sense to warn them of inevitable and imminent danger, these patients typically become hyperfocused to pick up other clues from the environment, mostly through sound. As a result, I don't typically introduce deep state training until my patient trusts me and the treatment surround enough to be able to comfortably close her eyes. The patient needs to feel secure in the holding environment that is our relationship.

Alpha usually represents a state of physical and emotional relaxation—clearly not a strong suit for trauma survivors. It is also thought of as the bridge state between the unconscious (delta) via the subconscious (theta) to the conscious (beta). As we fall asleep, we drop from beta (awake) to alpha (relaxed) to theta (hypnogogic) and then into delta (sleep), and we reverse that process as we are waking up. People who make sufficient alpha as they ascend from sleeping to waking will remember their dreams. Remembering dreams may, in fact, offer us a template for the efficacy of alpha–theta training. When we train alpha, we are strengthening the bridge between the conscious and the subconscious, giving us greater access to the information coded there. When we train theta, we gain access to the rhythms beneath consciousness, which hold, at least as the theory goes and as practice suggests, a storehouse of early implicit memory.

Before we venture further into theory, let's get a picture of how this process proceeds. In my practice, I work with my patients, using eyes-open training and psychotherapy, to stabilize fear and reactivity and to acquaint their nervous systems with a state of calm before we do any deep state exploration. I introduce deep state training only when my patients are no longer reactive—that is, when they inhabit a nervous system in control of itself. As you'll soon see, I learned this the hard way. This preparation will help patients assume and maintain a "witness position," rather than becoming, yet again, an unwilling participant in horror, should training in theta exhume early disturbing events. They can look at events that arise as if they were passively watching a film. Bill Scott describes it this way: "Because they are in a quiet state, people don't have flashbacks or re-experience the trauma. They become emotional, and they'll cry, but they won't re-experience. They process it cortically" (as cited in Robbins, 2000, p. 170). This has been the case most of the time in my practice too, but, as we will see shortly, not always.

Images, memories of a sort, can arise spontaneously with alpha–theta training. Recall the woman described earlier who watched her father molesting her as a baby as she hovered at the ceiling (Chapter 3). Images also often arise in the dreamscape the night of, or following, an alpha–

theta session. One woman, who was troubled by ongoing doubt about the impact of early trauma on her and her two siblings, reported the following dream the night after one of her early alpha–theta sessions:

> I was driving with a friend on a mountain road in a Third World country. As we came around a corner, we saw a huge boulder, three stories high, rolling down the mountain right at us. My friend swerved the car to the edge of the drop-off, and the boulder rumbled past us. I was afraid to get out of the car because I thought I would fall off the cliff, but when I opened the door, I saw it was just a gentle, grassy slope down to the forest.
>
> I joined my friend at the back of the car and asked her if the boulder had scared her too. She said that it hadn't; that she'd had a different life from mine. We walked down the road toward a small ocean beach. There was no sign of the boulder; no scarring of the trees along the road or marks in the sand. There were three children playing on the beach. I felt confused because there was no sign of the boulder. I commented on this to my friend, but the question was addressed by a man I couldn't see. He told me to look at the mountains that stretched out into the sea. I saw a chain of ragged peaks right under the surface of the water. The man said, "It filled in a space in the chain, so you can't see it."

She awoke suddenly from this dream (which, oddly, she never experienced as a nightmare) in a state of terror. In talking about it, she realized that there were two chains of mountains and that they looked like the double helix. She had, it seemed, dreamt her cellular memory not only of the impact of trauma, but of the impact of denial.

Neurofeedback literature is replete with these kinds of reports. Both of these women felt relieved that they "knew" and understood their experiences more deeply. Unfortunately, however, knowing does not always promote resolution. This is true in the developmental trauma population as a whole. Some are freed by knowing, and others experience knowing as further assault. Those in the latter category report that before they remembered what had happened to them, they were living apparently normal lives. After they discovered their histories, they experienced breakdowns. Both potentialities, I suspect, arise in the theta realm. Theta may well be the frequency of knowing as surely as beta is the frequency of thinking. I don't recommend alpha–theta training until the nervous system is stable and can protect the patient against adverse reactions to any new discovery.

For this training, the patient lies in a reclining chair that cradles the body. I have used earphones, eye shields, and eye pillows but most of my patients who have lived on such a thin tether to reality prefer not to be further cut off. They close their eyes and listen to the sounds from the computer. PZ–A2 is the site most commonly used. There is an argument to be made, however, that P4 may be the better site, particularly when working with early-encoded memory. The RH is the learning center for infants and toddlers before the age of 24 months as well as the center of primary process and implicit memory. Nancy White uses P4–A2 because it is "near the area of the brain associated with boundaries of the self," the precuneus (White & Richards, 2009, p. 146). Whatever aspect of self we may be addressing, it does seem that P4 sits atop the epicenter of the preverbal unconscious, and if this is so, it is exactly where we want to be.

I reward alpha at 8–11 Hz and theta at 4–7 Hz, and I inhibit 2–5 Hz to help my patient resist sleep and stay out of the depths of delta, at least initially. I use 15–22 Hz inhibit to quiet mental chatter. The interplay or "crossover" (the term used) of alpha and theta bands is the dance between the unconscious and the conscious, between not knowing and knowing, and between the subcortical and the cortical rhythms. Typically patients begin with alpha amplitudes higher than theta amplitudes, but over the course of some minutes the alpha will drop and the theta will rise slightly, signaling a state of consciousness deeper than relaxation. There is a sub-set of patients whose theta begins higher than their alpha and stays that way throughout the session(s). This seems to be a normal variant, and we are still looking not only for a drop in alpha, but for a rise in theta, and of course the patient's report of subjective experience. It is usually during this crossover that patients experience vivid trauma imagery, but neither crossover nor images are essential for alpha–theta training to be helpful. As suggested by the vignette above, people can also experience images from alpha–theta training in their dreams following sessions.

In his book, *Getting Started with Neurofeedback*, John Demos (2005) describes five classes of response to alpha–theta training as:

the client with negative experiences, such as painful imagery or body sensations; the client with frustration who remarks, "I just can't get deep"; the client who goes to sleep; the client with no experiences but who reports a state of deep relaxation; and the client with excellent experiences, such as insight and the unlocking of repressed memories. (p. 194)

I have seen the same, but the negative responses are almost always related to fear. On a couple of occasions, patients have pulled off the electrodes, due to mounting but nonspecific, nonverbal sensations of terror.

Although intuitively we would expect that crossover and access to "repressed" memory would be the most beneficial, it is not clear if one of these responses better predicts resolution of trauma. It does seem clear that the brain is actively engaged in decisions on how to manage its introduction to these new depths and some patients, as we will see, want nothing to do with the dive.

There is an added dimension in alpha–theta training. The reward sounds in the EEGer—the sound of a brook and a bing for alpha and ocean waves and a gong for theta—not only alert the brain to the changing amplitudes of alpha and theta, but reinforce these frequencies. The brook and the bing are at about 10 Hz, and the waves and the gong are at about 6 Hz. This process, called *entrainment*, is not a learning process, and its effects alone are much less substantial than training the brain, but the resonance of the rewards may smooth the descent and deepen access to the sub- and unconscious realms.

Like the Greens, most neurofeedback clinicians believe that alpha–theta training opens the brain to new learning by giving it access to theta. In this regard, it may be somewhat akin to hypnosis. Both seem to allow rescripting of old events and our reactions to them. I work with my patients to develop their own personalized scripts. Some prefer to read their script to themselves as they practice quieting their breathing before we begin training, and others prefer that I read it to them. It is important to note that the unconscious seems to screen out qualifiers. If you say to yourself "I don't want to feel afraid," the unconscious seems to hear "*feel afraid*," reinforcing the very message we want to change. So the script should read more like "I am calm when. . . . " Scott (as cited in Robbins, 2000, pp. 172–173) teaches that the new script should include images of the desired personality, instructions to the unconscious on new ways to handle material that might come up, and clear images of a safe place.

I have mentioned the story of a young adult who had been abandoned as a day-old premature infant and found in a shoebox on the steps of a police station, close to death. When I met her 20-some years later, she was extremely overaroused, agitated, and dysregulated, even after a year of inpatient treatment. She responded quickly to eyes-open training and made rapid gains in self-regulation, relationships, and academics. She was able to discontinue lithium and end day treatment within 4 months of beginning intensive neurofeedback and psychotherapy (three times a week).

She met all criteria, I thought, to benefit from alpha–theta training, which we did intensively over a weekend. She found it hard to settle in, and when she did all she could sense was the sound of moaning. When she came in for her regular appointment 2 days later, this normally well-dressed and carefully groomed young woman was noticeably disheveled. She was very upset about the alpha–theta training. It had left her feeling disorganized and what was even harder, distrustful of me. She refused to do any more training of any kind, and the therapy had to be devoted to the repair of our relationship. Three months later she told me that her dog, her most beloved attachment figure, was sick. It turned out that she hadn't been feeding him regularly. She also told me that she hadn't had her garbage removed for 3 months; that it was piling up in her garage! It seemed to me that she was reliving her experience in the orphanage; in fact, in every way but actual, she was in the orphanage. It seems that alpha–theta training took her there and left her.

Once she told me about what was going on, we were able to talk about it and begin the process of resolution. She immediately began to care for her dog and although embarrassed, got her rotting garbage hauled away. She was able to regain the present. But I was now directly associated with her torment, so repair was a complex and never fully completed task. (She did tell me later in a chance meeting that our time together was some of the best she'd had in her life.) Other patients who had experiences of early maternal deprivation also had negative reactions to alpha–theta training. The young woman who tore off the electrodes had been physically and emotionally tortured by her mother, and she was understandably reluctant to revisit that realm. (You can read about her experience in more detail in Chapter 9.) I use the word *realm* because theta holds more than memory. For these patients, neglected and abused in early childhood, it retains the gestalt of this experience, the unconscious or subconscious knowing, and for many it seems to hold this memory vividly, even without images.

Most people who have had successful alpha–theta experiences have had trauma histories, but in my practice there are a significant number of people who struggle with it. I suspect now that the degree of felt motherlessness is the variable, or at least supreme among the multiple variables, that predicts outcome. The absence or frightening presence of the mother is held in these developmentally early rhythms. The script process may offer a clue. The patient who has no coherent sense of self is asked to script a desired personality. Where would this come from? For these patients, the desired personality is conceived of only as a personality that is not theirs. It is constructed in the negative. Many have to stretch to conceptualize a safe place. *Safe* is a construct that emerges from an internal sense of security in the presence of others. A *safe place* has to act as a reminder of safety in relationship. And these patients often don't feel in a position to influence much of anything, particularly the daunting shadows of their unconscious.

It is unlikely that alpha–theta is a de novo state. As I wrote (Fisher, 2009):

> The experience one has is probably one already known to the brain/mind and recalled in this deep state training. If this speculation proves to be accurate, then we might assume that states of bliss and oneness, often reported by those training in alpha–theta, relate to early blissful fusion experiences between mother and infant. My adult adoptee had no such experience. (p. 330)

Instead she and several other patients seemed to be plunged into what they had experienced in their early childhoods: the uninhabitable territory of no mother—an endless, terrifying echo. Alpha–theta training invites surrender and encourages integration. Who would decide to surrender to this? And what would allow for integration? It may be that there needs to be enough sense of a safe "self–other" connection established for alpha–theta to be useful. There needs to be a good-enough mother encoded in this developmentally early theta for patients to visit there safely.

Alpha–Theta and Repressed Memory

Alpha–theta training takes the brain into theta, and early childhood memory seems to be encoded here, in this hypnogogic realm. Consider this quote by Lawrence Kubie (as cited in Green & Green, 1989) on the significance of this realm:

> The hypnogogic reverie might be called a dream without distortion. Its immediate instigator is the day's "unfinished business," but like the dream it derives from more remote "unfinished business" of an entire lifetime as well. . . . Whatever the explanation . . . with hypnogogic reverie significant information about the past can be made readily and directly available. (p.150)

This training approach sheds a new light on the process that we have thought of as repression. As we have discussed earlier, memory is state-dependent, and state depends on the frequencies at which our brain is firing. When we are infants and small children, or when we are adults in shock, we are making slow waves, delta or theta, as the primary rhythms. These frequencies hold the archives of how it was then and of what happened then. Alpha–theta training gives us access to these archives by giving us access to these rhythms. Atmospheres and events that are recovered are not so much repressed or even forgotten as they are inaccessible. Alpha–theta training gives us access.

As suggested above, there is an important clinical judgment to be made as to whether access will be beneficial. Alpha–theta training is no longer about affect regulation, although many will feel more regulated by it. It is about knowing. Your patient needs to come to a place where knowing or having a felt sense of experience will be productive. If you venture down this path and your patient is not ready or able to be curious about what arises—if he cannot be a witness—you'll know. There is nothing subtle about it. In most cases when this happens, we can train the patient with eyes open using the protocols that have already helped regulate intense affect, and she will again be able to quiet CNS reactivity, so imbedded in the experience that has just been touched on. For some, this kind of alpha–theta response suggests that we continue with higher frequency, eyes-open training and forgo alpha–theta. The brain is informing you of turbulence still too great to pursue. For others, particularly for those who want to do so, we can revisit alpha–theta after further calming, and for some, we can help by training with eyes open after a deep state session to firmly reestablish cortical control.

As with all other training, it is imperative to listen to the brain when you are training it to drop into its deepest recesses. There is mystery here and we cannot predict what we will find when we enter the ancient caves. But when your patient can use alpha–theta training, there is probably no deeper journey of consciousness.

Designing New Protocols

As you become increasingly experienced and proficient with neurofeedback, you may well become engaged in the design of new protocols. The three protocols I outlined above—FPO2, beta reset, and alpha down— offer a template for the process. They emerge from a knowledge of brain research—from an awareness of the specificity of different brain regions and the importance of brain networks—and from reading the literature in development and trauma, as well as in neurofeedback and body work—all seasoned with clinical intuition. Don't be overwhelmed. Few psychotherapists have any training in neuroscience, but you'll learn it. Certification in neurofeedback requires at least a fundamental understanding of neuroanatomy and neurophysiology. It is fascinating, particularly when you can translate what you have learned into a training hypothesis, which you can test, in yourself first, to see in this N of 1, if your hunch is correct.

Brain research (Lanius, Vermetten, & Pain, 2010; Porges, 2009; van der Kolk, MacFarlane, & Weiseath, 2007) highlights specific brain structures that are associated with developmental trauma, and we can include these areas as we consider developing new protocols: the insula (FT8–FT7 on the 10–10 system), the anterior cingulate (FZ), the posterior cingulate (PZ), and the precuneus (P4), to name a few. Emerging neuroscience and practitioner experience also suggest training the linkages to the cerebellum, which we may be picking up at the inion ridge. Brain science is evolving almost daily, however, and there will continue to be findings that relate to developmental trauma. When trying a new approach, it is compelling to have a rationale grounded in neuroscience but not overly defined by it. Neuroscience is just beginning to recognize the nature of the brain's frequency domain and networks. Not all that long ago electrical activity was regarded as noise. Forty years ago, researchers dismissed most of the human genome as "junk DNA" (Ohno, 1972; Orgel & Crick, 1980). This "junk" is now understood as the plastic element of DNA, the epigenetic realm that decides which genes are turned on and which turned off (Wells, 2011). We learn and when we do, paradigms change. Clearly, the brain's electrical activity is anything but noise.

Chapter **8**

The Integration of Neurofeedback and Psychotherapy

"I knew you were a good therapist and that you cared about me, but I didn't really know that you existed. Now you do and so do I."
—neurofeedback patient

This is a quote from a patient who suffered from dissociative identity as a result of severe maternal abuse and neglect, routine physical and sexual assaults, paternal abandonment, domestic violence, and poverty and food insecurity—the total catastrophe of developmental trauma. She is describing the core change I have come to expect with the integration of neurofeedback and psychotherapy: the emergence of a self and an other.

As we have seen, this emergence comes about through affect regulation, just as Schore, Siegel, van der Kolk, and others have said—most specifically, through regulating the circuitries of fear, rage, and shame that have been firing and wiring together since birth, or even earlier, since the birth of the amygdala at 5 to 6 months in utero. I have just not found this level of healing possible with psychotherapy alone. I have been able to help my patients understand both why and how these histories have affected them. I have worked with them dynamically and behaviorally to learn to ride these storm surges as best they can, but before neurofeedback I had no way to help them stop the surges where they begin: in the brain. It bears repeating that it is much easier to reach the mind through the brain than it is to reach the brain through the mind.

That being said, this developing mind is fundamentally relational and requires a relationship in which to grow, where it is understood, nurtured, directed, and supported to flourish. The regulated brain will give rise to the regulated mind, which, as we know primarily from meditation literature and practice, will then further regulate the brain. It is difficult to imagine how someone would emerge from the level of malevolent chaos this young woman survived without the attuned presence of an other. Put simply, she needed neurofeedback to organize her developmentally injured, disorganized, fear-driven brain; and to know that I existed at all, and she needed me to lend her my regulation; to embrace, understand, and nurture her emerging self; and explore with her, her increasingly complex and nuanced mind.

Even as we explore the interplay of psychotherapy and neurofeedback and the importance of this primary relationship, it is also important to note that it is likely, even in the near future, that neurofeedback will be available where psychotherapy is not. Psychotherapy is a Western tradition that is sparsely practiced in the rest of the world. Neurofeedback is cross-cultural: It doesn't depend on language, verbal processing, or cultural bias. Even without therapy, in as much as neurofeedback calms fear and reactivity, it facilitates the capacity for attachment, and it will be important.

Lack of self-regulation usually translates to behaving badly, erratically, and often dangerously. More often than not it leads to conflictual, need-based relationships, including those with therapists, and these conflicts routinely create even more amygdala-driven reactions. These patients are ashamed of being ashamed and afraid of being afraid. This is true for most of us, of course, but thankfully most of us do not feel these feelings with the same level of unremitting intensity. Rage often seems more syntonic, particularly for men and boys. It can pass as a narrative of power and fearlessness. It is always self-justifying, and it can mask shame. One boy in foster care described the "rage monster" that lived inside him. He felt at the mercy of his rage, and it was merciless.

This boy, as is true for so many like him, lost control, hurt someone badly, and ended up in juvenile detention only to go on to adult prison. At that time I could only help him understand the rage monster; I couldn't help him tame it. Understanding and interpersonal regulation helped him, but they could not suffice.

Trying to ride these primary negative emotions is like riding a tall, wild horse. The reactions to them, the emotions over having emotions, make the ride even harder. It is akin to putting a second wild horse on top of the first and trying to ride them both. This geometric propagation of negative affect is always at the ready because these patients live in kindling, reactive nervous systems. They live in reaction; it is their default mode. As we have discussed, our first task in life and in psychotherapy is affect regulation. Neurofeedback will help accomplish this. But as is true for young children, affect regulation is a necessary but not sufficient condition for self.

In this chapter, we consider how these two modalities complement the recovery, or in some cases, the birth of self. I explore the complicated but ultimately salutary effect of affect regulation on psychotherapy with these patients, including the way it can affect transference and counter-transference and, in that, how it is likely to affect the therapy relationship; the possibility of "transference cure"; and the impact of affect regulation on identity and how to anticipate and work with this impact in therapy. We also discuss the concept of inaccessible, state-dependent memory in contrast to the long held concept of repressed memory; how to help patients navigate a new relationship with their bodies and their access to body memory; and with all of this, how to foster the emergence of self and other and the capacity for attachment. The hallmarks of these changes in the nervous system are, of course, the symptoms we are faithfully tracking and addressing, and the alleviation of these symptoms will be enough for many. But the end of symptoms signals something much deeper, and if you and your patient are looking for it, you will be more likely to recognize it as it unfolds: the secure self and the secured other.

Fear as the Core of Transference

Transference in developmental trauma begins in the felt experience of "no mother." Motherlessness is the lowest ring of hell for a baby and small child, creating a background fear of death or obliteration. If this weren't enough, it leaves these children feeling either insatiably hungry for this primary connection or so damaged that they can no longer feel the longing. They are truly orphans in the storm and they need a mother. More precisely and importantly, they need to feel the way they would have felt, had they had a mother who could comfort their fears, understand and regulate their anger, soothe shame, and repair breaches. Many patients with developmental trauma dismiss or demean this need, but it is inevitable.

The transference is an expression of a biosocial truth: We need our parents, most intimately, our mothers. When they disappear emotionally or physically, or even worse, when they appear and turn against their child, the very best outcome is an agonized yearning for the mother: It means that they have managed to keep hope alive. It is remarkable, really, that most people with these terrible attachment histories still want this primary relationship and will utilize strategies that they learned as young children to try to get it. There seems to be less hope for those who, like Carl, don't experience the void. In these patients vacuity replaces yearning; they are antisocial and often so disconnected from others, so hollowed out, as to seem psychotic. These patients don't develop transference relationships; they develop instrumental ones. They don't yearn or love; they *use*.

All individuals with this history have their own unique experience of this void, and each will represent it differently, but if they still have hope and their strategies aren't threatening to us, we are likely to feel the pull to care for them as a mother would. This is the nexus of the transference and the countertransference. The patients with whom most of us work are not sociopathic. They can still yearn, if not always consciously, for a mother. At the depth it is felt, the yearning can never be satisfied. The goal of the neurofeedback is to quiet the alarm of the abandoned infant that drives the transference, rather than trying to address this terrible hunger with insight or transference-driven reenactments.

I don't want to be misunderstood here. I think that therapy can be very helpful. Feeling understood, cared for, and soothed goes a long way in helping even seriously disturbed patients, as can teaching them to practice emotion regulation skills. It cannot, however, quiet the deep, biological pulse of fear that drives their nervous systems. At best, it teaches them how to better live with it. I experienced a profound drop in my level of ambient fear after my neurofeedback weekend (described in the Introduction). But as it is a life-and-death matter, fear conditioning is difficult to extinguish. Ledoux (1996) seems to feel that once the amygdala is hijacked, it is hijacked forever. Jaak Panksepp, a researcher using animal models to understand the pervasive influence of fear, works primarily with well-cared-for rats raised in the lab. The young pups bond by engaging in what Panksepp (1998) calls "rough and tumble play" as a developmental matter of course. In this experiment, he introduced the slightest intimation of fear, a small tuft of cat fur, into their cage (they had never seen a cat). The rats stopped playing and reportedly never played with such abandon again, even after the tuft was long gone and they were fully mature. The well-cared-for rat pups had dramatic reactions to a fear stimulus that affected them throughout their lives. It is of little wonder that our patients, conditioned much more harshly, react to the slightest intimation of fear, and most have, long ago, forgotten how to play.

Everything I do now in psychotherapy and in neurofeedback I do to address fear, to try to establish that the survivors do not need to live forever ruled by the fierce whims of this circuitry. I don't know ultimately how successful this approach will be for any individual, but it is the goal. Or perhaps it is more accurate to say that I don't know how long this will take for any given person, but it is what I expect to happen. Constant fear just cannot be their inheritance. Fear reduction should be quite straightforward and received wholeheartedly by patients as the gift it is, but as we will see, it doesn't always go like that. It is the attuned relationship within the therapy that holds these patients as their nervous systems shed layer upon layer of fear.

Transference expresses the unmet needs of the infant. It is about dysregulation. In this paradigm we can look at transference as a nervous system seeking its own regulation from the other, almost always on its own dysregulated but insistent terms. Transference relationships that arise with patients who have suffered developmental trauma are fraught with expectations of mothering and intensified by affect dysregulation, distrust, and unbearable hunger. For both the patient and the therapist this transference can be challenging to manage.

Before I began to use neurofeedback, I regulated patients' effects as all therapists do and as best I could: with my state and my understanding. For many this eased the turmoil, but for some my receptivity would deepen the transference and its distortions. Recognizing and acknowledging the need for a mother did not alleviate their painful affects. Instead, this recognition often left patients feeling the need more strongly, laced with the inevitability of abandonment and harm. These are the dynamics of the survival (RH) amygdala, and I am no match for them—none of us is, whether patient or therapist. I take on these dynamics now with neurofeedback.

When I see an intense transference emerging, I take steps to minimize it, while still holding the needs and aspirations within it tenderly. Fear circuitry is inherent in this kind of transference, and I do everything I can to avoid the firing and rewiring of these patterns, while not turning away this orphan. I usually talk with these patients about embarking on a partnership in affect regulation, learning together what their nervous systems need to feel safe, calm and well organized. As we discussed earlier, this orientation is reassuring and affirming for some. They appreciate that the problem, which has been seen as located in their character or personality, is now relocated to firing patterns in their brains.

For others, however, it can feel like preemptive abandonment. They have come to find a mother (most often, unconsciously), not a machine, and understandably they can't see how they will get this through training their brains. I usually share my experience that when the brain feels regulated, a person feels mothered, not just in the present but back into infancy. But for this highly aroused group, identified completely with their arousal, this is like whispering to a tornado. They will need you to be the very present, attuned mother while their brains organize and get quiet enough to recognize that you even exist. As we have touched on throughout this book, fear reduction in those who feel that they are their fear signals what their fear always signals: their obliteration. More than one of my patients has asked, "Who will I be if I am not afraid?" The extinction of fear threatens extinction. But this is the amygdala's question, really, not theirs. When the time is right clinically, I will take all inquiry back to the unquiet firing in the subcortical brain. People caught in these states will forget that their brains are the primary culprits. I ask my patients not to believe any state that arises from fear, shame, or anger, but as we saw in Chapter 4, this is easier said than done. The amygdala does not readily cooperate with its own downsizing. But once again it is the goal. As much as we can feel otherwise, we are not our feelings.

Shame and anger infuse the transference but, as we've discussed, fear drives it. Before we enter even more deeply into the complexity of fear and its undoing in the transference, I think it is helpful to get a glimpse into the interior of the fear reduction process.

Although not diagnosed with developmental trauma, this next patient, a 36-year-old woman, came to me feeling overrun with fear and saying that she felt she was at the end of a fraying rope. She had been in therapy for 30 years to address her history of being mercilessly bullied almost daily in school. Her parents acknowledged her struggles and tried to help with practical steps and advice, but it never stopped and she felt pretty much left alone to manage it, day after day. By her 18th neurofeedback session, she told me that she was definitely calmer. She gave me the following example. She had gone out on a blind date with a man who liked to tease. The first thing she noticed was that she didn't warn him about her sensitivity. In the past, she had always warned people that she could not bear being teased. She reported that when he teased her, she felt the same terror that always arose, "but only for a millisecond and then it was gone." She went on to say: "I didn't know what to do then. There was a kind of emptiness where the terror used to be. I felt disconcerted, even disoriented, and kept expecting the response that didn't come." She summed up this experience by saying, "I feel disoriented but not disorganized." This woman, even with the disorientation, welcomed the absence of fear without ambivalence.

For patients with developmental trauma these moments can be more deeply unsettling. Unlike the woman in this vignette, they have no container of self when they feel this "absence of what used to be." It can resonate all too closely with the original state of no-self and be mistaken for the void. Their bewilderment can quickly morph into fear. As one of my patients said, "The fear doesn't want to lose itself." But these patients will also have this experience of fear shutting down. As it does, they are able to discern, usually haltingly, that this new experience is the opposite of obliteration. It is not an emptiness of self and other, but an emptiness of fear, shame, and rage. Initially, the amygdala responds to attempts to quiet it by reasserting itself. This is understandable. The amygdala is vigilant and dutiful, but it is not intelligent. There are times that I feel as if I am engaged in a full on wrestling match with the amygdala, trying to pin it, to let it know that it can rest. The more baseline terror, the more rounds we have to go.

In my experience, the fear of assault gives way first. These patients will lose their startle responses, their hyperalerting reactions, and self-harming behaviors pretty quickly. Several of my patients who had physically harmed themselves for years have used the identical statement, "I don't want to be hurt anymore." Over time these patients will no longer be triggered by signals that had sent them spiraling into terror or dissociation or both. After 25 sessions of neurofeedback my young patient with DID reported being able to watch zombie movies and to venture into her basement for the first time without terror. Another highly dissociative woman trained her brain using a game in which puzzle pieces came together every so often to reveal a shack in the woods or a photo of a climbing rose. Both scenes triggered her memories of childhood abuse. There were other games, but periodically we would use this one with its brief exposures to triggers. We could, I suppose, think about this as a kind of exposure therapy. I was not trying to desensitize her to triggers, per se, but to use the game as a measure of her reactivity. She was highly dissociative and every time we used it, we both approached it mindfully. She could close her eyes or practice slowing her breathing, and of course she could always decide to use a different game. As she quieted her nervous system, these provocative pictures lost their significance. At most they evoked a memory of having once been disturbing.

Another patient described the trauma mind beautifully as "endlessly evocative," and although she welcomed episodes of quietude, she missed it. It kept her miserable, but it kept *her*. She didn't quite recognize or trust the more peaceful mind that was developing, at first alongside the trauma mind and then slowly replacing it. One woman described this experience, saying, "One part of my brain registered that another part was dysregulated." Another said, "I have two minds—changes in the field, really—between old and new." This woman was beginning to conceptualize her states as fields that organized around her early trauma. Another patient shared a similar perception and told me that she was determined to "exit the 'traumasphere.'" We'll talk more about the powerful field properties of trauma later in this chapter.

After my first weekend encounter with my brain, I told friends that "my brain has a mind of its own." These changes in patterns can be both regulating and dysregulating at the same time. I can imagine the clash of new emerging circuitries with old established ones vying for space and neuronal attention within the brain. As we might imagine, this can be a daunting process, and it is important that the therapist recognize it, validate it, and encourage talk about it. Facilitate regulation. You may find yourself engaged frequently in reassurance that the end of fear is not the end of them, of you, or of your relationship.

As the anticipation of assault wanes, that fear yields to the deeper and even more pervasive terror of abandonment and loss. Abandonment is the ground of being for those with developmental trauma. Addressing fear at this level takes time, patience, and dedication. The therapy has provided a first home for many and, the therapist regardless of gender, the first mother. Absent their biological mothers, these patients have no relational trace of growing up, no internal track or gauge. Many were asked by parents or circumstances or both to be grown-up as very young children. One of my patients was cooking for her older siblings and parents when she was 7. These patients don't know what it means to grow up within a nurturing relationship and then to leave a parent at a developmentally appropriate time. These profoundly motherless adults, independent or dependent, functional or dysfunctional, have never grown up and left home. There was no brain pattern or psychic structure for this.

In these circumstances, the anticipated end of therapy threatens catastrophic loss. Over time, in their time, they come to know, viscerally, that they have me. It can be a surprising discovery that for most people is made anew many times. As they have been reducing fear, they have been internalizing me. When they know that this has happened, they will feel able to end therapy. In these earlier uncertain times, I tell my patients that they will leave only when the time is right, and the time will be right when they know that I am securely a part of them, and they, securely a part of me.

This maternal relationship between therapist and patient was birthed in terror. When the terror begins to ebb, patients may experience periods of confusion over who the therapist is and has been to them and shame about who they have been in this process. Growing up has been telescoped; patients have described themselves as Alice falling down the rabbit hole. Many have told me that they are experiencing all ages at once, as well as a speeded up developmental course. With neurofeedback we can address the earliest developmental needs at the same time as the patient begins to feel a sense of mastery, of adulthood and of a real self.

The pace of change that is typical with neurofeedback, although ultimately a gift, can be part of the problem initially. Because identity is bound up with fear and symptoms, as discussed in Chapter 4, a good neurofeedback response can promote a crisis of identity. It is a crisis you should expect in all of its individual variations once you adopt neurofeedback. After 75 neurofeedback sessions, a patient with DID told me that she was becoming "just your run-of-the-mill PTSD." Shortly after we began the neurofeedback sessions, alters visited and protested. They would express fear that they were disappearing. Alters are also manifestations of fear, and they give way as fear gives way. Her alters lost their distinctive edges and accents and over several months, became part of her, as every one of us experiences parts of ourselves. During these months her history became real to her and we talked about it. She was finally able to begin to grieve for herself and for her mother.

We also discussed her amygdala. The throes of amygdala reactivity can leave patients in terror at one moment and, as it subsides, in equanimity the next. Fear is habit, and equanimity is new. I acknowledge how real the fear feels but quietly and persistently side with peace in the kingdom. It is important to note here that substances, formerly tolerated well, can set off these fear bouts. Too much caffeine, sugar, or chocolate can trip this nervous system into high arousal, which can inspire the amygdala to prompt fear reactions and fear-filled narratives. Look for this as well as for new reactions to medications. ADHD drugs, as an example, can be processed as speed and unsettle rather than calm the system. It will be important to help your patients identify the source of their discomfort, so that they can avoid the substance and avoid setting off a fear response. When caffeine sets off an alarm, your patients can learn to recognize this as a state reaction. If the source of fear is unclear, it will redound to sense of self, and they could feel needlessly discouraged. They will give the amygdala reactivity meaning, because in its activation they cannot recognize that it is a false, substance-activated alarm. It is important to remind them gently of their brain, while not invalidating them. Reacting to a stimulant as a stimulant is, after all, a good sign. The nervous system is setting itself straight.

Negative Transference

For all too many people suffering from developmental trauma, the therapy flounders in the patterns of negative expectation that we call *negative transference*. Longing for the mother, now the therapist, brings fear and anger and shame with it, and as we have discussed, these states create a powerful narrative that doesn't yield readily to rational inquiry, insight, skills, or even patience. For some, everything the therapist does or says is suspect. At least initially, neurofeedback is not exempt from suspicion, even when this person has sought out the training. When fear is so intense that it can easily edge over to paranoia, change in state, no matter how deeply desired, will not be trusted. It will be feared and so will you. Most of these patients have highly reactive brains underlying these highly reactive states, and we can, unfortunately, expect negative effects, particularly as we are getting to know this brain. Harder still, we might make a mistake that leaves a patient feeling terrible. I have spoken about a young woman who came to me for uncontrollable rage. When I trained to raise her arousal slightly, she had the "worst night of my life; worse than the worst ever cocaine trip." Had she also been distrustful of me, this would have created a significant breach in our relationship.

I also talked about a young adoptee who hated the way she felt with alpha–theta training and stopped doing training altogether. To try to mitigate the fallout from negative effects and the distrust it can engender, I discuss the very real possibility of hard episodes with my patients early during our assessment. The problem is that states that are subcortically driven are utterly convincing and can be difficult to preempt. When an established patient arrives in the throes of negative emotion and transference, I will always train early in the session. That is the contract. We can talk about anything, but after we train. Given that the protocols are right, it will be a much more productive session after training than it could have been before. When the training has made them feel worse or when I have made a mistake, it is vital that we engage in repair, which consists of acknowledgment and validation and a recommitment to the process. I will remind them, if the time is right, about the plasticity of their brains and that all responses, even this terrible one, are data.

Positive Transference

In consultation, a young therapist talked about her patient, a middle-aged man who found himself much more at ease after beginning neurofeedback. He was striking up conversations at the coffee house he'd gone to alone for years. He was opening the door for strangers and found himself able to make eye contact. When she asked him about these changes, he said it was because she was such a good therapist. She indeed happened to be a very good therapist. But when I asked her what she thought, she had no doubt that neurofeedback accounted for the changes. She knew that we don't see these kinds of changes in psychotherapy. His increasing stability and sense of safety were promoting a positive transference. This too has its complications. This patient was still placing the locus of change outside his own brain.

As therapists, it is considerably easier to inhabit the positive transference than it is the negative, but both represent a distortion of the core reality that we are discussing here: We can change our brains and the minds they give rise to. On the therapist's end, with neurofeedback, we can feel overly identified with making this patient feel better and when we do, we can make the mistake of owning this or assigning it to the training and not to the patient's inherent capacity for change. It is therapeutically important, particularly with these uniquely disempowered patients, to remind them that *they* are the ones who are changing their brains. That being said, most of my patients still credit me more than they credit the training for their feeling better, and this too is OK. I know that I am central to the changes in state and in sense of self that they are feeling—just not as central as their newly self-regulating brains.

"Transference Cure"

Once he recognized the inevitability and power of transference, Freud proposed what has come to be called the *transference cure*. Simply put, he thought that when patients came to understand the needs and desires that drove the transference, they would be done with the neurosis. I actually have never seen this occur, or for that matter, ever experienced it, before I started neurofeedback. With training, as fear dissipates, transference dissipates. I actively encourage the growing peerage in the relationship, to the extent that a patient can hear this over, or under, the clamor of abandonment fear. For many patients with developmental trauma there is a conundrum: Each developmental step that the reduction of fear allows signals the inevitability of loss—again. There are many levels to this fear, beginning with the radiating power of the original abandonment through to the reality of the therapy relationship coming to an end. *Termination*, that unfortunate, harsh word, will evoke abandonment fear in most people with these histories. But with attention over time, the evocation becomes less and less intense and with intensity and urgency dropping away, the present-day relationship with the therapist can be experienced more completely. At some point the patient will look for the transference surround and it won't be there. When patients no longer live in an insistent past, it means they don't need it. Regulation is the mother. The hunger is deeply met. Reactivity ceases. Slowly, in awkward developmental steps, they can come to experience that we are in this healing venture together, as equal adults, without fearing loss.

Countertransference

In terms of countertransference, the therapist should first consider the training as the cause of the problem, not the difficult patient. I have heard many therapists in this situation fall back on the idea of resistance or secondary gain, locating the problem in the patient rather than in his brain.

I used to believe in secondary gain. This is the notion that patients are reinforced in negative behaviors essentially by the attention they get as a result of them. I am sure that this happens, but even when it does, it begs the question of origin. A neglected and poorly regulated nervous system will give rise to both the diagnosed "illness" and the often insatiable hunger for attention. When the early deficit is a deficit of maternal attention, getting attention means survival. Most of my patients who have spent any time in institutions talk about the stigma they felt when one of the staff would inevitably say they were just "trying to get attention." They had all heard this as an accusation, and it induced shame in each of them. It happens so frequently, that you have to wonder if it serves any other purpose. The parasympathetic tone of shame can crash arousal and can get people to stop what they are doing. It can also set the brain on fire and send someone into rage. Invoking shame makes people who are already shame-based critically and desperately shamed, and they will react to that in whatever way they have habitually reacted—either withdrawal or explosion. It can feel cataclysmic to be caught in behavior over which you have little, if any, real control, and particularly in the behavior that reveals infant hunger and the need for the life-giving attention of the mother.

Secondary gain is a proposition most commonly entertained when the therapist is frustrated; I have certainly retreated to this ignoble construction myself. As mentioned earlier, we have a tradition in psychotherapy of blaming the patient when they don't get better. We call it resistance and/or the power of secondary gain. These concepts yield to our new understanding of brain dysregulation. If the patient is not getting better, then it means that the neurofeedback protocol we are using is not helping. This is not resistance or secondary gain. The neurofeedback therapist is either helping the patient to regulate, or not. These issues are, of course, complex but they are played out quite differently in therapy when you and your patient have access to the concept and the reality of brain regulation. Suffice it to say, that you might too become quite skeptical of the secondary gain formulation. It is always arousal and survival. And it is always first in the brain.

In this way, unique to neurofeedback, we can become part of the problem, but in a way, even more unique to neurofeedback, we can become part of the solution. Short of an irresponsible practitioner, there is no one to blame here; there is a brain working itself out. I think the major countertransference pitfall can be frustration with a patient who either doesn't seem to benefit as expected or doesn't recognize the benefits that she or he has had. I have had to remind myself that every brain needs the time it needs. There is no pushing this river. My sense is that something is always happening within this interface of brain and computer, or more accurately within the interface of the brain with itself, but it may not always be quickly or clearly experienced. I have joked in the past about expediting therapy by putting a sign behind me in my office reading, "What does this have to do with your mother?" In the neurofeedback room, I would add a sign for the therapist behind the patient reading "Patience and protocol."

Emerging from Isolation and the Art of Acceptance

Patients with developmental trauma, no matter how well they have managed their lives, even those surrounded by family and friends, live in isolation. They often don't recognize this isolation until they begin to make newly deep and real attachments. A man who began to train was able to see his grown sons, almost literally, for the first time and to feel love for them. As these patients train, they begin to see the world around them and discover that others also get flat tires or blisters or panic attacks—not them alone. Due to their isolation, few comprehend that they actually have an impact on others. Many don't know the social rules and will have to learn them, most often in therapy and all too often later in life than they would wish. One patient tried to teach herself the way of social engagement by watching "M*A*S*H" reruns and could not understand why this didn't work. She was so separated from the lives of others and afraid of the reality of others that she never thought to learn from her environment, *in situ*. She could not comprehend the relational gestalt of everyday life, loosely the RH, even as she negotiated it successfully, loosely the LH. No patient with developmental trauma that I have known expects kindness, and they all have some difficulty in engendering this in others. In the course of their training, they are met more often with kindness and with the challenges of kindness, in part because they become kinder themselves. They have to learn how to settle into a new relational matrix of self, other, and possible kindness, a matrix unknown to them but, it appears, always known to their brains, and in their time they do, so much so that they no longer comment on an act of kindness as a unique experience.

As they have gained regulation, many of my patients have asked, "Is this all there is?" I think it is safe to say that you can expect this crisis. When the fugue clears, the experience they have had of themselves becomes poignantly clear. They have lived cut off from the world and have looked into it, much as a poor child might look into the window of a locked candy store. One woman realized that she had believed that everyone else lived together in Disneyworld—her child version of utopia. Others have described a fantasy tribe from which they were excluded where everyone is other than they—which means happy, stable, secure, and ready to take care of the other.

It is, sadly, not uncommon for these patients to feel as if they have been expelled from the universe by their creator. Those children abandoned by their mothers feel abandoned by God. Many have expressed astonishment as they came to see that the world is a suffering place and when they recognize that most people are worse off than they. One patient had a sudden recognition that at that same moment millions of people were suffering as terribly as she was. She had not been pathologically delusional. She had known cognitively that this was a fact, but it was suddenly real to her. It was for her a flash of enlightenment, and it opened the door for her to the world as it is. From the position of isolation, patients with developmental trauma don't expect this. They have expected that recovering from their childhoods would mean admission to Disneyworld, not to the real world. Some have initially felt betrayed or resentful. It's not difficult to empathize with them; their intense lifelong struggle for emotional regulation has now spit them out onto the street (or at least, that's how it can feel), eyes open and feet under them, and they must begin, with the help of brain regulation and psychotherapy, to learn acceptance.

Ultimately, acceptance of what is grants us freedom, and learning to accept is an important part of the therapeutic process—not only for people suffering from developmental trauma, but for all of us. But even the idea of acceptance is not always readily accepted. One woman asked me how she could ever accept the Holocaust, in a tone of disbelief and a sense of pending betrayal. How can any of us accept the historical or personal holocausts that people inflict and people suffer? I asked her only to experiment and to feel for herself if acceptance made a difference.

Another woman became enraged and dissociative when she thought I was asking her to forgive her neglectful mother. If I was asking this of her, then I clearly had no idea what she had suffered. She felt terribly misunderstood. She had talked about her mother for 20 years without resolution, but after training for 2, she spontaneously called her mother, just to talk. She never had to engage in what was for her a tour de force: an act of forgiveness. Acceptance and forgiveness arose not because we had talked about them—we couldn't—but because they are prosocial emotions that are inherent and in wait. The world as it is came into focus. In her own time, my patient arrived at a new and genuinely felt understanding: "My mother did the best she could. She was a trauma survivor herself. No wonder she acted the way she did." These were all proposals that therapists had undoubtedly made to her over her long therapeutic course, but now they were arising spontaneously from within her.

She has come to accept her mother and her present emotional limitations. She reported that she didn't think much about their early failed relationship; it felt resolved. It was resolved because she feels mothered, in her CNS. Given how distrustful she was of anyone, a working alliance was initially difficult to achieve. At the same time, however, that she gained her mother she was gaining herself and me. Neurofeedback had given her what her mother had not been able to give her: primary self-regulation.

She began to inhabit herself and at first, she didn't know who this was. Recriminations dropped away and she began to use therapy to make sense of how her history has affected her, but now as part of her exploration of what to do with her life. She is hungry for meaning and is searching for ways she can best help others who are suffering, as she has done. She has moments of grieving, understandably, for all of the years lost to her in mental illness and other moments of impatience that neurofeedback was not available sooner for her and is still largely unavailable to others who have to deal with similar difficulties. My primary task now is to help her recognize herself in these changes and to challenge her when she slips even momentarily into her default setting of helplessness or hopelessness. (Of course, I am also, at the same time, assessing protocols.)

Idiot compassion is a Buddhist phrase that refers to practicing compassion without practicing equanimity at the same time. These patients can be overwhelmed by the compassion they feel, particularly when they are feeling it for the first time. Recall the man who was overcome by seeing a squirrel hit by the car in front of him. Before this moment, he'd been unfamiliar with the feeling of compassion. He developed this new capacity as it were, over night, and he had yet to learn equanimity, the acceptance of the world as it is. We need both. Without equanimity, no one can bear opening to the reality of human suffering. Compassion arises with self-regulation along with empathy. Equanimity, although also greatly enhanced, has to be learned and practiced. The therapeutic conversation that has been a looping reprise of deprivation and horror begins to turn toward discussions and practices of equanimity or, as Linehan calls it, toward *radical acceptance*, not only of your own circumstances but of the world as it is.

Regression: The Temporary Collapse of Emergence

To the degree I imagined it at all, I once imagined the healing trajectory as a linear course with the inevitable setbacks, and I think most patients imagine it this way too. But this is not the nature of quantum phenomenon. If there are, at a given moment in time, just one too many attractors (triggers), a patient with developmental trauma can fall back into the vortex of terror. The brain may default to the patterns it has practiced since early in life to deal with trauma. This can be deeply disheartening and disappointing. "I thought I was done with this!" is a common lament. It is interesting to note that, with protest, there is a new sense of separation of self from symptoms.

Such experiences look and feel like a relapse, and at these moments patients are likely to feel that they will never be free of their childhoods. Hold steady. There is a great deal of density in this history, and it takes the time it takes. Keep track of the field trauma has produced and how it is changing. Your accident-prone patient should begin to have fewer mishaps. Those who attract unsavory people will find fewer of them in their lives and will come to want nothing to do with them. When we see this, we are watching the trauma field shrinking. The density of early experience lessens, as does its ability to attract trouble. The responses that arise are evidence to me not of setback but of the power of the early terror. And this is exactly what we are addressing.

I think we are seeing a contest between newfound regulation, new oscillatory patterns, and the foundational patterns of dysregulation. We must of course always reconsider the protocols we are using when fear is ascendant. We could be making an inadvertent contribution by raising arousal. In these times, I often share a Buddhist teaching with my patients about a tulip. You will only see the tulip in the spring, because that is when the conditions are right. The tulip, however, is always there. When the conditions are right, this patient will feel the power of the early experience, even when she has resolved it.

For many, these replays serve as revelations that they have, in fact, survived these dreadful childhoods. These episodes used to disquiet me considerably, but now they feel inevitable. These are the rounds of releasing fear to which I referred earlier. But they do lose their power. Even when these moments are fully felt, they are not fully believed. These patients are learning to put distance between themselves and their amygdala-driven reactions. They are no longer fearing fear. I'll talk more about this phenomenon when we discuss the trauma body and body work a little later in this chapter.

Changes in Relationships

We have discussed some of the potentially profound changes that can occur in the therapy relationship. Other relationships change as well. Patients with developmental trauma usually lose their attraction to drama. Relationships that depend on shared urgency and reactivity typically don't survive. These are the relationships born in the insistence of repetition compulsion, in the loop of dysregulated affect.

The woman with the terrible history of incest made her life, such as it was, with a succession of sexually violent men. She came to me for neurofeedback, exhausted. Within 20 sessions she had made a plan to end her relationship with her abusive partner, and even though financially dependent and pregnant with his child, she found a way to extricate herself at Session 25 (more about this case in Chapter 9). The man who had described himself to me as "the prick of the office" became the man whom others sought out for advice and even comfort. He separated from his wife, ending a purely instrumental relationship, and made new relationships with his kids, siblings, and parents.

In my experience, reunions with family members are quite common after the nervous system quiets down. One woman who had had what she called an obligatory relationship with her mother, wanted genuinely to be *with* her. Although her mother had never engaged in therapy or training, she seemed to change as her daughter trained. Both mother and daughter became softer and more accepting. My sense is that the changes in the daughter required a realignment in the field between them and allowed new patterns to emerge. Their relationship, at least to the daughter, felt unprecedented.

A young mother, who had herself grown up without maternal attention, expressed her hurt when her toddler turned away from her and toward her husband. During the course of 30 sessions, her baby began to seek out her mother. Attachment circuitry was enlivened in both mother and her child. A teenager with Asperger's reported a changed reality between her sister and herself. She gave me an example, struggling to describe a feeling before unknown to her. "So that's what they mean by *empathy*!" she said, in the full flush of discovery of self and other. Not only did she become aware that her sister existed, she could feel what she felt. Many patients have described an increasing capacity to discern falseness and appreciate the genuine. Several have described themselves as having an enhanced "BS detector." People report being better tuned into others, and many describe becoming more intuitive.

These changers can either stabilize or destabilize. This patient is having a unique, private experience within her brain as well as within her constructed sense of self, and this is an experience that can be difficult to share with others. As they gain regulation, these patients are often losing the company they have kept. In these ways, neurofeedback training can be lonely. A woman in her late 50s described feeling alone but also strangely OK with this. It felt accurate now, when before training, it had felt singular and even tragic. She described walking in her town and feeling separate from all of those around her. She felt herself as the quiet in the storm. She told me that "there was no species barrier," but she did not recognize herself in any other way in the swirl of street life. In her newly arising self-regulation, she could not identify with the level of ordinary tumult in which others seem to reside. She wasn't drawn in or toward. This feeling of separation, like all feelings, gave way pretty quickly toward one of inclusion, but she reports that she still never feels drawn toward drama, the life bread of her relationships prior to training. Her feelings of loneliness ebb and flow. When they are flowing, they seem to be just what they are. She doesn't react. There is no wild horse. When there is no reactivity, the feeling just "is."

As we discussed, these changes can be quite disconcerting, but if the patient feels better as a result, they are not refused. As you proceed, it is important to talk with your patients about their internal sense of change (often not so easy to render verbally), the changes that you see in them, any fears of change that arise, and to help them validate and incorporate the newness as it arises in them. There will be a strong correlation between lowering arousal, symptom reduction, and an increasingly non-reactive and fluid sense of self. The organizing CNS allows for a new level of choice. These patients are no longer captive to impulse. I ask my patients to make every decision, from when they go to bed, to what they take into their bodies, to those they choose as friends, thinking about how it will impact their regulation. The rule is straightforward if not always observed: *Choose regulation.*

Shame and Blame

Throughout this book, we have focused mostly on fear, but shame is ubiquitous in this group and, like the fear of abandonment, seems to outlast overt expressions of fear. I talked earlier about watching for the leading indicators of arousal, and these are often in the realm of shame. The leading indicator of shame is blame. One of my patients admitted to looking for someone to blame when she stubbed her toe! But it would not have to be another person. I want to hear a reduction in reflexive judgments not only of the other but of the self. Appraisal is fine; assertiveness is welcomed; judgment is overarousal. I work with my patients to observe this in themselves and when they do, to begin to practice mindfulness. One recognized how much unhealthy bonding she did with her coworkers through making critical judgments of others. "With some of these people, I have nothing else in common." There is in fact a great deal of social reinforcement for whipping each other up and not much for quieting each other down. When they are no longer drawn to the high drama of these interactions, these patients can feel an acute sense of loneliness, particularly in the transition from high arousal to stable arousal. At this time, many of my patients have sought out or rejoined a spiritual practice for support along the path.

Trauma Memory in Neurofeedback

I have discussed the growing consensus that memory is state-dependent and that it seems to be coded in the brain wave frequencies available to the person at the time the remembered or unremembered events took place (van der Kolk et al., 2007, pp. 292–293). As we have seen, the frequencies of early childhood are not routinely available to adults. I think this phenomenon explains, better than repression does, the absence of memory or the fragmentation of memory that is ubiquitous in those suffering from developmental trauma. Repression suggests a psychological intentionality. We deploy repression to keep the awfulness away. I had always accepted this elegant formulation until I began to engage with the brain. Shock alters brain waves. Shock in childhood disorganizes brain rhythms, and enduring shock reinforces this disorganization. We know from van der Kolk's research (Rauch et al., 1996) that at the time of a flashback, the RH amygdala is firing and the LH frontal is not. Speech, even thinking, which requires words, is out of the question. The fMRI image in Figure C.2 confirms what routine clinical observation suggests: that other than sharing the same word to describe it, regular memory and trauma memory have very little in common.

And, of course, there are brain dynamics underlying these differences. Practitioners who have seen flashbacks during neurofeedback report significant and sudden changes in the EEG. One woman early on in her training at C4 at 12–15 Hz (often considered the "plain vanilla proto-col") experienced a full-blown flashback. Her slow wave, particularly low theta, burst to over 75 µV for about 40 seconds. Her flashback revealed an event that she'd dismissed when prior inklings arose. She saw herself as a young child dangling over a third-floor banister by one ankle and the shadow of the man holding her, loosening his grip and threatening to let go. Her breathing became rapid and shallow and her body tone rigid. She described the flashback as coming "out of nowhere." She was still in contact with a woman who had cared for her as a child, and she later asked her if the stairs were configured the way she saw them in the flashback. Her memory was confirmed, at least the memory of place. In this instance, trauma memory did not require an external trigger such as a smell or a shift in the light: We happened upon it, nested as it was uncomfortably in the networks of her brain.

I have checked with other practitioners who have witnessed these events, and they report a similar EEG pattern. In those who stay frozen, the theta amplitude drops a little but remains high compared to baseline. One clinician reported that she has also seen another EEG marker:

> One of my clients had a quite severe flashback during the EEG recording. At the moment of experiencing the flashback, her EEG had shown excessive lambda waves at the back of her head. Lambda waves are occipital slow sharp waves that usually occur with eyes open during the visual scanning of the complex picture. However, I've seen this several times with my hypervigilant clients when they are scanning the room with their eyes closed. The client who had a flashback during the EEG recording had the excessive amount of lambda waves, as if she was intensely visually scanning the environment. (Mirjana Askovic, personal communication, February 2013)

This is the EEG portrait of a dysregulated brain remembering something of what happened to dysregulate it.

We do not want, of course, to precipitate flashbacks. We are attempting to stabilize the brain against this very event. When a patient has a flashback during training, in the session or between sessions, I reevaluate protocols, looking to provide more stability against this seizure-like event. The woman who came to consult me after two decades of treatment was having flashbacks every day. It took over 300 sessions—longer than average—before she was free of them completely, but we could track almost from the onset of training that she was having fewer of them, that they were losing their intensity, and that the events were shorter in duration. She also became less frightened of them and less reactive when then did occur.

Neurofeedback can make trauma memory available but ideally in a way that does not further traumatize. Alpha–theta training takes us into the rhythms of early childhood. Before we take this particular path, however, patients need to feel on their feet and neurologically and psychologically stable—which, for these patients, could often mean several hundred sessions of eyes-open training. We don't want to evoke the destabilizing brain event of trauma memory before the patient's system can manage it, but we don't always have the last word. As we are stabilizing the brain against this buildup–discharge cycle, the brain will have episodes of buildup and discharge, until it takes control of itself, often for the first time. When trauma memory no longer erupts, it is no longer trauma memory. It becomes like any other memory, something faultily known and in the past.

One woman credits neurofeedback as well as her therapy for the end of her traumatic reactivity. It was my work with her that first introduced me to the inevitability of replay as the traumatized brain recovers itself. She no longer suffered fits of terror or rage and no longer lived flooded by ambient fear. After years of hospitalization and decades of treatment, she had recovered. She reduced the number of sessions, going from twice weekly meetings to twice monthly. When this following episode occurred, we were training as needed, usually less than once a month.

During a drive back from Philadelphia, she decided on the spur of the moment to visit her childhood home. She took the next turn off the highway, a road that hadn't been built when she was a child, and found herself in her old neighborhood within a block of her home. She was visiting the scene of the crime, the first time since the resolution of trauma and the second time ever. She gave the following account when she came in for her session.

Even with everything I've been through, I have only been depressed once [diagnosed as a postpsychotic, reactive depression]. Now it's twice. I made it through the holiday OK, but woke up the next morning in a deep depression. I felt desperate and was glad I was coming for training. I meditated [she had learned to focus her attention on her amygdala as a reactive structure in her brain and to quiet it: the amygdala meditation], calmed myself, and took a shower and by the time I was ready for work, it was over. I didn't feel sadness or fear but I just couldn't maintain my [physical] balance. I literally had a hard time walking in a straight line.

She thought of this as cerebellar memory of the abuse that she'd endured in her home and the neglect that had enabled it. Although she denied feeling reactive or even emotional, she found it hard to think clearly. It was as if she had become an observer of her brain's reactivity without, as it were, falling for it. She reported similar responses when she addressed trauma memory in her body.

The Trauma Body and Its Recovery

Patients with developmental trauma do not live in their bodies. They are, for the most part, unbearably disembodied. One patient described sitting at a playground watching her children and feeling the wind go through her. To me, this represents the original sensory registration of *no mother*. We discussed the common and terrible feeling that some of these patients have described, that their nervous systems extend out forever into space. They have no felt sense of physical boundary or of the physicality of self and other. There is no shape to being. Human beings need to inhabit a body to develop a self. The physical and psychological co-arise and both depend on the mother's holding, on her touch, on her presence.

Disembodiment gives rise to distinct symptomatic expressions related most commonly to self-harm and to eating. As the CNS quiets fear, shame, and rage, there is less and less call for self-harm. The impulse moves from acts that typically stop pretty quickly, to impulses without action, to thinking about self-harm when under stress, to no thoughts or impulses arising.

Chewing and swallowing normally induce a parasympathetic response. That's what we mean when we talk about *emotional eating*. In the midst of sympathetic arousal, we can use eating to nudge our CNS toward "rest and digest." Eating is primarily about affect regulation, not about nutrition, clearly, or even appetite. Eating disorders can be seen through this lens. Bingeing quiets arousal, and purging addresses the fear of gaining weight and gaining shame.

One patient described this cycle in herself. After the purge she would experience a split second of bliss, a split second that she, quite understandably, did not want to give up. (This is reminiscent of a moment that Dostoevsky would have after his violent seizures. When we got a clinical EEG of this patient, there was evidence of subclinical seizure.) Disembodiment may be a significant factor in all eating disorders; it definitely was in her. I have spoken of her before. She was born in an Asperger's brain, and she had been sexually molested before the age of 3. Absent her body, she borrowed her body imagine from the fashion section of the *New York Times*: heroin–starvation chic. (You can read more about her treatment course in Chapter 9.) Although eating disorders may not always be generated by trauma, disordered eating, body distortion, and hatred of the body are ubiquitous in developmental trauma and relate, I think, directly to disembodiment.

Thankfully, there is renewed attention to the body in trauma therapy. Talk therapy alone runs the risk of abetting disembodiment. One long-term trauma patient, who saw herself as a walking head, thought that her many years of therapy had allowed her to reclaim her thinking, but had, at the same time, further eclipsed her unknown body. Peter Levine (1997, 2010) and Pat Ogden (Ogden, Minton, & Pain, 2006), among others, are reintroducing their patients to their bodies. At van der Kolk's Trauma Center in Brookline, Massachusetts, therapists do much of their work with children in a sensory room (called The SMART Room), keeping them engaged with their bodies and balanced, often literally on child-sized physioballs, as they try to talk about what happened to them. Adult patients can take yoga classes to introduce the body gently to itself. Postures can be trauma triggers, so this yoga practice is trauma-informed.

Memory is stored in the disenfranchised body. The body does in fact keep the score (van der Kolk, 1994). In my experience, although very helpful, it is not sufficient to notice and address trauma indicators in the body, without touch. We are bound by professional practices to leave these un-nurtured bodies untouched, but these patients need therapeutic touch to begin to know the reality of their bodies. For those who are open to it, I make referrals for trauma-informed body work. I have come to believe that patients with developmental trauma need access to three avenues for their recovery:

1. Through the brain, obviously with neurofeedback
2. Through the mind and its behaviors with psychotherapy
3. Through the body with hands-on trauma informed body work. Memory is not only in the hippocampus or even in the distributed networks of the brain; it is distributed in the body.

One woman described her experiences with Rosen massage. At first she could not feel even the deepest pressure. She was not frankly dissociative—she had been, so she knew—but she was very far away from her sacrum, even as the practitioner pressed down on it with her elbow. My patient wanted her to break through to her unfelt body. She had over 100 sessions of Rosen massage, and at every second or third one, she would experience an explosion of trauma memory. She was initially overtaken by old terrors. It took her an hour and a half to go into this experience and, with the help of her practitioner, to find her way out again. The next session or two would be quiescent, which could be disappointing to her, and then another would burst forth, filled with horror lived again right then on the table.

This patient was able to profit from these demanding events, I think, because there was always some aspect of her that was not participating but observing. After the discharge, she described herself as "reorganizing along the thread of that observer presence." It felt to her as if it took 2–3 weeks for her body–brain to gather enough energy to discharge again. There was often a good deal of early memory retrieval, much of it seemingly repetitive, but often her erupting body had no narrative and no visuals, just the volcanics of fear. Initially she thought each time would be the last. It was she who explained her experience in terms of density:

It is as if each upheaval throws particles of this density out into space. At the beginning, the density of my early stuff pulled most of these particles back into it. Only a few escaped into the atmosphere. Then there would be slightly less density. As it diminished, it pulls fewer particles of trauma back to itself.

This could be metaphor but it could also be a description of how this process works. Similar discharges occurred in therapy. While she was talking about these events, this woman, who I mentioned earlier in relation to the banister memory, suddenly recognized that she had been hanging over the banister her entire life. She broke open and wept, and we guided her small body to *terra firma*. Her body memory arose in dysrhythmic cycles of buildup and discharge. She would often leave these sessions feeling exhausted and sometimes even postictal. Although she had these major emotional events, she did not identify with them. Terror arose and then fell away. She was not captured, and she did not suffer from it. Her body work was an archeology of terror, but she felt that because of the therapy she understood what was happening and because of the training she was stable enough not to believe the subcortical display.

Memory in the body is held differently than memory in the mind. This woman described that her practitioner could be pressing with her thumb straight down (it took a while, but she got to where she could feel the touch without the practitioner's full weight) and nothing would happen, and then she would press at the same place but with the side of her thumb and "all hell broke loose." She was having these experiences as she was beginning to feel emotionally and neurologically resolved about the trauma and neglect of her childhood. I have the sense that were we to have watched what went on in these sessions, we might have been become alarmed. She described screaming and crying with terror. But she wasn't alarmed. She was actually not afraid of being afraid. She was able to contain the explosion and observe it. Each time she said it felt like she'd "found another Japanese soldier on a deserted island that did not know the war was over and sent him home." And each time the experience lost some of its density. Each time she felt a little more freed from her history.

Trauma memory in the body seems to be more concrete, more literal, than trauma memory in the brain, and the body seems slower to acknowledge and release its cellular secrets. If these cellular memories go untouched and untreated, the concern is that they will, as predicted by the ACE study, morph into physical illnesses (Dube et al., 2009). My work with this woman and several others who have been able to explore these multiple pathways suggests that neurofeedback may not resolve the memory held in the body. Training may, as we have seen, reveal it, but it takes this kind of trauma-attuned body work to address it fully. This woman still goes for an occasional Rosen session and when she does, she just has a massage. She is fully inhabiting a nonreactive body. She invites touch; she can feel it and she can relax into it. After living a lifetime in a tangent alongside her body, I doubt that she could have ever felt so embodied without this hands-on engagement.

As fear quiets with neurofeedback training, the body begins to manifest. More than one adult patient has described suddenly discovering his own hand, much as a baby would. It has dimension, shape, and sensation there in front of his eyes. Patients begin to feel their bodies as part of themselves, as a place to *be* for the first time. They begin to take care of themselves, brushing their teeth, eating vegetables, taking walks. Self-care has little meaning when there is no self.

The regulating brain is helping the body to regulate, and the regulated body in turn provides ongoing feedback to the brain to stay regulated. We can expect somatic complaints, particularly those that are vagally mediated, to ease. The woman who was mercilessly bullied had a pounding heart, and I found myself training as much to her heart as to any other report she was giving me. By session 15, her heart began to settle into a new rhythm. Interestingly, even after a good few days, her heart would begin to pound as she sat down to train. It felt to me as if we were witness to her heart's wariness about change. By Session 25 she was barely noticing her heart; it was now beating normally most of the time. Digestive distress, constipation, and IBS are common in this population and commonly decrease in severity and, optimally, go away as the nervous system organizes itself. Sometimes chronic pain will lift, but at the very least reactivity to it will. These reductions in symptoms make the newly emerging body a more inviting place to live.

Emerging Self

We began this chapter with my young patient's reflections on her changing sense of self and other. She credits brain wave training for her own emergent self and with it the capacity to recognize my existence as well. She came to consult with me after her discharge from a residential program at age 18, as an outpatient. We'd first met when she was my patient in a residential treatment program. Although she was living in a town only a few miles away, she was late for her first appointment because she could not figure out how to catch the buses that went by her. "I just couldn't organize myself." After training twice a week for 18 months, she flew alone to join a peace march in Japan. "I found my way through Nerita Airport," she told me, "without too much trouble—and that's saying something." Her account reminds me of the drawings of the boy's family in Chapter 4 (see Figure 4.1, p. 120). It is almost as if I could see her nervous system organizing in these reports during this year and a half. She and I had begun our work together sitting on the linoleum floor in a seclusion room when she was 16 years old. She spent all of her adolescence in treatment centers. She is now 30, has gotten her bachelor's degree in a strenuous program, and she is praised for her work with her patients. She is weighing the possibility of beginning a family and starting graduate work in her field.

Another gifted patient with developmental trauma beautifully described the eruptions of fear and the subsiding of fear that had been her only sense of self:

> I feel an empty spaciousness. It's like after the storm has passed and you step out of your house and other people come out of their homes and there is carnage all around and lightning far off in the distance. You know there are others but you still feel the power of the storm and the peace, now that it has passed.

She described the changes she felt in the kindling response that she'd suffered all of her life: "I always felt like I could ignite a forest fire. Drop a match and it takes off. It starts still, but it stops and goes out." As she emerged from the time warp of her amygdala, she discovered her body: "I feel my body, and I feel myself within, collected and able to move more fluidly in space. I don't need to know what is coming next, which is wonderful but completely unknown." She has developed a self within our relationship, and she and I are working with her fears of losing me now that she has finally inhabited herself, and we intermittently discuss ending our work together. She will be ready and able to walk into her future without me when she knows viscerally that she has me within her.

I have worked with the aftermath of trauma and neglect for my entire professional career. When I discovered neurofeedback and experienced the dramatic shift in fear, I began to privately hope that neurofeedback was "the answer" to these childhoods and that therapy, with its tremendous demand on both the patient and the therapist, would no longer be required. Some people in the neurofeedback field seem to believe this. As I am sure you know by now, I don't. Therapy does become less challenging, but at least in the treatment of developmental trauma, the regulating, attuned presence of the therapist is vital.

In a talk she gave describing the rapid changes she had seen in patients with chronic developmental trauma after introducing neurofeedback, the fMRI trauma researcher and psychiatrist Ruth Lanius cautioned her audience: "Neurofeedback does not replace psychotherapy. I think it requires you to be an even better therapist." Neurofeedback, as we have seen, can bring about rapid changes, and the therapist must be prepared for these and agile when they occur. We need to know when to talk and when to train. One of my metrics for deciding this is how curious the patient can be about her experience. If she is primarily reactive and not able to be curious, I think it is more important to train than to talk. When she begins to be curious, then it is time to pursue the inquiry. When it is the brain that is most in need, then it is time to train. When it is the mind and identity that need to reorganize in response to CNS changes, it is time for psychotherapy.

Chapter 9

Three Women

Developing Selves

I have learned what I have shared here from my work with my patients, talks with neurofeedback colleagues, and training my own brain. Any case study of developmental trauma I choose would illustrate most of what we've explored so far, including enhanced affect regulation, increasing awareness and inhabitation of the body, changes in relationships, and changes in sense of self. I have selected the cases in this chapter because they shed additional light on challenges in trauma treatment and on how neurofeedback can help us meet these challenges.

The case studies that follow are of three women with severe histories of developmental trauma. Although I have worked with many men and boys with developmental trauma, the vast majority of my patients have been women and girls. For teaching purposes, I present each in a slightly different format. I take you through the first case session by session, focusing on the neurofeedback to illustrate week-to-week changes. I include protocol decisions and some of the rationales I used to make those decisions in the first case study only, to give the reader a glimpse into how I "think neurofeedback." This may be tedious for some. If it is, skip over it. Every individual will respond uniquely; it's not about learning protocols, per se, but about listening in on my conversation with this particular brain.

The second case focuses on severe dissociation as it is addressed during a period of intensive neurofeedback training. I focus on alpha–theta training, its benefits and its demands. Again I share a session-by-session account because training with neurofeedback typically promotes change with each session, but here I forgo notations about protocols to avoid tedium and to again remind the reader that every brain is unique. This vignette covers only a brief but very important part of a much longer therapy.

The last case of a girl with Asperger's syndrome, anorexia, bulimia, and developmental trauma illustrates a central tenet of this book: that these seemingly disparate diagnoses share the same neurological routes and are all disorders of overarousal. This patient's experience of motherlessness, which was profound, arose mostly from her Asperger's. She was born neurologically ill-equipped to recognize her mother's existence, and as a result, was bereft of it. That being said, as Eleanor emerged from the lock of trauma and Asperger's, she recognized that her mother too suffered her own "core emptiness," which of course had compounded this girl's reality of no self–no other. I am presenting her case study in a narrative form in part because that was how she constructed what passed for a sense of self.

Rennie and Madeleine: Challenging the Intergenerational Transmission of Trauma

Traumatized adults who have not adequately addressed the imprint of trauma in themselves will raise traumatized children. There really is nothing else they can do. "These patterns of communication [between parent and child] literally shape the structure of the child's developing brain" (Siegel, 1999, p. 21). This case study focuses on a patient who came to me exhausted from the effects of developmental trauma. This account follows her through the course of her neurofeedback training over a 20-month period. Of unique interest in this case study are the apparent effects on the course of her third pregnancy, on fetal and postnatal development, and on the mother–infant attachment. As it unfolds you will see how neurofeedback apparently reorganizes CNS-to-CNS transmission of trauma from mother to child in utero.

Background

I first met Rennie when she was admitted to the residential treatment center where I was the clinical director. She was then 16. She came with a history of severe sexual trauma that included being the incest victim of every member of her family: father, mother, and older siblings. Violence in the home was routine. Two of her brothers have spent significant periods of their lives in prison, and her sisters have both been psychiatrically hospitalized. As a child she was knocked unconscious on at least one occasion when she was intentionally struck across the head with a brick. She suffered significant impairment in memory, although less so for the almost routine traumatic events of her early life than for appointments, dates, and names in her present one, a problem that made school and the possibility of independent living difficult for her.

She was diagnosed then with severe PTSD, which we would now recognize as developmental trauma. She was alternately explosive and withdrawn and often required physical restraint. She was also emotionally warm. When she saw her new room in the treatment center, she started to cry, "No one in my family will ever live in a room as nice as this." At that time, we were not yet assessing our kids for attachment ruptures, but in hindsight it is unmistakable that she had an anxious/ambivalent attachment. She did become quite attached to me. She left the center at age 18, at which time she qualified for the Axis II diagnosis of BPD. She went into foster care where she was also able to make a strong attachment to her foster mother. But the need for replay was too strong—the circuits too practiced—and she found a man quite a bit older than she who was somewhat of a sexual deviant and who was also diagnosed with bipolar illness. She had two children with him.

She lived locally and would call me intermittently over the years. She was psychiatrically hospitalized several times as an adult and with the birth of each child, suffered a prolonged postpartum depression, also requiring lengthy hospitalizations. She called me to request neurofeedback to address the persistent symptoms of PTSD, as well as the problems with her memory that seemed to be getting worse.

Due, she thinks, to her therapy and to her ability to attach, Rennie was a good mother. Poverty, its pragmatics and its degradations, as well

as the men she was drawn to in the tragic human inevitability of reenactment have made her life hard. In terms of brain circuits and patterns, we
can look at reenactment as a kind of pattern match. She had barely
escaped being murdered in one situation, only to flee to a man who
extracted constant sexual favors in return for food and housing. Both
were "addicted" to sex, but he, unlike Rennie, was also prone to rages
and assault. She was making a conscious, if not entirely willing, compro-
mise in living with him to be able to provide her children with a decent
home in a good school district. She was doing the best she could for her
children and for herself, tolerating nothing worse than she had endured
all of her life.

Sex "addiction" is a topic that is beyond the scope of this book, but it
is central to this case and, as you will see, it is affected by the training.
For Rennie, sexual behavior functioned both as a replay or repetition
compulsion and as a primary attempt to regulate her terror-stricken
CNS. Rennie had been trained into this pattern as well. It was learned
and overlearned from the time she was a small baby. It was what she
knew. Sex was central to her dysregulation and her attempts to regulate.

Assessment

Although I already knew her, I gave Rennie a full clinical assessment. As
therapists we don't routinely factor the body in our assessments, but as
we saw in Chapter 6, we need to. Presenting problems included persistent anxiety (fearful), panic attacks, agitated depression, difficulty falling
asleep, preoccupation with sex, memory problems, and some specific
indications of unresolved PTSD, such as excessive startle responses and
the inability to use public restrooms. She presented with a habitual nervous laugh and with fingernails bitten to the quick. She suffered with
chronic constipation. She was in this relationship with an abusive man
but did not, initially, present this as a problem. It wasn't high on the list.
It was routine . . . inevitable.

Training Course

There were 37 training sessions over an 18-month period. This is far from
an optimal training regime—it would be much preferred to have many

more sessions closer together since this is, at base, a learning technology—but it was the best she and I could do. Given her history and her symptoms, I decided to begin training on the RH at the temporal lobe.

• *Session 1*. Protocol: T4–P4 for 3 minutes at 11–14, then for 3 minutes at 10–13, then for 2 minutes at 9–12, and finally for 7 minutes at 8–11. (Inhibits throughout are 0–6 and 22–36 unless noted otherwise, and all numbers are Hz, unless otherwise indicated.)

I was dropping the reward frequency in response to her reports that she wasn't feeling much of anything and my observation of her face and body. The first protocol can only be our best educated guess about the frequency and site that will calm this excitable nervous system. From then on we are guided primarily by the brain's response.

• *Session 2*. After the first session, she described episodes of anger (frequency too high?) and no changes in memory: "Bad now, always has been." Her depression has lifted (her brain is responding). She noticed that she was writing the amount of the check in her register three lines below where she should write it. (Idiosyncratic responses usually signify brain injury.) She also noticed that in doing a jumble word puzzle, she could see the word immediately. (Her brain quickly discerning figure from ground; it is beginning to organize.) This, she told me, "is completely new."

The episodes of anger and her initial responses during the first training suggest that she might do well with lower frequency reward, and I wonder if T3–T4 might offer her more stability as we search for the optimal reward frequency. When I am searching for the best frequency, I typically begin at the lowest frequency we trained at in the previous session. When we began training, she described being immediately much more relaxed than when she arrived. Her breathing slowed down and her shoulders relaxed some. Shortly into the training she began to cry, softly and deeply. She said, "This [crying] feels different. It didn't drag me down. It was appropriate." Crying this time, unlike in the past, seemed to help her regulation. "I feel alert and relaxed and aware," Her voice, however, is quite loud, and she is talking over me—signs of ongoing high arousal.

Protocol: T3–T4 for 9 minutes at 8–11 and for 9 minutes at 7–10, then for 3 minutes at 6–9 and for 3 minutes at 6.5–9.5. These changes in frequency followed changes I observed in her. I went up in frequency briefly at the end because she appeared a little snowed.

• *Session 3*. Rennie reports lots of situational stress. She also reports feeling very good after our last session. When we finished training today, she said, "I feel so much better. Much more relaxed. A little sad. Quieted." Protocol: T3–T4 for 15 minutes at 6.5–9.5 and for 6 minutes at 7.5–10.5.

• *Session 4*. Very stable mood. Sleeping better. Becoming more stress resilient. Still struggling with her memory, but notices that she is remembering names that she would not have remembered in the past. Easier to talk with people she doesn't know. She reports feeling friendlier and more at ease in these situations. She also reports having a harder time with the craziness of her relationships. Increasing levels of awareness and impatience with the behavior of the men in her life. Appetite is OK. "I'm eating what I need for my body. Healthier stuff." Generally, "I feel more competent. I can handle more stuff. I am much less reactive." After training she reports, "This is where I want to live." Protocol: T3–T4 for 27 minutes at 7.5–10.5.

• *Session 5*. Rennie reports feeling calm most of the time after the last session, even with a lot of environmental stress. Sleep OK, but not enough. Over time, I have learned to recognize this as a code for being sexually harassed by the man with whom she is living. Memory may be getting better, but not great. Protocol: T3–T4 for 24 minutes at 7.5–10.5.

Although I repeated the same protocol as the last training, toward the end she got cold and shivery and she felt a little spacey. It had the feeling of a recalibration. She called later to tell me that this state had passed and that she felt OK.

• *Session 6*. Maybe not a recalibration after all: She got drunk and she is not a drinker. She reports that she has been acting out sexually when her kids were away with their father. She was agitated and depressed the day after training. She didn't want to get out of bed. "I really wanted to be 'bad.'" She knew this was a state and knew it was from the training, but she felt compelled to do it anyway. She was revisiting familiar pattern formations in her brain and for a while they were ascendant.

Four days after the training all of this went away and she started feeling better and better. This has the feeling of an old pattern fighting to maintain or even strengthen itself, and it is often an indication, as mentioned before, that it is under challenge. She reports some tension in her chest and she has a cold coming on. In my experience it is not unusual for people to get sick when they begin training. The use of alcohol (a CNS depressant) and her acting out in some habitual but dangerous ways prompt me to lower the frequency reward.

During the last period of training she feels something "rearrange" in her brain. For people with brain injury, this is not an unusual report. No experience of cold or shivers. She reports feeling relaxed. Protocol: T3–T4 for 9 minutes at 6.5–9.5 and for 15 minutes at 5.5–8.5.

• *Sessions 7 and 8*. Rennie reports that she is getting sick of her boyfriend. It is feeling harder to make the compromises she has been making. When she and I began, we had discussed that she might find it difficult to make the accommodations necessary to stay with this man. It wasn't precognition on my part, but a recognition that this relationship was built on repetitive neuronal patterns of high arousal. She needed to be forewarned of this possibility because her life seemed to depend on the arrangement she'd made with him. My raising this possibility was part of the informed consent process.

She has been drinking some, an indicator of her stress level and that the frequency may still be too high. At Session 7, I lowered it. She was able to drop slow wave amplitudes (0–6 Hz) from 21 µV to 10 µV, but by the end, it was back at 19 µV. Excess delta–theta can be an indicator of both brain injury and psychological trauma.

In Session 8, Rennie said, "I'm able to take care of myself." She reports being honest with others and no longer being sexual with everybody. She is eating less and craving healthier foods. She reports feeling much less depressed but having moments of sadness, which she describes as "reasonable." I agree and as I have said, I don't think of sadness as a training indicator. Depression is, but not sadness. Sadness flows; depression doesn't. Sleep may be a little better, but she had trouble getting to sleep a couple of nights. She says, "I have better access to myself. I'm not hiding." Increase in self-esteem. "I'm enjoying people a lot more. I used to be afraid of them." No trouble using public restrooms. This was one of the reasons she had come for neurofeedback. "Not jumpy; pretty calm." Thinks more clearly and feels her judgment is better. Not much change in memory, but it may be a little bit better.

Session 7 protocol: T3–T4 for 6 minutes at 5–8, then for 5 minutes at 4–7, then 3 minutes at 3–6, ending with 3 minutes at 4–7. I am looking for optimal quieting without slowing the system too much or, given that she has had panic attacks, slowing it too rapidly. Session 8 protocol: T3–T4 for 30 minutes at 4–7 Hz.

• *Session 9*. She felt situational moodiness but other than that, pretty steady. Good time and connection with her former foster mother. She felt more competent and at ease. She told her about a therapeutic abortion she had had. After telling me her experience, she felt suddenly very sick, not unlike the way she'd felt after the original and traumatic experience (access to body memory). She was able to feel all the feelings she had about the abortion, which were many and difficult, and then felt herself move out of these feelings. During the training she was cold, shivering, and scared. We stopped the training early. I put pressure on the emergency point, the point in neurofeedback that we call *FPO2*. After 10 minutes, the event was over. She thought this episode was also related to the abortion. "The storm blew through," she told me. She was good when she left. Rennie's positive response to pressure at this site was a good predictor that she would respond to training at FPO2.

Protocol: At T3–T4, I tried several frequency rewards, beginning at 4–7 up as far as 5–8 and down as far as 3–6. All felt terrible to her, including panicky feelings and cold hands and feet, so I switched to T4–P4 for 3 minutes at 8–11, then 3 minutes at 7–10, and 3 minutes at 6–9. Some episodes such as this seem necessary. It is not always easy to know when they are happening, but many of these events turn out to be meaningful discharges that give way to new CNS potential. I learned that in part in working with Rennie.

• *Session 10*. She told me that she was remembering people's names readily and that she had stopped drinking. The training event of the week before was over by the time she had left my office. There were no "aftershocks"; no new buildup–discharge cycle. She reported that the pressure at FPO2 had felt good to her, easing the fear that had been mounting. And she reported some feeling of "stiffness" in the prefrontal area—not terrible, but noticeable. Some coldness in her hands as we are training.

Protocol: I want to try to continue to address the clear instability in her nervous system while bringing down her arousal, so I return to T3–T4 for 7 minutes at 4–7 and for 4 minutes at 3–6, T4–P4 for 8 minutes at 6.5–9.6, and 1 minute at 6–9.

• *Session 11.* She had strep throat but recovered quickly. She reports no sex drive at all. "This is unheard of for me. I just don't think about it. I don't care about it." She has had the first days ever in her life without sex. Still handling stress well. "I don't get stuck." Some episodes of blurry vision (this will now be added to my checklist of symptoms to track). "My house is clean." Her partner is away and she feels much better without him. This too is a first. "I'm quiet." She is watching much less TV and she thinks that her humor is more appropriate. She feels assertive, clear about her feeling states, and increasingly articulate. At the end of the session she feels good, neither cold nor tired. Protocol: T3–T4 for 9 minutes at 3–6, T4–P4 for 12 minutes at 6–9 Hz.

The next week, Rennie reports an odd phenomenon, something she has not experienced before: Her skin is blotchy. Her doctor is at a loss about what this is. It may be an idiosyncratic response to the neurofeedback. Sexual feelings have returned, but they do not feel as compulsive or degrading. Good assertion skills. Aware of times when the "old sense of being defeated" arises in her, but her new feeling replaces it: "I'm going places. I feel like I have a fresh young brain." Talk session to help her recognize and consolidate her gains. Rennie is very sensitive to neurofeedback, and she is an excellent reporter on her own states—better, it seems, with every session.

• *Session 12.* A month later and the blotches have not gone away. All blood work is negative. Rennie has become quite anxious, particularly prior to the blood work and specifically about the possibility of AIDS. Now she says, "I pretty much handle what comes up," but she hasn't been doing quite as well recently. Feeling more neediness and crying more. It looks like it was not such a good idea for us to skip training. She does, however, report fighting back when attacked physically by her boyfriend. "It's almost as if I have a different philosophy."

I added a minute of left-side training to address the possibility of allergy and depression. She leaves feeling good. Protocol: T3–T4 for 9 minutes at 3.5–6.5, T4–P4 for 12 minutes at 6–9 and 6 minutes at 5.5–8.5, T3–A1 for 1 minute at 12–15.

• *Session 13.* Rennie is pregnant. This is an unplanned pregnancy, but she wishes to have the baby. The father does not want the child; her oldest is in significant trouble psychologically; Rennie is living on disability, a pittance; she is in an abusive relationship with a man on whom she is entirely dependent financially; her kids hate this man; her former abortion may cause pregnancy complications; and she has no family support. She knows all this and comments on all of it, and yet she is steadfast and reasonable about wanting this child——whatever happens.

None of the training felt good today. She reports pressure, feelings in her chest, and then experiences a major emotional eruption that scares her. "Sometimes I feel better after these, but I hate going through them." It is likely that her pregnancy has brought on a shift in her brain and that we will need to reconsider protocols. While not contraindicated, using neurofeedback during pregnancy should be approached with care, and only if the woman and clinician agree that it's beneficial.

Protocol: T4–P4 at several frequencies ranging from 5–8 to 7–10; also at T3–T4, searching for stabilization. Nothing felt good.

• *Sessions 14 and 15.* Rennie reports that she is losing control with her boyfriend. She is finding it very hard to tolerate his obliviousness, his abusiveness, and his violence. At the end of Session 14 she describes that she is feeling much better, relaxed, even happier, and more like joking. But at Session 15, she arrives crying: "My life is coming apart." She called the police after her boyfriend punched her in the stomach, and both he and she were now being investigated by the Department of Social Services (DSS). As is true for many women who live in poverty and violence, she fears that her children will be taken from her. We spent some of the session talking and ended with training. She left feeling "stabilized, strengthened, and ready to face whatever life brings." Protocols for both sessions: T3–T4 for 6 minutes at 3.5–6.5, T4–P4 for 19 minutes at 5.5–8.5, and then for 2 minutes at 5–8.

• *Sessions 16 and 17.* Session 16 occurs a week later, and Rennie reports that her mood has held: She is doing well. She is energetic for most of the week. She mistakenly washed all of her kids' summer clothes in bleach instead of detergent and most are ruined. This is the kind of mistake she was prone to making in the past. She felt terrible but could talk to herself and begin to makes plans about how to replace them. She reports that she is unable to keep days separate, that they are blending together. These difficulties are likely to be a manifestation of the head injury and will work themselves out as her brain stabilizes. It is not uncommon in the course of training for such occurrences when someone has suffered TBI. Our operating assumption is that they will fade away as she continues to train and regulate her brain. She has been having trouble sleeping and mentions her anxiety about DSS. After training she says that she feels capable again. "I can do this. The neurofeedback really helps me."

At Session 17, the following week, Rennie tells me that everything is good. She feels that she is handling the multiple stressors of her life well. Her sleep is better. She is beginning to relate to DSS differently. She begins to see that they might be able to help her with the kids' clothes, with camps, with finding another place to live. As she was leaving, she said, referring to herself, "I feel like the system is quieter and I feel happier." Protocols for both sessions: T3–T4 for 6 minutes at 3.5–6.5, T4–P4 for 21 minutes at 5–8.

• *Session 18.* "I'm doing well, but it is all a little too much." She is looking for a place to live, dealing with the courts, making multiple medical appointments, and her car is breaking down. She reports that she is thinking clearly but forgetting things. She attributes forgetting to having too much to remember, and she says that she is less frustrated when she does forget. "I'm still afraid of some things, like thunderstorms and heights, but I can deal with it differently when I have to." Her use of language is more textured and more expressive with an increase in vocabulary. She heard her baby's heartbeat. (Throughout the remainder of this case study, I use *Baby* as if it were a name, as Rennie does.)

I introduced FPO2 into her training regime and she reported, "I feel wicked calm—a big difference [with this protocol]." Protocol: T3–T4 for 3 minutes at 3.5–6.6, T4–P4 for 12 minutes at 5–8 and for 9 minutes at 4.5–7.5, FPO2 for 6 minutes at 5–8.

• *Session 19.* I was away for 3 weeks. The session after the introduction of FPO2, another therapist saw her for neurofeedback. Two weeks elapsed from the last session to Session 19. Rennie reports that she has sustained a general feeling of relaxation, and things seem visually brighter (the clean windshield effect). She also reports a heightened sense of smell. The olfactory bulb lies directly beneath the training site of FPO2, and as we saw in Chapter 7, increased sensitivity to smell is not an uncommon effect. But she also reports having been sick for 7–10 days with headache. Rennie feels that these are probably tension headaches, but the therapist recommended, appropriately, that Rennie talk with me about these symptoms as they could be related to the training. In light of this report, she decides not to repeat training at FPO2. Protocol: T3–T4 for 3 minutes at 3.5–6.5, T4–P4 for 12 minutes at 4.5–7.5.

• *Session 20.* This is now a month since Rennie has trained and 6 weeks since the first use of FPO2. She describes being tired and that she has lots of pregnancy symptoms. She also reports feeling hypersexual. She has been able to get a lot done, despite much adversity and not feeling all that well. She reports, in fact, being able to do things she typically hates doing. In the past, she would have quit. Her boyfriend was at the house and despite a restraining order, refused to leave. She can't sleep when he is there and is still very stressed when he is around. But baseline, she reports, she is much calmer. Her speech continues to impress me as more complex and more fluent. She seems to be getting even smarter. She establishes herself readily in the training and finds a place of relaxed attention. After FPO2 she says, "I'm extremely relaxed and calm." Protocol: T3–T4 for 3 minutes at 3.5–6.5, T4–P4 for 21 minutes at 4.5–7.5, FPO2 for 6 minutes at 4–7.

• *Session 21.* Again, a month passes. Sexual feelings are very heightened, but she is experiencing these responses more toward women than men. In assessing this shift, it must be remembered that she was the youngest in a family in which all family members engaged in incest. (She originally came into treatment when, as a young adolescent, she made a crude sandwich board and wore it through the halls of her school. It said, "Fuck me.") In all other ways she reports doing very well. "It's amazing, I'm always on top of all the details of my life." She is better organized. She reports that this baby is very active and describes the kicking as aggressive. "It hurts me, and it feels different than with either

of my other kids. Much more active and much more, well, almost hurt-
ful. I don't believe this, but it's almost like it wants to hurt me." It is
important to remember that Rennie and this baby were punched by the
baby's father.

The baby became very active with RH training. Rennie describes the
movement as rough. She can feel its elbows, knees, and heels. At FPO2,
Rennie became deeply relaxed. "I'm much better than when I came in.
It's as if I'd been on a vacation." As we trained at FPO2, fetal movement
quieted. Rennie commented, "It's like it stretched, rolled over, and fell
asleep." Protocol: T3–T4 for 3 minutes at 3.5–6.5, T4–P4 for 21 minutes
at 4.5–7.5, FPO2 for 6 minutes at 4–7.

• *Session 22.* Three weeks later: Rennie reports having had a pretty
severe panic attack. It was hard for her to breathe. We discussed the
circumstances that gave rise to her panic, and how she handled them,
but as is clear throughout this book, I thought first about her brain. I
assessed the last protocol in terms of her report (her feedback) and made
decisions on how to proceed with training, given her continuing CNS
vulnerability. Other than that episode, which was very difficult, she
reports handling stresses well. During the training she experiences something like waves going down her body. Her feet and hands become cold.
As we continue at the right temporal lobe, the baby begins to move.
Rennie feels like smiling. "Happiness," she says. Over time, both mother
and baby relax. With FPO2, she reports feeling a little sleepy. "I like
this." Both mother and baby seem to agree. Movement is slow and easy,
with no kicking. Protocol: T3–T4 for 6 minutes at 3–6, T4–P4 for 18
minutes at 4–7, FPO2 for 6 minutes at 4–7.

• *Sessions 23 and 24.* No recurrence of panic, although she has had to
deal with the main cause of her stress: the abusive boyfriend. She is sad
about him and unable to accept that it is unlikely that he is going to
change, even with his attendance at the court-ordered group for battering men. She seems more subdued to me. Baby is no longer kicking
violently. She thinks her memory is better. Again, movement quiets and
gentles during FPO2. Between these two sessions, the baby is moving a
lot, but not aggressively or violently. Baby is moving as we train, but
slowly, stretching and turning. "FPO is awesome. The baby feels just like
me. A happy baby. Happy mom; happy baby." Session 23 protocol: T3–

T4 for 6 minutes at 3–6; T4–P4 for 18 minutes at 4–7; FPO2 for 1 minute at 3.5–6.5 and for 5 minutes at 4–7.

At Session 24 Rennie asks not to train as low: T3–T4 for 3 minutes at 3–6, T4–P4 for 3 minutes at 4–7 and for 18 minutes at 5–8, FPO2 for 6 minutes at 4–7. When my patient begins to get involved in protocol decisions, it is another indication to me that training is "taking," and given that patients are living this experience, their preferences are important data.

• *Session 25.* Rennie "kicked him out." The abusive boyfriend is still supporting her but no longer living at the house. She reports handling this major event well. Her kids are relieved he's gone. Baby is asleep but wakes up and begins to move as we begin to train. Rennie describes the baby as awake and calm by the end of right-side training, moving lightly, and Rennie uses this description, "She is tapping at me." Baby moved throughout FPO2 training, and the mother reports that she feels relaxed but not as much as last time. Protocol: T4–P4 for 24 minutes at 4–7, FPO2 for 3 minutes at 3.5–6.6 and for 6 minutes at 4–7. I lowered the frequency at FPO2 by a shade to honor her request not to train as low and to honor the data from the brain, and perhaps the baby, that we hadn't quieted Rennie's arousal quite as much as we would have liked.

• *Session 26.* Five weeks from due date. "I'm better. I'm on top of things." Rennie's memory is much better. Even when she has a hard time, she recoups quickly and gets herself back in control. She describes the baby as calmer. We often assume that we have to address cognitive problems by training on the "cognitive" verbal LH. It's important to note here that as her arousal gets quieter, her memory improves. She is, I think, much less distracted by the implicit memories in the RH, so better able to focus on the explicit memory required for her daily life. It was Rennie who taught me that we help some memory problems, particularly in developmental trauma, through quieting arousal on the right. Protocol: T4–P4 for 24 minutes at 4–7, FPO2 for 9 minutes at 3–6.

• *Session 27.* The baby was not in position to be born and had to be repositioned last week. This is a painful process, with some risks attached to it, but Rennie and the baby held up well. It was successful. The head is now in a downward position. Rennie has some apprehension that the baby won't stay in position, but not undue anxiety given what she has endured—essentially, two labors. Sleep has improved, but it is hard for her to get comfortable.

She reports that she feels much better after 21 minutes of right-side training and that the baby is calm. I paid particular attention to the movement of the baby during FPO2 as I dropped the frequency. Quieter at 2–5 Hz. Rennie thinks it might be too low for her, so I move up to 2.5–5.5 and then back to 3–6 Hz. Movement is gentle and rolling at 3–6 Hz.

Protocol: T4–P4 for 21 minutes at 4–7, FPO2 for 5 minutes at 3–6 and for 35 seconds at 2–5 (she didn't like it; even 35 seconds could factor when you are assessing the effects of this training the following week), and then for 2 minutes at 2.5–5.5.

• *Session 28.* Rennie tells me that she is dealing with enormous stress, including a theft and threats from the baby's father. (So much for anger management classes!) She may be experiencing some lethargy. She feels the baby is doing well. "Calm, like I am . . . I'm OK most of the time. My stress is when he is around." She also reports, a little shyly, that she still feels hypersexual toward women and that the nature of the feelings is "a little perverted." Baby is quiet, as is the mother throughout the training. Baby moving lightly at the beginning, but then seems to fall asleep. The mother–baby dyad quiets significantly. Protocol: T4–P4 for 21 minutes at 4.5–7.5 and for 3 minutes at 4–7, FPO2 for 9 minutes at 3–6.

Three weeks later, Rennie brings her week-old baby girl, Madeleine. She reports that labor was unusual, as if this baby didn't want to leave the womb, but she had to and she did. She is a healthy baby. Rennie had been given a prescription by her OB for antidepressants due to her history of severe postpartum depression. She had decided not to take the medication, because she was no longer prone to depression, due, she felt, to neurofeedback. I saw no sign of depression.

She describes Madeleine as attuned to her in ways the other children were not. She says that she makes eye contact, is expressive, and is easily soothed. "She cries when she needs something, I give it to her, and she's fine. There is no more crying, no extra." She turns her head to follow mother's voice and can almost, at 6 days, hold up her head. Rennie feels there is something special about this infant. She is quiet, calm, and responsive. Her two older kids adore the baby. Rennie credits neuro-feedback for a lot of this, as well as for the complete absence of postpar-tum depression. "This baby is making everything more cohesive. 'T' [the boyfriend] was in my life just to make this baby possible."

• *Session 29.* I trained Rennie with Madeleine lying on her chest. This is her report at FPO2:

> She got more regulated too. I could feel it. She felt my heart beat and I could feel hers start beating the same way. And her breathing, too. This is so different from my other kids. I love them so much, but this baby is just different. I am different. I didn't know that there was this way to be, this place to be in. I didn't know it existed. I am attuned with her and she is attuned to me; I regulate her and she regulates me.

After training she says that she feels really good. "Excellent!" About the FPO2: "It's better than dope." Protocol: T4–P4 for 12 minutes at 4.5–7.5 and for 9 minutes at 4–7, FPO2-for 9 minutes at 3–6.

• *Sessions 30 and 31.* These sessions are 2 weeks apart. Rennie says that neurofeedback makes her life more possible. But the stress doesn't let up. She has a positive pap smear, the first one ever, and has to have a colposcopy. The hot water heater broke and the older kids are sick. Troubles continue for her older daughter at school. Everything about her housing is uncertain. She has no money except that which the father continues to provide, but he expects sexual favors in return. She is coping with it all, and her infant daughter and she are closely bonded. During FPO2 training, she had Madeleine on her chest and she could feel her getting heavier as she, Rennie, relaxed. The baby, as well as the mother, seems particularly responsive to her mother's training at FPO2. Protocol for both sessions: T4–P4 for 21 minutes at 4–7, FPO2 for 3 minutes at 3–6 and then up to 3.5–6.5 for 5 minutes.

• *Session 32.* Two months postpartum: Rennie is sleeping well and the baby is sleeping through from 10 P.M. to 5 A.M. No depression. Mother reports that Madeleine is making up games to play with her. She kicks off her blanket and then smiles at her mother. Rennie puts the blanket on again and Madeleine kicks it off—"She loves this game." Madeleine laughs as she kicks it off. She is attempting to turn over. When she is on her belly, she pushes up with her hands and turns her head. She remains very easy to soothe. Rennie tells me that she will put her to bed, rub her stomach for a moment, say it's time to sleep, and Madeleine goes to sleep. Rennie is doing well; she is amazed at this child. Protocol: T4–P4 for 9 minutes at 4–7 and for 12 minutes at 3.5–6.5, FPO2 for 1 minute at 3–6 and for 8 minutes at 2.5–5.5.

• *Session 33.* Rennie has a bit of her characteristic nervous laughter back. She reports that Madeleine was very reactive to shots: She was screaming, and this baby never screams. After the shots, she developed hyperstartle responses before falling soundly asleep. Rennie checked her breathing because her sleep was long and hard. She awoke, regulated. Rennie is OK too. She is engaged in creative problem solving, and feels she is moving ahead. She trained at FPO2 while nursing. "I'm now relaxed," she said. It was hard to get up after the training. Madeleine fell asleep, but there were little startle responses that I hadn't seen before.

Protocol: T4–P4 for 9 minutes at 4–7 and for 12 minutes at 3.5–6.5, FPO2 for 1 minute at 3–6 and for 8 minutes at 2.5–5.5. I am trying to nudge Rennie's CNS into repose without a kickback, so I am being creative with splitting times at different frequencies, to see what she can tolerate.

• *Session 34.* Rennie was sick last week with flu, a fever, and a headache. All sexual stuff feels under control. In fact, sexual trash talk is very irritating to her. She's not interested. "It's just not where I am at. I can be alone now, so I appreciate alone time, particularly with the baby." Madeleine is happy and smiley. Very focused, very attuned. Both baby and mother seemed to regroup pretty quickly after the "shock" of the shots. Protocol: T4–P4 for 21 minutes at 3.5–6.5, FPO2 for 3 minutes at 3–6 and for 6 minutes at 2.5–5.5 "Good. Quiet."

• *Session 35.* "I want to do a lot, maybe too many things. I want to go to school; I want to learn to do therapy and neurofeedback. Sebern, I am close to being all right. I'm not quite there. A little bit more and I will be. I used to be overwhelmed by everything, even a small apartment. Now I can handle. I feel more creative, more quick-witted. I am able to talk to anyone." She feels very "able." She feels more aware and she's sleeping better at night. Rennie reports that Madeleine seems to understand cause and effect. She also seems to recognize another close family member's voice on the phone. She recognizes the word *kisses*. She opens her mouth when her mom asks, "Can I have a kiss?" Protocol: T4–P4 for 21 minutes at 3.5–6.5, FPO2 for 3 minutes at 2.5–5.5. She has a little tension in her jaw, and I drop the reward for 6 minutes at 2–5. Better lower. "Very peaceful, relaxed, quiet and at ease. Better after the FPO2."

• *Session 36.* Rennie reports that her jaw has been tight since the last training and that she's tired. She says, "I know this could be a weird question, but could neurofeedback be changing the shape of my head? I would swear that my forehead is bigger, like I had more frontal lobe." We talk about this possibility—it is not impossible—and she feels quite sure that something is changing, that her forehead is rounding out.

During the training Rennie experienced a sudden "energy rush." She felt destabilized, her hands were shaky, and she looked panicky. I stopped the feedback. She thought she would get sick. I was holding the baby and she was looking over my shoulder away from her mother. She too became distressed. I stayed the calmest of the three and quietly talked Rennie through the episode. She went into the bathroom to try to calm herself further and to wash her face. I held the baby, speaking with her, rocking her, and reassuring her, but to little avail. However, as Rennie calmed, so did Madeleine. Both restabilized within 10 minutes and, it seemed, at the same moment in time, even though they were separated by two walls. Of course, I was part of this mixture, and I am sure that my state quieted too as Rennie pulled out of the anxiety attack. Protocol: T4–P4 for 14 minutes at 3.5-6.5.

Rennie and I decide to put neurofeedback on hold for several reasons, one of which was her response to the training. She is responding to it in less predictable ways, and this is likely due to postpregnancy hormone fluctuations. (Hormones are neurotransmitters and will affect other neurotransmitters such as serotonin, gamma-aminobutryic acid [GABA], and dopamine.) She came with the baby. Her mood is steady through the ongoing rockiness of her life. No depression. Energy is better. Her relationship with the baby's father has taken a remarkably positive turn, and she describes being both quite wary of him and hopeful that these changes will last. He is taking genuine interest in his daughter and he is treating Rennie with a newly found respect (a change in the field between them?). She is proceeding with her plans to find a place of her own, but subsidized housing is scarce.

Madeleine is almost 6 months old. She is plump and strong and smiley. She makes exceptionally good eye contact with her bright, deep-blue eyes. She seems to me, in this period that Daniel Stern (1985) describes as the most social of a baby's life, to be one of the more, if not one of the most, related babies I've met. I asked her mother if she was still easy to soothe, and her response was interesting. She said that she didn't really know how to answer the question because she didn't really need to be soothed. Madeleine would cry to ask for something and as soon as it was provided, she was fine. She was weaned to the bottle at 3½ months without protest. She has two bottom teeth poking through and no evidence of teething distress as yet. She investigates with her mouth, but doesn't put everything that she comes across into it, and she doesn't suck her fingers or use a pacifier. She sleeps through the night and wakes up happy. She laughs out loud with her mother. There is something about this baby and whatever it is, she continues to manifest it. She does not seem to her mother to be the same baby that started out in utero kicking her so hard that it hurt.

Although, the mechanisms of intergenerational transmission of trauma are still debated, most would agree that the stress level of the mother is communicated to the baby in utero. Remember that fetal movement begins at 5-6 months in utero, which is the same time that the amygdala comes online in the RH. This case study suggests the possibility that neurofeedback training, particularly at FPO2, the site that seems to most effectively quiet fear, has a role to play in interrupting this transmission.

When Madeleine was 8 months old, Rennie was pushing her in her stroller in the grocery store when they ran into her biological mother and oldest brother. This brother was the most abusive of Rennie's siblings and had been incarcerated for molesting children. Although surprised to see him, Rennie reported that she felt unexpectedly calm. Madeleine, however, was anything but. She apparently took one look at this man, who she'd never seen before, and started to scream hysterically. She could not be comforted until Rennie took her out of the store, away from the brother, held her and soothed her verbally. She quieted quickly and returned to her baseline state of eager engagement with the world.

I mention this incident in the service of the general, ongoing discussion of intergenerational transmission of trauma in the field. Rennie did not think that her daughter was picking up anything from her, at least at that moment in time. But Madeleine did seem to recognize, at the very least, the danger that this man posed and was clearly expressing her own terror. We can only speculate on how she "knew." From Rennie's own increasingly well-regulated state, she was able to quiet her child's sudden and unexpected fear.

It seems fair to conclude that training the mother with neurofeedback, at least in this case, contributed to the child's regulation even before birth. If we accept the mother's report of her own state, she felt a heightened sense of attunement with this child, a bond that began after the FPO2 training. The baby herself was born highly self-regulating, a reality that enhanced the mother's ability to mother her. She was an exceptionally "easygoing" child. The week she learned to walk, Rennie found her with her brother's headphones on. She was dancing.

Cybele: Alpha–Theta Training in Dissociative Identity Disorder

Background

This young woman came to consult with me after she was discharged from the residential center at age 18. It had been a year since I had seen her at the center. She was the child of a dissociative, raging mother, who had provided her landlord with access to her daughter's body as rent payment. After her father left the family, they lived below the poverty line, often going with little food for days. When she was 6, her mother locked her in the attic for prolonged periods with a pot and her collection of decapitated dolls. She ran away from home at age 12 and ended up in a shelter for runaway teens. By 14 she was hospitalized and given the diagnosis of DID. She arrived in my center a few days before she turned 16, a vacant, terrified young girl. She was smart and pretty, but pale, hunched over, withdrawn, and overly compliant. Halloween, the season of dark arts and masked reality, was a particularly frightening time for her. For weeks she carried a small pumpkin wherever she went; it was hard to judge which was the more hollowed out.

In therapy, she would routinely fragment and send up an alter or alters to express and address her stress. Although she had had years of psychotherapy, she had no coherent internal narrative about what had happened to her and, of course, no cohesive sense of herself.

Assessment

Cybele and I had talked about neurofeedback even before I left the center. She didn't quite know what to think about brain wave training, but she felt she had to do something different. She was thoroughly ambivalent. She was afraid of losing her alters (her known "self"), but she also felt that she was at great risk of falling apart. Among her presenting problems were daily dissociative episodes, auditory processing delays, learning disabilities, spatial and sequential processing difficulties, memory impairment, autoimmune disease, and severe chronic constipation. She is touch averse and yet often "willingly" sexually exploited. She lacked any capacity to assert her own needs. She was taking anticonvulsants and atypical antipsychotics, which she stopped shortly after beginning neurofeedback.

This case outline covers 90 sessions, each split about equally between neurofeedback and therapy, and it represents the stabilization phase of our work together. We began with eyes-open training and then moved to alpha–theta and often used both in one session. I began training on the temporal lobes, but due to too much reactivity, mostly in the form of headaches, we did a lot of the eyes-open training on the central strip. Cybele was beaten around the head frequently as a young child; it is not unusual, in my experience, to see reactivity to training at the frontal and/ or temporal lobes when this is part of the history. The sessions varied in frequency from one to two times a week.

• *Session 1.* Dropped the frequency when she switched to May, a threatening adult alter. As mentioned above, I understand alters primarily as manifestations of terror. I spoke with May, asked her opinion about training, and sought to reassure her that neurofeedback was a good thing. She seemed unaware of any agreement to undertake this. As I brought the frequency down, she became less agitated. At the end of the session Cybele returned and described herself as less depressed.

• *Session 2.* Appetite felt more regulated. Felt feelings. Feels some depression and some sadness. Sleep is more restful. Not as exhausted. After training, she reports that she is "beginning to feel relaxed and OK about leaving" when our session is over.

• *Session 3.* Headaches that come and go in different sections of her head—left temporal, right parietal—everywhere, in general. "They feel like bruises." Aspirin helps. Appetite more regulated; more exhaustion than depression. After the last session, she had a near panic attack at the mall. She is more aware of physical discomfort and reports more body awareness in general. She is restless in school but notices that she has an easier time expressing her thoughts.

• *Session 4.* Reports feeling restless. She watched *Wuthering Heights*, which just made her sad, but not panicky as she would have expected. She reports handling fear better, being physically tired, and having fewer headaches. Her period started when it was supposed to, with normal flow and hardly any cramps. This is the first normal period she has ever had. Some premenstrual depression. Mildly depressed more often but can pull herself out of it. Able to nap for the first time in her life. Not waking as frequently. Feels fine on leaving.

• *Session 5.* May be getting a cold. Very vivid dreams. Ghosts of old people she knew. Headaches still and the question is whether this is the training or the cold coming on. As I mentioned in Chapter 6, neurofeedback is the first rule-out. All her senses are more engaged: She smells and tastes things, and she's enjoying color and "the scene" more (her sensory brain is waking up to the world around her).

• *Session 6.* She told me about spraining her ankle and laughing uncontrollably. (As mentioned in Chapter 4, body workers interested in trauma often focus on the ankles because they "hold" the disconnect between the body and the earth.) She was terrified during a backrub last night, but felt the fear without lapsing into depression. Describes feeling "unattached." "I feel very different." Spelling is getting better. Does not move in her sleep until early A.M. when she seems to shift into familiar restless sleep. Jumpiness around 10 P.M. on the Equinox (intrusion of trauma sensation?). Colors more vivid. Feels more coordinated, more integrated, more self-aware. Much more in touch with her body. (Her brain is beginning to reorganize.)

• *Session 7.* Can be held again and is comforted by it. Woke up less but still waking up. Her dreams are vivid and, for the first time, she experiences feelings in her dreams. Mood is pretty good. She is more often hopeful, less stressed, and feels better able to work out stressful situations. Drinking is not appealing to her. She "can't ignore [her] body." She's less scared in social situations. Depression is generally minor, but some episodes of major situational depression. Some nonlocal pressure headaches, but these are less also.

• *Session 8*. More able to tolerate feelings when triggered. "I *have* feelings now." More memories of being home and bad dreams. Sex drive way down. Wants to be touched and held. Fearful at night; begins around 8 or 9. Depression is minor. Knows when she is full and stops eating. Digestion is better. Constipation is eased. (The vagal tracks are beginning to respond.)

• *Session 9*. Feels emotionally stronger. Dissociative episode over the weekend. Thought process clearer. Ended a lover relationship she felt was destructive. She commented that she had never ended a relationship before. Painting a lot. Colors are still vivid. Wakes often. Less appetite. Drunk on two beers. Less afraid. Can sleep with the light off. Easiest menstrual period she's ever had—no cramps, no trouble with blood, which she has always been reactive to; mood steadier.

• *Session 10*. Episodic depression. Some memories coming up. Could function even though depressed. Did not dissociate during GYN exam but had to work at it. Feels as if spatial confusion—where streets are and distances between cars—is improving. Able to clearly see her own face and not those of the others (the alters). All are still there and boundaried and separate, but they act more in concert, more as a collective. We had not come close to this level of cooperation and integration with even the most intensive psychotherapy.

• *Session 11*. Cybele came in distressed over conflict with her housemate, but reports thinking much more clearly. Handwriting is flowing better. Gets to sleep OK buts wakes often. Housemate is sexually provocative, so sleeping situation is unsettled. Feels more intuitive, more tuned in, and more assertive. "I stopped carrying my knife because I feel safer. . . . I'm seeing the whole." This observation suggests that she is fragmenting less.

• *Session 12*. Very good mood; maybe a little hyper. Finds herself smiling a lot and people are smiling back. Much more assertive. Less ruled by fear. More alert and more talkative. After training, she reports feeling mellow.

• *Session 13.* Slept very well. Feels alert and rested this A.M. Quieter. Regular bowel movements—used to be every 2 or 3 days. I note during session that "this is the lowest overall slow wave and the most consistent." The wave form is much less erratic. Slow wave fluctuates up as she gets tired. Reports feeling calm and good now. I am not sure what these fluctuating slow waves mean.

• *Session 14.* (2 days later) Her alter May is back today. She is depressed. Unclear about how Cybele is doing, but notes that this is historically a time of terrible trauma. She also tells me that she feels full sooner, that her head is clearer, and that she feels less dependent and more assertive. She wants good food. After the training she reports, "I feel so calm, I don't need to be here anymore." May leaves and Cybele returns.

• *Session 15.* Awoke depressed today, fear that she's been taken advantage of, bad dreams of residential placement. Did not go to school. Depression lifted by midmorning. More active, more aware of her body's physical limits: "I've got a body. It's really weird." Solving problems better. Memory seems better. Coming out of a fog. Insights coming fast. She needs healthy food; listening to her body. Stops taking St. John's wort.

• *Session 16.* Cybele began to cry when verbally abused by former boyfriend; crying is unusual for her. She burned herself but stopped when it actually hurt, which it did this time. She felt overwhelmed by emotion, and the heat of the burned-up match snapped her out of it. Talked to a friend instead. Bad dreams that night. Doesn't like coffee anymore. Now feels much more clear emotionally and better able to come out of depression. Feels happier. Cybele is aware that she lives in a body for the first time, and it is also new for her to turn to a friend and talk to manage challenging emotional states. She would have felt too much shame.

• *Session 17.* Mood feels baseline OK but a bit zoned, may be dissociative. General daily memory is better. Vivid dreams and recall problems related to the past. Writing is coming easily. "Food tastes better; air smells better." Much less frightened. Mellow. More assertive. Sleep and appetite are good.

• *Session 18*. With period felt a little bit of a daze that could be dissociative. Real sadness today as she begins to assess the effects of her history. She reports feeling the importance of connectedness. Sleep is fine. No depression. Many insights. My note: "Sea changes in this girl."

• *Session 19*. Sad, depressed, and angry after being home. No sign there of her presence. Lots of signs of affluence, but father won't pay for her support. She reported: "My boundary and the boundary of the other is much more visible. I have more sense of my identity. I used to become the other and that doesn't happen anymore. I am just becoming who I am." She told me this at the same time as she said, "Patrick [a young male alter] was grieving that Dad doesn't love him." She feels good at end of session.

• *Sessions 20 and 21*. Felt depressed and sad and anxious most of the week, got drunk at a party and smoked pot. Relates this behavior to my being gone and seeing a disturbing movie. She had a dissociative episode in response to a switch in her friend with DID, which she describes as very scary. Tempted to cut, but "finding reserves of strength that I didn't know I have." Near anxiety attack but got through that too. "I wonder sometimes, am I saying this?"

• *Session 22*. "Things are shifting. I'm feeling more things." Began to wake up at 3 A.M.—this relates somehow to abuse—awakes with "a vague expectancy." A little scared about graduating. Can't shove things off; feeling mixed feelings much more often. Felt very depressed this A.M. and scratched herself. Bouncing back better. "It takes less to make me happy. . . . Easier to get angry . . . more assertive."

• *Session 23*. "I feel very sad." This is new. All emotions are much more spontaneous. Cutting episode last week that did not work to help her feel better, or to feel anything. Beginning to get memories of things she did while dissociating. Never wants to cut again. Feels better able to understand others. After training she feels relaxed, "Like meditation. Grounded. Refreshed."

• *Session 24*. Cybele was raped by a man she had trusted. She'd fought and protested, to no avail. She descended, initially, into shame and fear. She felt confused and deeply unsettled, but she took refuge with friends and found comfort in their company. When alone after the attack, she felt panicky and out of her body. She did not switch, but she was dissociative. When with her friends she just felt OK. "I know more." She reports that she is switching much less often and relying more on simple dissociation. Her "BS detector" is humming along. Considering everything, she is doing well. After the session she said, "It is as if the last 24 hours didn't happen."

• *Session 25*. Feeling good. Able for the first time to go to the basement by herself. "Once I caught up on my sleep, what happened didn't affect me the same way. I am really fine. Back to normal. Startle response is much reduced. Woke up wanting to paint animals." When we trained today, I asked her to reduce delta–theta—over 45 µV—and when she brought it down to 12 µV, she described a sudden intense energy in her chest moving up into her head. "It's like sparklers going off in my head."

• *Session 26*. No depression but she is grieving her history, something she has never done before, in or out of therapy. "Grieving is weird." "Poetry is pouring forth." Appetite is healthy and normal or maybe slightly less; wants green vegetables. Exercising regularly. Bad dreams. Sleep has been restless. Startle response less. "When I left here last time, I felt like I was sizzling—I have never felt so awake in my whole life. Acutely aware of color, of shading, of the air . . . Deep joy about everything . . . Like being born." And, of course, this is exactly what is happening.

• *Session 27*. Able to be alone in her house "without wearing steel-toed boots." Much better able to understand technical things, including math. Easier to pay attention. Nature of her poetry is changing—softer, more pastoral, sophisticated and beautiful.

Worked to bring slow wave down. When she does, even to 14 and 13 µV, she reports: "Every cell in my body is awake." Theta then pops back. "It's not bad; it is intense, though. A completely different state."

• *Session 28*. Poetry is changing and getting much better. "I don't know where some of this is coming from—profound and fluid thinking." Increasingly articulate. Much broader range of feeling. She is becoming real to herself. She also had a panic attack when she assessed the reality of her financial situation—hyperventilating and crying—but it passed within minutes. She does not believe she will have another one. She can tune things out at will. This has never been under her control.

• *Session 29*. Wild dreams. More easily agitated but always for an "appropriate reason." She developed a gag reflex, which she'd never had before. "I don't want to know why I didn't have a gag reflex. All this makes me so much sadder." She cries, rare for her. In the session, she becomes dissociative in response to remembering and to her grief. Switches to Patrick, and Patrick could see his own false self: He feared he would disappear if he brought down slow wave. By the end of the session, Cybele returns to tell me: "I can feel the knots in my shoulders," and then, "Actually I feel really good."

• *Session 30*. Lonely, but finds that she "perks right up" when she's around nice people. Some urges to hurt herself, which she sees as habitual—"It doesn't seem like it will go anywhere." Lots of sadness. Much more self-respect. Reports watching *The Sweet Hereafter* and being deeply affected by the incest scene and by two parents grieving. She has no comprehension of parents grieving, no capacity to understand this, no language for it. After training: "As good as I could be—actually, pretty good."

• *Session 31*. First alpha–theta training: She describes having crashed into a "destructive" (agitated) depression. "I am able to do a self-inventory." Stressed by money and relationships. This is our first deep-state training. I asked her to imagine her calm, stable, quiet, organized, lucid brain, "like my hands around your infant head." She looked immediately distressed and started to cry. She did not dissociate. She became agitated within 10 minutes into alpha–theta. At first she liked it. Very high amplitude delta and her theta is higher than alpha. I rewarded alpha only and inhibited delta. She asks to stop. Does not know the source of her agitation. A few minutes of eyes-open training to stabilize whatever she is experiencing and she reports: "Very clear!"

• *Session 32* (second alpha–theta session). Severe situational depression. Very anxious. She's had suicidal thoughts, but could not imagine cutting herself. Can't block out pain, either emotional or physical. Lonely. During the alpha–theta session she experiences a level of relaxation (perhaps too unfamiliar to be comfortable). At 8 minutes she comes out of it and says, "It's too weird. I feel agitated." I encourage her to go back, but after 14 minutes, she takes off the electrodes. The agitation is getting worse. "I feel like I have new limbs." As she is leaving she says, "Real awareness is more tiring than hypervigilance."

• *Session 33* (alpha–theta: 3). Good night until midnight, then she just began to cry under the stress of her life, past and present. High volume of emotion. Somewhat of a meltdown. Her friends are worried about suicide, but Cybele is not. With alpha–theta, she has unbidden memories of the landlord, and feelings about her mother and father's abandonment. Begins to breathe rapidly and couldn't continue past 15 minutes. With eyes-open training she talks with me about periods of real, un-self-conscious enjoyment—reading Calvin and Hobbes; walking downtown. She appears very stable, open, and emotionally in touch.

• *Session 34* (alpha–theta: 4). "Doing pretty well." Seems a little distanced to me, but otherwise OK. She reports being tired and out of sorts. No depression. Restless, not really able to do alpha–theta. In eyes-open training she talks about changes in her sense of self and about no longer wanting any violence in her life.

• *Session 35* (alpha–theta: 5). Doing well. Enthusiastic and talkative today. Feels very clear intellectually and emotionally. Able to see others much more clearly for who they are: father, stepmother, and friends. No dissociation. Some apprehension around alpha–theta: "I feel so much doing this. I do my best to ride it but . . . " Fears of monsters that used to overwhelm her are now bearable (but still believed). With alpha–theta: deep relaxation frightens her. She fears she will die. She is very sad about this. "I like SMR (eyes open) better."

• *Session 36* (alpha–theta: 6). Co-conscious with Patrick and didn't like it. It began when she read the opening line of the book *Fugitive Pieces* (Michaels, 1996): "Time is a blind guide." Realized that he, Patrick, was a 7-year-old, buried alive to be saved from her holocaust.

• *Session 37* (alpha–theta: 7). "Freaked out" by former boyfriend's sexual involvement with 16-year-old girl. Experiences him as a predator. Particularly upset by his rationalizing this relationship. In conversation with him, she switched to Julia, an adult, competent alter who can deal with this. She is co-conscious with Julia. She also switched today to Patrick to tell me of cutting incident. "Fear and anger got pretty big, and I turned it back on her." She describes overwhelming, powerless rage. During alpha–theta the cut on her leg began to hurt for the first time. We stopped the training when she began to cry deeply with the ongoing recognition of how terrible her childhood had been. After eyes-open training, she said, "It is as if my brain is combating my mind." I think she is commenting, at least in part, on competing neuronal patterns.

• *Session 38.* No alpha–theta today, at her request. Cybele broke down and wept with the pain of her abandonment, her father's betrayal in taking her back to her abusive mother. Also able to tell me about a sexual encounter that was a straight-out reenactment and she knew this. She did not dissociate until it became sexual and then "spaced out." She described consciously using DID to leave the situation. As she wept and talked, she felt integrated to me. Such full, complete emotion does not come from fragments. No part of her held this alone. She agreed tentatively with me, unable in some way to see her wholeness.

• *Session 39* (alpha–theta: 8). Many reenactments of sexual abuse. Aware that all of her alters, almost as a collective, were participating in these reenactments. Finally able to just stop. Generally aside from compulsive reenactments, she reports that her mood has been good and that she's actually been having some fun, even while coping with many ongoing present-day stressors.

• *Session 40* (alpha–theta: 9). Mood is good. Felt fine after session yesterday. We discuss establishing a "safe place." During alpha–theta, thoughts about sadistic abuse arise, and she wants to come out of that memory and state. She said that she is not able to have detached thoughts. We talked about her immense, disallowed grief at my leaving for vacation next week, about all the losses. During right-side training she cried deeply and fully, with terrible pain, incomprehension, and grief. Flooded, but kept talking and at her request, kept training. Extraordinary session. Slow wave dropped as she cried. At the end, she said, "I feel stable. It came up and I breathed and it's gone."

• *Session 41.* I have been away on vacation. When I come in, she is huddled in a corner. She has a bad cold and reports feeling dazed. She came out of this state as we talked, but reports being in and out of dissociative states while I was away. Along with the stress of my absence, it is likely that the virus dysregulated her brain. At the end of the session she says, "I feel really good. All in all, much better. Brightness is back."

• *Session 42* (alpha–theta: 10). "Good, tired." Came out of alpha–theta at 4 minutes. Said she was vibrating. "What was that?" she asked, somewhat alarmed. She pulled the sensors off at 11 minutes and looked scared. . She wanted to continue to see if she could finish a session this time. Couldn't do more than 14 minutes. My note: She seems to touch into a primal terror.

• *Session 43.* Depressed. Disappointing interaction with father, which she feels she handled pretty well. Felt lost at the university today, couldn't get her bearings. Felt dissociative and posttraumatic, but also reports feeling much better control over states. These sessions, which bridge my being away and the assault of the virus, illustrate the vying of new and old patterns for supremacy in her brain; in her.

• *Session 44* (alpha–theta: 11). Asks for alpha–theta today and lasted 7 minutes. Realizes how fearful and disoriented she has always been. She talks about literally being lost most of her life and now, most of the time being able to find her way.

• *Sessions 45 and 46* (alpha–theta: 12 and 13). Woke up this A.M. disoriented. Came 1 hour early for her appointment. She is experiencing darkness. I asked her if she could go into it and try not to flee. She wept with the horror at the abuse and abandonment. I have never seen her as in touch with what she went through. I question the alpha–theta training in my own head and wonder whether we should continue this. Is this release of fear or abreaction, the rewiring of fear?

• *Session 47.* Agitated on and off all day—"Just the time of year." It occurs to her to be destructive, but it is not driving her. She describes a "Zen running moment." And then: "My worst moments now were my best moments every other October." After training she is less agitated, but sad and lonely. It is hard for her to find peers.

• *Session 48* (alpha–theta: 14). "It is October and I am not baptizing myself in blood. I am doing well." She appears thoughtful and had a breakthrough that allowed her to comprehend the constraints of my position at the residential facility. This is the first time she has made that empathic leap. She said as well: "Your love for me, which was not allowed [at the treatment center], allows me to love [a child in her care], which will allow her to love." I note: One of the major shifts in this girl has been in empathy. Her face looks softer. When doing alpha–theta training, I asked her to imagine a pebble falling through the brook that is shimmering in the sun.

• *Session 49.* She is triggered by a conversation on the bus about teenage parents raising kids in gangs. Sad and a little dissociated. Add back in some left-side training for depression and auditory processing. For a few seconds, I forgot to change the filter so I was inadvertently training to raise arousal on the right temporal lobe. She said it felt like a pre-flashback state. This mistake had consequences. It is hard to know if this created undue suffering or was something she had to experience. I had, I think, amped up her terrible implicit memory system.

• *Session 50.* Posttraumatic recall. Spacing out. Shaking. Meltdown and dissociation during sexual encounter. Headache. Pressure in her head. Knee hurting when she woke up. She's come down with a serious virus. After training she reports, "not feeling well but not freaking out." Lots of posttraumatic memory, mostly around her mother. Stopped training to talk about what she was remembering.

• *Session 51* (alpha–theta: 15). Did very well with driving lesson. Less depressed after session. "I let myself feel better." In and out of darkness, then out. Came out of alpha–theta at about 6 minutes. "Oh my God, I know where Jenny [an alter] came from!" She told me for the first time about a particularly perverse and sadistic sexual torture she'd experienced. Jenny arrived and talked about her worry of being lost, of no longer being needed. Cybele may still need the alters, but even they are more regulated.

• *Session 52.* No alpha–theta due to concern over aggravation of DID. Reports that her period is regular with only minor cramps. Did not even need aspirin. She felt the shift down in reward frequency immediately: "You can't believe how good I feel." Prior to the shift she felt "cranked up."

• *Session 53.* Hard few days. Dissociative episode after party. Generally feels she is taking better care of herself. Making less food and eating less. After training, she reports, "Less hazy. I feel very in my body. I am nowhere else."

• *Session 54.* Hearing delay caused trouble at work. She couldn't follow briefing. She made a protocol recommendation and when I did it, she felt it immediately and positively.

• *Session 55* (alpha–theta: 16). Came out of alpha–theta startled. Talking now, more generally, about the terrible trauma of her childhood—

not about dissociative symptoms but about the extent of trauma and neglect. She can hardly take it in.

• *Session 56* (alpha–theta: 17). Arrived in good mood. She came out of alpha–theta at 10 minutes, describing the background of horror and some memory of an event. Still pretty even. As she left, in response to me, she said, "It isn't even like I need to hang in there. I'm not hanging by my fingernails anymore."

• *Session 57* (alpha–theta: 18). Arrives cold (physically), possible viral infection. Some depression. "Bad dreams about what happened to me. What's changed in them is that I can protect myself and others." The dreams feel understandable to her. She feels panicky and asks to lower the frequency. Stopped training briefly, and she was OK. I went to train on the right temporal and Cybele wept. I have never seen her cry so fully and deeply. Then she started to talk about it without triggering herself. We are both amazed at her changing capacity.

• *Session 58* (alpha–theta: 19). Describes herself: "Yesterday, I was bright-eyed and active." She did well with my being away and many interpersonal challenges. Today she is "a little bit out of it." Talks about her sense of abandonment. She came out after 5 minutes, agitated. She is making lots of high alpha (usually a sign of agitation). Even with inhibiting this more aggressively, she comes out again in a state of near panic. Severe anxiety. Flashes of living at her mother's. Panicked over losing things. We talked, and we can't get a handle on this. These are the times when you need real faith in brain plasticity.

• *Session 59* (alpha–theta: 20). Last night she had a major fight with abusive boyfriend. He burst into her room and refused to leave her alone, taunting her, and then continued to taunt outside her door. She had a dissociative episode and cut her leg. She reports recovering quickly. She was disappointed with her reaction but was able to regain her equilibrium even before we talked. She is able to understand and articulate that this would have an impact on me and did well with that also. Even when she organizes in old symptomatic patterns, it is clear to us both that her internal system is calmer than it has ever been. Terrible feelings in alpha–theta. Came out after 7 minutes. Verbally, emotionally, and intellectually flooded. After eyes-open training she is calm on leaving.

• *Session 60*. Tired when she wakes up. Sleeping a lot. Irritable until she eats. Some sweet craving but for juice and carrots. A little depressed but pretty much OK. With left-side training she tells me that it is harder to control panic responses. "Things are rustling around." Memories come up and terror with it with RH training. Lowering frequency eased her terror but may have interrupted emerging memory. She drops her delta–theta to 13 μV. Feels very good, particularly with this drop in slow wave.

• *Session 61* (alpha–theta: 21). "I'm surprised at how easy this is." She is referring to moving about in her life. She's sad more often. No panic. Some fear after bad dream about her mother. In the dream:

> In the dream, two little kids are always hanging around me. [Cybele has a younger bother.] My mother is sentenced to die—then it would be me that was going to die. I rescue them [the two kids] in a hot-air balloon. Fought physically with mother, threatened her. Unclear who was going to die, but the death is by stabbing or strangling. I looked for sleeping pills to give her. My mother is being chased by a tornado, then this becomes me. My mother is not attempting to hurt me.

After alpha–theta, "I feel 10 years younger." Very peaceful until last 2 minutes, when she felt "too much stillness."

• *Session 62* (alpha–theta: 22). Reports that she is still falling asleep within 10 minutes of going to bed. "Unheard of." Lonely and upset yesterday at all the misery, apathy, and dissociation she sees around her as she emerges from her own dissociation. Emotionally stronger, honest, and more assertive. Feels increase in self-awareness. "More clear-eyed." Multiple crossovers during alpha–theta. A large amplitude crossover remembering an incident with her brother. After eyes-open training, she says, "I'm feeling really good."

• *Session 63* (alpha–theta: 23). Many alters arrived after the last session. Julia came (Cybele was co-conscious of this), then Mr. No Name (sociopath), then Justine, and for a moment Tom (sad psychopath, named after her most sadistic abuser). She reports that afterwards she felt good. "I would have been hospitalized after such a session. No, I wouldn't have had such a session." Alters arriving to speak about terrible trauma. Julia being shot at. Mr. No Name witnesses and assists in a murder. He expresses a wish to continue with this process even if it puts their existence at peril. Reports too from some of the later alters. Tore off the sensors at 9 minutes of alpha–theta. Memories of sadistic abuse. Eyes open, she dropped slow wave to 11 μV: "Very, very clear."

• *Session 64* (alpha–theta: 24). Woke up this A.M. desperately wanting to be stable. Asks for alpha–theta. She's been sick with flu for 3 weeks; not taking very good care of herself. Seems depressed and also realistically overwhelmed by memories of trauma. A little bit of a dazed, hunched girl today, pale and sad. "This feels terrible, but it is 10 times better than it used to be. In the past, this would have been one of my good days." After training, feels less sick and calmer.

• *Session 65* (alpha–theta: 25). Slept 11 hours and then had to be woken. Still feels pretty bad physically but better emotionally. Looks better; more color. Mood is improved. Asked her to visualize being well during alpha–theta. Couldn't stay with it because she needed to blow her nose. With eyes-open training she quiets and gets tired.

• *Session 66* (alpha–theta: 26). Came out after a restless 10 minutes. "Terror . . . too many crossovers." When beginning eyes-open training, however, she says, "I am distant and calm." She told me of an episode with scissors and says that she now has a glimpse of "why I became the way I was." I note her use of the past tense, but don't share it. Pushed slow wave down at the end of the session; she could feel it in her stomach. As she was ending, she said, thoughtfully, "I love the details of people's lives. I love people. I even love the human condition." After a pause she added, "I may be doing neurofeedback too young. Who will I marry?"

• *Session 67.* Now on antibiotics. Worn out from being sick so long. Denies being depressed; more aware, not always happy, but now unhappy with things around her. "I am now practical." She is deciding her own protocol, and today it's not alpha–theta.

• *Session 68* (alpha–theta: 27). Assertive, clear, mature, and happy. Able to draw the boundary in sexual relationships. "I know what I want." I remind her of the date, and she burst out laughing, saying, "Yes, things have been more active, but I wasn't aware that it was the Equinox. It wasn't acute. I like how I have changed. I really love being alive." Many crossovers and a mixed experience. Made the brook (alpha entrainment) return when she wanted it and was proud of this. During eyes-open training she is able to drop delta–theta to 9 µV and reports seeing everything with a crystal clarity she's never felt before. Sad too, that this is the first time that she's lived in this reality.

• *Session 69* (alpha–theta: 28). Yesterday, Patrick was here. We spent most of the session talking about the realities of integration, her fears, her OK-ness, the sense that things are blending, that she is getting characteristics of her alters and their memories as well. Questions about who she is, what is her identity, and fears of her integration invalidating the reality of the horror of her past. After 5 minutes and many crossovers, she comes out to tell me that she felt "small and big at the same time, bobbing in the air, like seeing the scope of who I will be as all fifty parts come together . . . scary."

• *Session 70* (alpha–theta: 29). No nightmares. Sadness. "My worst problems now are from the stress of my present life." Neglect issues are surfacing over those of abuse. She is softer and lighter. "No hard edges."

• *Session 71* (alpha–theta: 30). Everyday this girl comes more into herself. She is assertive and kind, thoughtful, funny, and mature. Still some hint of cowering, but only a hint. Teaching herself the penny whistle. "Now that I don't spend every day trying to survive, I can do these things." Emotionally articulate and able to discriminate finely— like the difference between being helpless and feeling impatient. Does not want to kill her abusers; just wants them as far away as possible. She is *very* funny about *Angela's Ashes* (McCourt, 1996). Comes out of alpha–theta at 13 minutes, saying she's done enough, but then decides to finish the 20 minutes. "A sick, nervous feeling." Feeling good at the end. Focus is on the legacy of neglect.

• *Session 72* (alpha–theta: 31). Tired and sad. Not depressed. More like mourning over the state of the world. At 7 minutes comes out because of agitation, but quickly feels better and returns. Left feeling very good, laughing and "smart."

• *Session 73* (alpha–theta: 32). Good shape. Sadness about her own growing ability to connect and the inability of her friends to do so with her. During alpha–theta, many memories arise (none new) of mother's bizarre behaviors—those that made her realize that she was crazy. Very high delta during session, but low affect. "I know it is not happening now." A little internally "mad," almost manicky. Calms down with eyes-open RH training.

• *Session 74* (alpha–theta: 33). Mood up and down. Really contending with the sadness of the reality of life. Read a book very quickly. Grasping what she reads more readily. Has to stop alpha–theta: Her brain feels "riled." She has old impulses. Wants to run. Aroused. Her delta is once again higher than all other bandwidths. She leaves more agitated than I or she would like, but thankfully, she no longer poses a threat to herself.

• *Session 75* (alpha–theta: 34). Feels like she's turned another important corner. Writing is fluid and creative. States of withdrawal have gone. Detachment is gone. More able to pay attention, stay open, and be curious. Lots of new recognition of the reality of what she's been through.

• *Session 76*. Cybele reports a traumatic reaction to scene in the movie *Practical Magic* that reminded her of her mother—a rapid turn from affection to threat and sex. "Like a biological reaction—so extreme I couldn't shut it off. Not really dissociated." Seems like an unfamiliar experience. Got very stoned a few nights ago and it didn't have the same effect. It passed through her system more quickly and she could override its effects. Delta–theta still high (over 20 μV). As she was leaving, she said simply, "I am doing great."

• *Session 77*. "I'm not much of a multiple anymore. I need these guys—like threads pulled out of a tapestry, they are being pulled back in." Feels good on leaving.

• *Session 78*. She asked for the same protocol, as she was calmer in general except during "high stress times." She was knocked out by soccer ball. "Standard PTSD stuff" related to abusive roommate. Bad dreams. Now we have the possible complications of a new head injury.

• *Session 79* (alpha–theta: 35). Some PTSD intrusion around memories of her mother. Troubling, vivid dreams; in some she can fly. She wants to deal with these in alpha–theta. Very high delta amplitude, then theta, then alpha. At times alpha overtakes delta. After the session she reports: "For awhile it felt awful. Mother's beatings. Felt shuddery. Very high anxiety; then I calmed down . . . afraid, the 'corner of the eye fear.'" Some concern that she'd have a flashback during alpha–theta, but she didn't. Feels good after eyes-open training.

• *Session 80.* Burst of enormous creativity. Five poems in a week. Bad dreams are over but she still wakes up with a startle. "I hate apathy. I wish my friends would dig their hands into life." She called between sessions to tell me that her friend (and a patient of mine in the residential center) had hung himself.

• *Session 81 and 82.* We talked together about the boy who hung himself and had our own private memorial for him. In talking today more generally about all that has happened and about her dissociative states, she realizes that one of her male alters, named after her most sadistic abuser, felt like her last resource, like what stood between her and her death. "He wanted me to believe that, and I have." Suicidal thoughts are up particularly after her friend's death, but she was able to feel quieter after training.

• *Session 85.* She is stressed. She can hear "alters' voices in the background," but she says, "they are not DID enough to pay any attention to." They can't overtake her or take over for her.

• *Session 89* (alpha–theta: 36). During alpha–theta training she has memories of a babysitter who was kind to her, even tender and singing to her. She has had very stressful encounters with the men in her life and reports that "all the little ones feel betrayed. The room was spinning. I had to calm them down and they were all in my body. It was physical." This was to be the last report of alters.

• Session 90: "I am leading a charmed life now."

Eleanor: Neurofeedback for an Adolescent Suffering from Asperger's, Eating Disorder, and Developmental Trauma

Background

Eleanor was the ice princess. She lived inside a stone tower with one small window at the top. There were no doors and none required. No one came in and she never went out.

When she arrived at my office she was a pale, sunken, tired 16-year-old who pulled her dark, lanky hair away from her face with a rainbow barrette. She wore a bulky blue sweater, jeans, and clogs. Hand out, her chin up, she greeted me robustly. It was an unusual greeting for a teen-ager. It was a little too loud, but in all other ways seemed competent, more adult than adolescent. It was, as became evident, well practiced.

Until the months of crisis that were to come, she attended her sessions as dutifully as she did her advanced classes in high school. Early on, she let me know that therapy was a project, something to get done, like a term paper. She had been brought to me for this project and to try a new approach, neurofeedback, to address her severe bulimia and anorexia, now in its fourth year. She was bingeing and purging at least five times a day, and even though she wished to be cooperative, she could not imagine stopping. She did not know how she could stand to feel what she might feel if she stopped or how she would forgo the 10 seconds of ecstasy she felt at the end of a successful purge.

Her mother's visit preceded Eleanor's. Psychotherapy alone, she felt, was not helping her daughter. The eating disorder was her treatment priority, but she had other concerns as well. Eleanor was "different" and had seemed so since soon after birth. She described her as tactilely defensive, and told me that Eleanor used to cry hysterically at any loud sound. She did not, as a baby, fold into her mother's arms. She walked at 8 months and spoke in full sentences by age 1. When Eleanor was 18 months old, her mother attempted to return to her morning job. Each day during the 1 month it took until her mother quit, Eleanor would fling herself against the front door of the day-care center and sob for the entire 3 hours. When her mother returned to take her home, she said it was like carrying a plank of wood. Eleanor arched rigidly across her arms. Subsequent assessment revealed that Eleanor met 9 out of 10 criteria for Asperger's syndrome (now referred to as *high-functioning autism* per the DSM-5; American Psychiatric Association, 2013).

Her mother described Eleanor's father as a charming, complex, drug-involved sociopath. They were separated when Eleanor returned from a visit with him highly agitated. She became hysterical again at bath time. Later investigations concluded that the 3-year-old had been sexually molested. Her mother later moved and brought her then 5-year-old daughter to live locally with relatives. After several years of financial and emotional hardship, she remarried.

Eleanor had a different view of her father. She knew what had happened, but she wanted to return to him and to the life he represented (he was now very successful in the entertainment business). She kept herself bone thin to maintain the route back to him. She kept the body of a starving child, which allowed her to sustain the myth that she could resume her interrupted childhood and live the life that belonged to her, one that "glittered."

Her mother's remarriage and the subsequent birth of a sister challenged Eleanor's tenuous hold on stability. She choked the baby in her crib to make her cry so that she could soothe her. She convinced another child to cut all of her best clothes into scraps. She shredded the living room curtains. She had momentary "spheres of influence," but no friends throughout her childhood.

At the time of our first interview, Eleanor still had no friends. She did not describe herself as lonely, and I don't think she was. She didn't have the capacity to be lonely. She was very bright and she had learned how to engage adults at least at the level of precocity, a level that kept her teachers interested in her. She not only answered all the questions, she expounded on them. She didn't walk, she scurried, bent nearly parallel to the ground, toppled over by books and the burdens of Asperger's. She talked too loudly, too quickly, and to no one. Even when she looked at me, I wasn't there. There was no "other." She was the center of a universe that had no people in it and that did not itself exist. She lived behind the walls of the tower. She was obsessive and rigid. Foods touching on the plate would send her spiraling out of control. Her multiple fears; her lack of awareness of the reality of an other; her obsessions around food, clothing, and body size; the eating disorder in all its forms; and her raging tempers meant that she ruled her house. Increasingly, she had to be physically restrained. Family life was exhaustingly organized around Eleanor. If neurofeedback and I didn't help her daughter, her mother thought the only option left would be residential care.

Eleanor told me about choking her sister and her bizarre behaviors as a young girl, but it felt as if this report were well practiced, a kind of adornment of the narrative expected in psychotherapy. She was a fiction writer and her life was her first work. It was only as a writer that she seemed at all conversant with the emotional dimensions of her experience. She felt isolated from everyone, including her mother. She felt, as well, that her existence depended on keeping her mother's attention riveted on her through the eating disorder. Although Eleanor was suffering from Asperger's syndrome, ambivalent and traumatic attachment, life-threatening anorexia and bulimia, "explosive disorder," and developmental trauma, she was largely unaware of the seriousness of her situation or of the impact she was having on others. I was, at best, part of a task to be handled and, at worst, a tormentor who insisted that she relate to me, who insisted that she would change.

This was not setting up as an easy therapy. Change, the putative goal of all treatment, threatened her with oblivion, and she lived too close to that daily. She undercut the therapy through omission. It was not so much that she lived a secret life, but that she tried to keep her unrelated, isolated, obsession-bound life a secret, even as she desperately wanted to be caught, stopped, and contained. There was someone high up in the tower who wanted to be reached. "Catch me if you can; don't catch me; there is no one to catch; you don't exist; I exist only with my mother and I belong with my father"—these were the repetitive themes of our "relationship." She was dutiful, articulate, and hardly there.

Summations and highlights will have to suffice to describe the multifaceted and fascinating unfolding of this girl, the warming of the ice princess and the emergence of a young adult. I was still very new to the practice of neurofeedback when we started, and Eleanor had to ride out the consequences of some of my initial errors.

Assessment

Clearly, Eleanor was unable to regulate her arousal on her own, even with the attention of her parents and an empathic therapist. If neurofeedback were successful for her, I would expect to see a reduction in the number and intensity of explosive episodes, quicker sleep onset, reduction in bingeing and purging, quieting and slowing of her speech, improved prosody, and an overall reduction in her level of stress. I would also expect less rigid, obsessive ideation and, slowly, more relatedness. I could expect all of this because, although her symptoms crossed diagnostic lines, they were all symptoms of overarousal. With neurofeedback, Eleanor could teach her brain to regulate itself and in this, to lower her baseline state of arousal.

Training Course

Within 10 sessions, Eleanor reported that she felt more relaxed and that she was falling asleep easily. She told me that her social life had never been better, and by Session 19, she described herself as "a gazillion times" more comfortable with other kids. Her teachers began to report that she was no longer talking "at" other students. There was little change in her bingeing, but she did begin to report a "feeling of revulsion" toward her typical binge foods. At Session 28, I introduced alpha–theta training. She had vivid, cathartic dreams after these sessions. She told me, "I want to eat normally, not just pretend to eat normally."

We were then 3 months into treatment, meeting typically two times a week. Her eye contact had improved, and she was better able to engage with my persistent requests for her to be present and to be real. Presence is not an easy negotiation for most people, but it is a particularly difficult one for a girl with Asperger's and ambivalent attachment. She took refuge in her tower, and spoke to me from there about how she always scripted her encounters. She had never had the experience of a genuine or spontaneous interaction, except when she flew into a rage, and although spontaneous, these episodes could not qualify as interactions. They were more a discharge phenomenon than they were effective communication. She maintained her social gains (which rarely rely on true presence), made gains on eating, and then lost them. As she felt positive shifts in herself, she mounted a resistance equal to the shifts. Her symptomatic behavior had organized her relationship to herself, to her mother, and to her absent father, and she wasn't going to give it up without a fight. "The trouble with neurofeedback" she said, "is that it works." Finally, she confessed to me that she had been stealing food and money, both to further her eating disorder and her desire to defeat me. A good deal of the therapy was then, needless to say, devoted to these behaviors.

One of the single most important demands on a therapist who integrates neurofeedback into her practice is the need to discern the effects any given protocol is having on the state and the behavior of the patient. I needed to question whether neurofeedback was making a contribution to this new level of acting out. I came to believe that it was; that I had inadvertently pushed her into a more overaroused, antisocial state.

I changed her training protocol, and I witnessed an almost immediate positive shift in both her behavior and her relatedness.

During her 31st alpha–theta session, Eleanor reported feeling a panicky sense that she did not exist. She saw herself emerging from a well. "I am nothing, entirely blank. As I get smaller, a part of me goes higher and higher, into the white light." I asked her if she felt as if she were dying. She started to cry real frightened, sad tears, and said: "This [eating disorder] has me and I am afraid I am going to die; my father killed something; I am already dead." In the sessions that followed, she began to describe her own murderous heart. Eleanor now had access to a deeper region of self-perception. She felt she was a terrorist, cold at the core. She had no experience of loving, although she had a vague understanding that she was loved. Her world was one of clumsy seduction, control, and triumph.

By her ninth month of treatment, she was describing bingeing as "completely habit"—as something she could, but would not, stop. She had, for the first time in years, experienced herself as full, and now she had to eat over the obstacle of fullness. She admitted that she preferred her symptoms to any person or any other activity. As she gained more control over the eating disorder, she pushed further away from me. It was as I had feared: I was doomed to focus almost entirely on eating and throwing up. She would allow nothing else. She was maintaining the social gains at school and, more turbulently, at home, but she was no warmer with me.

I abandoned all LH training at that point, even though she liked it, to focus primarily on arousal regulation. Shortly thereafter, Eleanor confirmed that all left-side training had been a problem. "I felt like I was a criminal." This feeling hadn't bothered her; in a way it hadn't even been reportable, because it had been "her." (I have seen this "LH effect" subsequently with others who have experienced, for one reason or another, a significant degree of disordered attachment.)

With RH training, Eleanor began to experience herself differently. She was able to acknowledge that she felt calmer. Explosive episodes were rare. I was becoming important to her. She was slowly "coming awake" to a complex world, a world with people in it. Her social cueing improved, but it was at first neither dependable nor fluid. She practiced it as a new skill. She felt that now she was defending against relatedness, as opposed to the total absence of others when she felt no need to defend. Her eating improved, and it scared her. Always trying to optimize clinical effect, I made another shift in protocol (significantly lower frequency reward on the right), and almost immediately she began to say things such as, "I am experiencing an alarming turn toward normalcy." *Normalcy* threatened her with being forgotten, with all the years of suffering being swept away, with no longer being special. She was also struggling to hold onto her idea that her specialness was in her thinness, particularly as she emerged into the world that had been occluded to her and saw how "nonspecial" thinness was, how pervasive this problem was all around her.

As I touched on in Chapter 8, shame is a primary affect in any eating disorder. Shame lurks in desire, in appetite. Eleanor's fixed response to stress was to get thinner. Twenty-one months into treatment, she physically attacked her mother in an argument over the issue of clothing and weight. It was, in fact, an eruption fueled by her inherent shame over her body, as well as her shame and confusion over her increasing ability to eat normally and her refusal to do so. I made it very clear to her that her behavior was unacceptable, not only to her family but to me.

I also made another change in protocol. As discussed in Chapter 7, this protocol targeted the quieting of the amygdala at FPO2. (New data were implicating the amygdala in Asperger's syndrome, and as we know, it is always an issue in developmental trauma.) We were also preparing for an inpatient hospitalization that she very much needed to do—it was part of her script—and she had to be symptomatic to be admitted. With the protocol change, Eleanor reported, "I feel as if I am in a totally different brain. Like someone turned off the static. I dropped down to a place I'd forgotten existed." (This comments suggests, of course, that she had known this state at some point. It reminded me of the woman who said, "I have never been more myself and never known less who I am.") Feelings of desperation about getting through the day are gone. It's like being washed." She went on to tell me about wanting to begin a binge, but this time seeing how it would affect her stepfather. She told me, "I had my first experience of moral compunction." She did not binge.

As her symptoms subsided, Eleanor gained access to deep fears, primary among them that her obliteration lay in wellness. This belief made progress impossible. Once in the hospital, she was cooperative with the refeeding program, which apparently made her an unusual patient in this program. While at the hospital, she and I had phone consultations. She was now fully aware of the false note, the beginning of the script, and so was I. Each time she started it, I called it to her attention and asked her to speak only if it was genuine. Her arousal skyrocketed briefly—she wanted to throw the phone—and then she said, "But then there is nothing I can say." I coached her, "OK, so then say nothing." And we sat, each on the separate ends of the phone, in a silence more meaningful than any words she could script. After several minutes she sighed and said softly, "Thank you." That moment marked the beginning of the end of scripting. When Eleanor stopped violently disrupting her brain with bingeing and purging, and nourished it instead, she began to feel something new. It was as if all the neurofeedback training had slotted into place and was now providing her with a new capacity for stability, a new capacity for genuine self.

At each turn, I found myself hopeful that the eating disorder was over, and of course it was not. That was still 2 years off. She kept to the literal terms of her discharge contract, while remaining obsessively vigilant and hyperfocused on food, clothes, and weight. On other developmental fronts, however, Eleanor was making remarkable strides. She described the beginning of a bounded self, particularly in relationship to her mother—a relationship in which, for her, no boundary had ever existed. While driving to the library one afternoon, she became "stunningly aware" that no one knew, at that moment, where she was. Until then, even as the center of the universe, as the Grand Puppeteer, she had felt completely transparent to everyone. She was glass.

As her arousal decreased, she experienced moments of empathy. I had to help her identify these feelings because she had had no prior experience of them and no vocabulary. She was beginning to see the outlines of self and other. My note from the third year:

> It gets clearer and clearer that this girl is negotiating stark terror all the time, and that this is unbearably acute when her mother leaves. Without her mother in sight, she does not remember her. This is also the case with

me. We are beginning to exist as "other," but we disappear. She rehearses all interactions to make it through these transitions, and in this has believed that she was scripting every role. "Training," she reports, "is like grounding a live wire."

She arrived one day, genuine. She talked of seeing her mortality, of getting the fact of time, of wanting her life to mean something, of beginning to choose people because she could see them. Eleanor realized increasingly that she is not transparent, that skin is a boundary, and that other human beings are simultaneously living out their lives without reference to her. Further, she has become aware that when she gets upset, there is always a cause. The notion of causality relies, of course, on cause-and-effect thinking, which had not before been available to her, as well as on the recognition of the existence of the other, also unknown.

During this same period, she put her hand up about 3 inches behind her head and said, "This is where I am." She was living closer to, but not yet in, herself. Although increasingly rare, and brief when they happened, she still had episodes of rapidly escalating affect, usually to angry tears. By then, I was no longer taken by surprise, even though these episodes usually depended on some very rapid and occult Asperger's logic, not always readily accessible to me. Now that she was able to discern the meaning of the tone of my voice, she allowed me to soothe her, and it usually took only a few minutes for her to quiet. Increasingly there were moments when she could acknowledge what I had said with a sudden, quiet, "Oh." In the past this was the space that would be flooded by shame and rage.

Eleanor began college at a nearby school at the end of her third year in treatment. She was still able to come for weekly sessions. She was desperately homesick, and she was also able to move with and through these feelings. She could see that others were homesick and scared too. During this same period, she began to remember her mother holding her. Like a recovering amnesia victim, she began to reconstruct her emotional life. She discovered that she "was actually in the life [she] wasn't there for." She discovered too, while riding a bus, that she could locate herself geographically for the first time. But her central struggle was a poignant one: She had brought herself to college, her genuine self only months old, and she was trying to conform to the social insistence on falseness. This was a very different way of not fitting in than she had ever experienced, but it triggered the daily school experience of being the strange girl on the outside looking in. The stress became too much. She started to binge, and true to form, she didn't tell me. But this time, bingeing felt hard on her. With the discussion of rehospitalization (this time hospitalization was not part of her script and she now saw it as "futile"), another protocol shift, and multiple reminders to be in our relationship, she was able to bring the bingeing under control.

By Christmas and the turn of the millennium, she said: "This is very good. I feel happy. Nothing feels hard." She had made friends at school and been nominated for positions in several clubs. She found the idea that people had her on their minds, "stunning." She described a "neutral state" in which she felt "vastly peaceful and terrified of the peacefulness. None of it is what I thought it would be. It is not a movie."

Eleanor made her way through freshman year and, with some acting out of traumatic sexuality, the summer after it. At the beginning of her second year, she became upset when someone stole something from her. She managed the shift in focus without inordinate shame when I asked her about her own thefts. After a pause in which I could see her begin to struggle with control, she said simply, "I had to." And she did. Her brain, her arousal, her betrayal, her loss, her "stolen childhood," and the absence of any real "others"—all meant that she "had to." And now, she had to be responsible for it, all of it, and she was much better prepared to be so.

A month after September 11th, this young woman who had been diagnosed with Asperger's syndrome (I almost had to remind myself of this) said to me, "Relationship is the only harbor." As her fear continued to give way to regulation, she felt growing attachment. She could fold into our relationship for comfort. The urge to binge still passed through her, but there was "nothing to attach it to." The narrative that would have arisen from her fear, and that would have justified bingeing, did not materialize. She did not believe her state, and so she had room to let it arise and fall away.

Despite these gains, she was still struggling with obsessive thoughts about food and thinness into the fourth year of her therapy. Thinness is, of course, a cultural obsession, and she lived at college in a women's dorm—which is to say, in the white hot center of it. She did not, however, binge. She also described another phenomenon common to people working with neurofeedback: the need to continually update herself, in this instance from someone who had trouble with transitions to someone who was negotiating them better than most. Peers wanted to be with her, and this simple fact also required a constant process of updating and a fundamental restructuring of her self-definition. She turned corners, met herself, and surprised herself, almost daily.

Eleanor was now able to seek out others. But it wasn't easy, in this newfound regulation, to find company. She was lonely. Most of her peers were steeped in sex, alcohol, and self-abuse. They sought her out to help them stabilize, but this, she was recognizing, was not the same as company. The very changes that were providing her with herself compounded her loneliness. She met another young woman her age who was also using neurofeedback. Originally diagnosed with severe PTSD and dissociation, this girl, too, described herself as leaping across developmental milestones. She, too, could find little solace or interest in the normal commerce of adolescence. They became abiding friends, each insisting on the genuine presence of the other, and both able to understand the "self" and "other" redefinitions that neurofeedback often requires. This relationship has, for both of them, been an essential element in their "recoveries." I use quotation marks because recovery does not adequately describe the process. All three of the women in this chapter describe themselves as "new."

In the fifth year of therapy, Eleanor said, with an unveiled allusion to *The Sixth Sense*, "I see sad people. I see sadness behind the eyes, everywhere." Her own sadness is multifaceted. It is about watching herself grow up (psychically, a little like the bean stalk), something she intended never to do. It is the loss of the "safe" delusion that she would never have to inhabit the terrible sadness of the real world (she would live in the glitter and the glass), and it is the reality of all that has happened to her. It is the sadness that others are suffering needlessly, tinged with frustration that they are apparently so willing to do so. It is sadness that she has so little company. And she is, for the most part, not sad.

It seems increasingly incomprehensible to her how deeply organized and profoundly disorganized she was by the eating disorder. She no longer lives "behind her head" but in her body. She feels that her relationship with food is now ordinary. She looks forward to coming to therapy, to coming to see me. It is no longer a project; it is a relationship. She continues to deal with the legacies of her father, her increasing awareness of her mother's sad vacancy, the aftermath of severe anorexia and bulimia, and the fact that she was born with Asperger's. She said at one point in the fifth year, "I lived in the swirling chaos of Asperger's and trauma. It was so loud I couldn't hear the noise, like living in the eye of the storm. Now, I am just . . . present."

She also has had to contend with the fact that few people will believe she ever had this "incurable condition." Today she meets none of the criteria for Asperger's (or high-functioning autism). Eleanor has to find new words to describe her new sense of self, to help construct an identity that is at the same time both new and preexisting. Her therapy is not yet over, but now she is here to do it.

Some colleagues have asked me whether Eleanor might have made this progress with the therapy alone. I very much doubt that would have been possible. She was profoundly impaired in her ability to regulate affect and in her ability to use me to help her do so. It is clear to me and to her that neurofeedback allowed both to happen. Perhaps most importantly, neurofeedback allowed the therapy. As the only intervention, neurofeedback would have helped her to learn affect regulation. She needed psychotherapy to learn how to relate and, over time, to help her to integrate the significant changes she was experiencing in her sense of self. With both in place, she has learned the most important of life's lessons: that "relationship is the only harbor."

Afterword

Several years after beginning my study and practice of neurofeedback, I attended the Stephen Wolfram Science conference, held that year in Boston. A colleague was invited to present on neurofeedback to this highly receptive audience of physicists, mathematicians, and philosophers, and he asked me along to help demonstrate the training.

Wolfram, a distinguished scientist, inventor of computational software and the author of *A New Kind of Science* (2002), hosted this conference (and others like it) as an opportunity to explore the ways in which technical computing could be applied to a range of disciplines, from education to business, physics to philosophy, and to the brain. My colleague was asked to present because of Wolfram's interest in the connection between mathematics as he conceptualizes it and the electrical domain of brain function. As became clear to me at this meeting, Wolfram's work offers a metaphor, if not a model, for the liabilities and potential of the brain and the mind it creates. Math is, of course, quite a bit cleaner and neater than the bioelectrical body–brain–mind–genetic–epigenetic interactive fields that give rise to the EEG. It is clearer than we humans will ever be and fascinating in how it illustrates the inherent possibility of the emergence of brand new patterns.

Wolfram designed software that generates a simple geometric pattern with the possibility for multiple iterations. He found that one of four conditions will occur:

1. The pattern cannot replicate at all and it dies.
2. The pattern repeats itself without variation, endlessly.

3. Something new begins to happen; the original geometrics remain, but new patterns form.
4. Everything is new—unpredicted and unpredictable. There is no longer anything of the original pattern discernible.

As I am sure is abundantly clear by now, I am neither a mathematician nor a physicist, but I didn't need to be to be struck by the computer-generated art on the walls of the exhibit space demonstrating how these four conditions might manifest. It felt to me analogous to the unfolding we have been discussing throughout this book: the movement from repetition and rigidity in the brain—at its most painful in mental illness—to complexity, flow, organization, and newness culminating in optimal brain functioning, in optimal mental health.

Neurofeedback allows the brain to explore and establish potentially unprecedented and even beautiful new patterns. We could describe what happened for the three women we met in the last chapter and others in this book in these terms. With training, their brains jumped the ruts of their individual manifestations of the second condition—which we know as their symptoms—and moved them into the third condition. Developmental trauma exerts a persistent drag on this capacity for newness, but I think, given enough time and therapeutic help, most patients with developmental trauma will make the leap and some will even find themselves inhabiting the fourth condition, usually to their great surprise.

Many of my patients have reported just this phenomenon in language more familiar to them: "My fresh new brain"; "I don't know who said that"; "Who is this person?" These are the breakthrough moments in Wolfram's frame: the fourth condition. When we are working with developmental trauma we see patterns of change, the new, arising simultaneously with the old, repetitive and familiar ones. In Wolfram's language, we are exploring the third condition through most of the course of neurofeedback, with the emergence of new patterns out of the old as these brains push toward something completely new. Recall the young-adult adoptee who summed up landing in the fourth condition when she said, "I have never been more myself and never known less who I am."

We have seen that we can learn to quiet and organize traumatized brains and that neurofeedback makes this possible by direct appeal to the brain's organizing properties: its rhythmic oscillations. Neurofeedback provides the brain with information on itself, on how it is firing and how it can change how it fires, in the language it understands: in the declensions of frequencies. When the brain's dysregulation is primed by the wild firing of the RH or survival amygdala, it can take as many as 100–500 sessions, at least presently, to strengthen cortical control over these powerful subcortical pulses. All through the training process we will see changes that signal lowered arousal and enhanced regulation. Many of these changes will be in the realm of symptoms, but there are also subtler, more pervasive, and ultimately more important changes in the person beneath the symptoms. These are the changes in the sense of self.

Although we focus our attention on reduction of symptomatic behavior, in those who have suffered the ravages of developmental trauma we should be looking for and encouraging the emergence of a regulated self, a sense of the reality of the other, and the capacity for meaningful, empathic relationships. In the language of quantum physics, self is an emerging property, and as Wolfram's model suggests, we don't know an end point for emergence. When the brain learns to release itself from repetitive, self-reinforcing patterns, it discovers not only its own capacity for regulation, but its own unique trajectory of unending emergence. As one person described her journey, she began in "no-self," as described by Allan Schore (1994, 2003), and moved to an organized and relational "self," as we think of it in our Western psychological tradition, to still further, a "no-self," as proposed in Buddhist teaching. Imagine that! Whatever language we use, this capacity for unprecedented change must be encoded within the EEG, the most complex signal known in the universe.

A good deal of what we see as mental illness or as behavioral disorder has its roots in the density of developmental trauma, and thankfully, our field is moving toward "trauma-informed" therapy. Experience with neurofeedback suggests that trauma-informed treatment should also be brain-informed treatment—and not just to know that the brain is at issue, but to work *with it* directly. As we have been exploring, even those patients with developmental trauma who have access to psychotherapy (and most don't) are being treated without specific regard to their brains and even more specifically without regard to their wordless RHs and, even more specifically yet, to the subcortical storms that overtake them. It has become clear to me, and hopefully to you as well, that we need to address the fear circuitries directly. As therapists we've had only indirect access to the brain before the advent of neurofeedback. Now, with brain wave training we can reach what so deeply afflicts people who have suffered these childhoods: primal terror, shame, and rage. It is hard to imagine what mental illness would look like were everyone able to quiet fear, shame, and rage.

Whenever I talk to audiences about neurofeedback, someone invariably (and quite appropriately) asks me about research, so I just want to touch on it briefly. To date, research has been driven by the DSM consensus that we are dealing with discrete disorders that require discrete research. As we are discovering, the brain doesn't parcel out its problems in diagnostic categories. It suffers dysrhythmias, disconnections, and general disorder, yet all research has been tied to specific diagnoses. This seems to be shifting.

The National Institute of Mental Health (NIMH) recently changed its guidelines for mental health research to look for common factors, rather than discriminating factors, in mental illnesses:

> Strategy 1.4 of the NIMH Plan calls for new ways of classifying psychopathology based on dimensions of observable behavior and neurobiological measures. . . . In brief the effort is to define basic dimensions of functioning (such as fear circuitry or working memory) to be studied across multiple units of analysis, from genes to neural circuits to behaviors, cutting across disorders as traditionally defined. (http://www.nimh.nih.gov/research-priorities/strategic-objectives/strategy-14.shtml)

The practice of neurofeedback suggests, of course, that one primary and critical common factor is the failure of cortical brain structures to regulate subcortical ones, with significant behavioral, emotional, and cognitive consequences. Neuroscientists have known this for over a century. Neurofeedback reveals that with accurate feedback, the brain can learn to strengthen cortical control and quiet subcortical eruptions.

Brain dysregulation is the core factor in all mental illness, and as we have seen, even severely dysregulated brains can progress toward regulation, and typically, if given enough time, a supportive environment, and therapeutic guidance, can achieve it. When I began my training 16 years ago on how to influence neural circuits, there was little if any discussion of neural circuits in our field. It is still more common to hear references to *brain chemistry* than to hear *brain circuitry*, but this too is changing. In a recent TED talk, Tom Insel (2013), Director of NIMH, spoke about mental illness as "disorders of the human connectome." The *connectome*, he explained, "is the wiring diagram of the brain." In neurofeedback we are directly addressing "the human connectome," allowing it to explore, connect, and order itself. Neurofeedback makes this seemingly esoteric information available and therapeutically useful to us now.

As we have seen in the ACE study (2003), developmental trauma has profound effects not only on the individual but on the society. We could discuss its costs through many different lenses including addiction, criminal justice, and health care. But I will end with just one example of the heavy toll of developmental trauma on those of us here in the United States.

James Heckman (2006), a Nobel prize-winning economist at the University of Chicago, used his award money to investigate a disturbing reality that does not bode well for the economic strength of the United States. There are estimated to be 1.2 million high school dropouts every year, or 24% of all students (Black Public Media, 2013). This is a very expensive problem for the individual and for society as a whole. Heckman's investigation concluded that the main reason that children fail in school is that they are coming from dysregulating environments:

> Because of the dynamics of human skill formation, the abilities and motivations that children bring to school play a far greater role in promoting their performance in school than do the traditional inputs that receive so much attention in public policy debates. . . . The families and not the schools are the major sources of inequality in student performance (p. 1901)

Heckman's work, like Sroufe's, emphasizes the devastating effects of poverty on family cohesion. I think it would also be safe to say that the majority of dropouts are dealing with developmental trauma histories that affect impulse control, cause-and-effect thinking, and their ability to learn the lesson, social or academic. Dropouts typically make little if any contribution to the economy and all too many will require system support for most of their lives. Heckman makes a compelling case for programs tailored for these at-risk kids to keep them in school and learning. Although he doesn't use this language, Heckman's primary goal for these interventions is to help disadvantaged children learn to self-regulate. He is an economist and he has done the math. Even intensive one-on-one support programs throughout the school years are less expensive than letting these kids flounder and fail.

Neurofeedback may well offer an alternative. Although it is clear to me that neurofeedback is best provided within the context of a psychotherapy relationship, it is a learning technology, and those teachers trained in special education, as well as school counselors, would be well equipped to provide it, once trained in neurofeedback and with appropriate mentoring. The experience of neurofeedback practitioners across clinical populations indicates that people cooperate with training their brains. They show up, because it feels good to them to have access and control over their own brains, over themselves. And, I have to admit, I do like the acronym for brain wave education in school: BE.

One young patient who had suffered most of the assaults and degradations of developmental trauma was able to complete her dissertation, interestingly in the field of education, in record time. She arrived one afternoon after a testy student faculty meeting and dropped into the training chair. She looked up at me and said, "I can't wait until we have a neurofeedback nation!" One day, we might realize her vision, but in the meantime it is important for us as therapists to understand that none of our patients (none of us) can be better than their brain and that we now have the opportunity to converse with it directly as it seeks its birthright: regulation and human connection.

Neurofeedback Assessment Questionnaire

Date of Assessment: ____/____/____

Name: _____ Age: _____

Birth Date: ____/____/____

Address: _____ City _____

State ____ ZIP_____

Phone: H: ____-____-_____ W: ____-____-_____ C: ____-____-_____

Legal guardian: _____

School & grade: _____

Occupation: _____ How long? _____

E-mail _____ Do you check it regularly Yes No
(circle one)

Sex: M or F   Handedness: L__ R__ Mixed __ Blood Pressure_____

Presenting Problem(s): _____

_____

_____

_____

_____

In the following lists please circle any symptoms that you have ever experienced. It is important to know whether you have any of these symptoms
presently, or have *ever* had them.

Name: _____

ATTENTION SYMPTOMS

• ADD (inattentive subtype)
• Inattention
• Daydreaming
• Poor concentration
• Lack of motivation
	• ADHD (attention deficit/
	  hyperactivity disorder)
	• Hyperactivity after sugar
	• Hyperactivity after sedatives
	• Overwhelmed by stimuli
	• Hard to make decisions
	  (executive function)
	• Disorganized
		• Impulsivity
		• Distractibility
		• Stimulus seeking
		• Thrill seeking
		• Competing
		  thoughts; too
		  many thoughts

Assessment notes (practitioner):

_____

_____

_____

_____

_____

Name: _____

SLEEP SYMPTOMS

• Night sweats • Frequent waking during night (without agitation) • Sleeping lightly • Sleeping too much • Sleep apnea • Snoring • Not rested after sleep • Waking early • Difficulty falling asleep (mind quiet)	• Night terrors • Nocturnal myoclonus (jerking or moving while asleep) • Sleepwalking • Sleep talking • Narcolepsy (falling asleep frequently or suddenly) • Too busy to sleep (manic quality) • Night sweats • Bed-wetting (enuresis) • Sleep paralysis when awakening; still dreaming when awake	• Difficulty falling asleep; mind busy • Hot flashes during sleep • Physically restless sleep • Nightmares (bad dreams) • Bruxism (teeth grinding) • Restless leg syndrome • Vivid dreams • Clenching jaw • Waking with agitation • Vigilant sleep

Do you nap? Yes No Sometimes

How long does it take for you to fall asleep? _____

How many hours of sleep do you get a night? _____

What time do you tend to go to bed? _____

What time do you get up? _____

Do you dream in color? Yes No Sometimes

Assessment notes (practitioner):

_____

_____

_____

_____

_____

Name: _____ _____

EMOTIONAL AND BEHAVIORAL SYMPTOMS

• Anxiety (worry) • Depression (blue, low, helpless and hopeless) • Irritability • Feelings easily hurt • Perfectionist • Remorseful after tantrums • Cries easily (feelings hurt) • Rumination • Guilt • Withdraws when stressed • Passive • Wishes was dead • Grumpy • Thinks little of self • Performance anxiety • Shy • Seasonal affective disorder • Fidgets • Whining • Tired, listless • Obsessive thoughts	• Binge eating • Anorexia • Bulimia • Panic attacks • Encopresis (soiling) • Irritable bowel syndrome (IBS) • Bipolar disorder • Dissociative identity disorder (DID) • Borderline personality disorder (BPD) • Posttraumatic stress disorder (PTSD) • Developmental trauma • Rages • Antisocial personality disorder (APD)	• Anxiety (fear) • Depression (agitated) • Agitation • Mania • Paranoia • Suicide thoughts or actions • Shame • Compulsive behavior • Involuntary movements or tics • Impatient • Aggressive; initiates conflict • Jealous/envious • Angry • Lacks remorse • Hates self • Dissociative • Exhausted • Lacks empathy • Lacks cause-and-effect thinking • Manipulative, controlling • Holds a grudge • Poor comprehension and expression of emotions • Lacks body awareness (pain, discomfort, appetite) • High pain threshold • Loud, unmodulated voice • Poor eye contact • Poor social awareness

		• Autistic symptoms
		• Humorless
		• Road rage
		• Hair pulling or twirling
		• Nail biting, nervous habits
		• Attachment disorder (history)
		• Developmental trauma

How fast do you drive? _____

Assessment notes (practitioner):

_____

_____

_____

_____

_____

_____

Name: _____

COGNITIVE SYMPTOMS

• Dyslexia • Indecisiveness • Poor word fluency • Poor sequential processing • Poor sequential planning • Poor reading comprehension • Difficulty decoding words • Poor arithmetic calculation		• Nonverbal learning disabilities • Poor spelling • Poor visual–spatial skills • Poor sense of self in space • Poor tracking during reading • Lack of prosody in speech (monotone) • Poor drawing • Loud voice • Inability to write neatly (even slowly • Poor fine motor skills • Poor sense of direction • Poor math concepts • Left and right are not automatic

Assessment notes (practitioner):

_____

_____

_____

_____

_____

Name: _____

PAIN SYMPTOMS

• Chronic pain with depression • Chronic aching pain • Tension headache • Low pain threshold	• Fibromyalgia • Reflex sympathetic dystrophy (RSD) • Trigeminal neuralgia • Migraine • Headaches • Jaw tension • Motion sickness	• Chronic burning pain • Chronic throbbing pain • Chronic stabbing pain • Chronic shooting pain • Sciatic pain • High pain threshold • Peripheral neuropathy pain • Emotional reactivity to pain • Reflux

Cursive or print handwriting?

Compare geometry to algebra (spatial–linear to computational–abstract)

Assessment notes (practitioner):

_____

_____

_____

_____

_____

_____

Name: _____

NEUROLOGICAL AND MOTOR SYMPTOMS

• Left-brain seizures • Left-brain stroke • Left-brain TBI (traumatic brain injury • Right body paralysis or paresis • Enuresis (urinary incontinence)	• Generalized seizures • Absence (petit mal) seizures • Tonic–clonic (grand mal) seizures • Temporal lobe epilepsy • TBI with brainstem injury • Vertigo • Tinnitus • Motion sickness • Tics	• Right-brain partial seizures • Right-brain stroke • Right-brain TBI • Left body paralysis or paresis • Spasticity • Tremor • Poor balance • Poor coordination • Involuntary regurgitation • Nervous habits/laugh • Reflux • Hiccups

Assessment notes (practitioner):

_____

_____

_____

_____

_____

Name: _____

IMMUNE, ENDOCRINE, AND ANS SYMPTOMS

• Sugar craving • Immune deficiency • Low thyroid function • PMS, depressive symptoms: 　—Irritability 　—Insomnia 　—Sugar craving 　—Cramps 　—Pain • Postpartum depression • Insomnia • Intolerant of alcohol, other sedative drugs	• Hypertension • Hypotension • Incontinence • Severe PMS (mood swings, migraines) • Chronic fatigue syndrome (CFS) • Irritable bowel syndrome (IBS) Autoimmune disorders: 　—Type 1 diabetes 　—Lupus 　—Rheumatoid arthritis 　—Crohn's disease 　—Multiple sclerosis • Intolerant of coffee, alcohol, and many medications • Multiple chemical sensitivities • Asthma	• Irregular menstrual periods • Racing thoughts • Mania, rage • PMS—high arousal: 　—Agitation 　—Mania 　—Rages 　—Racing thoughts • Menopausal hot flashes • Skin allergies, eczema • Heart palpitations • Pounding, racing heart • Constipation • Intolerant of coffee and other stimulants

Assessment notes (practitioner):

_____
_____
_____
_____
_____

Name: _____

PERSONAL HISTORY

Prenatal, birth events, and/or injuries such as maternal stress, accident, drug exposure, difficult labor, forceps delivery, breech birth, induced labor, Pitocin, anesthesia, anoxia, premature/late delivery, or postbirth problems? Other? Please describe.

_____

_____

_____

_____

Problems with growth and development, such as severe or recurrent illnesses or infections, allergies, emotional difficulties, behavioral problems, appetite/digestion, language/speech, coordination? Walking or talking early? Walking or talking late? History of ear infections? Please describe.

_____

_____

_____

_____

Physical trauma, injury, head injury, TBI, coma, accidents, high fever, serious illness, surgery, CNS infection, poisoning, anoxia, stroke, heart attack? Ever broken your nose? Have you ever been to the emergency room? Please describe.

_____

_____

_____

_____

Recreational drug use? If so, when, what drugs and how did each effect you? Drug overdose?

_____

_____

_____

_____

_____

Sensitivity to light such as discomfort with fluorescent lights, glare, or computer screens? Do things seem too loud? Bothered by tags or seams? Any sensory or auditory processing problems? Please describe.

_____

_____

_____

_____

_____

Psychological stresses/life changes during childhood, such as a death, parent's divorce, losses, moves, or school changes—or in adulthood, such as, job change or loss, loss of love one, illness, or financial stress? Did you experience emotional or physical abuse or neglect? Did you witness acts of violence? Please describe.

_____

_____

_____

_____

_____

Sexual history. History of sexual abuse? History of sexual dysfunction? Do you have concerns about libido?

_____

_____

_____

_____

_____

Family history. Have any close relatives experienced problems such as epilepsy, autism, Asperger's, alcoholism, mental illness, depression, suicide, incarceration, or any of the other problems reviewed in this assessment? Please describe.

_____

_____

_____

_____

_____

Name: _____

MEDICAL and THERAPY HISTORY

Are you currently or recently on any medications, drugs, hormone replacement, allergy or asthma treatments, alternative therapies, nasal sprays, or any regular use of OTC medications? Please list name, dosage, and indication for use:

_____

_____

_____

_____

_____

Any surgeries, hospitalizations, or medical treatments? Was either general or local anesthesia used? Please describe.

_____

_____

_____

_____

_____

Are you currently under treatment or supervision by a health provider? For what condition(s)? Who is your primary health provider?

_____

_____

_____

_____

_____

Have you participated in any psychological therapies (with a psychologist, social worker, counselor, family therapist)? Are you currently in psychotherapy? If so, with whom? Have you ever been given a psychiatric diagnosis?

_____

_____

_____

_____

Have you had any educational therapies (tutors, special schools, resource teacher, vision or speech therapy, occupational therapy, etc.)? Please describe.

_____

_____

_____

_____

_____

Have you ever had any neurological or educational testing? Do you have copies
of these tests or the results?

_____

_____

_____

_____

_____

Name: _____

LIFESTYLE INVENTORY

Do you drink alcohol?   If so, how often?   How much?   How does it affect you?

Do you drink caffeine (soda, tea, coffee, energy drinks)?   How much? When in the day?   How does it affect you?

Do you smoke?   If so, how many cigarettes per day? How long have you smoked?

Do you like sweets/sugar?   If yes, what is your daily sugar intake? How does it affect you?

Do you eat chocolate?   How much and how often? How does it affect you?

Do you crave salt?

What foods do you favor?

Do you use supplements? If so, for what?

How many hours do you watch TV on weekdays?   On weekends?

Do you play computer games?   How many hours a week?

Do you read for pleasure?

Do you exercise?   What form(s)? How many times a week?

Name: _____

What do you do to relax?

(Practitioner only)

Summarize findings (include CPT, qEEG, mini Q, or other psychometric find-ings)

_____

_____

_____

_____

_____

_____

_____

_____

Initial indications for left hemisphere training:

    Initial indications for placement:

    Initial indications for frequency:

Initial indications for right hemisphere training:

    Initial indications for placement:

Initial indications for frequency:

Initial indications for interhemispheric training:

Initial indications for frequency:

Initial indications for placement:

Assessment completed by_____Date_____

Appendix **B**

Frequently Asked Questions

What is neurofeedback?
Neurofeedback, also called EEG biofeedback, is a learning technology that enables a person to alter her brain waves. When information about a person's own brain wave characteristics is made available to her, this person can learn to change them. You can think of it as operant conditioning of the brain waves and as exercise for the brain. Frequencies at which our brains fire underlie every thought, feeling, and behavior. Brain dysregulation underlies emotional, cognitive, and behavioral disorders. The choice of which training approaches are appropriate for a particular individual depends on a professional assessment of symptoms and history. Neurofeedback training should take place only under the supervision of a properly trained professional.

Can a successful outcome be predicted?
It is not possible to predict with certainty that training will be successful for a particular individual. The effectiveness of the training, however, can usually be assessed early on in the course of training. Adverse effects are rare, and when they do occur, they can be reversed because neurofeedback promotes brain plasticity.

Why does neurofeedback work?
The brain is amazingly adaptable or "plastic" and capable of learning. It can learn to improve its own performance, when it is given cues—feedback—about what to change. All learning actually depends on feedback, and the brain is the

part of us that is most devoted to learning. By making information available to the brain about how it is functioning, and asking it to make adjustments, it can learn to do so. When the brain is doing a good job of regulating itself, the person will feel calm, alert, and attentive. Each session challenges the trainee to maintain this "high-performance" state. Gradually, the brain learns, just like it learns everything else, and with sufficient training, it typically retains the regulation it has gained.

How long does training take?
EEG training is a learning process, and therefore results are seen gradually over time. Indications of progress, however, can be seen usually within 10–20 sessions. Developmental trauma can require over 100 sessions, but the trainee will know it is helping long before all symptoms remit.

How frequently should training sessions occur?
In the initial stages, the sessions should be regular, optimally two times a week. Think of learning to play the piano. After the brain begins to consolidate its new learning, sessions can be less frequent. There is no way to anticipate how many sessions an individual will need.

My doctor is skeptical about neurofeedback. What should I do?
Your doctor may not know of this specific type of biofeedback. He or she should maintain a healthy skepticism about any new approach claiming these kinds of benefits across disorders. Ask your doctor to examine the recent research on the effectiveness of neurofeedback in treating various disorders such as attention deficit disorder, PTSD and epilepsy. It is most readily available at www.isnr.org/resources/comprehensive-bibliography.cfm. Additional websites include:

www.aapb.org
www.aboutneurofeedback.com
www.eeger.com
www.treatmentoftrauma.com
PubMed at www.ncbi.nih.gov/pubmedhealth

You can find many testimonial videos on YouTube.
Enjoy this journey into the regulation of your brain.

Appendix C

FPO2 Protocol Guide

FPO2 (frontal pole-orbital on the right) is a site that can be used in those cases that indicate an overactivation of fear circuitries in the brain, such as in those suffering from developmental trauma, posttraumatic stress, reactive attachment disorder, personality disorders, anxiety disorders, and depression characterized by high arousal (see Figure 7.2 on p. 223). The amygdala is the part of the brain that learns and holds fear memory. FPO2 lies within "the greater amygdaloid region" (Schore, 1994, 2003) or the very part of the brain that is responsible for mediating the reactivity of the amygdala. Training at this site often quiets the fear driven brain.

Cautions: Training at FPO2 has been known to activate fear memory as well. This is not necessarily negative, but you have to be in the position to deal with these memories, should they arise. There have also been two anecdotal clinical reports of precipitation of a seizure when training at FPO2. The amygdala is highly susceptible to kindling. Seizure history may be a contraindication for FPO2 training, at least until there is more overall brain stability.

Site: FPO2 stands for *prefrontal occipital* (frontal pole) and 2 signifies the *right side*. The site is at the juncture of the nose and the brow bone, immediately adjacent to the eye socket. There is often a small notch in the bone or a spot that is sensitive to pressure right at that "corner." This is where you place the electrode.

It is best that the trainee is lying back, to make the placement easier to secure and also to recruit slow wave activity. We naturally make more slow waves when we are lying down. A properly placed headband can help hold the electrode in place.

Training with eyes closed is recommended for the same reasons: more naturally occurring slow wave activity and less chance of paste getting in the eye. Some people, however, are afraid to train with their eyes closed, and you should respect this. (They will make more artifact with eyes closed than eyes open.) The effects do not seem dependent on the eyes being closed.

Rewards: Depending on tolerance and overall arousal of the trainee, rewards may be anywhere from 8 to 11 Hz (too high for most) and as low as 0–3 Hz (too low for most). Usually people will feel the effects within 3 to 6 minutes. If they don't, it could be an indicator that you are rewarding at too high a frequency. Most people will like how they feel if you find the right frequency. As with any protocol, trust the trainee's report. If it's a negative report, don't persist.

Inhibit: 0–6 Hz. This inhibit is in place to protect against abreaction. Even when the reward and inhibit overlap, as they often do in this protocol, the inhibit is protecting against excessively large amplitude or bursting slow waves— those that would tend to destabilize. The inhibit band actually allows 75% of the inhibited frequency through. We are only inhibiting 0–6 Hz, 20–25% of the time. In short, it works to have reward and inhibit frequencies overlap. (The brain figures this out, even if, at this moment, you can't.)

Time: FPO2 can be a very powerful training. Most people begin to feel the effects within 3 minutes, and 3–9 minutes is probably enough. If the trainee wants more, less, or none, trust that response.

FPO2 effects noted to date:

Positive effects

- Reduction in fear
- Calming/equanimity
- Reduced inflammation
- Increased creativity
- Access to emotional memory ("opening")
- Appetite reduction
- Reduction in pain
- Increased sensitivity to smell
- Releasing of fear memories
- Bliss

Negative effects

- Triggered seizure (two cases known to date); stop training
- Triggered release of fear memories
- Sense of smell too strong
- Syntax/language problems (can be addressed with left-side training at T3, F7, T3–F7)
- Impacts on short-term memory (can be addressed with left-side training at T3)
- Disinhibition, such as swearing or shopping
- Apathy

References

Acri, A. A., & Henretig, F. M. (1998). Effects of risperidone in overdose. *American Journal of Emergency Medicine, 16*(5), 498–501.

Ainsworth, M. D. S., Blehar, M. C., Waters, E., & Wall, S. (1978). *Patterns of attachment: A psychological study of the strange situation*. Hillside, NJ: Erlbaum.

Amen, D. (2001). *Healing ADD*. New York, NY: Berkley Books.

American Psychiatric Association. (1980). *Diagnostic and statistical manual of mental disorders—third edition*. Washington, DC: Author.

American Psychiatric Association. (2013). *Diagnostic and statistical manual of mental disorders—fifth edition*. Washington, DC: Author.

Anda, R. A., & Felitti, V. J. (2003). *The adverse childhood experiences study*. Atlanta, GA: Centers for Disease Control and Prevention (CDC).

Askovic, M. (2013). Personal communication.

Ayres, A. J. (1979). *Sensory integration and the child*. Los Angeles, CA: Western Psychological Services.

Baumeister, J., Reinecke, K., Leisen, H., & Weiss, M. (2008). Cortical activity of skilled performance in a complex sports-related motor task. *European Journal of Applied Physiology, 104*(4), 625–631.

Black Public Media. (Producers). (2013, March). *180 days: A year inside an American high school* [Television broadcast]. Arlington, VA: PBS.

Bluhm, R. L., Williamson, P. C., Osuch, E. A., Frewen, P. A., Stevens, T. K., Boksman, K., et al. (2009). Alterations in default network connectivity in post-traumatic stress disorder related to early-life trauma. *Journal of Psychiatry and Neuroscience, 34*(3), 187–194.

Bostan, Dum, & Strick. (2010). The basal ganglia communicate with the cerebellum. http://www.ncbi.nlm.nih.gov/pubmed/20404184

Bowlby, J. (1988). *A secure base*. New York, NY: Basic Books.

Budzynski, T. H., Budzynski, H. R., Evans, J. R., & Abarbanel, A. (Eds.). (2009). *Introduction to quantitative EEG and neurofeedback: Advanced theory and applications*. New York, NY: Academic Press.

Buzsáki, G. (2006). *Rhythms of the brain*. New York, NY: Oxford University Press.

Carlson, E. A., Collins, W. A., Egeland, B., Englund, M., Simpson, J. A., & Sroufe, L. A. (1975–present). *Minnesota longitudinal study of risk and adaptation (case study)*. Minneapolis, MN: Institute of Child Development at University of Minnesota.

Craig, A. D., Chen, K., Bandy, D., & Reiman, E. M. (2000). Thermosensory activation of insular cortex. *Nature Neuroscience, 3*, 184–190.

Cook, P. S., Petersen, R. C., & Moore, D. T. (1990). *Alcohol, tobacco, and other drugs may harm the unborn*. Rockville, MD: U. S. Department of Health and Human Services.

Damasio, A. (1999). *The feeling of what happens*. New York, NY: Harcourt.

Davidson, R. (2004). Well-being and affective style: Neural substrates and biobehavioural correlates. *Philosophical Transactions of the Royal Society B: Biological Sciences, 359*(1449), 1395–1411.

Demos, J. (2005). *Getting Started with Neurofeedback*. New York, NY: Norton.

Diamond, D. M., Campbell, A. M., Park, C. R., Halonen, J., & Zoladz, P. (2007). The temporal dynamics model of emotional memory processing: A synthesis on the neurobiological basis of stress-induced amnesia, flashbulb and traumatic memories, and the Yerkes–Dodson law. *Neural Plasticity*, Article ID 60803. http://dx. doi. org/10.1155/2007/60803

Doppelmayr, M., Finkenzeller, T., & Sauseng, P. (2008). Frontal middleline theta in the pre-shot phase of rifle shooting: Differences between experts and novices. *Neuropschologica, 46*(5), 1463–1467.

Doyon, J. (1997). Skill learning. In J. Schmahmann (Ed.), *The cerebellum and cognition: International review of neurobiology* (pp. 273–291). New York, NY: Academic Press.

Dube, S. R., Fairweather, D., Pearson, W. S., Felitti, V. J., Anda, R. F., & Croft, J. B. (2009). Cumulative childhood stress and autoimmune diseases in adults. *Psychosomatic Medicine, 71*(2), 243–250.

Dube, S. R., Felitti, V. J., Dong, M., Chapman, D. P., Giles, W. H., & Anda, R. F. (1995–1997). *The Adverse Childhood Experiences Study*. Atlanta, GA: Centers for Disease Control and Prevention & Kaiser Permanente.

Duffy, F. H. (2000). The state of EEG biofeedback therapy (EEG operant conditioning) in 2000: An editor's opinion. *Clinical Electroencephalography, 31*(1), v–vii.

Egner, T., & Sterman, M. B. (2006). Neurofeedback treatment of epilepsy: From basic rationale to practical application. *Expert Review of Neurotherapeutics, 6*(2), 247–257.

Faulkner, W. (1951). *Requiem for a nun*. New York, NY: Random House.

Fehmi, L., & Robbins, J. (2001). Mastering our brain's electrical rhythms. *Cerebrum*, *3*(3). Retrieved from http://www.dana.org/news/cerebrum/detail.aspx ?id=2984

Fehmi, L., & Robbins, J. (2007). *The open focus brain: Harnessing the power of attention to heal mind and body.* Boston, MA: Shambhala.

Felitti, V. J., & Anda, R. F. (2010). The relationship of adverse childhood experiences to adult medical disease, psychiatric disorders and sexual behavior: Implications for healthcare. In R. Lanius, E. Vermetten, & C. Pain (Eds.), *The impact of early life trauma on health and disease: The hidden epidemic* (pp. 77–87). New York, NY: Cambridge University Press.

Ferguson, P. (2009, November 28). *Ted Kaczynski: Evil man, or tortured soul?* Retrieved from http://www.cnn.com/fyi/school.tools/profiles/kaczynski/index .story.html

Fields, A. D. (2010). *The other brain: The scientific and medical breakthroughs that will heal our brains and revolutionize our health.* New York, NY: Simon & Schuster.

Fink, G. R., Markowitsch, H. J., Reinkemeier, M., Bruckbauer, T., Kessler, J., & Heiss, W. D. (1996). Cerebral representation of one's own past: Neural networks involved in autobiographical memory. *Journal of Neuroscience*, *16*(13), 4275–4282.

Fisher, S. F. (1985). Identity of two: The phenomenology of shame in borderline development and treatment. *Psychotherapy*, *22*(1), 101–109.

Fisher, S. F. (2009). Neurofeedback and attachment disorder: Theory and practice. In *Introduction to Quantitative EEG and Neurofeedback: Advanced Theory and Practice* (pp. 315–335). New York: Academic Press.

Fitzgerald, K. D., Welsh, R. C., Gehring, W. J., Abelson, J. L., Himle, J. A., Liberzon, I., et al. (2005). Error-related hyperactivity of the anterior cingulate cortex in obsessive–compulsive disorder. *Biological Psychiatry*, *57*(3) 287–294.

Fogel, A. (2009). *The psychophysiology of self-awareness.* New York, NY: Norton.

Fonagy, P., Steele, H., & Steele, M. (1991). Maternal representations of attachment during pregnancy predict the organization of infant–mother attachment at one year of age. *Society for Research in Child Development*, *62*, 5, 891–905.

Gedgaudas, N. T. (2009). *Primal body, primal mind: Beyond the paleo diet for total health and a longer life.* Rochester, VT: Healing Arts Press.

Gray, J. A. (1987). The psychology of fear and stress. New York, NY: Oxford University Press.

Green, E., & Green, A. (1989). *Beyond biofeedback.* Santa Barbara, CA: Knoll.

Gruzelier, J., Egner, T., & Vernon, D. (2006). Validating the efficacy of neurofeedback for optimizing performance. *Progress in Brain Research, 159,* 421–431.

Hagmann, P., Cammoun, L., Gigandet, X., Meuli, R., Honey, C. J., Wedeen, V. J., et al. (2008). Mapping the structural core of human cerebral cortex. *PLoS Biology, 6*(7), 1479–1493.

Hammond, D. C. (Compiler). (2013). *Comprehensive neurofeedback bibliography*. Retrieved from http://www.isnr.org/resources/comprehensive-bibliography.cfm

Harlow, H. F. (1958). The nature of love. *American Psychologist, 13,* 673–685.

Hebb, D. O. (1949). *The organization of behavior.* New York, NY: Wiley.

Heckman, J. J. (2006). Skill formation and the economics of investing in disadvantaged children. *Science, 312,* 1900–1902.

Henriques, J. B., & Davidson, R. J. (1991). Left frontal hypoactivation in depression. *Journal of Abnormal Psychology, 100*(4), 535–545.

Herculano-Houzel, S. (2010). Coordinated scaling of cortical and cerebellar numbers of neurons. *Frontiers of Neuroanatomy 4*(12), 1–8.

Herman, J. L. (1997). *Trauma and recovery: The aftermath of violence from domestic abuse to political terror.* New York, NY: Basic Books.

Hippocrates. (1886). *The Genuine Works of Hippocrates* (F. Adams, trans). Vol. 2, 344–5. (Original work written 400 B.C.E.)

Inanaga, K. (1998). Frontal midline theta rhythm and mental activity. *Psychiatry and Clinical Neuroscience, 52*(6), 555–566.

Insel, T. (2010). Faulty circuits. *Scientific American, 302*(4), 44–51.

Insel, T. (2013, January). *Toward a new understanding of mental illness* [Video file]. Retrieved from http://www.ted.com/talks/thomas_insel_toward_a_new_understanding_of_mental_illness. Html

Izard, C. E. (1971). *The face of emotion.* New York: Appelton-Century-Crofts.

Kaiser, D. A. (2013). Infra-low frequencies and astrocytes. *Neuroconnections,* (Fall), 14–16.

Kluetsch, R. C., Ros, T., Théberge, J., Frewen, P. A., Calhoun, V. D., Schmahl, C., et al. (2013). *Direct modulation of the salience and default mode networks following EEG neurofeedback in posttraumatic stress disorder.* Acta Psychiatrica Scandinavica, in press.

Kolb, B., & Whishaw, I. A. (2001). *An introduction to brain and behavior.* New York, NY: Worth.

Koob, A. (2009). *The root of thought: Unlocking glia—the brain cell that will help us sharpen our wits, heal injury, and treat brain disease.* Upper Saddle River, NJ: FT Press.

Kounois, J., & Beeman, M. (2009). The aha! moment. *Current Directions in Psychological Science, 18*(4), 210–216.

Lanius, R. A., Vermetten, E., & Pain, C. (Eds.). (2010). *The impact of early life trauma on health and disease: The hidden epidemic*. New York, NY: Cambridge University Press.

Ledoux, J. (1996). *The emotional brain: The mysterious underpinnings of emotional life*. New York, NY: Touchstone.

Legarda, S. B., McMahon, D., Othmer, S., & Othmer, S. (2011). Clinical neurofeedback: Case studies, proposed mechanism, and implications for pediatric neurology practice. *Journal of Child Neurology*, 26(8), 1045–1051.

Levin, F. M. (Ed.). (2009). *Emotion and the psychodynamics of the cerebellum*. London, UK: Karnac Books.

Levine, A., & Heller, R. S. (2011). What attachment theory can teach about love and relationships. *Scientific American Mind*, (Jan/Feb), 22–28.

Levine, P. A. (1997). *Waking the tiger: Healing trauma*. Berkeley, CA: North Atlantic Books.

Levine, P. A. (2010). *In an unspoken voice: How the body releases trauma and restores goodness*. Berkeley, CA: North Atlantic Books.

Linehan, M. (1993). *Cognitive-behavior treatment of borderline personality disorder*. New York, NY: Guilford Press.

Llinás, R. R. (2001). *I of the vortex: From neurons to self*. Cambridge, MA: MIT Press.

Maguire, E. A., Woollett, K., & Spiers, H. J. (2006). London taxi drivers and bus drivers: A structural MRI and neuropsychological analysis. *Hippocampus* 16(12), 1091–1101.

Main, M., & Solomon, J. B. (1986). *Discovery of an insecure-disorganized/disoriented attachment pattern*. Westport, CT: Ablex.

McCourt, F. (1996). *Angela's ashes: A memoir*. New York, NY: Touchstone.

McEwen, B. S., & Stellar, E. (1993). Stress and the individual: Mechanisms leading to disease. *Archives of Internal Medicine*, 153(18), 2093–2101.

McFarlane, A. C., Weber, D. L., & Clark, C. R. (1993). Abnormal stimulus processing in posttraumatic stress disorder. *Biological Psychiatry*, 34(5), 311–320.

Michaels, A. (1996). *Fugitive pieces*. New York, NY: Vintage Books.

Neugebauer, V., Li, W., Bird, G. C., & Han, J. S. (2004). The amygdala and persistent pain. *Neuroscientist*, 10, 3221–3234.

Ogden, P., Minton, K., & Pain, C. (2006). *Trauma and the body*. New York, NY: Norton.

Ohno, S. (1972). So much "junk" DNA in our genome. In H. H. Smith (Ed.), *Evolution of genetic systems* (pp. 366–370). New York, NY: Gordon & Breach.

Orgel, L. E., & Crick, F. H. (1980). Selfish DNA: The ultimate parasite. *Nature*, 284(5757), 604–607.

Ornstein, R. (1997). *The right mind*. New York, NY: Harcourt Brace.

Othmer, S. (2008). *Protocol guide for neurofeedback clinicians*. Los Angeles, CA: EEGInfo.

Othmer, S. (1999). Personal communication.

Panksepp J. P. (1998). *Affective neuroscience: The foundation of human and animal emotions.* New York, NY: Oxford University Press.

Pavlov, J. P. G. (1928). *Lectures on conditioned reflexes: Twenty-five years of objective study of the higher nervous activity (behaviour) of animals.* New York, NY: Liverwright.

Peniston, E. G., & Kulkosky, P. J. (1989). Alpha–theta brainwave training and beta endorphin levels in alcoholics. *Alcoholism: Clinical and Experimental Results, 13*(2), 271–279.

Peniston, E. G., & Kulkosky, P. J. (1991). Alpha–theta brainwave neuro-feedback therapy for Vietnam veterans with combat related post-traumatic stress disorder. *Medical Psychotherapy, 4*(1), 47–60.

Perry, B. D. (2003). *Effects of traumatic events on children.* Available online at www.childtrauma.org.

Porges, S. (2011). *The polyvagal theory: Neurophysiological foundations of emotions, attachment, communication, self-regulation.* New York, NY: Norton.

Poskanzer, K. E., & Yuste, R. (2011). Astrocytic regulation of cortical UP states. *Proc Natl Acad Sci, 108,* 18453–18458.

Rauch, S. L., van der Kolk, B. A., Fisler, R. E., Alpert, N. M., Orr, S. P., Savage, C. R., et al. (1996). A symptom provocation study of posttraumatic stress disorder using positron emission tomography and script-driven imagery. *Archives of General Psychiatry, 53*(5), 380–387.

Robbins, J. (2000). *A symphony in the brain.* New York, NY: Atlantic Monthly Press.

Ros, T., Theberge, J., Frewen, P., Kluetsch, R., Densmore, M., Calhoun V., et al. (2013). Mind over chatter: Plastic up-regulation of the fMRI alertness network by EEG neurofeedback. *NeuroImage, 65,* 324–335.

Roth, S. R., Sterman, M. B., & Clemente, C. D. (1967). Comparison of EEG correlates of reinforcement, internal inhibition and sleep. *Electroenceph. Clin. Neurophysiol., 23,* 509–520.

Rothschild, B. (2000). *The body remembers.* New York, NY: Norton.

Sacks, O. (1985). *Migraine: Understanding a common disorder.* Berkeley, CA: University of California Press.

Sapolsky, R. M. (2004). *Why Zebras Don't Get Ulcers.* New York, NY: St. Martin's Press.

Sapolsky, R. M. (2005). *The Neurological Origins of the Self* [CD]. Chantilly, VA: Great Courses.

Sarang, S. D., Osipova, D., Bertand, O., & Jerbi, K. (2013). Oscillatory activity of the human cerebellum: The intracranial electrocerebellogram revisited. *Neuroscience and Biobehavioral Reviews, 37,* 585–593.

Sasaki, T., Kuga, N., Namiki, S., Matsuki, N., & Ikegaya, Y. (2011). Locally synchronized astrocytes. *Cerebral Cortex, 21*, 1889–1900.

Schmahmann, J. D. (Ed.). (1997). *The cerebellum and cognition: International review of neurobiology.* New York, NY: Academic Press.

Schmahmann, J. D. (1998, May–June). The sorcerer's apprentice. *Harvard Magazine.* Retrieved from http://www harvardmagazine.com

Schmahmann, J. D. (2000). The role of the cerebellum in affect and psychosis. *Journal of Neurolinguistics, 13*, 189–214.

Schore, A. (1994). *Affect regulation and the origin of self.* Mahwah, NJ: Erlbaum.

Schore, A. (2003a). *Affect dysregulation and disorders of the self.* New York, NY: Norton.

Schore, A. (2003b). *Affect dysregulation and the repair of the self.* New York, NY: Norton.

Scott, W., Kaiser, D., Othmer, S., & Sideroff, S. I. (2005). Effects of an EEG biofeedback protocol on a mixed substance abusing population. *American Journal of Drug and Alcohol Abuse, 31*, 455–469.

Shalev, I., Moffitt, T. E., Sugden, K., Williams, B., Houts, R. M., Danese, A., et al. (2013). Exposure to violence during childhood is associated with telomere erosion from 5 to 10 years of age: A longitudinal study. *Molecular Psychiatry, 18*(5), 576–581.

Shelley, B. P., Trimble, M. R., & Boutros, N. N. (2008). Electroencephalographic cerebral dysrythmic abnormalities in the trinity of nonepileptic general poplulation, neuropsychiatric, and neurobehavioral disorders. *Journal of Neuropsychiatry and Clinical Neurosciences, 20*, 7–22.

Sheth, B. R., Sandkuhler, S., & Bhattacharya, J. (2009). Posterior beta and anterior gamma oscillations predict cognitive insights. *Journal of Cognitive Neuroscience, 21*(7), 1269–1279.

Siegel, D. (1999). *The developing mind: Toward a neurobiology of interpersonal experience.* New York, NY: Guilford Press.

Skodol, A. E., & Bender, D. S. (2003). Why are women diagnosed borderline more than men? *Psychiatric Quarterly, 74*(4), 349–360.

Spitz, R. A. (1945). Hospitalism. *Psychoanalytic Study of the Child, 1*(2), 53–74.

Sroufe, A. (2012, January 29). Ritalin gone wrong. *New York Times.* p. SR1

Sroufe, A., Egeland, B., Carlson, E., & Collins, A. (2005). *The development of the person: The Minnesota study of risk and adaption from birth to adulthood.* New York, NY: Guilford Press.

Stein, G. (1937). *Everybody's autobiography.* New York, NY: Random House.

Sterman, M. B. (2000). Basic concepts and clinical findings in the treatment of seizure disorders with EEG operant conditioning. *Clinical Electroencephalography*, *31*(1), 45–55.

Sterman, M. B., & Egner, T. (2006). Foundation and practice of neurofeedback for the treatment of epilepsy. *Applied Psychophysiology and Biofeedback*, *31*(1), 21–35.

Stern, D. N. (1985). *The Interpersonal World of the Infant: A View from Psychoanalysis and Developmental Psychology*. New York, NY: Basic Books.

Suetsugi, M., Mizuki, Y., Ushijima, I., Kobayashi, T., Tsuchiya, K., Aoki, T., et al. (2000). Appearance of frontal midline theta activity in patients with generalized anxiety disorder. *Neuropsychobiology*, *41*(2), 108–112.

Surmeli, T., & Ertem, A. (2009a). QEEG guided neurofeedback therapy in personality disorders: 13 case studies. *Clinical EEG and Neuroscience*, *40*(1), 8–10.

Surmeli, T., & Ertem, A. (2009b). Post WISC-R and TOVA improvement with QEEG guided neurofeedback training in mentally retarded: 23 cases. *Clinical EEG and Neuroscience*, *40*(1), 32–41.

Szaflarski, J. P., Binder, J. R., Possing, E. T., McKiernan, K. A., Ward, B. D., et al. (2002). Language lateralization in left-handed and ambidextrous people. *Neurology*, *59*(2), 238–244.

Tan, X., Uchida, S., Matsuura, M., Nishihara, K., & Kojima, T. (2003) Long-, intermediate-, and short-acting benzodiazepine effects on human sleep EEG spectra. *Psychiatry and Clinical Neuroscience*, *57*(1), 97–104.

Tansey, M. A. (1991). Wechsler (WISC-R) changes following treatment of learning disabilities via EEG biofeedback training in a private setting. *Australian Journal of Psychology*, *43*, 147–153.

Teicher, M. H., Anderson, C. M., & Polcari, A. (2012). Childhood maltreatment is associated with reduced volume in the hippocampal subfields CA3, dentate gyrus, and subiculum. *Neuroscience: PNAS Plus*, *109*(9), 563–572.

Teicher, M. H., Anderson, C. M., Polcari, A., Andersen, C. M., Navatta, C. P., & Kim, D. M. (2003). The neurobiological consequences of early stress and childhood maltreatment. *Neuroscience and Biobehavioral Reviews*, *27*(1–2), 33–44.

Teicher, M. H., Glod, R. N., Surrey, J., & Swett, C. (1993). Early childhood abuse and limbic ratings in adult psychiatric outpatients. *Journal of Neuropsychiatry & Clinical Neuroscience*, *5*(3), 301–306.

Teicher, M. H., Rabi, K., Sheu, Y.-S., Seraphin, S., Andersen, S., & Anderson, C. M. (2010). Neurobiology of childhood trauma and adversity. In R. A. Lanius, E. Vermetten, & C. Pain (Eds.), *The Impact of Early Life Trauma on Health and Disease: The Hidden Epidemic* (pp. 112–122). Cambridge, UK: Cambridge University Press.

Tronick, E. Z. (2007). *The Neurobehavioral and Social–Emotional Development of Infants and Children*. New York, NY: Norton.

van der Kolk, B. (1994). The body keeps the score: Memory and the evolving psychobiology of traumatic stress. *Harvard Review of Psychiatry, 1*, 253–265.

van der Kolk, B. (2005). Developmental trauma disorder: Toward a rational diagnosis for children with complex trauma histories. *Psychiatric Annuals, 35*(5), 401–408.

van der Kolk, B. (2009, June). *Developmental trauma disorder*. Paper presented at the International Trauma Conference, Boston, MA.

van der Kolk, B., Hostetler, A., Herron, N., & Fisler, R. E. (1994). Trauma and the development of borderline personality disorder. *Psychiatric Clinics of North America, 17*(4), 715–730.

van der Kolk, B., MacFarlane, A. C., & Weisaeth, L. (Eds.). (2007). *Traumatic Stress: The Effects of Overwhelming Experience on Mind, Body, and Society*. New York, NY: Guilford Press.

van Lier, H., Drinkenburg, W. H., van Eeten, Y. J., & Coenen, A. M. (2004). Effects of diazepam and zolpidem on EEG beta frequencies are behavior-specific in rats. *Neuropharmacology, 47*(2), 163–174.

Wells, J. (2011). *The Myth of Junk DNA*. Seattle, WA: Discovery Institute Press.

White, N. E., & Richards, L. M. (2009). Alpha–theta neurotherapy and neurobehavioral treatment of addictions, mood disorders and trauma. In T. H. Budzynski, H. R. Budzynski, J. R. Evans, & A. Abarbanel (Eds.), *Introduction to quantitative EEG and neurofeedback: Advanced theory and applications* (pp. 143–164). New York, NY: Academic Press.

Wise, A. (1995). *High-performance Mind: Mastering Brain Waves for Insight, Healing and Creativity*. New York, NY: Penguin Putnam.

Wolfram, S. (2002). *A New Kind of Science*. Champagne, IL: Wolfram Media.

Wyrwicka, W., & Sterman, M. B. (1968). Instrumental conditioning of sensorimotor cortex EEG spindles in the waking cat. *Physiology and Behavior, 3*, 703–707.

Index